3.00

Lives in Progress

A STUDY OF THE NATURAL

GROWTH OF PERSONALITY

ROBERT W. WHITE

HARVARD UNIVERSITY

THE DRYDEN PRESS, NEW YORK

Typography and format by
LEONARD W. BLIZARD

Manufactured in the United States of America

Preface

For fifteen years I have been making case studies of normal people. Some of these people were studied when they were college students, others were seen when somewhat older, and a small number—eight cases thus far—have been studied intensively on two separate occasions from five to ten years apart. This book is based on my collection of case studies, and it may serve as a kind of progress report on research that is still going forward. My purpose in writing it, however, is more general: the book is intended to provide a brief introduction to the whole field of personality. Case histories furnish the factual foundation, but they are used to introduce and illustrate the general ideas, drawn from a variety of sources, that go to make up a scientific account of personality.

How should a person be introduced to the general subject of personality? My preferences with respect to this question can be indicated by mentioning four features of the book.

In the first place, I have concentrated on three case histories rather than attempting to summarize a larger number. I chose this plan because it seemed to provide the best way of basing the exposition on a solid foundation of fact. The initial facts of personality are the lives of people, and lives cannot be adequately understood unless they are described at considerable length. The case histories are designed to constitute a groundwork of carefully observed facts on which to anchor the discussion of concepts and theories, and I have tried to maintain a close connection between general ideas and their particular embodiments in these three lives.

Secondly, the lives reported here were studied on my initiative rather than on that of the subjects, and they were studied on two separate occasions. These circumstances are important, in my opinion, in making the case histories broadly representative of the facts of personality—a field in which too much of our knowledge is based on clinical case records taken at a time when the patient, overwhelmed by difficulties, is completely preoccupied with the problem of getting well. Clinical histories concentrate on the origin of the disorder and build up to the climax of explaining the patient's present plight. Then they stop; or at best continue with the sparse information that a few years later the patient was understood to be feeling better. No matter how strong the historical orientation, a clinical case history can almost never do justice to the fact of change, except perhaps such change as occurs under the artificial circumstances of psychotherapy. Yet temporal development is one of the central facts and central problems of personality.

In the third place, I have favored a broadly inclusive approach to the understanding of lives. Personality is open to a multitude of influences, shaped by a multitude of forces. Repeatedly we say that it is complex, and this means that it cannot be properly envisioned from a single provincial point of view. I am glad that my professional associations have included a Department of Psychology, a Psychological Clinic, and a Department of Social Relations. This has helped me to utilize appreciatively the biological, the psychodynamic, and the social and cultural points of view and to realize that the problems of multiple influence, conflict, and organization are crucial in understanding personality.

Finally, I have laid a good deal of stress on natural growth and constructive activity. Personality does not stand still; under certain conditions it evolves in the direction of greater maturity, effectiveness, and contentment. The study of relatively normal people and the study of these people at two different points in time provide favorable conditions for examining the process of natural growth. The person, furthermore, is not always a passive victim of the forces that influence him. He is himself a center of energy and an active agent in changing the surrounding environment.

In the last chapter I have drawn together some ideas about growth and activity, organizing them by means of the general concept of growth trends.

The life histories in this book are not fiction. Any resemblance between the three principal characters and real living individuals is far from coincidental; it is the result of a painstaking attempt at faithful description. It will be realized, of course, that I have taken steps to conceal the identities of these three people, and that the purpose of the disguise would be defeated by explaining how it was done. On this point I must ask to be trusted for having fulfilled my obvious obligation to the subjects without making changes that would significantly alter one's understanding of the cases. The subjects have seen the chapters about themselves and have consented to the publication of their histories. "Nothing requires a rarer intellectual heroism," said Santayana, "than willingness to see one's equation written out." This book is dedicated to the three subjects, with my respect and affection.

In gathering my collection of case histories I have had the assistance of well over a hundred people. I am greatly indebted to the staff members, research assistants, volunteer workers, and graduate students who at various times formed part of the diagnostic team. In my final working over of the present case material I was reminded anew of my helpers by seeing their names on the reports of test sessions and interviews, and I kept realizing how often I was using their thoughts in piecing together my own. Of outstanding importance were the contributions of Dr. Donald W. Fiske, Mrs. Annette R. Silbert, Dr. Pauline B. Hahn, Dr. Ruth-Jean Eisenbud, Dr. Margaret R. Riggs, and Dr. Robert M. Ravven. I exempted myself from all worry about the typing of the manuscript by turning it over to Mrs. Esther L. Smith. My wife, Margaret L. White, was one of those who helped gather and interpret the case material, and her editing of the final draft was a strong influence in the direction of clarity.

R. W. W.

Concord, Mass.
April, 1952.

Contents

vii

1. The Understanding of Lives

> To know the truth partially is to distort the Universe.
> . . . An unflinching determination to take the whole
> evidence into account is the only method of preser-
> vation against the fluctuating extremes of fashionable
> opinion.
>
> A. N. WHITEHEAD

Man's understanding of himself is one of the central problems of our time. This book is an attempt to forward that understanding. It undertakes to do so in a particular way and with a particular kind of observations not hitherto well represented in the study of human nature. Its method of attack is that of the intensive case study, using a variety of techniques designed to disclose the individual patterns of personality. Its subjects are young adults, relatively healthy and relatively successful, who have been studied on two separate occasions, once when they were college students and again five to ten years later. Its emphasis is on growth, on changes in personality occurring under natural circumstances over periods of time. In order to keep the discussion in close touch with the facts and complexities of individual lives, three case studies are given in great detail. The cases provide a proving ground on which current ideas about personality can be put to work. These ideas come from diverse sources: biological research, experimental psychology, the study of children, the treatment of neurotic patients, field trips among primitive peoples, and the study of the structure of society. Central to the purpose of this book is the often neglected task of bringing these diverse contributions to bear all at once on the study of the individual. Better understanding cannot be expected unless we cover the whole biosocial range, extending our observations all the way from organic foundations such as drive and temperament to social shaping forces such as class status and cultural pattern.

Much as we know about personality, there is a serious gap at the very center of the subject. Individual lives moving forward normally amid natural circumstances have received almost no scientific

3

study and have played almost no part in our current understanding. It is easy to see the reason for this gap. To some extent scientific research takes directions pointed out by human need, and the natural growth of personality has not been a pressing problem. Recent trends in world affairs, however, have broadened the scope of what we want to know about human nature. Now that man has become so troubled about himself, so alarmed at his ineptitude in organizing a social system to suit the small world created by modern communication and modern scientific discoveries, he urgently needs to know more about his own potentiality for constructive growth. He can no longer afford to distort the universe by knowing truth partially, to distort his self-knowledge by leaving out those very features of his development that give him a chance to guide his destiny. He deserves a picture of himself that will not omit the highly human qualities of trying to understand things and change them for the better. Yet if he tries to build up this picture out of the materials of present scientific knowledge he discovers a dismaying paradox. The scientist has almost never studied ordinary people as they increase their mastery of the ordinary problems of daily life. Still less has he studied the investigatory activity of scientists, and he has thereby overlooked one of the most devoted, persistent, honest and selfless forms of human behavior. There are scarcely any systematic case records of great fortitude, rare heroism, unusual contribution to the arts, or special success in grasping and solving important social issues. The natural growth of personality and the higher flights of human achievement have been given almost no representation in man's current ideas about himself.

The consequences of these omissions are serious. The sciences of man have learned many things of great value to human welfare, but their partial view of human nature has added to the anxiety and pessimism of our times. We know a good deal about the ways in which conditions mould men, and this knowledge is important; we know very little about the ways in which men mould conditions, and this knowledge can hardly be called less important. It is grimly unfortunate that in a period when rationality, insight, and creative social invention are in such urgent demand, science is prepared to throw light mainly on man's irrationality and helplessness.

The material chiefly needed to start filling the gap in present knowledge is *the study of lives in progress*. In this book we shall examine three such lives. It will be our first goal to understand them

as fully as possible in the light of existing ideas derived from biological research, psychopathology, and the social sciences; our second goal, to consider some of the ideas that need to be added in
order to account for natural growth. Before we begin the study of
our first example, however, it will be well to assemble in a brief survey the ideas that make up our current stock in trade. In later chapters these concepts will receive fuller evaluation in the light of the
case studies. Here we can do little more than call the roll and sketch
the broadest outlines. Yet in this brevity may lie a special advantage:
that of setting out our resources where they can be grasped almost
at a glance and thus better marshalled for effective teamwork.

THE BIOLOGICAL VIEW OF MAN

One of the major revolutions in scientific thinking occurred in
1859, when Darwin published *The Origin of Species* with its impressive evidence for a theory of evolution. The effect of this work was
to plant man firmly in the animal kingdom. His cherished notion of
himself as a separate kind of creature, endowed with altogether superior faculties, had to be abandoned in the face of evidence that he
had evolved from an earlier primate form. Instead he was forced to
regard himself as one of the animals, distinguished from the rest of
the kingdom only by certain quantitative advantages, such as his
more mobile hands and more spaciously developed brain. However great these advantages, the roots of his being and the reasons
for his existence were identical with those of all living creatures. He
could be studied just as animals or plants were studied without in-
voking special principles such as soul or spirit. This general idea,
now implemented by nearly a century of research, constitutes what
we shall here call the biological view of man. It underlies the momentous accomplishments of the biological sciences, including experimental psychology and medical research.

If man is an organism, he is engaged on the task that is common
to all organisms: growth, maintenance, reproduction. Taken over a
short span of time the activities of an organism seem adequately
covered by the concept of homeostasis, the maintenance of an internal equilibrium in the face of changing tissue needs and changing
external conditions. Body temperature, for example, has to be
maintained within narrow limits, and the tissues must be kept nour-
ished by periodic taking in of water and food. Viewed over a longer
period, the life of an organism can be seen to exhibit further

trends: growth to maximum size and efficiency, and reproduction of its kind. In all such transactions the organism takes an active part, responding sometimes with great vigor to conditions both internal and external, especially those which seriously threaten its well-being. Its energies are not called forth in random and indiscriminate fashion; rather, there are certain conditions to which it is highly sensitive, which release large amounts of energy, and which make for persistent behavior until the situation is changed. The concept of *drive* refers to this selective mobilization of energies.

Considering the matter abstractly, one might suppose that the biological view of man would necessarily be founded on a clear understanding of his innate drives. If these could be listed, we would know the raw material out of which experience fashions the complex motives of adult life. The earliest attempts at such a listing emphasized the continuity of man and animals by using the concept of *instinct*, but it soon became apparent that man possessed none of those clear-cut unlearned sequences of behavior that appear, for example, among the insects. The concept of *drive* thus came to be preferred in describing human urges, which are initially more blind but capable of great elaboration through learning. The goal of preparing an exhaustive catalogue of drives, however, has shown itself to be something of an illusion. One can be sure of an innate drive only when it is possible to specify bodily structures and tissue conditions which set off persistent lines of behavior. These tissue conditions can be approximately specified for certain important visceral drives such as the needs for air, food, water, sex, and lactation. But we have no right to assume that our present knowledge of the human tissues is so complete as to exclude the possibility of other important innate drives. Is there not an innate need for exploratory activity, as well as for visceral satisfactions and for repose? When we think of everyday behavior this seems probable, but there is no way to be certain about it as long as we cannot identify the tissue conditions that would make for exploratory activity.

In spite of the difficulty of listing human urges, the concept of drive is fundamental to any understanding of behavior. Its value becomes fully apparent when it is placed in conjunction with learning. Man with his highly developed brain is the animal above all others capable of learning elaborate channels of expression for drives. He can learn the most complex routes to their gratification;

he can delay and deflect them, combine them in patterns of joint satisfaction, build them into motives many steps removed from their original sources. Yet even when all this complex organization has been achieved, it remains important to understand the elements of primitive drive that may still be contributing to behavior. However susceptible to change through learning, the human motivational system has roots in the simple necessities of growth, maintenance, and reproduction. The value of this idea is particularly apparent with respect to the sex drive. Some parts of nineteenth-century society treated this need as if it could be wholly subordinated to motives of other kinds. The difficulty in working such a policy became clear first through the study of neurotic illness and then through biological research on the nature of drives. During the last half century these two influences have revolutionized the attitude of our culture toward sex.

The scientific investigation of *learning* is one of the chief concerns and accomplishments of experimental psychology. An early landmark was Pavlov's well-known work on the conditioned reflex. This was the starting point for an array of researches on animal and human versatility in picking up cues which are of service in the pursuit of satisfactions or safety. Other important lines of research emphasized the effects of practice and repetition in the building up of habit sequences such as the several turns in a maze or the order of items in material committed to memory. Another landmark was established when Thorndike studied the efforts of hungry cats to get out of cages in order to reach food. This work brought to sharp focus the relation between drive and learning. The only way to understand the cats' slow but successful mastery of the intricate mechanical problem was to suppose that the reward— reaching the food—strengthened the last few acts, including the ones that had opened the cage. In more general language, the selective reinforcement of certain responses resulted from their having just preceded a reduction in the tension inherent in a drive.

This version of Thorndike's original "law of effect" has wide applicability in understanding even the more complex features of human behavior. When properly amplified by some of the findings of Gestalt psychology, which emphasized the patterning of the learning process and the possibility of sudden new solutions to problems through perceptual reorganization, it provides a valuable groundwork for studying both normal development and its aberrations. As we advance through this book we shall increasingly appreciate the crucial significance of learning.

The study of personality is in part the study of individual differences. Inasmuch as each person has his own particular history of learnings we would expect him to be different from anybody else. Biological research, however, shows plainly that no two individuals of the same species are precisely alike even in their structural properties. Present knowledge about the laws of inheritance shows that the genes are combined in constantly novel patterns rather than being arranged to produce a standard article. Just as we would like to work out an exhaustive list of innate human drives, so we would like to have a complete account of those differences in natural endowment which might affect the development of personality. But the goal of completeness is here even less practicable, depending on a refined knowledge of the structure and functions of the body, a knowledge which we are infinitely far from possessing. Individual differences in temperament and ability are strikingly obvious in every day life. To decide whether they spring from innate tissue and biochemical differences, or whether they result from the slow cumulative effects of experience, remains a baffling and elusive problem.

Earlier in this century there was a time when the problem of individual differences in temperament seemed well on the way to definitive solution. It was discovered that the endocrine glands were extremely important in regulating growth, mood, and the tempo of behavior, and this led to the hope of a simple endocrine theory of temperament. According to such a theory, individual differences would be attributed to the size or functional capacity of the different endocrine organs, and extreme deviations might even be corrected by medication or by surgical reduction of over-active glands. When one considered the tense agitation and restlessness that went with an overactive thyroid, the dull apathy and poor growth that accompanied thyroid insufficiency, the formidable stature developed by pituitary excess, the very direct dependence of sexual characteristics on the gonads, and the vital contribution of the adrenals to energy level and to reactions under stress, it seemed reasonable to suppose that the endocrines held the key to individual differences in temperament. Perhaps we shall eventually reach a duly sophisticated version of this theory, but at present the problem seems to be to find the key to the endocrine system. More precise research has shown that most of the glands secrete several different substances having different effects; furthermore, the glands regulate each other in a complex fashion that makes it necessary to investigate the properties of the system as a whole. The situation is typified by recent findings concerning ACTH—the adrenocorticotropic hormone—which is secreted by the pituitary gland but activates and regulates the adrenal cortex, one part only of the adrenal glandular system. Indeed, the biochemistry of the body proves to be a good deal more complicated than at first appeared, but this does not diminish its importance. Perhaps we shall eventually be able to untangle the ways in which our lives and fortunes are influenced by internal biochemical happenings.

In the realm of abilities, great progress has been made since the beginning of the century in the measurement and analysis of intelligence. Innate endowment clearly plays a large part, though not an exclusive one, in the individual differences revealed by intelligence tests. Other kinds of ability are not so readily brought to crucial measurement. It is clear that even in early childhood there are differences in the time and rate at which capacities unfold. Some children walk before they talk; others reverse this order. Every child learns some things with ease and pleasure, other things with difficulty and pain; but no two children seem to have precisely the same pattern of ease and difficulty. It is almost impossible to work out the origins of such differences. Except for those few that can be perceived at birth, they must be studied at a point where experience has covered the ground with footprints and thus made it impossible to isolate innate predisposition. The aptitudes and lack of aptitudes displayed by adults have obviously evolved far from possible organic roots. It would be a great boon to guidance programs if the innate element in aptitudes could be better assessed. But we are still far from knowing what can and what cannot be changed.

MAN AS SEEN BY DYNAMIC PSYCHOLOGY

Dynamic psychology is the title generally given to that field of inquiry in which the individual and his motives are the objects of central concern. This field occupies a position between biological and social research. At one edge it touches the biology of drives and makes extensive use of the concept of learning. At the other edge it runs into the study of social shaping forces, especially the family circle and the human environment of childhood. Its center of interest, however, has always been the person as we know him in every-day life—a creature of hopes and fears, loves and hates, frustrations and struggles, failures and triumphs. Originating in the practice of psychiatry, dynamic psychology's major task has been the under-standing of disordered development, but its findings are vitally im-portant for the general study of personality.

The strongest and most lasting impetus to dynamic psychology came from the work of Freud. A physician interested in the cure of neurotic patients, Freud began his labors at a time when doubt was first beginning to be cast on the organic or disease-like character of neurosis. Instead of being, like other diseases, the surface manifes-tation of a disordered bodily state, neurosis appeared to have its roots in the patient's thoughts and feelings, and there were a few bits of evidence that exploration of the thoughts and airing of the feel-ings might produce a cure. Freud's career of discovery really began when, after several false starts, he invented a way to surmount the obstacles offered by patients to having their intimate thoughts and feelings explored. His invention, the technique of free association, seems an amazingly simple device to have produced such momen-tous consequences. It consisted of nothing more than asking the pa-tient to put aside his usual goal of reporting about himself with logic, order, coherence, and propriety; instead, he was to give his thoughts the utmost freedom, telling the listener about the images, feelings, and day-dreams that streamed through his mind, no matter how haphazard and insignificant they seemed to be. The material produced in this way soon proved to be anything but meaningless. By eliminating the effects of logical habits and of fixed pictures of the self, Freud successfully brought into the open the feelings, im-pulses, anxieties, and defenses that operated all the time behind this customary facade and that under just the right combination of cir-cumstances produced a neurosis.

Free association did not, of course, provide a rapid and easy march into the patient's inner life. Giving such license to one's stream of consciousness proved in itself a difficult accomplishment against which heavy resistances were mobilized. At first it often seemed that the patients wilfully disobeyed the instructions and showed no persistent interest in working to be cured. If their objec-tions could be overcome and their resistances dissolved, however, they would begin to recall incidents which obviously involved great frustration, pain, and fear. Their difficulties with free association sprang from anxiety rather than from a perverse unwillingness to get well. It proved possible to move by slow degrees, always through barriers of resistance, from one emotionally charged topic to another, often far back into childhood, laying bare whole chains of frustrating and frightening situations which had caused development to take a neurotic course. Moreover, the patients experienced again the tangled patterns of love, hate, and fear that had generally characterized these incidents, acting out in their relation to the physician the crucial struggles with parents and other important figures of their earlier years. This renewal of contact with the emotions and urges which they had earlier shut out of their development was in many cases the means of promoting a new growth toward health. The cure of neurosis was more difficult and time-consuming than was at first hoped. Psychoanalysis became in fact a thorough exploration of the patient's emotional life. This very fact, however, increased its contribution to the study of human nature.

Leading Ideas of Dynamic Psychology.—The ideas developed by Freud to explain the findings of psychoanalysis have been expanded, criticized, amended, occasionally even subjected to experimental study, so that the dynamic psychology of today has become the work of many hands. The whole movement has enjoyed extraordinary success. Its leading ideas are no longer the property of specialists but have entered widely into current thinking about human behavior. Foremost among these ideas is the notion of the constant play of impulse beneath and through the rational, conscious, goal-directed activities of everyday life. The central place is given to motivation rather than rationality, to drive rather than intellect. Beneath the surface of awareness lies a zone of teeming emotion, urge, fantasy, from which spring the effective driving forces as well as various disrupting agents in our behavior. At first it seemed that this zone was chiefly inhabited by sexual impulses, but soon the finding was generalized to include aggressive urges, dependent tendencies, and any other strivings which, for reasons either external or internal, could not be permitted free egress into behavior. The new image of man was beautifully dramatized by Eugene O'Neill in *Strange Interlude,* in which the characters speak to each other in ways dictated by reality and propriety but also give long asides to the audience in which they display their hates, fears, vanities, and sexual involvements. The centrality of striving, the understanding of behavior by finding out how it is motivated even though the operation of the motives be devious and unconscious, remains one of the leading ideas of dynamic psychology.

Another leading idea is that of defense mechanisms. Freud was aware of two stages in the development of his thinking: one in which the chief interest lay in unmasking the patient's unconscious strivings, another in which the focus of inquiry shifted to the defenses set up to check and control these strivings. This advance was necessary in order to understand the neuroses, many of the symptoms of which represent the effects of overworked defenses rather than the disguised expression of impulse. The defense mechanisms which Freud first recognized in his work with patients—such things as repression, projection, and reaction-formation—were gradually expanded to accommodate some of the more complex aspects of personality organization.

Wilhelm Reich introduced the notion of *character armor* to describe features of everyday behavior that had been built up as a protection against anxiety, then rendered automatic and unconscious through long practice. Haughty aloofness and carefully measured speech, for example, he perceived as protective devices utilized to keep others at a distance and the person's own emotions in check. Similarly he interpreted submissive friendliness as an habitual method of placating suspected hostility in others.

Karen Horney used the concept of *neurotic trend* to describe lines of activity in which the ordinary motives were augmented by the necessity to control anxiety. The struggle for professional success, for instance, sometimes carried the added meaning of a vital personal vindication, a denial of inferiorities that had produced rage and panic in childhood; thus the person became highly vulnerable to even the smallest hint that his success was incomplete, and he drove himself relentlessly to make his triumph perfect. In such ways the whole pattern of personality came to be perceived as accomplishing not only the satisfaction of urges but also the maintenance of defenses.

A third major tenet of dynamic psychology is that the earliest learnings are extremely important in the shaping of personality. The free associations of neurotic patients led back constantly to the earliest years and to memories in which the members of the family circle played a paramount part. The first five years of life, formerly brushed aside as a time when the child was too young for serious learning, suddenly sprang into focus as the period in which the great problems of impulse and defense received their vital first solutions. Parents and siblings served as chief characters in the infant's emotional dramas, giving him his first experiences in human relationship. Repeatedly it was found that neurotic difficulties in adult years arose from the continuing effects of infantile learning. A patient's troubled relation to his women friends, for example, would prove to come from an almost literal repetition of the attitudes and expectations he had learned in his childhood experiences with his mother. Such behavior could be understood not only by perceiving the impulses and defenses that were involved but also by discovering the historical origin of the pattern in the learning situations of the nursery. Particular significance came to be attached to the manner in which the major frustrating episodes were traversed: weaning, toilet training, punishments and discipline, birth of siblings and adjustment to their presence, jealousies and rivalries including the "eternal triangle" of child and parents which Freud picturesquely called the Oedipus complex. It was clear that the attitudes shown by the parents constituted an extremely important influence. Many studies pointed to the damaging effects of emotional rejection, overprotective zeal, tyrannical dominance, and the atmosphere of uncertainty created by parental friction and the breaking of the home. Conversely, a combination of love and firm yet kindly discipline was indicated as the pattern most conducive to healthy development. Such circumstances favored *sublimation*, the relinquishing of unsuitable goals and the channeling of urges into lines of action that would yield both satisfaction and social approval.

These ideas had their origin in the attempt to understand and cure neurotic patients, but it has proved possible to give them much wider application. Many problems earlier conceived in a quite different way have been brought to real illumination through the insights of dynamic psychology. Chronic alcoholism, for example, used to be explained as an addiction into which a person fell because of bad habits and weakness of will. Today the problem can be approached both with more sympathy and with more likelihood of giving help. This change has occurred partly through considering the purposes served by drinking, the fears and conflicts that find temporary relief under alcohol. A second example of widening application is to be found in current ways of dealing with school disabilities. Failure in school work has been found to occur for many reasons other than limited innate intelligence. If a child feels, for instance, that his parents press him too relentlessly for high marks, he may express resistance in the form of apathy toward lessons, with consequent failure to mobilize his true ability. These examples typify the contribution of dynamic psychology to the understanding of man's behavior. It is always necessary to consider the striving that is involved, the goals that are being sought, the dangers that are being avoided, the motives that are at work—whether they be conscious or unconscious, realistic or archaic, integrated or full of contradiction.

THE SOCIAL VIEW OF MAN

It is impossible to understand a person without understanding the social environment in which his life is led. Man is an organism, but his most distinctive characteristic is his capacity to learn; and his whole career of learning takes place in an environment well populated by other human beings. From the start he is highly dependent on human ministrations. His learning is first closely guided by those who provide for his immediate wants, later increasingly by larger segments of the society to which he belongs. For the most part his voyage of life does not cross unexplored oceans; rather he sails along dredged and buoyed channels, guided by a carefully prepared social chart.

The Culture Concept.—Our rapid sketch of the social forces that shape personality will begin with the concept of *culture*. This concept has been put forward primarily by anthropologists as a means of understanding some of the features of primitive societies. The field study of primitive peoples has played a part here somewhat analogous to free association in dynamic psychology. Just as free association eventually crumbled our fictions about ourselves as individuals, so the study of other and simpler cultures at last set aside our blindnesses as regards our own culture. The culture concept has had an enormous influence on the understanding of personality. It opened another of those areas to which we had previously paid little heed. Not that the effects of culture are remote and obscure; quite the contrary, they are everywhere in our daily lives and were overlooked simply by being taken for granted. The comparative study of primitive societies necessitated the emergence of culture into our consciousness.

Culture is used here in a broader sense than that of everyday speech. We often use the word to distinguish people with trained interests in knowledge and the arts—"cultured people"—

from the less-trained majority of the population. The culture concept in anthropology refers to training in a much wider meaning: all the training that an individual receives because of his membership in a human society. This includes routine matters such as eating with the fingers or with chopsticks or with knife and fork. It includes beliefs about the nature of the world and the means of propitiating hostile forces: ceremonial dances, or employment of medicine men, or support of scientific research. It includes ideal patterns of conduct, such as gentle cooperativeness or warlike assertiveness or individual enterprise and self-reliance. In this sense no societies, however simple, are without a culture, and no individuals are uncultured. The concept of culture refers to the total way of life of a society, the heritage of accumulated social learnings that is shared and transmitted by the members of that society. To put it another way, a culture is a set of shared plans for living, developed out of the necessities of previous generations, existing in the minds of the present generation, taught directly or indirectly to new generations. Without such plans the life of a society would become impossibly confused. The culture provides pretested solutions to many problems and allows us to learn without endless trial and error what to expect of others and of ourselves.

The most dramatic examples of the quiet but forceful impact of culture on our lives come from comparisons with other societies where customs are radically different. Rattlesnake meat is in some places a delicacy; by fancying our own reaction to this tempting dish we can appreciate the horror and disgust felt by members of other cultures on seeing us eat the unclean pig or the flesh of the sacred cow. The religious practices of other societies, or their customs as regards the burial of the dead, serve further to remind us of the wide differences that exist in what is felt to be right and natural.

More important for the understanding of personality are those parts of the plan for living which have to do with the socialization of children and the setting of ideal standards of behavior. Some societies train children through sharp punishments and the evoking of fears; others are more lenient, using gentle persuasion and bribery. Some cultures make courtship and marriage a matter for individual enterprise; others assign matrimony to parental decision, regarding mutual attraction and romantic love as irrelevant to this grave social institution. As Benedict, Mead, and others have shown, some societies train children to shun individual success and prominence. The goal of life is to be pleasing, generous, cooperative; to put people at their ease, be thought a good fellow, and avoid all signs of arrogance or strong emotion. As adults, children trained in this tradition try to avoid marks of distinction and consider it a miserable sacrifice if they are elected to public office. Other cultures look upon such behavior as repulsively weak and abnormal, training their children instead to climb to the top through sharp practice, theft, and the use of magic. Elsewhere the prescribed route to self-esteem may be individual excellence in hunting edible game, in human head-hunting, or in accumulating wealth which is then wastefully destroyed in a public display. Thus the culture bears down on its individual members, indoctrinating them with the plan of life they will be expected to follow.

The study of culture, mostly in simpler societies, and the study of dynamic psychology, mostly in neurotic patients, seem to have little in common, but in certain respects they have had a similar impact on the understanding of personality. Both challenged man's claim to conscious, rational self-direction. Dynamic psychology disclosed the irrational grip of urges, anxieties, and overworked protective devices. The study of cultures brought out a similar tyranny, this time of custom, belief, and moral precept learned half unconsciously from the older members of the group. Large sections of our behavior were unmasked and found to be anything but expressions of free choice or adjustment to the clear dictates of reality. The culture concept shows us how closely we live according to the habitual life plans prevailing in our society, even when changed conditions make these plans inappropriate.

Clyde Kluckhohn has described a young man of American origin, the orphaned child of missionaries in China, who was brought up from earliest years in a Chinese family. When he visited the United States as an adult he was completely bewildered by American ways. In spite of blue eyes and light hair he seemed more Chinese than American, even in his style of gait, arm and hand movements, and facial expression, to say nothing of his modes of thought and sets of values. He had been forcefully shaped by the culture in which he was reared, and it was virtually impossible for him to change.

In another respect dynamic psychology and the culture concept have made an overlapping contribution. Both have turned a searchlight upon the earliest years of life and upon learnings that take place within the family circle. For the child the first transmitters of the culture are his parents, just as they are the first participants in his emotional development. The initial impact of the culture comes through the behavior and attitudes of the parents. It comes charged with all the importance and authority that the young child necessarily attributes to his parents. For this reason cultural dictates often acquire the force of moral imperatives and become resistant to critical appraisal. What first impinges on the child is always a parental version of the culture, possibly somewhat different from the overall pattern that is characteristic of the society as a whole. In a small and uniform society it is not likely that parental versions will stray far from the general pattern. When it comes to understanding a person in our own vast and differentiated society, however, we have to specify with great care the portion of the culture, the particular sub-culture, which the parents represent. Cultural pressures vary widely among different regions, social classes, ethnic and religious groups. But the search for these sub-culture patterns quickly takes us into the whole question of the social structure and its effects upon personality.

Social Structure.—If a society is to operate successfully, there must be a division of functions among its individual members. Even the simplest society does not make the same demands upon all, for instance upon men and women, or upon infants, children, young adults, and older people. Age and sex put the individual in a definite position with respect to the other members of his society. Different behavior is expected from the occupants of different social positions, and the individual personality cannot be fully understood without taking these expectations into account. With a more complex division of labor, future social and occupational positions can often be anticipated in advance, so that from the very beginning the child is trained for a specific part. Our own society favors the abstract ideal that each individual shall be free to choose his life work. Nevertheless it is obvious that the child of wealthy professional parents and the child of an itinerant farm laborer are not reared in the same framework of expectations for the future. In a society with highly developed division of labor the specialized position occupied by the individual member becomes a major influence in the shaping of his personality.

Much light has been thrown on this problem by recent studies of *social class*. Our democratic ideals incline us not to speak openly of classes and barriers, but there is no doubt that social stratification exists and that it exerts a powerful influence on individual behavior. Students of social structure, notably Warner and his associates, have recently been active in working out the precise nature of social classes in various American communities. The findings are disheartening to those who would like to consider our society classless. Marked social stratification was found in every community, and its effects were pervasive and anything but democratic. Other workers, in particular Davis and Dollard, have repeatedly pointed out that each social level has its own set of values and ideals, which differ sometimes sharply from those of adjacent levels. A child grows up not merely in the American culture but in the sub-culture of his social class; we cannot hope to understand him without taking account of these direct pressures and traditions.

Similarly, we cannot expect to understand an adult without taking account of his *occupational status.* The more organized occupations, especially the professions, tend to impose very definite roles upon their members. Living within the role means restricting for the most part one's goals and one's notions of success to the goals and success patterns favored in the occupation. An occupational role confers numerous privileges but it also imposes a series of obligations which are maintained not only by internal standards but by the expectations of everyone on the outside. The force of these expectations as regards roles can be illustrated by considering our attitudes toward answering questions. How would we feel if our lawyer asked us about habits of eating and excretion, if a loan officer inquired into our sexual adjustment, if a doctor wanted to know the terms of our will? Each occupational group is privileged to work with its clients in one particular way and is not expected to go outside definite limits. The whole pattern of privileges and obligations reacts strongly on the member's personality. He is progressively shaped by the requirements of his role and increasingly motivated to live his life within the framework of his occupation.

In such fashion the individual personality is shaped by social forces. Much of the shaping takes place unconsciously. Through the constant process of social interaction a person comes gradually to know what others expect of him, what he may expect of others, what roles he can play satisfactorily, and how these roles fit into the roles of other people. In this subtle process of learning, memberships in groups play a significant part. Second only to the impress of the family is the moulding influence of groups in childhood and especially in adolescence. In attempting to understand an individual life it is important, though often difficult, to work out the history of group participations and to establish their effect in forming the personality. Equally important is the appraisal of current memberships, which often have a great deal to do with stability, contentment, and the person's conception of himself.

COMBINING THE THREE VIEWS: A SAMPLE PROBLEM

The need for at least a threefold approach to the study of human nature is well illustrated by the problem of development during adolescence. There is an old tradition in our culture that adolescence is a period of emotional storm and stress, marked by difficult behavior, a rebellious outlook, and a great deal of internal conflict and suffering. In the nature of things, according to this tradition, adolescence is a trying period that must be endured as best one can. Let us now briefly consider what the biological, psychodynamic, and social sciences have contributed to our understanding of this phase of growth.

Viewed biologically, adolescence signifies the attainment of adult stature, strength, and mental capacity, together with the final maturation of sexuality and reproductive functions. The child finishes his period of growth and becomes ready to assume an adult role. Studies of intelligence show that mental capacity reaches its maximum during the 'teen years; the youngster becomes as bright as he will ever be, though naturally not as wise nor as experienced. Part of the storm and stress might be attributed to the rapidly expanding mental horizons: there is so much to be taken in and assimilated by a mind freshly able to perceive things in their full dimensions. Part of it might be due to the difficulty of getting used to adult stature and overcoming the clumsiness of the awkward age. A substantial part might come from the strengthening of the sex drive, which upsets not only the accustomed pattern of interests but also the established balance of the endocrine system. Adolescence can be perceived as a kind of biological turning point, and its problems are in part the results of this crisis in organic growth.

When we take the psychodynamic point of view the problems of adolescence appear in a somewhat different light. The adolescent must learn to manage a newly strengthened and somewhat tumultuous drive, but his difficulties in doing so spring chiefly from the fact that this drive has a previous history which has channeled it in ways no longer wholly suitable. The sexual interests of early childhood, somewhat forgotten during the so-called "latency" period from the sixth year to puberty, are reanimated by the waxing sex urge. But now they are a source of even more severe conflict, especially if they continue to involve family members or friends of the same sex. Anxiety and guilt are frequent by-products of infantile sexual interests, and these painful feelings return to plague the adolescent while he is attempting to get used to his new erotic status.

A second important problem is that of outgrowing his dependent needs. The surly and exaggerated rebellion that is sometimes displayed may well represent an angry attempt to cut the ties that still inwardly bind him to the benefits and exemptions of childhood. Parental psychodynamics need to be added in order to complete the picture of adolescent storm and stress. It is not easy for the parents to withdraw protective supervision at an appropriate rate, to respect the new-found powers of their young, or to avoid disquieting contrasts between the fresh energy of youth and their own advancing middle-age.

These problems could easily be misconceived, however, if we failed to transcend the limited perspective of our own culture. It is here that anthropology makes a significant contribution. Field studies among primitive peoples show that adolescence is by no means always a period of storm and stress. In some societies it is traversed with a calmness quite at odds with our own expectations. The problems of adolescence are highly relative to the values of the culture. Many societies have elaborate puberty rites which serve to mark sharply the entrance of the erstwhile child into full adult status. Very likely the young person ceases to live at home and becomes the object of a wholly different set of attitudes on the part of other people. Perhaps this institutional recognition makes it easier for the adolescent to accomplish the necessary growth; at all events, it creates a very different situation from that which prevails in our society, where there is no clearly defined transition from childhood to adult status. Cross-cultural studies reveal also great differences in the cultural attitude toward sex. When this attitude is highly tolerant there seem to be no signs of the "latency" period assumed in our own culture to be more or less biologically determined. Sexual interests flourish during late childhood and make a smooth transition to those of adolescence. The "latency" period turns out to be a cultural rather than a biological phenomenon.

It is impossible, finally, to complete one's understanding of adolescent development without placing it in the framework of the social structure. In the course of establishing his independence from adult constraints, the adolescent in our society tends to identify himself very strongly with other adolescents. He becomes a loyal and highly conforming member of the local youth culture. His conformity, so at odds with his negative attitude at home, suggests that an emotionally difficult piece of work is going on, and we can grasp its difficulty when we notice two features of the American social structure: the small isolated family with its strong emotional ties, and the still highly competitive economic system with its requirement of independent enterprise. The adolescent must leap from the family nest into the employment jungle. He must pass from a highly protective domestic system into a particularly unprotected social and economic system, where he must set up his own independent home and find his place as a worker. No wonder that for a time he feels disoriented and becomes excessively dependent on the circle of his peers. The transition is particularly sharp when the situation prevails that is not uncommon in the large cities of today: a small family living in an impersonal environment isolated from relatives and friends, constituting a tight though not necessarily harmonious emotional unit; in contrast, a competitive universe of specialized, impersonal jobs offering little emotional anchorage or sense of security.

The three views of man are all of value in understanding development during adolescence. It is essential to include the biological, the psychodynamic, and the social evidence, remembering that man, the animal, is a very complex animal who lives in a society having a history and tradition as well as a contemporary structure. Human nature cannot be understood in a narrower perspective. Perhaps it cannot be understood without broadening the perspective still more. Much as we have gained by combining the three views of man, we must not hastily conclude that we have taken everything into account.

THE CRUCIAL GAP IN PRESENT KNOWLEDGE

The progress of science is necessarily halting and uneven. Scientific research has scarcely any resemblance to a well-planned military operation in which forces are deployed and equipment brought up in such a way as to move the line steadily forward to complete conquest. It is much more like the small and scattered penetrations of a few tiny exploring parties working against the almost overwhelming obstacles of a rugged uncharted wilderness. Many of the parties are thrown back because they cannot improvise the means for overcoming the climatic and geographical hindrances with which they are confronted. At only a few points occurs that happy combination of technical invention and hospitable terrain which permits the explorers a major advance. Thus at any given moment the line of scientific progress takes an extremely jagged form. Here and there a few long fingers reach into the wilderness without being able to drag other parts of the line forward. Such a situation is not favorable for understanding the wilderness as a whole, certainly not for making authoritative pronouncements about it. Of the many conceivably relevant facts, science can offer but a small selection, chosen because they lend themselves to investigation. It is particularly important to bear this in mind when attempting to assess results at any given moment and to fit them into a broad picture of the whole.

At the beginning of this chapter mention was made of the gap at the center of our knowledge about personality. This gap can now be identified with more precision: it is a gap at that point where it becomes necessary to consider the continuous development of personality over periods of time and amid natural circumstances. Obviously this topic offers rough ground for scientific exploring parties, and until recently the techniques for studying personality have hardly been strong enough to promise substantial progress. Furthermore, no single branch of science has included the natural growth of personality as one of its immediate goals. Biological research does not assume the task of explaining the unique course of individual lives; rather, it deals with man as an organism and searches for the common basic mechanisms of his behavior. Experimental psychology has generally turned away from the complexities of adult life, seeking facts more ripe for control and measurement in animal experiments, the behavior of infants, and the simplest mental operations. The social sciences are not concerned with the single individual, giving attention rather to groups of similarly situated people and discovering what these people have in common. Only dynamic psychology has regularly kept the individual at the center of interest and tried to bridge the chasm between biological and social ways of thinking. But dynamic psychology had its origin in the attempt to treat neurotic patients; it is still largely based on the study of blocked and disordered behavior. Thus it comes about that the searching eye of scientific research has barely glanced at everyday lives in progress, to say nothing of lives marked by unusual happiness or major social contributions.

It is more than historical accident, however, that this gap remains unfilled. The scientist, like anyone else, prefers victory to defeat. He wants to work with facts that can be controlled, with determinants that can be determined, with outcomes that can be predicted and measured. He wants to arrive at general concepts and general relationships, searching out the lawfulness beneath the multitude of surface events. In consequence of this bias, the scientist is inevitably disposed to deal selectively with human nature. He can do little with the fact that each person is acted upon by a tremendous multiplicity of influences, becoming as a result a unique individual. He can do hardly more with the circumstance that both person and environment undergo continuous change—that personality is a constantly evolving system. He is extremely reluctant to go beyond the task of explaining the forces that affect the person in order to consider how the person in turn affects his environment. The scientific approach to personality, therefore, has thus far greatly favored the simpler and less flexible aspects of behavior, giving scant attention to multiplicity, individuality, continuous change, or to the person as a source of action.

The extent of this bias can be appreciated by contrasting the scientist's approach with that of the novelist, dramatist, or writer of biography. The literary man is usually interested in the changes that occur in his characters as they live through a series of complex important events. He tells us about the way such events affect the characters and the way the characters affect the events. Our interest is not merely in what the characters are but also in what they do and in what they become. Growth is a prominent theme in novels of strongly autobiographical flavor, and it becomes particularly insistent for the writer of biography, who usually sets himself the task of understanding a life marked by noteworthy accomplishment. If his work is to be complete, the biographer must try to account for transformations such as that of Abraham Lincoln from a moody, reluctant, indecisive young man into a President distinguished for passionate conviction and vigorous leadership. Change, whether it be growth or disintegration, is a central concern in literature. Of a writer who does not depict change in personality we are apt to say a little scornfully that he deals only in caricature. The minor characters of Dickens, like Mr. Micawber, who at each appearance reiterates his bland assurance that something will turn up to rescue him from poverty, illustrate this inferior though often amusing treatment of personality. An artist would certainly be overlooking the richest qualities of his material if he made his central characters behave with such monotonous rigidity. The scientist, however, is under tremendous temptation to practice the art of caricature. It would be vastly easier to explain and predict behavior if everyone acted like Mr. Micawber and if no one had any particular effect on the conditions surrounding him. It is not surprising, therefore, that scientific study has been directed chiefly at the fixed, the repetitive, the unrealistic, and the unspontaneous in human relations.

Most of the ideas discussed earlier in this chapter put emphasis on the kind of learned behavior that is unwitting and irrational. The subtle impress of the culture is most readily perceived when it produces automatic behavior that is not adapted to existing conditions. Behavior indicative of social class is unconsciously absorbed from the environment and sometimes occurs in contradiction to the person's professed ideals. Role expectations are not laid down in black and white to be learned by conscious act; they seep into a person's life from sources he does not always recognize and with a force he may sometimes regret. It is much the same story with emotional attitudes early learned in the family circle and with the unconscious conflicts, anxieties and defenses that figure in neurotic maladjustment. Similarly the biological foundations of behavior have been examined in their more primitive manifestations where their command of conduct is most autocratic. In short, the scientific student of personality has been most interested in the things that freeze the learning process and that sneak into it by channels not consciously discerned. This direction of interest has become fully explicit in psychopathology, where it is recognized that most of the facts of individual maladjustment can be understood as blockages in the learning process. Here, however, balance is provided by an equal interest in the process of cure, which is conceived as the creation of a new learning situation in which the blockages are removed so that the patient becomes able to resume his development. The study of psychotherapy has begun to contribute helpful insights into the constructive aspects of human learning and thinking.

In this book we shall make a direct study of lives, choosing ones that exhibit a certain amount of growth under natural conditions. We shall study them over the course of time, using methods designed to reveal the multiplicity of influences surrounding them, their individuality, their gradual or sudden change, and their effect on their environments. To these lives we shall apply the social, the biological, and the psychodynamic views. We need to seek all possible benefit from what is known, while at the same time testing current ideas against concrete fact and looking for the interactions among various classes of fact. We shall also watch for the gaps left by such an account and do our best to make a place in the scientific understanding of man for the changing, growing, planful, farsighted, creative aspects of behavior. Any single contribution to this problem must necessarily be a small one, but the general subject is neither small nor unimportant. Toward the end of the final chapter we shall raise some basic questions about today's philosophy of human nature and consider specific ways in which its one-sidedness is doing serious harm.

SUGGESTIONS FOR FURTHER READING

The most pertinent book to suggest for further reading at this point is Ralph Linton's small but illuminating volume, *The Cultural Background of Personality* (New York & London, D. Appleton-Century Co., 1945), which undertakes to build bridges between the study of society and the study of the individual.

In the present book the biological view of man will be considered at greater length in Chapter 6, the psychodynamic view in Chapter 8, and the social view in Chapter 4. Suggested further readings are given at the end of each of these chapters.

A broad survey of adolescent development will be found in *The Adolescent Personality* by Peter Blos (New York & London, D. Appleton-Century Co., 1941), pp. 228-270.

2. Hartley Hale, Physician and Scientist

> I like the world as it is. For as it is it offers competition and insecurity, and it's the battle to overcome each of these that makes life worth while.
>
> HARTLEY HALE

A number of years ago, twenty Harvard undergraduates were engaged through the student employment office to serve as paid subjects in extensive studies of personality. One of these young men was Hartley Hale, a twenty-one-year-old junior who was concentrating in biology and planning a career in medicine. The studies proceeded at a leisurely pace up to the time of his graduation. Ten years later, just after his thirty-third birthday, he came to Boston to read a paper at a medical meeting. He was prevailed upon to extend his visit by two days so that he might be made the subject of a second study, compensation being offered at a rate appropriate to his current earning capacity. This time the interviews and tests were packed closely together, but all the sessions were electrically recorded, and this together with Hale's good-humored and generous participation permitted the study to be searching and comprehensive. What we know about this man thus rests upon two separate series of observations, one made when he was a premedical undergraduate, the other when he had become a physician and scientific investigator well-established in his profession.

To understand as well as possible the natural growth of even a single personality is a task of no small magnitude. In order to concentrate fully upon it we shall not stop to make explicit in this chapter either our methods of examination or our guiding concepts. These problems will occupy us later. Our present purpose will be more strictly biographical. We want to understand one man, Hartley Hale, as well as it is possible to understand him with the materials at our disposal. We want to know the story of his life and to search behind that story for whatever we can find by way of explanation. Before we can move in a responsible manner in the realm of general ideas it is necessary to become exhaustively acquainted with at least one fact, and if personality is our theme this fact can be nothing smaller than a person's whole life in all its uniqueness and all its complexity.

Part One: THROUGH COLLEGE

THE HALE FAMILY CIRCLE

One of the first tasks assigned to Hale in the undergraduate study was that of preparing an autobiography. He started with the family circle. He told of his paternal ancestors, who herded cattle in the Scotch lowlands, and of his grandfather, remembered as a "stern straight-laced old Scotchman," who settled in a fair-sized midwestern American city and established his own wholesale business. He described his father's career at a large university, a career which included both scholastic attainments in the classics and success in the hockey rink. After a short period of teaching, the father was persuaded to enter the wholesale business, where he "started at the bottom" and "struggled upward" until he became, on the grandfather's death, general manager of the company. Hale's father was forty when he met and courted his future wife, an artist of twenty-seven for whom "critics were predicting a bright future." Born in Iowa, this talented young woman had received most of her education and all of her artistic training in Chicago, and had but lately moved to the smaller city with her mother following the latter's second marriage. So energetic was the father's courtship that she was persuaded to drop her career in favor of marriage. Three years later a daughter was born, and after another five years, when the father was forty-eight and the mother thirty-five, Hartley arrived on the scene. "As my mother remarked many years after," he wrote, "I was late on this occasion just as I have always been late for everything else."

Hale's father conducted his business with energy and devotion. Most of the profits were ploughed back into the company to expand and strengthen its position. But he was much more than a business man. His son wrote:

> Dad is a scholar in the old meaning of the word. The house is filled with bookcases, which in turn are filled with books, all

of which he has read. He even sometimes picks up Latin books and reads them. He is young-minded, forward-looking, interested. His mind is sharp and fast; his temper, when roused, likewise. He is seldom unreasonable. Operated on for appendicitis two years ago (when 69) he was sitting up in bed smoking a cigar on the second day, home and around on the sixth. He is half a head shorter than I; thin, active, a burner of midnight oil.

Hale admitted later that his father's quick temper was sometimes disturbing. The father's scholarly tendencies, perhaps also the fact that he was by no means a young man while his children were growing up, caused him to want peace and quiet in the home and to be unduly irritated by noise. "He'd get quite angry at us," Hale declared; "it always used to sort of shock me when he'd get that angry." What shocked him most in these incidents, however, seems to have been his father's lapse from a standard of reasonableness which at other times conferred a considerable feeling of security. On the whole he considered his father an unusually just man as well as a model of energy and competence.

The mother appeared in the autobiography in a somewhat less favorable light. The son's pen sketched as follows the contrasting personalities of his parents:

> Mother is undecided, opposed to unknown change. She is afraid of airplanes, having never been in one. Dad went up in an open two-seater when I was four years of age, just to see what it was like. Mother's mind usually makes a quick stab at the answer, and then retreats while she thinks it over and answers again. Dad's mind pauses momentarily and then comes out with the right answer. This point is readily apparent when one plays bridge with the two of them. I can never remember seeing Dad play the wrong card. Mother often plays and then gasps as she sees that she has played the wrong card.

If the father's standards of quiet were a little high for a growing boy, the mother's standards of cleanliness were even more formidable. In the second study Hale told us that she kept the house "absolutely spotless," cleaning it twice a day, polishing the furniture, insisting "that no piece of dirt be allowed to lie in a place for more than thirty minutes." She was also "a great dictator: she told you when the weather was cold, what you should put on, whether it was myself or my father, and that's a very irritating quality." In other ways, however, she figured as an interesting and satisfactory member of the household, where on the whole the children felt themselves to be liked and cherished. This was summarized as follows in the autobiography: "Mother is interested in art, music, books; Dad in nearly everything; both in Connie (my sister) and me."

Different as were the two parents, they managed for the most part to present a united front in matters of discipline. "They pretty much got together on punishments," Hale told us; they always carried out whatever disciplinary measures they had threatened to use, and this gave to the punishment program a reliable character which allowed the boy as he grew older to weigh in advance the pleasure of misbehavior, the pain of punishment, and the chances of being caught. He felt that his punishments were deserved and that there was no particular favoritism between himself and Connie. Methods of punishment included spanking, scolding, being sent to his room, denial of some pleasure, being made to feel that he had fallen short of expectations; but no methods were used, as far as he could recall, which emphasized sibling rivalry or possible loss of the parents' love. Hale looked upon his father as the final authority and as the more reasonable disciplinarian. If his father lapsed from rationality, he protested angrily and might even refuse to obey. He recalled an incident in his adolescence when his father had forbidden a radio in the car. This unjustified ruling he evaded by hooking up his own portable radio temporarily when he had the car for the evening, and his father, though well aware of the ruse, never caught him in the act and never punished him.

Both parents seem to have played a part in creating what Hale rather oddly described as an "atmosphere of cultural unrest." This expression signified an emphasis on intellectual and artistic accomplishment; for instance, "I had read, or had read to me, most of Shakespeare, had learned to draw and play the piano, and could quote quite a few poems by the time I finished with primary school." He claimed to have memorized almost the whole of *Horatius at the Bridge* before he could read. Artistic and musical instruction was undertaken by the mother, but she was an impatient teacher whenever the learning progressed slowly. Hale's early literary heroes were Horatius, Ben Hur, and several of the characters of Kipling. He wrote that he "liked and admired justice, hated injustice and cruelty."

The high cultural standards of the home did not preclude interests of a more childlike and spontaneous kind. Hale wrote:

> I loved animals. Any kind of animals. I used to read stories
> about them by the hour, draw pictures of them, own as many
> of them as I could convince the family we had to have. This in-
> cluded several birds (one of which we had for 13 years, and
> which would come out of the cage and sit on our fingers), two
> dogs, white rats, turtles, gold fish, a cat. They vetoed a skunk.
> An English setter was, and is, my idea of a perfect pet.

That his parents limited the domestic zoo only by prohibiting the
skunk suggests that his father's love of peace and his mother's devotion to neat cleanliness were counterbalanced by considerable
appreciation of the natural interests of childhood.

In one important respect the family circle failed to provide a
feeling of security. Every so often its harmony was disrupted by a
parental quarrel, and these quarrels frequently started over
Hartley's misbehavior and disobedience.

> But there was a general tension in my home life. I was a
> rather stubborn, know-my-own-minded little child. I used to
> distress mother no end, which distressed dad no end, which led
> usually to an argument. Dad, an introvert, would say things
> and then sit there reading; mother, an extrovert, would go up-
> stairs (where I then went) and tell me what she felt, upon
> which I would act as a sort of peacemaker. I, strangely enough,
> felt malice toward neither of them; partly because harmony be-
> tween the two of them was uppermost in my mind, and partly
> because I felt that mother was wrong in saying what she did
> in the first place, and then that dad was wrong in saying what
> he did. So that about evened the score. These 'outbreaks' didn't
> happen often, but I had a certain fear that they might at any
> time. It was a tension.

Nothing further was said in the autobiography, but in the second
study a decade later Hale told us a great deal more about these
quarrels. "I never felt that things were too safe and too happy,"
he said; the whole thing seemed to "make my own future so uncertain, as a result I spent a lot of time thinking about it." From the
later vantage point he was able to see the relation between these
quarrels and the recurrent nightmares which he had reported in his
autobiography:

Our house was a big wooden frame structure. I was born in the very room I occupy when I'm home. I always loved the house, and the only nightmare I can remember having fairly often was the one that would cause me to run crying to my parents' room to be reassured that we weren't going to move out of the house.

When in the second study we reminded him of this excerpt, he said that his parents sometimes talked of moving, especially his mother who wanted a smaller house. He said:

Whenever they did talk about that, it used to scare me, used to scare the hell out of me, I didn't want to move, I was very much attached to the old house. For no special reason; it had no particular gratifying features about it: big frame ugly house with high ceilings and poor heating, no heating as a matter of fact until I was about 14, and there wasn't much to recommend it except that my sister liked it . . . I never felt too secure about life in general, and the talk about moving was taking away the most secure part of my life, which was that house.

The effect of these quarrels on Hale's development was evidently a profound one, especially from his tenth to twelfth years when they came to their peak. We shall return to them when we reach that point in his career.

It was important that his sister liked the house. From this remark we might infer that his sister occupied a position of prestige and respect. Connie resembled her father, having his "quick mind and temper;" she got high grades in school but also excelled in the art and music first taught by her mother. "She was very good looking," wrote Hartley, "and I liked her, though we were never especially close due to age differences." One of her endearing traits was her tendency to stick up for him when he was out of parental favor. But her most drastic influence occurred in what we shall refer to as the "backbone incident."

Probably the greatest influence she exerted on my young life was the installation of a backbone in me. I shall never forget the incident:

I was thin and small when young. One day when I was about 8, I guess, I was playing with my cousin, a girl half a year older than I. One of the bullies of the neighborhood came over and began making unpleasant remarks about what he was going to do to me. Betty (my cousin) stuck up for me and held him off until I could make my escape. I ran home as fast as I could. Mother wasn't home, but Connie was. I told her the story, expecting sympathy. To my utter amazement she accused me of cowardice and shamed me for 'hiding behind a woman's skirts.' She told me if I had any courage I'd go back there and assert my rights. This I did, I must admit with fear and trembling inside of me, and when I called his bluff with no changes in my anatomy occurring I found that my terror of him vanished; and from that time on I never again feared him and never again ran from fright in a fight.

Hale attached to this incident an importance almost equal to that of the parental quarrels. Before we attempt to evaluate its part in his development, however, we must consider in more detail the events and chronology of his childhood.

EARLY CHILDHOOD

Hale remembered two episodes which occurred when he was two years old. One of them involved the enjoyment he felt in playing around a country summer cottage with a little girl of his own age. In the other we find him in the role of investigator: he stood on his kiddy car to peer through a garage window in order to see what was going on inside, but the car went out from under him so that he fell and cut his head. For the next year his memories were more numerous. His sister and another girl wanted him to ride in a baby buggy and pretend to be a baby; though greatly offended, he consented in return for a suitable bribe. He recalled swinging and riding a velocipede, eating grapes from the vine and picking dandelion greens with the family. These scattered early memories presently give place to more definite and more connected episodes. An important landmark was the Christmas when he was four years old:

> I got a fire engine, a wagon I could sit in and ride, with a ladder sticking way out behind. For four years I went all over the neighborhood. Everyone in the neighborhood used the fire engine. Next summer I got an Indian suit. I couldn't decide whether to be an Indian or a fireman.

Noteworthy in this memory is the easy making of the masculine identifications implied by the nature of the gifts he received. Also to be inferred from this recollection, as from his earliest memory of the little girl, is an easy and comfortable feeling about other children: he expressed no fear or resentment over the borrowing of the cherished fire engine, basking instead in the popularity and distinction which it conferred upon him.

By the end of his fourth year his memories begin to testify to a tremendous interest in things mechanical. The mastery of machines is the theme of a whole series of pleasurable recollections. When he entered kindergarten, the blocks with wheels, holes, and axels arrested his attention: "I built carts every day and rode on them." He used to slam the cupboard doors after putting the blocks away, but one day he happened to close them quietly and the teacher praised him and held him up as a good example, after which he took the lead in quiet closing. His memories of machines continued with the receipt of an electric train for Christmas. This gift had hitherto been considered too dangerous by his parents, so although he was dubious about the existence of Santa Claus he decided to go over his parents' heads by writing a direct letter.

> The train was there, with a letter from Santa Claus saying how we had foxed my parents. I was jubilant; I wouldn't leave the train for a minute, and it was hard to shake my faith in Santa Claus after that. I was just about nuts.

Before he could read, a friend of the family gave him a book on electricity, which his parents read to him while he looked at the diagrams. Thus instructed, he tried to build a motor that would run without an outside source of power, but he experienced all the difficulties that beset earlier inventors of a perpetual motion machine. At seven his appendix was removed, an event which he remembered chiefly because it prevented him from celebrating the Fourth of July. During convalescence he continued to design the machine, even though his nurse said that it looked like a mouse trap.

> I was all pepped up again about my machine. So I sold stock, 5 shares at a nickel, which gave me a quarter. I worked all summer and it wouldn't work. The stockholders began to clamor for their quarter. So I talked to Mother about it. She usually tried to shut me up on things she didn't think I could do. So she said if I could make a boat that would go twice around the bathtub she'd give me a dollar. I got a clock motor and did it, and the stockholders got twenty cents on their nickels.

Later in the year he began building model airplanes, a craze in which he was joined by two other boys. At nine he received a book on radios and built first a crystal set which did not work, then a one-tube set which was a great success. Quite early he seemed to possess the spirit of a true mechanic. He did not require quick success; it was the planning and building and tinkering and experimenting, together with the vision of some ultimate success, that kept him on fire with enthusiasm.

Meanwhile he was going to school, where his studies were successful but his deportment record horrible. He used to "act up in class" and "raise as much hell as possible," as a result of which he spent a great deal of time standing in the corner or sitting in the principal's office. "I got interested in girls about this time," he said; "I used to grab them when they came into the coat closet and kiss them." At six he worshipped from afar a platinum blond three years older than himself. At seven, however, his affections came to rest on a young lady a year younger who was "cute," whom he "led around by the hand." From this point on he was never without a girl friend. He was equally unabashed about investigating the possibilities of tobacco. At eight he and his cousin Betty were irked because his parents would not let them join in a game of bridge. To get even they smoked a couple of cigarettes. When Hartley's mother detected the smell of smoke, he expected a severe punishment, but instead she merely explained why it was an undesirable thing and told him not to do it again. Soon afterward, however, he resumed cigarette smoking, sometimes with Betty, more often alone behind the barn. It is interesting to note that by the time he reached college he had become a moderate smoker who chiefly enjoyed an occasional pipe.

Hale's proficiency as a fighter, first demonstrated in the "backbone incident," received considerable development in the years immediately following. He wrote:

> The neighborhood, though fine to the west of the house, became a very tough district only a block to the east. Gangs came out of the east to cloud our youthful horizon, and many a heated fight occurred. I still felt afraid while we were bandying words, but as soon as the actual fight started the fear vanished, and I bored in with a verve that earned me a better-than-average percentage of wins. I grew stronger.

His parents differed in their attitudes toward this phase of his social development. "Mother didn't like me to fight," he told us. "Dad

didn't care too much; he actually paid to have me take some boxing lessons at one time, which helped quite a lot."

LATER CHILDHOOD

Although Hale's interest in mechanisms continued unabated
through the later years of childhood, the events that stood out in his
mind between the ages of nine and thirteen had to do chiefly with
athletic and social ventures. His school career continued to be tem-
pestuous. According to his own account his behavior record became
worse and worse. Without much effort he was able to keep up such
a good scholastic record that he skipped half a grade in the fourth
grade and stayed consistently on the honor roll. He said little about
this and seemed inclined to attribute it more to his skill in human
management than to either scholastic aptitude or effort: "When I
wasn't cutting up I played the teachers for all I was worth."

At the age of nine Hartley joined the "Y" and went to "Y" camp
the summer he became ten. Here he met a boy named Dan, who became for many years his best friend: "a hellion, a daring sort of a
chap; we got into more trouble than anyone who ever lived." Following Dan's bold example he would perform feats such as diving
from the top of a windmill tower into the water tank many yards
below. It was also in Dan's company that Hartley overcame a long-
standing fear, that of moths alighting on his face. One night at
camp they got the cabin full of moths so that Hartley even
swallowed one while talking. Dan lived only four blocks from the
Hales, but in an easterly direction so that Hartley's parents did not
know his parents. At the end of the camp period he joined with
Hartley and the two friends of the model airplane days to make an
adventurous foursome.

It was at the "Y" that still another fear dropped by the wayside.
Attempts had been made since the age of four to teach Hartley to
swim, but he was deathly afraid of the water.

> At the "Y" I began playing at the shallow end of the pool.
> One night there was a swimming meet of 10-year-olds, and one
> side was a man short. So the instructor asked me to join but I
> said I couldn't swim. So he coaxed me to dive across the pool,
> which I did, struggling across to the other side. Then they put
> me in the 60-foot race and I beat the fellow I was against. I
> almost dropped dead from surprise.

There was one branch of learning which Hartley pursued with great vigor during his later childhood, choosing for the most part his own sources of instruction.

> I was from the earliest time curious about sex. Due to my insistent demands my mother started to teach me something about it, but the gutter was so much more rapid that I finally abandoned instruction in favor of it. When I went east a block, I found that knowledge and near-knowledge were quite easily attainable, and with my natural curiosity the two of us soon got together. When I learned a new word one day I went and looked it up in the Century Dictionary which was on our library shelf, and the paragraph about that mentioned some other word, and so on, so that in two hours' time I had learned all the scientific names, though I wasn't just exactly sure how the whole thing worked yet. By the time I was twelve I had read a book on prenatal care, one on childbirth, and one on 'what every married man should know,' and that, added to all the jokes I had heard, gave me a pretty comprehensive knowledge for one of my age. I was thinking about it one day when I realized that of course my parents must have done it, but though it seemed sort of strange to think about it, it didn't shock me at all.

His knowledge served to immunize him against terror on the subject of masturbation, about which he merely felt that "it was something I shouldn't tell anyone," but at puberty he gave up, at least for the time being, both masturbation and smoking when he read that they interfered with athletic ability. Of his first nocturnal emission, which occured at about thirteen, he said: "It didn't worry me because I had been expecting it ever since I read about it the year before."

With other children he felt that he was on the whole quite popular. "Among my close friends in youth," he wrote, "I was more often than not the goat, but this really never bothered me—I sort of liked it." The role of goat is not usually a child's spontaneous first choice, and the willingness to play it can usually be interpreted as a sign of urgent need for acceptance by the others. With the passage of time, however, Hartley was no longer obliged to swallow his pride; he became increasingly "competitive and outspoken." "I was cocky," he said in the autobiography. "As I grew older, approaching twelve, I was very very cocky. This almost always antagonized older people with whom I came in contact. But the few older people who took the trouble to break under the shell of cockiness became among my staunchest friends."

One highly important problem of Hale's childhood was completely omitted from his autobiography. In fact he did not disclose it at all during the undergraduate study; it came to light only in the last interview of the second study when, to the utter amazement of the interviewer, he suddenly said:

> When I was very young I stuttered extremely badly. I stuttered badly all through grade school, and I stuttered pretty badly all through high school. Although I was able to overcome it on a few occasions and get myself up on the stage, it was always with a great deal of effort, and I usually forced myself to do those things with the hope that I would ultimately overcome those feelings, but it didn't work out as rapidly as I thought it was going to, and I was stuttering when I came to college. I didn't have as much difficulty when I was among friends as I did when I got myself out on a limb, when I was in class or something of that sort. But I've done a reasonably good job of overcoming it now.

Asked if it was not quite a handicap when he was in grade school, he replied:

> Oh boy! I'll say it was tough. It was very tough. And I'm sure it arose from the general insecurity of my home surroundings. That's why it started, I'm sure. But even that knowledge, even the fact that I had that knowledge, even when I was a little kid, didn't help me as far as the stuttering was concerned. Nothing I could do about it myself, no one I could go to to help me. And as a result it's been tough.

Hale did not, of course, stutter in any of the undergraduate interviews. Nothing in his speech suggested a history of stuttering even to interviewers accustomed to take notice of such things. It is interesting to inquire why he suppressed this particular piece of information when he seemed otherwise so free in relating the facts of his life. Evidently he found the speech difficulty peculiarly humiliating. We can assume that as a child he had been mercilessly ridiculed. His difficulty in wielding the weapon of speech doubtless contributed to his anxiety when a fight was in the stage of "bandying words" and his joyful relief when he could bore in with his unstuttering fists. At the time of the first study he was still not quite sure that his victory over stuttering was securely won. He preferred to tell us about his historic victories: his conquest of the fear of moths, his mastery of swimming, his triumph over cowardice in fights. There was no evasion of his failures and setbacks provided he had finally mastered them, but he was not disposed to bring into the discussion a personal battle in which the issue was still in doubt. Stuttering bears a peculiar relation to the building of a favorable self-picture. It lets one down and exposes one to ridicule precisely at those moments when one is attempting self-display, assertion, and competitiveness. It is also involuntary and uncontrollable, likely to be made worse by effort and tension, thus resistant to those techniques of vigorous direct action and mastery which Hale used so successfully upon his other problems. Here, then, was a source of grave feelings of inferiority and helplessness, a severe blight on the career of an energetic growing boy. We can better understand his hunger for respect, his earlier willingness to play the goat, his pride in mastering adversities, and his omission of the still dangerous weakness when painting for us the picture of the man he hoped he was becoming at the age of twenty-one.

Hale himself related his stuttering to the insecurity of his life at home. The parental quarrels constituted another threat which he usually could not control. In the second study, further removed from their impact, he was able to tell us a great deal more about these squabbles which reached their height when he was ten to twelve years old. Apparently his mother and father came fairly close to an actual break-up during this period. He attributed the difficulty to their differences in temperament. As mentioned before, he himself was one of the main causes of strife, which made the situation all the more trying. He said:

I was a bone of contention because my mother was a very cautious person, and her general reaction to anything new is a negative one. And her general attitude toward me was one of protection and of not wanting me to do anything that was bad for me or anything, and I was by nature slightly venturesome, so this attitude used to annoy me considerably. And as a result, instead of calming me down any, it made me considerably more venturesome than I would have been. And I went out of my way to do things that I knew would—that she didn't want me to do, simply because she didn't want me to do them. I'd go ahead and do these things anyhow and then I'd usually go them one better, and that would get her very upset. She'd get very upset, and then that would upset my father because he didn't like upsetting things . . . He never liked to have arguments at the dinner table, it was very annoying to him, so then he'd get mad at my mother, and then she'd get mad at him for getting mad with her, and then they'd forget about me.

One of the worst features of the quarrels, especially after Connie had gone away to school, was that the entire burden of restoring peace fell on Hartley's shoulders. "It was difficult being caught in the strife," he said, "and having to take care of it and not having anybody to help me." As with the stuttering, he did not see what he himself could do and he could not turn to anyone for help. He felt responsible for the continuing existence of the family.

The thing that used to bother me the most was the uncertainty of when the thing was going to explode. I could never be quite sure. I didn't like to go to bed, and I used to read until I could hear my parents coming upstairs, and I'd put out the light and lie there, and I could hear them as they were getting undressed, and I'd never be sure when they'd start talking about it, they could almost never talk without there being some kind of an argument. And I could always recall lying there in bed wondering whether it was going to develop into an argument or whether it wasn't, a point about which I am so conscious that we make it a very definite point now with my own children never to argue in front of them.

Hartley's anxiety was clearly intense, but it is significant that he did not discontinue the venturesome and defiant behavior which was so often the immediate cause of the arguments. Whatever his initial bewilderments, he eventually placed the whole problem on a reflective plane and consciously decided against toning down his own behavior.

I realized that if I were the model child perhaps that would quiet down the arguments, because it was always—it was often made fairly clear to me that I was the cause of the arguments. But I quickly discarded that thesis and decided that after all I couldn't go that far. I decided that I had my own life to live after all, and by God I was going to live it, and by God I did. An awful lot of the things that I did were things that I wouldn't have done if it hadn't been for this opposition; I just went that much further as an extra effort of defiance.

He was inclined to agree to a suggestion that in some respects his early trials might have had a stimulating effect on his development. "I think that probably by birth I was endowed with some of my mother's qualities, caution," he said, "which without that opposition might have held me back to some extent." He was clearly resentful of what he described as "being held down," resolving not to give in at any cost. Describing his own eldest child, he said:

> She is very much like I was when I was young, very anxious to be grown up, and very anxious to assume responsibilities for things, and likes very much to be around grown people and so on. I was myself always held down in those things, anything I wanted to do I was held back in, used to irritate the hell out of me, with the result that I usually went ahead and did it anyway, and I always made up my mind that if I had any children that wasn't going to be the case with them.

In some of our tests in the earlier study which called upon him to make up or to complete stories he utilized the theme of being held down and made his heroes stubbornly pursue their own way to worthy ends. We also noticed at that time that all the marriages which came into his plots were either explicitly or implicitly unhappy.

To accomplish his extensive program of resistance and rebellion Hartley fortified himself with a large circle of friends. We have already noted the strengthening effect of his daring friend Dan, who was, however, merely the most prominent representative of his many contacts to the eastward. Hartley's choice of friends often upset his mother and thus led to quarrels at home, but he rejected the friends she preferred for him and found a welcome life of his own among the gangs and on the baseball teams of the less pretentious end of town. He said:

> I got a chance to get a circle of friends around me that sort of buffeted me from my family, that my family had no connection with . . . It gave me a circle of friends of my own which I could use between my family and myself. . . .

> Once I got into high school I was able to build up my own circle of friends against my family. Then I wasn't so much embroiled in the family as I had been. And then I was happier.

In this case also it seemed to him that his departure from family ideals had a beneficial effect on his development. He learned about the rougher side of life, proved his capacity to deal with it, and at the same time gained sympathy and respect for people living in economic circumstances less favorable than his own.

HIGH SCHOOL: THE HAPPIEST YEARS

Hale remembered his high-school years as the happiest time of his life. "I was struck with the idea," he wrote, "that one should try to indulge in as many outside activities as possible, raise hell, have a good time. This I did." In later retrospect he attributed his happiness to "the complete and utter irresponsibility of those years": "nobody did much work, there were a lot of outside interests which made it happy. I enjoyed working on theatrical productions, working on the newspapers, going to parties, driving an automobile rapidly around corners, things of that sort." He looked back on high school as a place where he had learned nothing but had had a wonderful time.

He was still able to make good grades in his studies without serious effort. Disliking chemistry, he did no work and got a "D," but the courses he enjoyed, such as physics and English, yielded him a harvest of good grades which offset his failures. He carried extra courses and could have graduated half a year early except that his parents thought him too young and he himself wanted to graduate with his class. When he graduated, it was with considerable distinction: he had achieved an average of 90 and was also voted the most popular boy in the class.

His heart was in extracurricular activities. He took particular pleasure in dramatics, in which he rose to the position of stage manager. Quite a little space in the autobiography was given to describing the up-to-date high-school auditorium, which had stage facilities to delight the heart of a mechanically inclined manager. "Working out startling lighting effects and staging plays," he wrote, "was one of the major joys of my life, and I worked hours on it." He did not participate as an actor, which is not surprising in view of his tendency to stutter, and in the second study he told us of an incident which must have given him a decidedly poor reputation as a public performer. The wording of a stimulus phrase in one of our association tests struck him as funny; he responded humorously and then became seized with a fit of uncontrollable laughter. When he finally brought his mirth under control he explained the seizure as follows:

> I've always had trouble with laughing. When I was a kid in school I used to get started laughing and couldn't stop. The more the teacher would get mad at me and try to make me stop, the harder I'd laugh, and it was just fantastic, and I was afraid I was going to get started again, I haven't done that for years. I was afraid I might laugh half way through a record for you. The first time I was ever on the stage, one of our school plays, my lines were after several other people had spoken, and I thought to liven up the ceremony a little bit I'd shoot a spit ball at one of the other characters on the stage. So I rather surreptitiously shot the spitball, and it hit him right behind the ear, and he let out a howl—this was before about 1500 people—and just about the next instant was my line, and I got so convulsed with laughter that they had to bring the damn curtain down and call the whole thing off; I couldn't go on.

Even if this yarn contains a bit of picturesque exaggeration it testifies to a number of interesting traits in our subject and certainly suggests that he was better placed behind the scenes than in front of them.

Equal in attraction to Hale's work as a stage manager were his activities as a high school journalist. He became humor editor of the monthly magazine, editing the humorous contributions and drawing cartoons. He also wrote an anonymous column filled with spicy bits of gossip and scandal. It amused him to hear the persons who appeared in this column expressing their annoyance and saying what they would like to do to the author, but the editor-in-chief, who alone knew the authorship, faithfully kept the secret. Hale was irked that some of the most fascinating gossip was deemed unsuitable for publication in the school magazine. To remedy this situation he got out a single sheet of his own, prepared by hand and circulated among the students. He was asked about it in detail during the second study, and said:

> That was a sort of little scandal sheet. I'd collect embarrassing things about people and then make some drawings and write it up and circulate it. It would circulate to most everybody in the school except the person about whom it was written, who would get it only at the last minute and be quite angry but

generally keep the paper. I got a big kick out of it and I think most of the other people did too.

> I would try to find out something about someone that nobody else knew, sort of scout around and see what was going on, see what they were up to, and trail them around for a while. Sometimes I'd go and follow them in the car at night and see what they did and where they went. It was especially nice when I could get something they thought nobody else knew, and which they were trying definitely to keep secret. The sort of thing that I particularly liked was somebody who would be going steady with some gal and two-time her, go see some other gal, something of that sort. That was especially choice.

The authorship of this sheet was no secret, yet Hale was not disqualified from being chosen the most popular boy in the class. It is justifiable to assume that his relations to his fellow students contained friendlier elements which did not, however, lend themselves so well to lively narrative when viewed in retrospect.

That Hale was not wholly occupied with hell-raising comes out in his description of his girl friends. He started having dates at thirteen but went always with the same girl for the next three years and was therefore "considered slow." This girl was a year older and did not take much interest in her young suitor; their relationship was somewhat shy and distant. It was in fact with another girl, a casual acquaintance met while crashing parties at the age of fifteen, that Hartley overcame his shyness about kissing.

> She said it was New Year's Eve and it was the custom to kiss girls on New Year's Eve, and, well, I'd been brought up to be a gentleman. I must have been pretty poor because she asked me if she was the first girl I had ever kissed, and I just barely recovered in time to say 'Don't flatter yourself' and really kiss her.

This incident is curiously parallel to the "backbone incident" at eight years. Again the woman defines the masculine role, in which Hartley is failing, and again he meets the challenge by swift direct counteraction. At sixteen he met a girl a year younger with whom he fell in love, "if one may be said to do that at sixteen." He described this girl as very goodlooking.

> She was likewise very emotional, though reserved and cautious. She held her head high, talked easily, said the right things,

danced well. I walked home with her every night, a mile out of my way, and I saw her 'by accident' between every class.

> One night after I had known her about a month (but had only had three dates with her because she was very popular) I called her on the phone. During the conversation she mentioned that she was having trouble with her mathematics. I really wasn't supposed to go out on school nights, but then . . . It didn't take long to solve the problem; I had had the course the year before. It took longer to solve the problem of leaving. I wanted to kiss her, but had talked that very day with someone who was usually successful along those lines and who had failed when he tried it with her. But she seemed co-operative, and I finally got up enough nerve to try. I was successful, and from that time on it was just a question of gaining momentum.

He went with this girl steadily until his second year in college when, although they had considered themselves engaged, they both agreed to call if off in view of his prolonged absences and formidable course of professional training. The relationship was a source of great happiness to him:

> We seldom quarreled. We laughed too much to quarrel. We both liked the same things and we were both crazy about each other. Neither of us could stay mad about anything for long. Sexually I think I shall never meet anyone who appeals to me more. The only emotion I can ever remember having had after a sex experience with her was one of intense pleasure. Neither of us ever felt shame, remorse, or revulsion.

The decision to part was a hard one, made several times and then reversed before it finally stuck. Discussions about it sometimes made him feel so weak that he could hardly talk or stand. The discovery of an enjoyable and lovable girl companion, who put him ahead of her other male friends and with whom quarrels could be avoided, seemed to do a lot to soothe and stabilize the rambunctious young man whose path through high school so closely resembled one of his responses on the Rorschach ink-blot test: "a bullet going through mud, splattering, traveling at high speed."

COLLEGE: THE EMERGENCE OF SERIOUS PURPOSES

Graduating from high school at seventeen, Hale went for a year to a nearby junior college before making application to Harvard.

His experience with the high-school magazine, and a course in journalism which he found "sensational," had caused him to select advertising as his life work. He enjoyed the idea of selling things, of "presenting things in attractive form," of writing copy and making drawings, and in addition he liked the prospect of what he called "the hectic life, the upside-down hours, the peculiar existence." At junior college, however, he elected a course in biology, more to round out a program than because of any previous interest in the subject, and this brought him into contact with a teacher who had a marked effect on his career. When questioned in the second study about people who had influenced him he spoke as follows:

> Some people that I admired most were my teacher of physics in high school and my teacher of biology in junior college, both of whom were men and both of whom were very inspiring teachers. Both were intensely interested in the subjects that they taught and both were intensely interested in individuals, which is a rare quality in a teacher, and I did well in those subjects because I liked both teachers so much.

Evidently these two men broke through the shell of his cockiness; certainly they became his very good friends with whom he visited whenever he returned to his home city. To the biology teacher he assigned credit for getting him into Harvard: as a result of his tutelage Hale wrote an entrance examination in biology that earned highest honors.

> This guy got me so darned interested in the course that I used to sit up nights looking through the miscroscope, and I went out into the field to collect things and all that kind of thing. By the time I got done I'd really learned a little biology, and gotten intensely interested in it.

The thought of changing to medicine crossed his mind, but he was still headed for the advertising business when he entered Harvard.

The news of his admission to Harvard was one of the major positive events in his life. But when he learned that his best friend Dan had also been admitted, he was completely overwhelmed. "I have never regretted," he wrote, "the tears of joy I shed" upon hearing the second piece of glad tidings. The two boys continued to be friends at college, but they made the decision not to room together, their plan being that each should build up his own circle of friends and then share it with the other. Apparently the plan worked well, and the friendship was still in force at the time of the second study. Hale was enchanted to find that there were no required courses. "That's wonderful," he said, "it gives you a wonderful sense of freedom and it makes you very enthusiastic. You can wade out into the middle of things and get as wet as you want to in as many things as you want to." He used his freedom chiefly to take extra courses in biology.

During his freshman year he plunged more heavily than before into athletics. This had some curious consequences. He worked hard all season to make the freshman football team, but on the morning of the final game he was so late for the bus that the team had to leave without him so that he never got his numerals. He then worked furiously for the track team and was in every meet except the one with Yale, for which he failed to qualify by the narrowest last-moment margin. "That was a bitter pill to swallow," he wrote, "but fortunately my spirits don't stay down for long." That he should twice have failed on the very threshold of success suggested that athletic achievement was not entirely free from conflict and anxiety. He told us that he never lost sleep over sports but that he was always very nervous, in fact "practically a wreck," just before an important game. He also said that he often deliberately got himself late so that he could drown the anxiety by rushing around and arriving ready at the last possible moment. But his anxieties did not generally interfere with top performance; quite the opposite, they added energy to the battle and zest to the ultimate victory. He was not sure that sports would be worth while if they did not contain the element of anxiety and its conquest. The two incidents of the freshman year were certainly not typical of Hale, not typical even for the rest of his athletic performance that same year. Yet they happened, and they gave him a severe feeling of frustration; furthermore, they found an echo in several of the plots he devised two years later in our tests of creative imagination.

Given the picture of a man climbing a rope, for example, and asked to make up a story for which the picture might be an illustration, he told of a powerful young Negro athlete who sneaked into the gymnasium reserved for white people because his own gym was not equipped with a rope. The story continued:

> He is nearly at the top when the door of the gym opens and the keeper comes in. He sees him from his lofty position and his

brain gropes madly for a method of escape. He fears that if he does not find any the rope will be around his neck rather than in his hand. But he is only severely reprimanded and sent back to his own gym where he contents himself with doing push-ups.

The very next picture in the test showed a man bent over a table, his face buried in his arm, surrounded by strange hovering birds and bats. Hale perceived the man as an author who is also an opium fiend; the author is "approaching the climax of his most brilliant story" when his drug-poisoned body collapses "and his mind is filled with horrible visions," as a result of which "the story remains unfinished." Hale's reported anxiety connected with competitive struggle, the two instances of last-minute failure, and these two unusual imaginative plots, together suggest the presence of an inner obstacle which is occasionally large enough to trip him up at the threshold of success, although for the most part he functions with great effectiveness in competitive situations. We shall return at a later point to this curious problem.

It was also during his freshman year that Hale came to his decision to be a doctor. His conversion, we learned in the second study, occurred in a quite unusual way. Across the hall in the dormitory lived a student who enjoyed argument. Hale also enjoyed argument, and he particularly liked debating with this neighbor who was always reasonable and therefore did not irritate him and throw him into stubborn negativism. As a result they sometimes spent most of the night in arguments. Hale reconstructed for us as follows the crucial incident:

> One night for some reason or other, this was out of the clear blue sky, I don't know why or what brought it up, he decided, he got it in his mind, that I should be a doctor instead of going into advertising. And so he started to argue with me about it, and when morning came I agreed that he was right. He did a very logical, very thorough job on me, and so I went down the next day and I changed my field of concentration to biology. Then I called up my family and told them what I'd decided, which they didn't like.

Asked if he could recall the course of the argument, he said that his friend began by declaring him to be chiefly interested in medicine. Hale countered by pointing out that he was concentrating in English, going into advertising, and not taking a premedical program.

His friend then called attention to his honors entrance-grade in biology and observed that he must like his biology course the best of any he was taking because he spent the most time on it and talked about it at the greatest length.

> And after thinking it over pretty seriously I had to admit that I was pretty interested in that course. And he said, 'Now look what you've outlined for next year, all these biology courses, why are you doing that?' And I had to argue, had to admit that he was right, that perhaps I was slightly interested in the subject. And then I went on to the fact that it was going to take too damn long, that I didn't want to go through all the business of going through medical school, and that in addition the field was overcrowded, and so on, and he went on to argue that that didn't make for much difference, that if I did well at it I wouldn't have any trouble getting ahead, and that doctors don't usually starve. And he said that in addition it was his personal conviction that I was suited psychologically to be a doctor, so I went on to argue that I wasn't in the slightest suited to be a doctor, and . . . I've forgotten just what points he brought up about it but he made a pretty good case.

It is not without interest that Hale forgot the content of the arguments just at the point where they involved his own personal characteristics. He may have halted here because the friend's arguments were filled with embarrassing praise. We learned with surprise that the friend was not himself going into medicine, rather into law for which he considered himself psychologically better suited. His only connection with medicine was his great admiration for the doctor in his home town, a man who had done a great deal for the community and stood as a "very heroic figure in his mind." It was this picture of the medical man with which the friend enticed Hale, who had always previously thought of doctors as "a little too stolid and fixed," "tied up in their work," "not very interesting people," "dull people." Hale thought that his tremendous interest in biology might eventually have led him to choose medicine anyway, but the argument with his friend greatly hastened his seeing of the light.

Hale was not in the habit of responding submissively to the advice of others. In the early study he did not mention the part his friend played in the shift from advertising to medicine, allowing the decision to sound like one that he reached of his own accord. Why was he so decisively influenced on this particular occasion? Partly because he respected reasonableness and could see that his friend had no ax to grind. Partly because an appeal was made to inclinations already at work though not formulated in his own mind. But perhaps the strongest impact came from the element of flattering challenge that was implicit in what his friend had to say. The friend was arguing, in effect, as follows: "Medicine is a great career, an heroic one, not a dull one; I have been observing you, and you have the qualities that fit you for this great and heroic career." Through the combined appeal of logic, fact, and the display of personal interest, Hale was converted from a lower to a higher calling. Advertising represented to him an easy, exciting, profitable way of continuing the brash irresponsible life of his high-school years. Medicine appealed to something different in his personality, the thing that had been touched by the physics teacher and the biology teacher who had broken through his shell of cocky rebelliousness. It mobilized his capacity for deep absorbed interest, patient continuous work, dedication to goals of discovery that transcended the immediate satisfaction of personal needs. It eliminated certain doubts he had entertained about the ethics of advertising, and it gave to his college career a feeling of purpose and direction.

Having overcome, in what was for him routine fashion, his parents' objections to the new and bolder plan, Hale plunged enthusiastically into his biology courses. Sometimes his other work was neglected, especially if he did not see its relevance to his career, but he continued to do first-rate work in biology. He presently began work with a teacher who resembled his two previous models: highly competent and enthusiastic in his field, but also interested in his students and what they could accomplish.

During his junior year Hale became interested in a research project involving bone growth in animals, and his teacher allowed him to pursue it the following year as a senior honors thesis in spite of the fact that he had failed in sociology and therefore did not have quite the grades required to qualify as a candidate for honors.

As it turned out it was all right, I got two A's and two B's. That was really a lucky break in which he sort of took a gamble on me. There've been a few people along the line who've taken a gamble on me, it's been necessary two or three times, and I always feel a great sense of responsibility toward those people, and I think that every time that's happened I've come through.

Interestingly enough, although he "came through" with more than the required grades, the honors thesis itself was not completed on time. We inquired closely into the reasons and were forced to discard our first guess that once again he had been compelled to fail on the threshold of success. His research problem was sound, but the technical difficulties were very great and he did not have time for all the false starts, changes of method, and checking and rechecking of results, that go with honest scientific inquiry. If again he did not "get his numerals," so to speak, it was this time because he was too good a scientist, and he did not lose the esteem of his teachers for holding back an incomplete piece of research.

Hale's busy life as a premedical student cut into his athletic career, but he did not allow it to interfere too seriously with his social life. He took an active part in the affairs of his House, knew and regularly spoke to at least 250 of the 300 students who lived there, and was always seen in the dining hall in lively conversation with the students around him. He also made time for two or three dates a week. His dates would generally be with some favorite girl of the moment; "usually," he said, "it would take a minor upheaval to get going on a new track." These friendships did not supplant the relationship with the girl in his home city until the beginning of his junior year. When that relationship was finally terminated, he gave his full attention to a new girl who was still his regular date up to the time of graduation. He was quite fond of this girl but not at all inclined to consider marriage in view of the long professional training that lay ahead. During our senior year interview in which his girl friends were under discussion he rather unexpectedly volunteered the following piece of information:

> One other girl I liked better than any I've ever met. She's the only one I'd consider asking to marry me. She was the sister of a kid I grew up with and used to play with ever since I was five. She was about eight years older but she was at ease with us as with anyone else. She is more unselfish, more gracious, more talented than any I've ever met. There is so much more to her. She paints and plays the piano. She has the rare quality of making anyone from one to ninety feel that there is nothing more interesting in the world than talking with them. She has the disposition of an angel and a marvelous sense of humor.

Now nearing thirty, married, and with her own children, this "girl" was obviously not a potential partner. Some of her qualities were those of an ideal mother, yet Hale described his interest as being anything but ethereal.

Hale's conception of himself at the time of the undergraduate study can best be conveyed by quoting the closing words of his autobiography.

> I like the world as it is. For as it is it offers competition and insecurity; and it's the battle to overcome each of these that makes life worth while. When one gives up the fight he's through with this 'mortal coil,' and with security comes senility.
>
> The world thinks of me as happy, as seldom worrying; they laugh at and with me and I like it. They usually respect my judgments. They like me, I think.
>
> I swear too much, I procrastinate, I tend to exaggerate, I dramatize, I'm stubborn, I daydream. I'm optimistic, I'm honest (except when exaggerating), I'm fair. Life is sweet.

Analysis of responses on self-rating questionnaires did not substantially change this picture. He gave himself fairly high ratings with respect to most abilities, though quite low ones on a few. He pictured himself as intense and impulsive yet also capable of endurance, but he made only modest claims to organization and continuity. In the sphere of motives he thought of himself as highly active, assertive, dominant, yet friendly and nurturing; his low self-ratings piled up in the area of dependence, avoidances, and fears. He felt that he had won most of his developmental fights up to the present and could face those of the future with confidence and zest.

AVAILABLE CAPACITIES AND EXISTING LIMITATIONS
AS A COLLEGE SENIOR

Before we undertake to deepen our understanding of Hale's development and to carry his career forward another decade, we must stop to take a brief cross-sectional view of his capacities and limitations. In making this appraisal we do not assume that we are dealing with fixed innate endowments. We are concerned rather with the capacities and skills, whatever their origin, which were available to him and capable of mobilization at the time he was a college senior.

Physical Traits.—Hale was of average height and weight, with a bodybuild well-suited to athletic achievement. He carried no excess weight, was broad in the shoulders, narrow in the hips, muscularly strong in arms and legs. When younger he had been of less than average stature, but a marked growth spurt at fourteen brought him well up to average. He had participated in a great many different sports, usually with considerable success though rarely with outstanding distinction. No unusual or serious illnesses had marred his excellent health record. He seemed full of restless energy, describing himself as "a very impatient sort of fellow" who hated to sit and wait and always wanted to take action of some kind. His preference for vigorous action showed itself in many ways, serving among other things as his chief method of dealing with obstacles and frustrations.

Affective Qualities.—Hale's days were full of events from most of which he received satisfaction and pleasure. His prevailing mood could best be described as zestful. From rare experiences of dejection his spirits tended to bounce back quickly. It was interesting to notice that in his imaginative productions there were frequent themes in which dejection and despair visited the characters as a consequence of failure, isolation, and the lack of an appreciative audience. Sometimes his characters were so overwhelmed by these misfortunes that they elected to kill themselves. It was evident that Hale was not a stranger to dark moods, but it was equally clear that his energetic and sociable way of life effectively counteracted most of the conditions which proved so disastrous to his fictional characters. Hale said that sad stories and sad scenes in the movies never made him feel like crying; they simply depressed him. He was more apt to cry when flooded by sudden happiness, as when he learned that his best friend was admitted to college, or when transported out of himself by beautiful music. He specified as follows the most specific stimulus to tears: "when somebody goes out of their way to do something nice for me," or when a character on stage or screen "goes out of his way to be awfully good to someone who doesn't expect it." He was also able to specify the condition most conducive to furious anger: "when I think some injustice has been done." His temper could be easily aroused, though if necessary he could control it by being "very quiet and very firm." For the most part he believed in expressing his anger and then forgetting about the episode, lasting resentments being unusual in his experience. Mention has already been made of his anxieties in competitive situations and his control through procrastination and distracting activity at the last moment.

Intellectual Characteristics.—Hale's intellectual competence has already been attested by his effortless climb up the educational ladder and by his occasional outstanding performances such as the entrance grade in biology. Standard intelligence tests placed him in the *very superior* category with an I.Q. of 130; performance on the different parts of the tests showed a fairly even distribution of skills with no areas of marked weakness. Characteristically he used his mind in rapid, direct, concrete fashion, sometimes even to the extent of a careless disregard for details and a willingness to leave hasty replies uncriticized. He showed little disposition toward either cautious planning or complex theorizing; his test performances were those of a doer rather than a thinker. He seemed to have difficulty, relative to the rest of his capacity, in organizing separate items and in arriving at general patterns. In tests of imagination he was free and creative. It was characteristic of his stories that they took full account of whatever facts were offered him in the first place. If he was shown a picture, for example, he told a story which included everything that was in the picture; he unleashed his imagination only after having paid full respect to the objective stimulus. Impressive also was his preference for objects as against human figures in the Rorschach ink-blot test. He managed to find quite a few mechanical objects in the roughly-formed, unmechanical ink-blots. His test performances showed the same mechanical and objective preferences that had appeared in his autobiography. We were reminded of his extensive description of the stage in the high-school auditorium and his objective way of contrasting the characteristics of his parents through their behavior in a bridge game.

Special Abilities.—Hale's history gave abundant evidence of his early and lasting interest in the understanding of mechanisms. When he said that he put a reverse switch on his electric train at the age of seven, we thought of his remark that he was always honest except when exaggerating; but even if he did it only at nine or ten, we must still count it as testimony to considerable aptitude. The record is full of his fascination by mechanical objects, his rapid but patient mastery of their intricacies, his creativeness in thinking of new devices and working out new triumphs of technique. His absorption in biology seemed to be a continuation and development of the same kind of interest, shifted from the inanimate machine to the even more intriguing machinery of the living organism. In interviews he was more apt to talk about his dramatic adventures in the social sphere, but his hours in the laboratory were clearly a deep and lasting source of satisfaction.

In the arts Hale preserved a more completely amateur standing, but his interests and energies overflowed even in this direction. Though not really a good singer, he got considerable pleasure out of his efforts and found time to write a number of songs during his college years. He greatly enjoyed good painting and good music, to which his parents had introduced him early in life. Occasionally he turned his hand to poetry and occasionally to drawing, the latter talent eventually being diverted into the making of biological drawings in his courses. Considering the high artistic standards of his home he seemed to have accepted relative mediocrity in the arts with fairly good grace. He could usually take pleasure in artistic activity regardless of the competitive merit of the product.

Social Skills and Attitudes.—It was plain from his school and college histories and from our own observation of his behavior that Hale was unusually gregarious. Companions and friends were involved in almost everything that he did; in fact, he expressed a definite distaste for being alone, and it was the lonely characters in his stories who fell prey to dejection and despair. Even his most absorbing mechanical and scientific interests were apt to be shared with others, especially in subsequent conversation. He reported several incidents in which he displayed social initiative, though he confessed that his first enthusiasm sometimes waned before the project reached its fulfilment. He said, and we observed, that he could often keep the whole table laughing in the dining hall, and he enjoyed presiding or serving as master of ceremonies at meetings. Those of our questions which were designed to bring out his capacity for intuitive, empathic understanding of other people he reinterpreted in more congenially objective terms. "I can't know anyone without analyzing him," he said; "I tear people to pieces all the time in my own mind."

Then he spoke of his quickness to detect unpleasant traits such as "social climbing," "selfishness," "narrow-mindedness," and "excessive ambition, not the kind that inspires you to work hard, but an over-reaching one." With regard to such traits he was a determinist: "It's pretty hard to change them, almost impossible. I've tried." These excerpts, taken together with the fact that he never felt moved to tears by sorrowful scenes, suggest a low capacity for sympathetic understanding and a tendency to look upon people objectively with emphasis on the annoying features of their behavior. Nevertheless, we noted that his companionship was valued and that his friendships with both men and women tended to be of long duration.

FIRST INTERPRETIVE SUMMARY

Hartley Hale's life has now been described through its first twenty-two years. We have brought him to the point where he was about to graduate from college, with medical school and a long period of professional training lying ahead of him. Before making his story any longer let us attempt to strengthen our grasp on what we already know. Thus far we have not fully exerted ourselves to search out the significant connections among the events of his life. We have not tried to work out in consistent detail an explanation of the course taken by his development. Closer inspection may help us to understand better how he came to be the kind of person he was at the age of twenty-two.

In making this closer inspection we shall inevitably find ourselves attempting to reconstruct his past history. What he is today grew out of what he was at earlier points in his life. Such reconstructions always contain a substantial amount of guesswork, and we should not deceive ourselves into thinking that we can be certain about what really happened. Nevertheless we are justified, if we pay proper respect to all the facts at our disposal, in trying to increase our understanding by weaving into an intelligible fabric the loose strands of event, attitude, and feeling that have made up the narrative of Hale's career.

So much in personality is closely interconnected that it is often hard to find a suitable starting point for a discussion of this kind. Here we can do no better than follow Hale's lead and begin with the situation which he himself considered crucial in his childhood: the quarrels between his parents and the terrific feeling of insecurity which they engendered in him.

Hale's parents often made it clear to him that his own venturesome and mischievous behavior was the subject of their quarrels. The sequence of events usually started with some act of rebellion on his part; then followed upset feelings in his mother, which upset his father, which precipitated a quarrel in which Hartley was forgotten. The mother then retired to her room, whither the son followed with a view to restoring peace, but there was little he could do beyond listening to her protests and self-justifications. Hale told us that his sympathies were evoked on both sides, that he judged both parents to be wrong in losing their tempers, but that he did not feel resentment against either of them. This is surprising, especially when we recall that he himself had often been punished and sent to his room for the very same crime of losing his temper. But the situation aroused anxiety: there was danger that the mother would leave and the home break up, and there was fear that he would not be able to make peace in these quarrels which obviously involved more than his own misbehavior. If he did not feel anger, it must have been because he did not dare to feel it lest he heighten the quarrel and ruin his own efforts at conciliation. Experienced marriage counselors do not consider it easy to deal with marital strife, even in the subsequent detachment of the consulting room. Hartley was called upon to cope with the problem in its moments of white heat, himself fully involved, his own security hanging in the balance, and with only a child's resources for understanding what it was all about. The foundations of self-respect as well as the cornerstone of security must have been severely shaken as he struggled with these unmanageable situations.

If this sequence of events and emotions occurred in a quite young child it would probably bring about an inhibition of the stubborn rebellious behavior that precipitated so many of the quarrels. When assertive behavior brings on the threat of parental desertion, the feelings of guilt and anxiety become insupportable and the child strives to become everything that his parents desire.[1] In Hale's case we have to explain why this did *not* occur. He refused to relinquish his right to independence and rebellion; quite consciously he decided not to become a model child. This means that he was in some way able to control the guilt and anxiety set off by the quarrels. We can reject on his own showing any hypothesis that Hale was naturally fearless: he feared water, moths, fights, and a

---

[1] This outcome is well illustrated in the case of Albert Rock, who also was forced to deal with parental quarrels. This case is described by Smith, M. B., Bruner, J. S., & White, R. W. in *Opinions and Personality*, New York: to be published 1953, ch. 8.

reasonable number of other threats. His power to control anxiety must be explained in some other way.

One method by which he supported his independence and controlled his guilt and fear was to form an active alliance with friends of his own age. He was quite explicit in pointing out this function of his circle of acquaintances. His friends became an alternative source of human support, taking the place of that which was threatened by the parental quarrels. To emphasize the opposition he chose friends of whose social class his parents disapproved. Many of his adventures, much of his growing self-assertion, took place in the company of these friends and enjoyed their express approval. Bold companions like Dan helped him greatly to overcome his shortcomings and master his fears. Even though he carried the grave social handicap of stuttering, he poured great energy into his activities with others and derived great satisfaction from them. He did not have to sustain single-handed his refusal to become a model child. Probably he could not have done so—like his fictional characters he would have fallen into deep dejection—if he had found himself without friends, without audience, without some measure of success.

Once again, however, we encounter something of a paradox. When a child's feeling of security is heavily dependent on his social relationships we can expect a marked hunger for group approval and a strong fear of group rejection. Conformity becomes peculiarly urgent when group membership is being used to ward off anxiety and guilt. Hale's relation to his age-peers does not seem to have shown this compulsive quality. It is true that he sought group approval by active means—humor, hell-raising, defying the teachers—but apart from evidence that earlier he played the goat, he does not appear to have been inhibited from expressing self-assertion, cockiness, and aggression in relation to the group. He declared himself to have been outspoken and competitive with his friends even at the time when the parental quarrels were at their worst, and he certainly ran chances of group disapproval by his eagerness to win and poor acceptance of defeats. We must conclude that he could control guilt and anxiety in relation to the group just as he could control it in relation to his parents.

These considerations force us to look back to the earlier part of his childhood. We are trying to understand how he was able to maintain so much independence, defiance, and assertiveness in the face of circumstances so threatening that docile conformity would seem a more likely outcome. Understanding would be easier if we could believe that before stuttering began, before the gangs from the east clouded his youthful horizon, Hale developed a feeling of confidence and self-reliance which could not be wholly shaken by later events. On what, in his case, could such secure confidence be based? There is evidence, in the first place, that his parents were interested in their children, fond of them, and able to discipline them without creating a fear that love would be withdrawn. In the second place, there is evidence that Hartley was happy and comfortable in his early relationships with other children. Here were two conditions highly favorable to the development of a feeling of security and confidence. Furthermore, inspection of his record suggests that several conditions existed which encouraged him to rely on himself and on his own power of mastery. Consider the punishment program, for example. He remembered his punishments as realistic and reasonable, clearly related to the offenses, a sort of transaction with his parents who defined standards to which he must live up but who did not threaten dire and catastrophic consequences if he failed. Sometimes his father allowed him to choose a form of punishment appropriate to the offense, and always he felt that he could object and perhaps convince if the punishments appeared unreasonable. Conducive also to his feeling of strength was the knowledge that his sister would sometimes lend aid. Both the father, as in the case of the boxing lessons, and the sister, as in the backbone incident, appear to have held standards of assertive accomplishment before him but left him to fight his own battles. In particular we must not overlook certain incidents which show clearly that Hartley's parents respected him, understood his interests, and were not disinclined to let his initiative prevail. They let him persuade them to keep pets, they allowed him to feel that he had outwitted them in the matter of Santa Claus and the electric train, and they encouraged him to substitute a still-challenging mechanical achievement, the boat that would go twice around the bathtub, when his perpetual-motion project was stalled.

From such evidence it seems permissible to hazard the guess that quite early he was able to build a firm core of self-respect. Though it took effort, he was successful in memorizing the poems and making the drawings that his parents expected of him; he was also successful in mastering the intricacies of the mechanical world. He took pleasure in using his skills and increasing his mastery over things; the story runs consistently from the block carts in kindergarten, through model airplanes and radio, to his stage managership in high school, and his work in the college biology laboratories. Any sequence of events that ran from bafflement to mastery gave him great satisfaction. When the emotional climate grew more difficult, his reliance on his own competence was put to severer tests. He was peculiarly gratified when he found it possible to master human situations by action and manipulation: his physical fear by counterattack, his shyness by kissing, his poor deportment record by playing the teachers. The advertising business he conceived as a lively continuation of his pleasure in manipulating and mastering the human environment. In contrast, he was peculiarly frustrated when either his human environment or himself proved refractory to such treatment. The parental quarrels he could not seem to master, nor could he bring under control his own tendency to stutter.

Our search into early childhood has thus far yielded one possible reason for Hale's ability to maintain his independence: he was actually encouraged along lines of mastery and self-respect. His independence was seriously challenged, however, by his mother's cautious, apprehensive, but dictatorial attitude of protection and restraint. As the scope of his boyish venturesomeness increased, he felt more and more held down by his mother's tidy rules and fears of danger. He seems to have felt that his father did not disapprove of his independence but that it was difficult to win open support against his mother because of his father's distaste for argument and domestic upset. Thus the mother seemed likely to prevail in her attack on Hartley's cherished delight in mastery. In short, the early alliance between his parents and his assertiveness broke down into serious opposition. We need to scrutinize this situation with some care. It was here that he launched forth on the career of rebellion and defiance which we found him so sturdily maintaining in the stormy years of later childhood.

We should first notice that the behavior of which he most complained in his mother was not such as to imply that she did not or would not love him. On the contrary it was marked by great solicitude and fear lest he come to harm. The danger, as he first sensed it, was probably not that she would desert him but that she would fatally interfere with his urges to activity and his enjoyment of masculine roles such as fireman, Indian, and adventurer. His rebellion

was first directed against a smothering of his initiative and assertiveness, privileges worth defending even at some risk. We can hardly
assume, however, that a young child could oppose a generally loving mother without emotional cost. He took the bold rebellious way,
but there is every evidence that in doing so he experienced severe
conflict and had to carry on a running campaign against his own
feelings of guilt and anxiety. The situation must have created a powerful temptation to give in and preserve affectionate harmony as
well as an urge to break out and continue the life of adventure.
That his mother's restraints could make him so uncomfortable probably added to his hostility toward them. To compromise, to give-and-
take in a situation of this kind, would certainly be difficult for a
young child. We can make the guess that Hartley was forced into
a radical solution, that of affirming and asserting his independence
while attempting to repress his guilt and anxiety and his longings
for a dependent relation with his mother.

The probability that this guess is correct would become greater if
we could show (1) that the assertive and independent behavior became forced and exaggerated, (2) that there were signs of general tension, (3) that dependence, guilt, and anxiety were strongly
denied in word and deed, but (4) that these tendencies reappeared
in some indirect form such as dream and fantasy. All of these manifestations were characteristic of Hale, although it is not now possible
to pin them all down to the time in his childhood, say the third to
the eighth years, when the hypothetical development took place.
That his assertive independence was exaggerated came out in his
own testimony that the desire to outrage his mother kept forcing him
into ever wilder enterprises, and that his deportment in school was
practically the worst on record. That he felt great tension is suggested by the fact that stuttering began during these years, and is
certainly demonstrated in the school mischief and laughing jags
whereby he infuriated his teachers. Dependence, guilt, and timid
avoidances were systematically denied in his self-ratings as a college
junior and were admitted to his autobiography only when they led
up to a masterful triumph. The reappearance of anxiety was shown
in the nightmare that the family would move, and the continuing
existence of dependent longings came to light in certain features
of his fantasy life. His cherished image of the much older girl whom
alone he would want to marry, who made him feel that he was the
most interesting person in the world, probably harks back to the

mother as she was remembered to be before he began the battle for independence. In our tests of imagination he made up stories in which older men through kindly interest guided younger ones toward success, and this particular theme found real enactment in his relationship to certain of his male teachers.

An interesting sidelight on rebellion and guilt in relation to the mother is furnished by a story which Hale derived from a picture that is often perceived as a son breaking bad news to his mother. The mother, he said, had long hoped that her only son would become a doctor or lawyer.

> One fateful night he comes home to tell her that he has become a boxer. She can't believe her ears and is stunned by this statement. He feels badly that he should have to thus wreck her hopes but he knows that boxing is the only thing for him. Though he later rises to the top of the boxing pile, she never quite forgives him this breach of faith.

The same picture was used in the retest ten years later, and once again Hale represented the young man as disappointing his mother but going firmly away to do what he had planned. The second version differed only in that the emotional tension was not so fully concealed.

> She has undoubtedly said, 'If that's what you want to do, all right, go ahead, don't worry about me,' in a voice that implies he ought to be worrying about her, and he is therefore upset at the dilemma in which he finds himself.

But he has already decided what he is going to do, and he does it anyway.

We have now worked out two possible reasons for Hale's independence. He was early encouraged, in a secure environment, to develop initiative and self-respect, and he was then able to defy his mother's apprehensive interferences because the gravest threat, loss of the mother's love, did not present itself as an imminent danger. By the time parental quarrels became severe it seems likely that a new complication had entered the picture, one that may have made it easier for him to hold his own course and that counterbalanced the increased danger created by the sister's absence and the real possibility that the family would break up.

Hale's account of the later quarrels made it clear that he sensed issues between his parents that were much more far-reaching than his own fractious behavior. In the course of their arguments they forgot him and went on to deeper grievances. His picture of himself listening nervously for an argument to start when his parents came upstairs to undress and go to bed suggests that sex was one of their bones of contention, and that Hartley was extremely curious, baffled, perhaps frightened and perhaps angry about this mysterious element in their lives from which he was completely excluded. We know that Hartley became inordinately curious about sex, that during childhood he combed the available literature, that in high school he trailed couples at night in order to obtain copy for his scandal-sheet. Very likely he perceived still other issues between his parents, but this one was peculiarly apt to create jealousy and a feeling of exclusion. It seems important that the parental quarrels reached their peak at a point where Hartley was old enough to discern that matters beyond his own misbehavior were involved. He must have felt a burning sense of injustice when his parents blamed him for their quarrels, and he must have felt an added urge to defy, even at the cost of great anxiety, the people who blamed him and did not tell him what was really at stake.

We have already considered the fact that Hale counterbalanced his disappointments at home by means of an active, gregarious life. We need to explain, however, his uneasiness in the competitive aspects of this life, as shown in the anxieties he reported in connection with athletic contests and presumably also in the two curious incidents of last-minute failure during his freshman year. The available evidence on the origins of his fear of competition is not very clear, but two things at least must have contributed to a sharp feeling of inferiority: the early incursions of tough and menacing boys from the east, and his own stuttering. We can infer that during the middle years of childhood, in contrast to the earlier ones, he had a hard fight to establish respect, and with it self-respect, among boys of his own age. He triumphed in this campaign, but it is not inconsistent with victory that there should be residues of anxiety in the presence of any new challenge.

One of the most significant sequences in Hale's life was his progress from a brash irresponsible high-school student to a young man of rather serious purposes in college. In general such a sequence is not unusual, though sometimes with a serious-minded high-school student it works in exactly the opposite way. Development does not have to be exceptional, however, in order to deserve explanation,

and in Hale's case there is the added interest that the progress involved a change of vocational goal to one of the hardest and most
exacting professions, a thing that must have astonished most of his
high-school teachers and friends, though perhaps not his physics and
biology teachers.

The understanding at which we have arrived shows Hale as rely-
ing heavily upon himself. He had learned to depend a great deal
upon his power of action and mastery, his ability to attack and solve
problems, his capacity to check and counteract emotions that might
otherwise betray him. He was certainly successful, but any adjustment must be regarded as a not wholly stable balance, liable to tip
in one or another direction whenever the weights are changed.
Looking at Hale's career we can observe a rather frequent, though
by no means fatal, tendency of his adjustment to shift in the direction of greater assertiveness, self-display, and aggression, with the
resulting danger that he would become separated and isolated from
his human supports. We know from his statements and from his imaginative productions that he dreaded such isolation, associating
it with depressed feelings and despair. But it was hard for him,
given an audience, not to overplay his bid for applause, hard also
not to mingle in his assertive self-display a large measure of hostility. It was difficult for him, for instance, to keep his humor from
hurting as well as entertaining, and to prevent his outspokenness
from angering others as well as winning a certain respect. The hard
battle of his development had left a legacy of hostile feelings which
had a tendency to creep into his relations with other people. When
his adjustment tipped in this direction, he became uneasy, drove
things all the harder, and was unable to relax sufficiently to pursue
constructive interests.

From this situation he could be rescued only by a real display of
kindly personal interest. The interest might be directed toward him
as a person, as was the case with his girl friends, or it might be directed toward his skill and capacity for learning, as was the case with
the three teachers who affected him so profoundly. That he really
hungered for this kind of thing was indicated by his statement on
what most readily made him cry: someone's going out of his way to
be unexpectedly kind. At all events the effect of another person's
deep interest was to calm him down, remove his uneasiness, and free
him for absorption in some kind of continuous work. One of Hale's
assets was his capacity to become deeply absorbed and fascinated by

scientific pursuits. This capacity, however, could actually operate only in a situation that contained a definite income of reassuring esteem. Whenever he was forced into cockiness, his power of productive work was impaired. Whenever he felt assured of some respected person's esteem, whenever he felt that someone was willing to take a gamble on him, his productiveness sprang into high gear. One of his stories, set off by a picture showing an older man talking to a younger man, bears striking testimony to this connection:

> The younger man in the picture is an intern who has been working since graduation from medical school in a large and very modern hospital. Like all young interns he is ambitious and has already formulated many ideas about how to better the medical profession. His favorite scheme has met with rather cold disdain from the higher-ups in the hospital. He feels bitter about this rebuff and is contemplating changing hospitals when an older doctor, who when he was the age of the young intern felt the same way and who realized how the young man must feel, knocks on his door. The young man opens the door and the doctor comes in. The older doctor talks to him and shows him why his scheme was not accepted, and explains to him that every young man in his position must expect to meet with many rebuffs before one of his suggestions is finally met with approval. The young man loses his bitter feeling to some extent and determines to go back and work even harder on his experiment.

Perhaps it was not coincidence that between the ages of sixteen and twenty-one, during which time he enjoyed the affectionate interest of his first important girl friend and had successive gambles taken on him by the high-school physics teacher, junior-college biology teacher, friend who urged him into medicine, and college tutor in biology, his stuttering steadily declined so that we did not observe it in our interviews.

Part Two: FROM 23 TO 33

MEDICAL SCHOOL

Hartley Hale's career as a medical student began with a series of frustrations. He had wanted above all things to get his medical training at a leading school in New York, but his overall college record was not quite good enough and his application was rejected.

This was, he said, "a pretty bitter pill to swallow; in fact, one of the major failures of my life." He found himself living in a city where he was a complete stranger, attending a medical school which, though excellent, was not his first choice. The living conditions were uncongenial. "I was in a room by myself," he said, "which I never like; I don't like being alone." His freedom was restricted by grave financial embarrassment. His father, having reached the age of seventy, was in process of liquidating his business and for the time being could give him no help. Hale obtained a tuition scholarship, but he had to take on outside jobs, such as washing dishes in a restaurant, that totalled forty hours a week. He was also obliged to enroll for an extra course which most of the medical students had already taken. "I hated to have to go over there when nobody else did," he told us, and as a result he skipped the final exam, failed the course, and lost his scholarship. The first term at medical school was "pretty unhappy," indeed one of the darkest periods of his life.

Hale's response to these discouraging circumstances was as usual an active one. He made friends with several of his fellow medical students and had beer parties with them on his weekly night off. When the school authorities expressed distaste for beer cans strewn outside the windows on Sunday mornings, he and two friends seized the opportunity to take an apartment off campus. Required to repeat the course he had failed, he this time gave it full attention and secured a very high mark. The most important step that he took, however, was made possible by the research he had done during his junior and senior years at Harvard. He approached one of the medical professors whose own research lay in the same field, explained the work he had done on the growth of bone cells, and asked whether he might have the opportunity to continue it. He was soon provided with space and equipment, and shortly thereafter with a small paid job as assistant in the laboratory, which helped to ease his financial difficulties. In spite of his extremely crowded schedule he was able, mostly during the night, to keep up a certain amount of work on his research.

By the time he reached the third year things began to go really well. He enjoyed clinical experience much more than book work, and he felt that this part of the training was particularly well handled inasmuch as "the teaching was personalized," "we got a lot of attention," and "we were let do quite a lot of things." His record had been good but not outstanding during the first two years, but his success with practical work in the clinics eventually placed him among the top five men in his class. The wartime shortage of medical personnel was already beginning to be felt, and this opened unusual opportunities for responsible work. On one occasion near the end of his third year, for example, replacement of an intern was delayed for several weeks; Hale volunteered to assume the duties during the interim, and carried them off in a way that delighted the astonished chief of the service. "I've felt many times since," he remarked, "that it was very lucky for me that I went to that school. It was one of those things which started out badly and turned out well."

For a while he was neutral toward surgery. "The student's-eye view of surgery," he said, "is that of holding the retractors and standing long hours in the operating room, looking over somebody's shoulder and not seeing much." He preferred to work on the general medical service, where the diagnostic problems seemed to be more difficult and challenging. During the fourth year, however, his preference swung definitely to surgery. "I've always liked to do things with my hands," he reminded us, and then he enlarged on the differences in personality between men who go into general medicine and men who go into surgery. The former, in his view, "like to sit around and talk about things and think about things," whereas the surgical people "like to go and do something about them." As his medical course drew to a close, Hale became increasingly certain of where he belonged, and he applied without hesitation for a straight surgical internship.

We shall later describe in detail the subject of Hale's marriage, but in order to keep the chronology straight we must insert here the information that his wedding occurred in the middle of his fourth year at medical school. At this time he was serving as a paid assistant in a laboratory course for first-year students, and he was hoping to be relieved for a fortnight's honeymoon. Shortly before he planned to put in his request, however, the professor in charge of the course announced that he was going on a two-weeks' vacation and asked Hale to take over his sections of the laboratory course. "So there I was," said Hale, "and we had only seventy-two hours for a honeymoon."

PROFESSIONAL APPRENTICESHIP: INTERN AND RESIDENT

Feeling that his medical school record had been strong, Hale re-stricted his applications for internships to three hospitals in New York City. "I suppose because of my failure to get in there in the first place," he said, "I set my heart on going to New York." In spite of wartime restrictions on travel he took the initiative in securing interviews and pressed his cause so successfully that he received one of the most coveted appointments. Upon arrival at the hospital, he was immediately thrust into a terrific round of duties which kept him going all day and most of the night, so that although in theory he was entitled to every second night off it was actually several days before he saw his wife again. The pace did not continue quite so vigorously, but everyone in the hospital was over-worked and each new assignment seemed to plunge him into a thousand obligations. Earlier than usual he was assigned to the out-patient department.

> At first I was pretty lost down there, but I got to liking out-patient a lot because I was left to my own devices and I could do what I wanted to, and I could see the patients and make diagnoses on them, which was fun, and we did a lot of minor surgery down there. And I had time to read, I stacked a lot of books down there and read about things I didn't know about, in fact I used to sleep down there a lot of the time on one of the cots because then I could be there when the patients came in and I could read until they came in.

Because of this reading he was able to recognize that one pa-tient, treated unsuccessfully for many previous weeks, had been wrongly diagnosed and actually had a rare disease seldom seen at the hospital. This disease was treatable, though by a different method, and Hale soon had the satisfaction of seeing the chronic pa-tient become a well person. "I had a good time there," he said; "things went very well."

In the operating room things went if anything even better. "When we finally got to operate," he reported, "I found that it was very easy for me, I did quite well in the operating room." The war-time shortage of personnel was a real boon to this part of his train-ing, because there was no choice but to press promising young sur-geons as rapidly as possible toward more difficult assignments. "I love to operate," he told us, "so I used to stick around at odd hours and do things when other people would go to bed, so I got to do more than the others." This helpfulness was much appreciated by the harassed staff. "They welcomed enthusiasm, and I was nothing if not enthusiastic at that point."

When the period of internship ended, Hale found himself retained for another year as assistant resident, a rare honor for someone not trained in the leading metropolitan medical schools. His work was praised by some of the visiting physicians. The residency was a stimulating experience. Sometimes he was in the operating room most of the day and part of the night. Little time was left over to be at home and to make the acquaintance of his small daughter.

> As you can imagine, I didn't see much of either my wife or my child. As a matter of fact I never saw the child when it was awake until it was a year old, I think, because I always got up at around four-thirty or five in the morning, and even on my nights off I didn't get home until nine or ten, so I never saw the kid except when it was asleep, but it seemed to be a fairly quiet, nice baby.

The young lady here referred to as "it" was thus badly handicapped in working her way into her father's affection, the more so, no doubt, because he had really wanted a boy and felt quite outraged at first that fortune had decreed otherwise.

At the end of his residency Hale was called into the service and assigned to a military hospital in the South. His first placement was not in a surgical service, but the chief encouraged him to examine patients who might be in need of surgery, and all of the older staff members were impressed by the thoroughness of his work. His training at the hospital in New York had been extremely rigorous. The most careful checking and rechecking, the greatest exactitude was expected in every case, no matter how routine, and the interns and residents received merciless criticism if their work showed haste or carelessness. "I thrived pretty well in that system," he commented, "I don't mind working that way; in fact I actually like it, it's a challenge to get everything as perfect as you can." His detailed and up-to-date knowledge also proved to be a great asset. One day a patient was brought to the military hospital in coma. The commanding officer, an earnest man but not very well trained, could not determine the cause, and in great agitation lest the patient die he summoned all staff members on duty to his aid. Hale had seen a few such cases in New York and quickly administered the proper treatment, as a result of which the patient within an hour was markedly improved and well out of danger. This incident led to Hale's being put in charge of a ward of his own and gave him a second opportunity to astonish his chief. He was transferred to his ward at three o'clock in the afternoon. Next morning the commanding officer made rounds and discovered that Hale knew each of the hundred patients by name, had talked with each one, knew the contents of each record, and had examined all the relevant X-ray plates. One might suspect that in telling this story Hale was exaggerating again, but the sequel shows that at all events the commanding officer was greatly impressed. He wrote to Washington about Hale, and as a result the next assignment was to an overseas rear hospital specializing in some of the most difficult branches of surgery.

In his new post Hale continued to work and to learn. Typical of his devotion to his work was his handling of a patient who had been in an extremely severe jeep accident and had "everything in the books wrong with him." Since the patient obviously could not be pulled through without constant care, Hale put a cot in his room and attended him almost without interruption for four days and nights until he was out of danger. In the course of three months, five operations were necessary, but the patient finally made a complete and lasting recovery.

At the end of his overseas service Hale returned to New York, where he picked up the threads of the research he had done in medical school on bone growth and development. The research went well, and this strengthened his desire to become an orthopedic surgeon.

MARRIAGE AND FAMILY LIFE

The foregoing narrative of a crowded medical life naturally begins to make one wonder what was happening to young Mrs. Hartley Hale. Before we inquire how she managed the difficult assignment of being Dr. Hale's wife we must go back to find out how she came on the scene and how her predecessor in his affections left the scene. It will be remembered that he went fairly steadily with one girl during his last two years of college. She was to accompany him to his much anticipated senior spread. The day before the spread she telephoned to say that she had a good business offer in New York and was leaving at once. Hale commented:

> Of course there was no possibility of getting anyone else at that time. I was without a date to my own senior spread. That was quite a blow. And I was a little disappointed that she thought more of her career than she did of coming to senior spread with me, although I realized that that was a selfish point of view.

Correspondence continued during the summer, but Hale became sidetracked from a projected visit because of his growing interest in a new girl, several years younger than himself, who had previously been a casual acquaintance. The girl in New York began to repent her haste and offered, when Hale went to medical school, to have herself transferred to another office so located that they could live together. In the loneliness of his first year Hale "thought about that for a long time," but he finally decided that it was "not really very fair to her" inasmuch as he had pretty well decided not to marry her.

In the next two years letters and occasional visits strengthened his interest in the new girl. One summer they had a month together and became engaged. In speaking about their courtship Hale mentioned the attraction of her family circle, so different from his own.

> One of the things that attracted me, oddly enough, was her family situation. I mean her family always had such a good time, and they always seemed so happy, and they always had so much fun together, that it made it very pleasant to be with them, and I would still much rather be with her family than with mine.

His future wife, however, possessed numerous pleasing qualities in her own right. In retrospect he enumerated them as follows:

> And I was very strongly physically attracted to her; she's good-looking, and she's very very attractive. And then another thing was the fact that things didn't bother her too much, they didn't seem to bother her too much when I was courting her, at least. If we decided at ten o'clock at night to go for a sail we went, and that was fine and nobody got excited about it; and if we decided to jump off the end of the dock and take a swim, why, nobody was upset, and that all seemed great. And

then she has some insight into the trials and tribulations of doctors because of her father being one. I think that those are the
main things that attracted me. She likes parties, likes to go out,
likes to see people. She's very gregarious.

Reviewing these grounds for attraction one cannot escape the feeling that Hale already sensed something of the terrific demands he
would make upon a wife both because of the nature of his profession and because of his own absorbed devotion to it and determination to do well. It is almost certain that he did not reason it out in
this way, but he seems to have tried to select a girl who would make
him a blithe, happy, sympathetic companion while not being bothered by erratic hours nor demanding of his time and attention.

Whatever his wife may have known about the trials and tribulations of doctors, she had little conception of what being a doctor
meant to Hartley Hale. Frequent moves to new places, cramped
wartime housing, and a husband who practically never came home
from the hospital, soon began to bother her a good deal. "Our marital life," Hale admitted, "was fairly strained for the first few
years." His wife, he now began to realize, had been accustomed to
much loving care and protection at home. "To be out in the cold
cold world all alone was quite a shock to her, and she hadn't been
very well suited for that sort of life." Throughout his internship
and first residency it was impossible to get off for more than a
single afternoon at a time. When he was called into the service he
managed to get a fortnight's vacation and for the first time got acquainted with his fourteen-months-old daughter. It was not until he
became established in research, however, that the marital situation
really began to improve. They took a house in a pleasant suburb
where they were more or less surrounded by professional people and
where for the first time Hale could be at home long enough to take
an interest in his family and community. His wife at last found a
congenial circle of friends and a chance to do things occasionally
in her husband's company. But if she hoped that his interests would
stay in the laboratory and not encroach upon their domestic life she
was soon disappointed. He set up a photographic workshop in the
attic and began to process pictures for his experiments.

> I often come home at 10 o'clock and go up to the attic
> and work until 2. My wife likes to go to bed at 8:30 or 9,
> so that it usually irritates her when I come home at 9, say,

and go up to the attic. I put an easy chair up there for her and I got a radio, and I try to induce her to come up and sit in the chair and listen to the radio while I work. She does sometimes, but occasionally I've got to take her out or come downstairs and talk to her, occasionally I have to do that. So that's the only cloud on the horizon; she hates to see me get buried in the attic. I spend a lot of time up there; I enjoy it very much.

In spite of the cool self-centeredness of the last declaration, Hale was not entirely at peace with his own proclivities. In one of our free-association tests his thoughts arrived at the topic of buying an expensive new piece of equipment for his shop. This called up misgivings: he considered it "pretty purely selfish" to want such elaborate equipment, and he told us how "miserable" it usually made him feel to buy articles for the shop when the money could have been used for things around the house that would benefit the whole family. In another part of the tests, when associating to the phrase *others expect,* he said, "Well, my wife expects me to spend more time with the family." What he admitted his wife might rightfully expect of him, however, still looked small when compared to what he expected of her, as shown in his associations to the phrase *a wife should.* Her primary duty was bearing, bringing up, and providing for the children. "Her secondary job is taking care of the husband" by getting his meals, running the house, and so forth.

And, thirdly, I think that wherever possible she should be companionable, should go along with the things her husband likes to do as much as she can, and be enthusiastic about the things that he does. And I think, fourthly, that she should as much as she can remain attractive, and make herself desirable as far as her husband is concerned, and do everything that she can to make him proud of her so that he's anxious to show her off to other people.

In several parts of our conversations Hale contrasted his own and his wife's temperaments. His wife differed pleasantly from his mother in that she took care of the house in a casual spirit, getting the work done reasonably well without fussing over details. Hale's own thorough and meticulous tendencies, derived from his mother, have often bothered him considerably. "I realize why I do it and I still can't stop it," he said, "and it's been a hell of a thing for me." Another difference between them was their attitude toward adversity:

his wife was somewhat timid and unaggressive, inclined to retreat from difficulties and "fold up when things get bad," whereas he, "stubborn and obstinate," was more apt to "go charging ahead in the face of adversity." "She has no spirit of competition," he complained, a trait which seemed to irk him considerably. At another point he remarked: "She's very feminine and has most of the feminine shortcomings which, oddly enough, rather attracts me."

Real difficulty had arisen over their differences in daily cycles of energy. His wife arose cheerful in the morning, while he himself was then tired and irritable. Early in the evening, however, his wife became tired and wanted to go to bed, whereas he was all ready for several hours in the attic. A good many times Hale mentioned this problem with respect to the hour of retiring. Usually it was solved by his wife's going to bed early while he stayed up until twelve or one o'clock; fortunately, he added, she was not averse to being waked up when he came to bed. "I think she's reasonably happy these days," he judged. "We like long walks and riding, we both like the kids, we like to go to parties, and we like the same people, so that's quite a lot in common." The main problems appeared to him to have been solved. "It looked bleak for a while," he concluded, "but it all worked out very well."

At the time of the second study Hale had three children, two girls and a boy. He had been quite disturbed by the birth of his second daughter. Having a girl rather than a boy the first time had been something of a disappointment, causing him to feel, as he put it, "slightly cheated," but the news that he had had a second daughter left him "completely crushed." "I wasn't prepared for anything like that at all," he told us, "and it took quite a while for me to get over it." He was naturally overjoyed when the third child proved to be a boy. "I wanted to have a boy sometime," he said, "at least one boy." He considers his children a source of great enjoyment.

> The two things I enjoy most about my children are the fact that they seem happy in their surroundings and the fact that they're always glad to see me, the fact that they're nice to me. This is very pleasant. And I enjoy teaching them. They very often come to me and ask me questions, and I like to sit down and talk to them; they seem to enjoy it, I enjoy it. I like to tell them stories. I like to take them with me walking and riding.

He undertakes to provide for them a better home atmosphere than that which he remembers to have prevailed in his own childhood. In particular he avoids open argument with his wife, tries not to hold down the children's venturesomeness, and does what he can to be more companionable with his children than his own much older parents were with him. He believes that on the whole his children are developing excellently. "I'm very proud of them," he remarked; "I like to see them develop along the lines I think they ought to."

Dealing with his children has made Hale aware that he sometimes involuntarily behaves as his own parents used to behave.

> The thing that usually tips me off is that the children act exactly the way I did under the same circumstances. And I stop and think, 'Well, now, why is that child acting like that?' and then I suddenly realize that I've done exactly what my parents would have done in the same situation. Then I usually make a conscious effort not to act like that.

He perceives that his elder daughter works hard to be considered mature and independent, just as he himself did as a child. Sometimes this independence makes him angry:

> I get angry when my children don't do what I've told them. The oldest child in particular is inclined to do exactly what I did as a child, and that is to go out of her way to appear unimpressed by what I tell her to do, and to make every effort to show me that she's doing it not because she thinks that I'm right but only because she has to. She can sometimes be very very annoying in that respect. The case in point especially is when you tell her to hurry, when she's doing something, and she then proceeds at the slowest possible pace, just barely moving one foot in front of the other. This makes me quite angry.

The vigorously assertive older girl and the charming and popular baby boy do not show signs of insecurity, but the second little girl is not without her troubles. Caught between the greater privileges of the older sister and the greater indulgent attention received by the baby, she alternates between belligerence and thumb-sucking and has become the object of no little parental solicitude. "She definitely has a feeling of insecurity," Hale told us, "and we all work on it all the time. I often go out of my way to take her by herself some place so that she'll feel that she's the center of attention for once." He assumes that "every family has that sort of problem" and is optimistic about the outcome of his own and his wife's efforts to do something about it.

Hale is much pleased with the suburban community where his home is now located. He described with pleasure the backyard picnics at the outdoor fireplace and the friendly way in which neighbors, young and old, drop in for casual conversation. He has participated in public meetings summoned to discuss the affairs of the borough such as the zoning of school districts. Much as he likes his dwelling place, he goes ahead in fantasy to what he calls his "ultimate house," which without being isolated from other homes or inconveniently remote from his work and from shopping centers would enjoy some of the advantages of the country. He imagines a hill and a view, a good-sized garden, perhaps a barn and some animals, certainly a stream or pond that could be stocked with trout. He also cherishes the fantasy of going off somewhere to write a book, not necessarily a medical book although he hopes later to contribute to the professional library. To some extent he keeps up his singing, and he owns a good many records. He gets great pleasure out of drawing, but this art has been wholly subordinated to his professional activity. The exacting demands of his profession have restricted considerably the range of his outside activities, but his restless energy still pushes out in fantasies of new territory he would sometime like to explore.

GROWING RESPONSIBILITY AND POWER

Although Hale was happy in a life centered on research, he felt that his professional future depended upon holding at some time the position of orthopedic resident in a hospital. This post was recently offered to him, and he gladly accepted it. He was at once precipitated into a schedule of work more demanding than anything he had yet encountered. "You don't really get to the top in surgical matters," Hale informed us, "until you run the whole show yourself, and you don't really run the whole show until you're the resident." He described as follows his life in this new and gravely responsible position:

> You run the ward, you see all the patients, you decide what's going to be done to them, and you decide who's going to operate on them, who's going to help who, who you want to do yourself, and you make rounds every day on every patient, decide what portion of their treatment you don't like, what you want changed, and that sort of thing. And you're always on call, you're never off, and although I go home almost every

night I don't usually get home until nine or ten o'clock, because when you finish the day's work you have consultations on the medical service, and sometimes they're problem cases and it takes you a while to work things out and get x-rays. And then some nights you've got patients that are pretty sick and you stick around to see what's going to happen, and we do quite a lot of emergencies, night work, and although I don't operate on most of those patients, the interns do that, I always want to see every patient, just so I can say 'O.K., go ahead with it,' so that they're protected in case anything happens, and I usually stick around until after the operation is done just in case something turns up that's unexpected so that they need me.

It's a busy time but it's a good time. You do what you want to, and it's a chance to really get out and do surgery that you might not ever do elsewhere.

Among the duties of the orthopedic resident is the training and supervision of residents and interns. Hale tries to deal with his subordinates as he himself liked to be dealt with when he occupied a similar position. When a new man comes into his charge he tries to put him on his mettle. He tells him in explicit detail how he would like to have things run, emphasizing that he would like to have the younger man take just as much responsibility as possible. He indicates that he will be appraising efficiency especially when rounds are being made. If everything seems well organized and if questions about the patients and their treatment can be promptly and adequately answered, so that the rounds proceed with despatch, he will judge his subordinate favorably and give him opportunities to do more surgery. He explains that there are always twenty things to do in a ward and that time must be carefully organized to get the important things done first and all the things done in the end. Hale laughingly admitted that this matter of organizing time had been one of his own most difficult problems. He tries to help his subordinates with it, but some do not seem to be able to achieve good organization. He pictured for us his impatience when rounds went slowly and the needed information had to be pried out of the intern or sought from the nurse.

It just makes rounds pretty tedious and I don't like it, and it's hard on them, the intern feels he isn't doing a good job, in fact he isn't, whereas with other boys they'll learn so that you can make rounds on the ward in fifteen minutes, and they'll have all the facts for you; they'll just reel it out as you stop at each bedside, and you can just nod to the patient and move on. The boys who don't ever get that I'm sure feel somewhat brow-beaten, because I usually am a little hard on them. But the ones who do a good job feel very happy; I usually give them a lot of responsibility in the operating room, and they get a good deal out of it.

Hale enjoys the respect of his subordinates not only for his skill but also for his defense of their interests in conflict with the hospital management. No novice at battling with authorities, he takes a strong attitude when things are needed to improve the efficiency and comfort of the service, and this makes the house staff feel that he is on their side.

Hale's strictness and his tendency to be angered by inefficiency come to their fullest expression in dealing with the nurses. When given the phrase *I hate* as a stimulus to free association, he said, "I hate stupidity," and when pressed to continue his associations he mentioned the nurses at the hospital. "I sometimes get very angry at them," he said, "when they do stupid things, which they do about twenty times a day." Elsewhere he described himself as sometimes screaming at them and frequently criticizing them, with the result that he was far from popular with most of the nursing staff. Good nurses he respects, taking active steps for their advancement, but the poor ones become the chief targets of his irritation. Hale is not perfectly at peace with the idea that the poorer nurses dislike him. He says that he quickly forgets his own outbursts and harbors no grudges, and he reassures himself that "most of them know it, so that there aren't too many who really dislike me intensely." The same misgivings cross his mind about those interns and residents who receive his disapproval. He expresses his belief that their resentment is "fairly quickly forgotten," his evidence being that they show no sign of it at social gatherings. On such occasions he himself steps widely out of his professional role in favor of fun and conviviality.

Among his patients Hale has the reputation of being the kind of doctor who cares about their lives as well as about their diseases. A number of people whom he first treated on the ward have come to him later as private patients. More than once he has lent a hand in finding a job or helping to solve some other personal problem. At the time of the first study we believed that Hale had little capacity for empathic response. The desire to help people, however, always formed part of his motive for entering medicine, and in the relationship of doctor to patient he seems to have found a welcome opening for his nurturing needs.

VALUES AND IDEALS

To the value which he esteemed most highly in his professional life Hale gave the name "integrity." When asked to specify this value in more detail by giving an example of behavior which lacked it, he first mentioned doing a careless job in working up a patient's diagnosis. He remarked:

> I sometimes stop and ask myself whether I'm being honest with all my patients and I sometimes find that I am starting to slide over things a little bit, and I force myself to go back and double-check on everything to be sure that I'm not missing anything.

As discussion continued he amplified his conception of integrity so as to make it include the willingness to attempt a difficult operation when you judged that it stood a fair chance of prolonging the patient's life but knew that a bad outcome would injure your reputation. He blamed a feeling of insecurity about one's reputation for any lapse of this kind from the standard of integrity. In general it appeared that he identified integrity with an absolute subordination of oneself to the welfare of the patient, a devotion into which the physician's ease, comfort, timidity, and concern for reputation must never intrude. This is, of course, the spirit of the Hippocratic Oath, and if Hale gave it a personal slant it was only in the intensity of his affirmation and in his choice of examples. He had been somewhat upset in the earlier days of his medical work to see the extent to which petty rivalries, jealousy, and factionalism discolored the atmosphere of hospitals. "It's like anything else," he commented, "but that isn't the way it's made to appear." The image of the completely dedicated physician had evidently served him as a strong guiding ideal, and it was his purpose to keep his own behavior close to this formidable standard.

We asked Hale whether he would still have made integrity his central value if he had gone into advertising. He laughed uproariously at such an idea, but then revealed that he had done quite a lot of thinking about the ethics of advertising during the time when he expected to make it his life work. He greatly disliked, even in those days, the idea of selling people things they did not need, of entangling them in installment buying, and of creating anxiety as a means of inducing people to buy. He had solved the problem in this way: he would select first-rate and necessary products, then go out and actively solicit the advertising for them, knowing that the sales he might bring about would be at the expense only of rival manufacturers whose products were not as good. His service would be that of promoting better products in situations where people were likely to buy something anyway.

Hale began an interview devoted to his opinions on public affairs by disclaiming any proper knowledge. He represented that a man who spent most of his time in a hospital, in an attic studio, or reading medical journals could hardly have well-crystallized views on the world at large. The exposition of his ill-crystallized views, however, occupied nearly an hour and was characterized by definiteness of statement and vigor of partisanship. Ten years earlier the most marked feature of his opinions had been his uniform opposition to government interference of any kind. He seemed to treat government interference with the same angry contempt that he had shown toward maternal interference. In the course of a decade his opinions had become better differentiated, but he still viewed with disfavor anything that suggested interference with freedom of enterprise, especially when it touched his own activities. The two objects of his bitterest wrath were Communism and socialized medicine. He favored the tougher parts of United States foreign policy, but he deplored the trend of events in the Far East where he felt the spread of Communism was being but weakly opposed. He did not, however, favor supporting the Chinese Nationalist Government, asking rather for a more long-range program of offering the Chinese people advantages that would successfully compete with the inducements of the Communists. He felt that Russian designs were wholly imperialistic and that a third world war would inevitably take place, but he rejected, chiefly because of our poor preparedness and the danger of retaliation with atomic weapons, the idea that we should consider a preventive war.

Although firmly a Republican, Hale was severe in his criticism of Republican policies, which he characterized as a stupid mixture of waving the flag for the good old days and trying to outdo the Democrats in conferring federal benefits. "We've got to stop screaming to get the labor unions throttled," he said; "it's more a matter of getting them managed well, actually helping them rather than hindering them." Labor leaders he considered too powerful, but he was not at all sure that the real interests of labor were sufficiently represented in the American economy. He interrupted us when, thinking that he had finished with this topic, we suggested another one:

> I'd like to say one final word. I have a very definite feeling that labor was not getting the break it deserved in the past, one of the reasons being that I worked on a lot of jobs with a lot of people, and I've gotten a pretty good idea of what it was like, and I worked many hours for 35 cents an hour while other people were doing work which was a great deal easier and no more skilled and getting 3 dollars an hour. It's a very annoying thing, and a very unfair thing, I think. It's a good thing that wages have come up the way they have, so from that point of view I'm more in favor of getting the labor unions organized and supporting that part of the system.

The ideal in Hale's mind was clearly the establishment of a fair balance between the interests of management and those of labor. He did not believe that large-scale government interference was the proper method of achieving such a result.

SECOND INTERPRETIVE SUMMARY

Toward the end of the final interview we asked Hale, mildly deprecating the journalistic sound of our question, to what he attributed his success. His answer to this question may well form the starting point for our second interpretive summary. Certainly his still young career in medicine has been by all ordinary standards a tremendous success, and it is just as much our task to understand success as to understand failure. Hale was of the opinion that the decisive thing in his career had been his research. He said:

> I didn't do brilliantly in medical school. I think that the only reason that I've gotten most of the things that I wanted was because of the research I did. If I hadn't done that I wouldn't have stood out above anybody else. When I came to get an internship, certainly. It gave me a chance to get myself a little above my classmates.

He traced the crucial role of his research interests, showing how in medical school they drew the attention of certain professors, brought him a chance to assist in teaching, and led to strong recommendations for the internship. His present prospects and growing eminence in the profession depended, he believed, more on his work as a research scientist than on his ability as an orthopedic surgeon. He considered it a "lucky break" that part of his experiments had come out well and that they had "dovetailed so neatly" into other ongoing research, a circumstance which enabled him to seek and obtain financial support for the continuing of his investigations. His research was thus the central reason for his success, but he did not deny the importance of his surgical skill and devoted hard work, especially at the critical point where, following his initial internship, he was retained at the hospital in the capacity of assistant resident.

> That choice came out in my favor mainly because I was enthusiastic and worked hard and enjoyed the work, and because I was also lucky again, I was able, without much difficulty, to do pretty well in the operating room.

When asked whether he had put an unusual amount of energy and time into his work he denied being a hard worker, characterizing himself as in most respects "a lazy guy at heart." He attributed his zeal at the hospital to an intense interest in everything that was going on.

Hale's own account of his success does full justice to the elements of good fortune in his career: his luck with the research, and the advantage of being trained in wartime when opportunities opened more rapidly than would have been possible under normal conditions. What he did not perceive so clearly, or at least emphasize so strongly in the interviews, was the contribution of his own behavior and his own personality to the success of his career. He called it "luck" that he was able to do well in the operating room, but this is certainly an insufficient explanation. Perhaps he had unusual dexterity, but we know that ever since early childhood his hands had been practicing the delicate manipulation of mechanisms and the art of drawing, and his research in college involved refined surgery on experimental animals. Skill in surgery, furthermore, is not simply a manual skill; it involves qualities of boldness, confidence, self-reliance, freedom from squeamishness, and willingness to assume responsibility in a situation where life is at stake. Hale did not sense that he possessed such qualities in rather unusual measure, just as he did not sense that, relative to others, he seemed practically a stranger to fatigue and welcomed the challenge of those critical situations that constantly arise in the daily and nightly life of a large hospital. He also did not think it unusual that he was capable of the absorbed interest, patience, and eternal struggle with baffling problems that characterized his behavior as a research worker. Like most people, indeed like most students of personality, he took for granted a great many of the qualities that are responsible for success.

We shall not try to work out here all the possible reasons for the pattern of traits shown by Hale in his professional life. This will concern us in later chapters when we use Hale and our other subjects as a proving ground for general ideas about personality. It should be noted, however, that his behavior as a physician and scientist was not created suddenly as a response to the demands of the profession. His traits go far back in his history; we have already discussed all of them when summing up his personality at the end of his college years. The profession of medicine influenced him in a favorable direction, bringing forward his steadier and more constructive qualities and permitting his disorganized rebelliousness to recede. It exerted a selective effect, but the selection was made from a pool of qualities already well developed. Before he became a doctor he lived a life marked by high energy and zestful interest, by wide gregarious contacts, by deep absorption in scientific problems, by lasting curiosity and a joy in mastering mechanisms, by direct action and counteraction in the face of difficulties, by self-reliant independence, and by subordination of feelings of guilt, anxiety, and inferiority. When he was in college we noticed his relative obtuseness toward the inner feelings of other people, and we were not surprised to learn a decade later that he had never liked nor respected psychiatry. His desire for challenging action first inclined him to general medicine but later, when he graduated from passively holding the retractors, swung him decisively toward surgery. Thus even the pattern of his interests within medicine reflected traits which were clearly discernible during the undergraduate study.

To what extent, it may be asked, was Hale's success the result of calculated ambition? Did he, in medical school and later, behave in a way that corresponded to "playing the teachers" in his earlier school career? This question can be more sharply specified by asking whether he deliberately chose to play up research and whether the alleged interest that caused him to be at all times an "eager beaver" was in fact a design to impress his superiors and secure his advancement. In Hale's case the answers to these questions seem fairly clear. The ability to do creative scientific research is not a thing that can be conjured into existence by even the most flaming ambition. Hale possessed this special pattern of interests and skills before he entered medicine, and a great deal of his satisfaction in doing this kind of work must be rated as strictly intrinsic. Much the same can be said for his skill as a physician. Thus it appears that Hale was well able to deliver the goods as a physician and scientist because of qualities long prepared in the course of his development, qualities that were clearly apparent before he decided to enter medicine. Granting this, however, it is also true that he cared a great deal about success. It was extremely important to him to stand out above the others. Finding in himself the power to deliver the goods in so many respects, he did not hesitate to use it as a means of impressing his superiors. Still another of his pre-existing traits, however, made this a natural and spontaneous, rather than a cynical and calculated, way for him to behave. As we have already noticed, he took great satisfaction in the interest and respect of older men, reaching his best level of constructiveness when some mentor became willing to give him unqualified encouragement. Hale's whole personality was so well-adapted to making a success that we do not need to accuse him of devious design in forwarding his career.

The roots of his ambition can best be understood by considering some of his faults. We asked him the reasons for his success but we did not spare him questions about the things in himself that had hindered success. The fact that a person accomplishes a job and fulfills a role does not mean that there is nothing further to say. We must be on the lookout for signs of wear and strain in even the most smoothly working machine.

Hale was able to give us, both in interviews and free associations, quite an extensive account of his faults. He complained, for instance, about a trait which he described as "my constant procrastination which keeps overcoming me." He related his struggles against it, especially when he was an intern and found himself overwhelmed by the number of things to be done. Often he would get behind schedule; then he would make out a list, forcing himself to cross out each item before going to bed even if that meant, as it several times did, that he stayed up all night. "So that was a hard thing to fight against," he concluded. Then he mentioned a quality of obsessive neatness which had bothered him a great deal. It struck him as strange that in some respects he could be very untidy, for instance with clothes and with things around the house, but that when it came to making anything, whether bookshelves, drawings, or pieces of apparatus, every detail had to be absolutely perfect. Even in school he used to tear up drawings and start afresh because he had made some tiny mistake. He believed that his "meticulous attention to details" was derived from his mother, whose extreme neatness we have already described. Today he still sometimes finds himself completely unable to check this trait even when he realizes that speed is the main requirement, and he characterized it as "a terrific handicap" and "a hell of a thing for me."

Hale complained also about a certain inefficiency in the workings of his mind. His memory does not always serve him with the facts and details it would be convenient to have available, especially in scientific arguments. He furthermore deplored what he called his "vagueness," a quality possessed by his mother but admirably absent from his father and sister. He reflected as follows on this trait:

> I'd like to be somewhat less vague than I am, somewhat more like my father than I am. He very rarely made a statement that wasn't right, or that he didn't have pretty good proof for. . . . The thing that I principally don't value is the general tendency to speak first and think afterwards, and the tendency to be somewhat vague, as against knowing what you want to say at once and knowing what you want to do at once, and not having any indecision. I would rather be as decisive as my father than the way I am, although I'm nowhere near as indecisive as my mother, fortunately.

We were not surprised, in view of his history of stuttering, that he included among his ideals that of being "an easy and gifted speaker who is never at a loss on his feet, able to say whatever he wants to at any moment." It was clear, however, that Hale's feelings of inferiority had roots deeper than his stuttering, however much this handicap may have enhanced such feelings. In the family circle he had perceived the contrast between his alert, self-possessed, ever competent father and his vague, fussy, indecisive mother. He had apparently felt the same contrast between his clear-minded sister and himself. The desire to be unlike the mother and equal to the father and sister seems to have acted as a spur to action, yet left him with a frequent sense of shortcoming, residues of which persist today.

Even now, when he enjoys the respect of colleagues and the outspoken admiration of patients, he is not always satisfied concerning his adequacy. The bothersome thought now and then crosses his mind that people think he is better than he really is, and when he sits down to analyze himself he is forced to conclude: "I never am quite as good as they think I am." The ambition which has carried him so far, which has made him fight so hard to subdue his stuttering, vagueness, procrastination, and obsessive meticulousness, seems to spring from a deep-rooted necessity to prove himself a masterful human being.

It was interesting to discover that Hale feels disquieted when everything is going well. He spoke as follows:

> Everything is just a little bit too smooth now. I don't like it like that, I feel a little nervous about it. I don't have any real problems right now, and that's not good. . . .
>
> It's always been much harder for me to be on top of the pile than to be down in the pile. Once I get on top of the pile I don't know what to do with myself, and I very soon don't do anything, and it very soon catches up with me again. And I feel more at home when I'm submerged and when things are closing in on me, when I feel myself cornered. Then I sort of gird my loins and look for ways out and there always seems to be one. It's a miserable way to live; I don't know why I do that, but I've always done it that way. . . .
>
> There's almost nothing that I've ever done that held any sustained interest for me that I was not also afraid of. It's true even in my present position. It's true of horseback riding; I love to ride, but still being on horseback often sort of scares me. But the general sort of situation that I find myself propelling myself into, whether it's by obsession or desire I don't know, is one in which I'm in the middle of a situation which terrifies me—not necessarily terrifies me, but frightens me to a certain extent—but which I can ultimately set to rights and get out of. I don't know what force propels me into them, but I've always gotten in them and I seem to always get out of them.

Hale described vividly his terror at stages in operations when everything seemed to be getting out of hand. He is able to fight down panic by working all the harder, by reminding himself that the responsibility belongs to him alone, by urging himself to keep going as best he can. He always prepares himself with the utmost care for a difficult operation: reviewing the relevant anatomy, searching the relevant scientific papers, making exhaustive tests on the patient. He told us also that a certain anxiety was involved in his research activities. When offered in one of our tests the phrase *my greatest fear* as a stimulus to free association, he thought immediately of his current research. He fears that his findings will not be confirmed by the work of others. He reported being very upset when another laboratory published results at variance with his work, then much relieved when still another laboratory brought out findings in agreement with his own. "Quite a lot of one's career depends on research," he remarked, "and I would hate to see the whole thing come tumbling down like a house of cards."

These disclosures demand the most careful analysis. Let us begin by noting that Hale does not seem to be quite accurate when he relates all sustained interest to anxiety. His original interest in biology and his undergraduate research grew under circumstances virtually free from threat. His fears about research seem to arise from the possibility of finding himself alone and rejected by other scientists and from the possibility that failure might wreck his career. We should further note that Hale's remarks about being at the top of the pile do not seem to imply anxiety specifically at being ahead of other *people*. He uses the analogy of a pile to suggest circumstances, demands, crises, details that require attention, in short the whole impact of events as one feels it in a busy institution such as a hospital. Having made these two reservations, however, we must still be impressed by what Hale has here told us. He has said, in the first place, that he feels impelled to get into a turmoil of events, not knowing what to do with himself and even experiencing nervousness when this external pressure is lacking. Secondly, he has declared that anxiety and the chance to conquer anxiety are very important elements in his satisfaction with life. It almost seems as if the sequence of inviting anxiety and then conquering it had become an end in itself. He attested its presence in riding, a pure recreation unrelated to the serious concerns of his life.

The need for outside turmoil and pressure suggests a certain lack of internal organization. We can infer that when Hale's life is not forcibly structured for him by the pressure of events he falls into the grip of his various "faults"—procrastination, meticulousness, vague indecisiveness—and is unable to pull himself together for effective action. Mild weakness in the organization of his mental processes appeared in the results of his intelligence tests, and his choice of surgery rather than general medicine revealed his strong preference for dramatic action together with his distaste for elusive diagnoses and slow methods of treatment. Hale seems to need pressure and excitement to energize and direct his action. It is not easy to be certain of the cause of such a trait. Perhaps he is an innately scattered, impulsive sort of person; perhaps his restless impatience is a part of constitutional endowment. On the other hand the nature of his "faults" suggests that certain emotional intrusions might be at work to hinder organization and disturb peace of mind. The obsessive character which he himself recognizes in these "faults" counts as evidence in favor of this interpretation. He needs external pressure in order to neutralize and dispel these intrusions.

Hale's need to invite and conquer anxiety represents a slightly different though probably not unrelated problem. It will be recalled that his undergraduate autobiography contained several incidents in which he felt anxiety but was able to emerge victorious. His interest in college athletics was, he believed, to some extent dependent on the fear he experienced before a contest and the joyful triumph over fear that could be achieved by vigorous competition. This long-standing pattern of behavior might be interpreted as a habit broken loose from its original importance, repeated merely as a matter of pleasure. Its force, however, suggests that it has a more strictly contemporary function in Hale's adjustment to life. He seems to require constant proof that he can repeat his old triumphs over fear, as if some traitor within his personality kept whispering that he could not win. One way to beat these hidden traitors is to look for external threats and keep proving that one is their master. Perhaps what he is really proving is that he can still rule the household of his personality.

Concerning the origin of the obsessive traits and anxieties which bother Hale we can offer the following hypothesis. In his earliest years he was encouraged to become self-reliant and to take pride in his power of accomplishment. In the course of time, however, maternal solicitude and autocracy began to insult this pride. He reacted by rebelliously increasing his independence, but the inner conflict and hostility generated by this bold course led to the appearance of obsessive traits and indecisiveness which constituted a still further insult to his pride. The inner stress gave rise also to inexplicable fears of the dark and of water, later on of having to move to a new house. Pride was again insulted when stuttering appeared, a grave and uncontrollable social handicap. The final insult came when he could not control his fear of the boys from the neighborhood to the east, and his ultimate conquest of this fear, in the "backbone incident," stood out as the major triumph of his childhood. It is slow work to overcome traits which have been implicated in the emotional crises of childhood. Hale still needs to strengthen his mastery of anxiety by inviting and overcoming it, to counterbalance his earlier speech handicap by volubility, and to beat out his obsessive traits by immersing himself in a turmoil of dramatic and demanding events.

One of the traits which Hale criticized in himself was his general irritability. He said:

> I'd like to have a somewhat more even temper. I get fairly annoyed at some situations, and I think it's very advantageous not to be bothered by little details that keep cropping up; lots of little things annoy me, and that's very wearing, to be annoyed by lots of little things. I'd rather not be.

It seems reasonable to assume that Hale's associates share his negative attitude toward this trait and that everyone would be happier if he could change it.

We have already discussed, in the first interpretive summary, his association of solitude with dejection, his need of friendly social support, and his tendency to injure social relationships by too free a display of assertiveness and aggression. His attitude toward solitude and toward being set apart from the group came out with striking clarity during the unhappy first year at medical school, but it appears that from now on solitude is likely to be the least of his worries. The only danger that is today actively present is that of alienating the group and creating a sense of isolation by being too critical and too aggressive. In the past this tendency has been balanced by the presence of older men who were willing to take a chance on him: professors at medical school, commanding officers in the service, senior physicians in the hospital. His term of duty as orthopedic resident, when he runs the show more or less alone, is a crucial test of his ability to function without the active support of an older man and still to check himself from assertive and aggressive displays toward his staff. Like most things in life the test is not pure, because he enjoys the implicit support of the surgeon-in-chief who granted him the flattering appointment, but he has never before faced so clearly the relative isolation that is the lot of a top administrative officer. We have seen that he experiences distinct strain. He is irritable, he criticizes his less competent lieutenants sharply, he is at times violently aggressive with the nurses, and he is anxious about the effects of all this, hoping that his victims harbor no grudges and doing his best in the relaxed atmosphere of social occasions to cancel any injuries he may have inflicted.

His capacity to be demanding of himself has made him a demanding task-master, impatient with stupidity, awkwardness, and incompetence. He wishes that he did not have to keep things stirred up in this way. Nevertheless he carries on successfully and seems likely, insofar as we could tell at the middle of the term, to finish his tenure as orthopedic resident with an exceptionally good record. He has made some progress in the management of aggression.

When we turn our attention to Hale's children, we discover another realm in which he is making progress. Although at first it seemed that he had scarcely time to become aware of his children, later he began to take considerable pleasure in their company, giving them trips and instruction in return for their gratifying quality of being nice to him. From his eldest daughter's annoying displays of independence he is slowly learning not to repeat his mother's errors in child rearing, and his sympathy for the insecurity of the second child has somewhat opened his mind to the sort of problem that is dealt with in psychiatry. Hale's own life has been built on action and the mastery of the external world. It is through bringing up his children that he is beginning to learn more about the inner world of feelings.

The point of least progress in Hale's life seems to be his relationship with his wife. Attention has already been called to the unusual features of his courtship: the appeal of his girl friend's harmonious family life, and the subtle influence of his estimate, doubtless unconscious, that his girl would be able to endure the slim emotional pickings of being a doctor's wife. She was charming, erotically attractive, and congenial to the gay social life he hoped to lead when off duty. The trouble was that once he got launched in his medical career he literally had no time off duty. Even on the occasion of the honeymoon he placed considerations of being a good medical subordinate ahead of spending time with his new wife. When this kind of thing seemed likely to continue indefinitely, his wife showed signs of rebellion, but Hale seemed to have great difficulty in contemplating that her complaints might be justified. Only slowly has he conceded that it is necessary for him to give more thought to her happiness.

In many ways his lack of consideration can be traced directly to his relationship with his own mother. Because of her over-solicitude and threat to his boyish spirit of adventure, he was obliged to develop a precocious capacity for independence, suppressing both his dependent longings and his feelings of guilt over his own defiance. He became an expert in leading his own life regardless of a woman's demands. In one of his test stories he depicted a son who disappoints his mother's hopes by becoming a boxer, feeling only a transient regret as he embarks on the course he knows is right for him. Hale thus acquired a kind of insensitivity which carried over into his own married life when that life began to replicate the original pattern of stress: domestic demands versus the man's right to do what he wanted.

At first glance one might suppose that the conflict was simply between incompatible duties, the claims of a wife and the claims of a hospital with its sick people for whom the husband is professionally responsible. Every doctor's family knows this kind of conflict. Closer inspection shows, however, that the freedom Hale expected went far beyond the legitimate demands of his job. He was not required to do the photographic work connected with his experiments and scientific papers. He did these things because he wanted to, and it was hard for him to realize that a wife's objections sometimes had to be taken seriously. Occasionally he was aware of guilt feelings over his preoccupation with the attic workshop. But he was an old hand at disposing of that kind of guilt feelings.

In considering the life adjustment of a single individual we are inevitably drawn into weighing the correlated adjustment of those people who constitute his social orbit. Hale's way of leading his life involves certain strains in himself, although these are for the most part well-mastered and do not interfere with successful accomplishment. It also involves strains in others, particularly his wife, the hospital nurses, and the less competent members of the hospital's house staff. For them, adjustment to Hale must often be a difficult and vexing problem. But if we are to include the social orbit, it is hardly fair to consider the strains Hale imposes upon it without remembering also the services that he renders. He does much to advance the fortunes of the better nurses and more gifted house-officers, he runs his section of the hospital efficiently, he contributes possibly lasting benefits to mankind in his research, and he takes care of his patients. Our portrait of him includes his night-long study in preparation for a difficult piece of surgery, his four-day vigil at the bedside of the injured jeep driver, and his casual remark that "some nights you've got patients that are pretty sick and you stick around to see what's going to happen."

3. Resources for Understanding

> To know that we know what we know, and that
> we do not know what we do not know, that is true
> knowledge.
>
> CONFUCIUS

In order to concentrate fully on describing and understanding Hartley Hale we excluded from the last chapter any discussion of the sources of our knowledge. No doubt this created an air of magic and omniscience with which no one should remain satisfied. In this chapter we shall try to clear the air by stating how our information was collected. It will at once become apparent that our study falls far short of being a definitive investigation. By subjecting Hale twice to extensive studies, and by reflecting carefully upon the results, we have probably been able to understand certain things about him that would not otherwise be apparent. But we had to use such tools as were practicable for us. As in any scientific investigation, what we know about him is the kind of thing our methods made it possible to know. An explicit statement of resources for understanding must always accompany the claim that something has been understood.

A full survey of methods for studying personality would keep us too long from the central theme of this book. Excellent accounts of the topic are available elsewhere.[1] Even from what we say here, however, it will be clear that the study of another person is a difficult undertaking which cannot be handled in a cut-and-dried fashion. Perhaps the very first thing to consider is the other person's motivation for taking part in such a study. Unless his interest is enlisted to a rather unusual extent he is not likely to be disposed toward whole-hearted participation and candid self-disclosure. Even when cooperation is perfect, a further difficulty arises from the

[1] For a brief systematic survey see Allport, G. W., *Personality: A Psychological Interpretation*, New York, Henry Holt & Co., 1937, ch. 14. A more extensive weighing of methodological problems is given in McClelland, D. C., *Personality*, New York, Wm. Sloane Associates, 1951, chs. 1-4.

very nature of the material. No interviews or available tests, no existing methods of observation, can possibly be considered complete or definitive. Furthermore, all methods yield information of a sort that leaves much to be judged and interpreted by the examiners. In this way the frailties of the examiners enter the study and constitute a liability in reaching valid conclusions. It clearly behooves us to reflect a little on what is involved in trying to understand other people.

METHODS OF GATHERING INFORMATION

Interviews.—Any attempt to study other people must rely heavily on interviews. There can be no adequate substitute for the obvious procedure of asking the subject to tell all that he can about himself and his environment. The present project began with a written autobiography, but the subject's story was then amplified by means of extensive interviews covering the family circle, the personalities of the parents, discipline and ideals, early memories, school and college history, social relationships, health and sex, emotions and their control, current interests and problems, opinions and general outlook on life. A similar series of interviews, preserved verbatim by electrical recording, formed the backbone of the second study. We began with the history of the intervening years, then sought more detailed information concerning relationships with parents and siblings, marriage and family, ideas and practices as regards bringing up children, occupational satisfactions and frustrations, social life, amusements, participation in community affairs, opinions about world events, personal values and ideals. Abundant time was allotted to the interviews so that both subject and examiner could feel free to explore whatever topics entered the conversation.

It is sometimes felt that the interview method puts the examiner at the mercy of whatever fictions the subject chooses to set forth. When we ask someone to tell us what he considers to be the characteristic and essential features of his life, we certainly give him an opening to regale us with falsified pictures, selected events, and highly colored interpretations. Even when he intends to tell nothing but the truth, we cannot expect him to cancel his unwitting defenses or set aside his cherished illusions. Under favorable circumstances, however, this very real defect in the interview method can be greatly diminished. Much depends on the subject's motives and the relationship he establishes with the examining staff. Some people do not really like to have their personalities studied. They feel defensive and would prefer to study the examiners while keeping secret their own true qualities. Others participate willingly so long as they can fathom the purpose of the procedures but become resentful if they suspect the examiners of trying to learn something which they themselves do not know. The subjects described in this book were relatively free from these forms of resistance. The process of being studied was congenial to them, satisfying important needs and thus evoking their fullest cooperation. The pattern of favorable motives was quite different in each case, as we shall see in later chapters, but it was always such as to dispose the subjects toward judicious candor in discussing themselves.

For Hartley Hale an important attraction was the opportunity to talk about his successes. He felt encouraged to describe exploits which it would have been boastful to relate under ordinary circumstances. Finding himself appreciated, he progressively relaxed his defenses and became able to discuss his faults and even his failures. He gained needed reassurance from the discovery that his faults were accepted calmly, without censure or criticism. Hale thus obtained both pleasure and increased confidence from putting his personality under the microscope. It was also important to him that his chief listener in both studies was a man older than himself. The situation resembled those earlier ones in which an older man took a chance on him, respected his ultimate worth despite current defects, and thus brought out the best features of his personality. External motives of money and of service to science were not without effect, but in Hale's case they were strongly supplemented by a favorable pattern of inner needs.

Motivation of this kind goes a long way to minimize the faults of the interview method. It would be a mistake, moreover, to think of interviews merely as fact-gathering procedures in which the examiner has no way of sifting out the truth. The subject's behavior includes much more than the imparting of information; he displays feelings and gives the examiner abundant opportunities to read between the lines. Especially when the session is recorded so that the transcript can be studied at leisure, the examiner will observe peculiarities of phrase, odd sequences of topics, abrupt changes of theme, errors and self-corrections, hints of anxiety, and many other signs which indicate how the subject feels about the things he is discussing. Close inspection will reveal unspoken assumptions and unwitting ways of looking at things which may be of great importance in the subject's personality. Hartley Hale never told us, for instance, that he regularly placed the demands of his profession ahead of the demands of his wife, but this generalization was obvious from specific events he described and from the character of his transitions between the two topics. Only toward the end of the study did he speak of his strong conscience with regard to patients and his sharp anxiety over difficult pieces of surgery, but these feelings could easily be inferred from his earlier narrative of events.

Tests and Observations.—In spite of the central position of interviews and the richness of understanding to be derived from them when subjects are favorably motivated, the study of personality would be incomplete without a considerable use of other methods. There are plenty of things which people cannot tell about themselves and which cannot very well be inferred from interviews. One of the best ways to extend the search is to make a study of imaginative productions. The general idea behind tests of imagination—the *projective tests* that have recently come into popularity—is to confront the subject with ambiguous material of some kind and ask him to do something with it. In the Rorschach Test, for instance, he is asked to tell what he perceives in a series of actually meaningless ink blots, while in the Thematic Apperception Test he is shown pictures susceptible to many different interpretations and is invited to make up stories about them. The ambiguous character of the material precludes merely conventional answers and forces the subject to fall back on his own preferred ways of doing things. He is thus apt to reveal certain covert features of his personality, for example his unsatisfied desires, suppressed anxieties, preferred patterns for perceiving the world and the people around him.

Hartley Hale in the Rorschach Test made a strenuous effort to perceive mechanical objects in the unmechanical ink blots. He also had difficulty in achieving good organization among his percepts. Both of these clues pointed to traits which were important in understanding his personality. In his stories for the Thematic Apperception Test he regularly attributed dejection, despair, and suicidal thoughts to lonely characters, thus significantly amplifying his direct statement that he hated to be alone. Significant also were those plots in which sons ran counter to their mothers' wishes, showing determined independence but also traces of uneasy regret.

The Rorschach and Thematic Apperception Tests were regularly used in the studies described in this book.[2] They were supplemented, especially in the earlier studies, by several other procedures involving imaginative production: sentence completions, story completions, story alterations, cloud pictures, and so forth. By these techniques we hoped to extend and deepen the abundant information gathered in the interviews. We also used with each subject one or both of two procedures based on Freud's original idea of free association. The first of these procedures called for continuous free association with a minimum of prompting. The second technique varied from the classic pattern by offering brief but significant phrases as a stimulus to association.[3] Examples of the phrases used in the latter session, and of the associations they stimulated in Hartley Hale, have already appeared in the preceding chapter.

In attempting to assess the abilities of our subjects we relied upon a combination of standard tests and performance in everyday life. With respect to physical abilities we obtained standard somatotype photographs according to the technique devised by Sheldon, and we took careful note of the health and athletic histories.[4] For an estimate of intellectual status we used the Wechsler-Bellevue Adult Intelligence Test, generally supplementing it with several other measures.[5] One of these supplemental examinations was the Vigotsky Test, a difficult problem in concept formation which generally creates considerable frustration and tension before the correct solution is reached.[6] A test of this kind has the special value of

[2] These two procedures are briefly described in Hunt, J. McV., ed., *Personality and the Behavior Disorders*, New York, The Ronald Press Co., 1944, Vol. 1, ch. 6.

[3] Ravven, R. M., *The Phrase Association Interview*, 1951, unpublished thesis, Harvard College Library, Cambridge, Mass.

[4] A brief account of Sheldon's method will be found in his chapter in Hunt, *op. cit.*, vol. 1, ch. 17.

[5] For a brief description of the Wechsler-Bellevue, with illustrative results, see Rosenzweig, S., & Kogan, K. L., *Psychodiagnosis*, New York, Grune & Stratton, 1949, pp. 24-32. A fuller account of intelligence testing is given by A. Magaret in Pennington, L. A., & Berg, I. A., *An Introduction to Clinical Psychology*, New York, The Ronald Press Co., 1948, ch. 15.

[6] Rosenzweig & Kogan, *op. cit.*, pp. 66-70. For fuller information consult Hanfmann, E., & Kasanin, J., Conceptual Thinking in Schizophrenia, *Nervous & Mental Disease Monographs*, 1942, No. 67.

showing the extent to which intellectual processes become disrupted by stress. It is of interest that Hartley Hale dealt rather successfully with this problem. Baffled for a while, he showed distinct signs of mounting annoyance and confusion, but he firmly pulled himself together and worked with resolute concentration until he had mastered the problem. In estimating intellectual competence we included the school history, the imaginative productions, and such evidence as we could obtain by discussing intellectual interests with the subjects. We sought in these ways to draw a qualitative picture of the subject's actual use of his mind.

To facilitate comparisons between our subjects and larger populations we used a certain number of standardized self-rating scales, particularly the Bernreuter Personality Inventory and the Allport-Vernon Study of Values.[7] The fullness of our interview material, however, freed us from having to depend heavily on self-ratings in understanding the individual cases. We endeavored to observe the subjects in spontaneous social situations and to secure the opinions of other people about them. Whenever possible we became acquainted with parents, friends, and others who might contribute to our understanding. Our own sessions, being conducted by several different people, provided a chance to notice differences in a subject's attitudes toward men and women, for instance, or toward older people and contemporaries. During the undergraduate study the subjects participated in whatever experiments were going on in the laboratory, for example hypnotic susceptibility, level of aspiration, and tests involving competition and frustration. Such participation provided further opportunities to observe their behavior under various pressures.

Comparison with Other Methods.—These were our methods and the sources of our knowledge. It is hardly necessary to add that we did not know everything about our subjects and that our understanding of their lives cannot be certified as either complete or accurate. No single research project on personality can be in a position to use all of the best methods that are currently available. The study of psychodynamics, for example, is most fully accomplished by the technique of psychoanalysis. This means perhaps two or three

[7] Short accounts are given in Rosenzweig & Kogan, *Psychodiagnosis, op. cit.*, pp. 95-96, 103-107. The original sources are Bernreuter, R. G., The Theory and Construction of the Personality Inventory, *Journal of Social Psychology*, 1933, Vol. 4, pp. 387-405; Vernon, P. E. & Allport, G. W., A Test for Personality Values, *Journal of Abnormal & Social Psychology*, 1931, vol. 26, pp. 231-248.

years of daily meetings between patient and analyst in the course of which the intricacies of the patient's emotional life are slowly unfolded and slowly changed. This laborious delving, with its ample opportunities to appraise early inferences by waiting for further material to emerge, leads to a desirably deep insight into the inner workings of personality. But no one would be willing to submit to a process so painful and protracted unless he were driven by the most powerful motives, such as recovering from a grave disorder which could be cured in no other way. The ideal technique for studying psychodynamics is simply not available unless the subject is seeking treatment, or perhaps being trained to give treatment.

A parallel situation exists with regard to placing subjects in prepared social situations or under realistic stress. Great success was achieved with this kind of technique by the Assessment Staff of the Office of Strategic Services during World War II, the candidate being put through a series of difficult lifelike tasks requiring action, alone or in groups, under genuinely trying conditions.[8] Such methods yield information that can never be reliably obtained through interviews, but their success depends upon unusually compelling motivation on the part of the subjects—a zeal equivalent to that which was evoked by the challenge of selection for special assignments in wartime.

Again, the study of social behavior and the social orbit is best carried on when the examiners can function as participant observers and can secure expressions of opinion about the subjects from the people amongst whom they live. A high standard in this respect was set by Jones in the Adolescent Growth Study at the University of California.[9] Ratings made by teachers, reputation among classmates, position in the pattern of friendships, and spontaneous behavior observed at the school clubhouse all contributed in this study to a detailed knowledge of each subject as a member of the school society. Such excellence can be achieved, however, only when the research project has invaded the community and secured a rather unusual degree of cooperation from everyone concerned.

Still another important branch of personality study, parent-child relationships, calls ideally for a similar kind of participant observation. The studies of child development being carried on by the Fels Foundation at Yellow Springs, Ohio, have brought to a fine point the observation of parents and children at home and the systematic recording of their interaction.[10] This technique again calls for unusual community cooperation and is most successful when the children are quite young. It is hard to conceive of a single study which could utilize all of the best contemporary methods for understanding other people.

The preceding paragraphs have called attention to a number of ideal methods for studying personality. If in so doing they have constituted a criticism of the case studies reported in this book, which rivalled none of these ideals, we are the more justified in mentioning a special virtue of our own enterprise. By using an abundance of interviews, by evoking strong personal interest in the proceedings, and by giving respectful attention to the subject's self-estimates, his hopes and fears, his plans and daydreams and deepest aspirations, we have been able to learn a great deal about the ego, self, and those other inner integrations which are so important in giving overall form and direction to a life. Furthermore, by starting with relatively healthy and able young people and by carrying the study on into their more settled young adulthood, we have been in a special position to observe the process of natural growth. Whatever potentialities there may be in human nature for self-direction, spontaneous insight, and constructive change, our methods have helped us not to overlook them. And natural growth is the most neglected aspect of personality.

PRECAUTIONS IN INTERPRETING INFORMATION

The final point to consider with regard to method is the judging and interpreting activity performed by the examiners. It is impossible to study another person without making evaluations, and it is hard to keep these evaluations from being seriously distorted by one's personal reactions to the subject. Hartley Hale, for example, is a man who evokes strong feelings in the people who become acquainted with him. These feelings in turn call forth definite preferences as to what the case material should reveal. Some people are impressed by his successes and admire his rapid climb on the lad-

[10] Baldwin, A. L., Kalhorn, J., & Breese, F. H., Patterns of Parent Behavior, *Psychological Monographs*, 1945, Vol. 58, No. 3. See also Buhler, C., *The Child and His Family*, New York, Longmans Green & Co., 1940.

der of professional status. Some are particularly taken by his vigorous self-confidence and capacity for independent and masterful action. Some tend to emphasize his service and self-dedication in the field of medicine. For people thus disposed it is natural to hope that the reconstructed story will be one of triumphs over adversity, a living proof that circumstances can be conquered by will power.

Other people react with envy to a life that has achieved the outward marks of success. They prefer to feel that Hale had an easy time of it. They contrast him with people whose financial difficulties were more acute and who faced other special obstacles such as ethnic prejudice. They experience a certain resentment that he constantly got by in school without working hard or even behaving well, that he was befriended by instructors, and that he took such great pains to win the approval of his superiors. People thus disposed feel almost gleeful when the material reveals anxieties, irrationalities, and other evidence of imperfect integration. They favor the idea that he is just a neurotic young man who by lucky chance has found a socially acceptable way of holding his neurosis precariously in check.

Others dislike him for his attitude toward clumsy subordinates and toward his long-suffering wife, feeling that he deserves the come-uppance of an unhappy future. Finally, his political views and values easily offend those who do not share them. Resentment may be felt over his opposition to socialized medicine, his Republicanism, his individualistic outlook, and his lack of interest in organized religion. In short, it is easy on the one hand to give him an admiration too uncritical, on the other hand to yearn angrily for the chance to teach him a thing or two.

The study of personality is one of the most difficult branches of knowledge in which to achieve a judicious outlook, free from invasion by personal preferences and personal feelings about the subject-matter. Even when the more obvious kinds of prejudiced thinking are overcome, there is still the danger of projecting one's unconscious problems and unwitting attitudes into the judgment.

There are only two ways in which this difficulty can be reduced to relatively harmless proportions. One of these is to neutralize the distortions by having several different workers collaborate in making the interpretations. Especially if these workers are of somewhat different backgrounds and training, they can, to a considerable extent, cancel each other's personal rigidities of judgment. The second way is that of progressively teaching the examiners to overcome their rigidities and to achieve greater judiciousness through increased familiarity with their own personalities. Such education occurs quite naturally in the course of team studies of personality, as in fact it does for many people simply through the experiences of everyday life. The studies described in this book are the handiwork of a large number of examiners. Several different people participated in giving the tests and conducting the interviews. The interpretation and integration of the findings was done in staff conferences attended by ten or a dozen workers. While this pluralistic procedure does not guarantee complete impartiality, it serves at least to diminish those errors of judgment that must be laid at the door of the examiners.

SUGGESTIONS FOR FURTHER READING

Further study of methods for the understanding of personality can well begin with the brief systematic survey given by G. W. Allport in *Personality: A Psychological Interpretation* (New York, Henry Holt & Co., 1937), ch. 14. A small book by Harold E. Jones entitled *Development in Adolescence* (New York & London, D. Appleton-Century Co., 1943) reports the study of a single case and is particularly strong on methods for observing social behavior and social reputation. H. A. Murray in *Explorations in Personality* (New York & London, Oxford University Press, 1938) describes a wide variety of methods designed to approach personality from all angles; see especially ch. 6. Methods developed by Murray and associates for the purpose of assessing personnel for strategic wartime services are given in chs. 3 and 4 of *Assessment of Men* by the O. S. S. Assessment Staff (New York, Rinehart & Co., 1948). Stress is laid on the performance of lifelike tasks in a social setting that permits frequent informal contacts between observers and candidates.

A brief introduction to projective tests is given by R. W. White in *Personality and the Behavior Disorders*, J. McV. Hunt, ed. (New York, The Ronald Press Co., 1944), Vol. 1, ch. 6. A new and authoritative survey of this field has recently been assembled by H. H. & G. L. Anderson, *An Introduction to Projective Techniques* (New York, Prentice-Hall, 1951).

For a reflective account of the problems involved in observing and understanding personality the best place to turn is David C. McClelland's *Personality* (New York, William Sloane Associates, 1951), chs. 1–4.

4. The Shaping of Lives by Social Forces

> Society and individuals are inseparable phases of a common whole, so that wherever we find an individual fact we may look for a social fact to go with it.
>
> C. H. COOLEY

It is the plan of this book to alternate between intensive case studies and the discussion of general ideas about personality. The present chapter will be devoted mainly to what we previously called *the social view of man*. It will be concerned with the ways in which an individual is shaped by the culture and society of which he is a member. We shall examine some representative ideas about social shaping forces, using Hartley Hale as a case in point. The proper evaluation of these ideas is a matter of great importance. It is essential to appreciate as fully as possible the contribution they make to the understanding of man's nature, but it is also essential to become wary of pitfalls that lie in the path when they are used in a fashion too reckless and too dogmatic. The important thing is to utilize the social view without excluding the other legitimate ways of looking at man.

THE GENERAL INFLUENCE OF THE CULTURE

Our first concern will be with the broad influence of the culture as a whole. How do the values and ideals of the American culture affect the course of individual development? To what extent, more specifically, can we see in Hartley Hale's personality the imprint of the culture in which he grew to manhood? Our inquiry would expand in all directions if we attempted to make it in any sense exhaustive. Fortunately the purpose of this chapter does not require us to examine more than a few outstanding characteristics of the culture. If we approach these in a spirit both appreciative and critical, they will suffice to give us the needed insight into the culture concept.

Competitive Enterprise.—One of the most frequently mentioned characteristics of the American culture is its emphasis on competitive enterprise. "The pattern of the culture," writes Lynd, "stresses individual competitive aggressiveness against one's fellows as the basis for personal and collective security. Each man must stand on his own feet and fight for what he gets—so runs the philosophy of the culture—and in this way the common welfare throughout the entire culture is best achieved." [1] For the most part success in the struggle is measured by money, but money easily serves as a symbol for other values such as prestige and power. The sharp cultural accent on individual enterprise had its origin in the conditions that prevailed on the frontier and in a rapidly expanding economy, but it tends to outlast these conditions. In the atmosphere engendered by this ideal the individual is encouraged to be much concerned about his competitive prowess and to seek constant proofs of his adequacy. He also tends to feel alone and isolated from others, who are his rivals rather than his associates in a common enterprise. To be able to compete successfully he must hold in reasonable check his dependent tendencies, his sympathies, and his desire to be loved by others. The ideal calls for high self-sufficiency and freedom from hampering restraints.

We need enlarge no further on this cultural characteristic in order to see how perfectly it is exemplified in Hartley Hale. His early independence and self-reliance, his embattled course toward childhood self-respect, his drive, his desire to rise above his fellow medical students, his suppression of the softer side of his nature, his conception of a proper economic order, all testify to the impact of the cultural ideal of competitive enterprise. A personality such as Hale's might be found in places other than the United States, but it is easy to think of cultures, for example the Chinese, Hindu, and Russian, in which a like pattern would be all but impossible.

Faith in Material Progress.—Another important feature of the American culture pattern is an optimistic faith in material progress. Two world wars and a severe economic depression shook but did not destroy this American article of faith. As Commager puts it, the American's culture is "still predominantly material, his thinking quantitative, his genius inventive, experimental, and prac-

---

[1] Lynd, R. S., *Knowledge for What? The Place of Social Science in American Culture*, Princeton University Press, 1939, p. 71.

tical." [2] In this cultural climate there is scant encouragement for contemplation and theorizing, which tend to be identified with the idle and the useless. Virtue resides rather in action, and this action must be directed primarily to changing the material environment for the better. The role of the inventor is honored and dramatized, as is that of the industrial pioneer who forwards technology and extends man's mastery of his world. Once again the description of a cultural characteristic sounds at the same time like a description of Hartley Hale. A few points will sufficiently recall the whole striking resemblance: his description of the ample high-school stage and of his joy in inventing new lighting effects, his research activities which included the building of apparatus, and his ultimate preference for surgery because of its active attack on the material sources of illness. The channels of Hale's interest and the directions taken by his energies again show the influence of the American cultural terrain.

Action and Rationality.—In our culture the optimistic faith in material progress is accompanied by a like faith in the energy and rationality of man. Making an effort and behaving with realistic common sense are so strongly valued as to constitute an essential part of our moral code. In Kluckhohn's words, "our glorification of science and our faith in what can be accomplished through education are two striking aspects of our generalized conviction that secular, humanistic effort will improve the world in a series of changes, all or mainly for the better. We further tend to believe that morality and reason must coincide." [3]

It is remarkable to see how fully Hale is a child of his culture with respect to this feature of its outlook. He feels almost completely detached from religion, declaring that he can get more inspiration from being out of doors than from being in church. Whenever we attempted to draw him into a discussion of moral and spiritual values, he plainly showed that he considered such topics both fuzzy and unimportant. In common with most of his sophisticated contemporaries he had dislodged sex from its pre-Freudian status as the cardinal sin and accepted it as a pleasurable part of man's biological endowment. If it is true, as Commager maintains, that Americans on the whole lack "either a sense of sin or that aware-

[2] Commager, H. S., *The American Mind*, New Haven, Yale University Press, 1950, p. 410.
[3] Kluckhohn, C., *Mirror for Man: the Relation of Anthropology to Modern Life*, New York, Whittlesey House, 1949, p. 232.

ness of evil almost instinctive with most Old World peoples," [4] then Hale must again be rated a typical American. But this does not mean that his conduct is without moral control. He has a sharp sense of fairness. Injustice is the thing above all others that makes him angry, and it was on grounds of unfairness that he refused to take advantage of the girl he had decided not to marry. In his dedication to this value he exhibits yet another culturally accented trait. According to Erikson, a common type of young American "does not know any kind of indignation in the positive sense of the violation of a principle, with the exception of *unfairness*." Perhaps this has its origin in the tribunal of the family circle; at all events this young American "becomes an advocate of fairness—unfairness, primarily in sports, is probably the only subject which would cause a facsimile of indignation—and then, of course, bossiness of any kind. 'No one can do this to me' is the slogan of such indignation." [5]

Hale's morality, however, does not stop at this point. As we have seen, his indignation can easily be fired by any lapse from that high code of professional ethics which he applies relentlessly to his own conduct. As a doctor and as a scientist he has submitted to as stiff a code of service and honesty as has ever existed. But it is a secular and humanistic code in which morality and reason are pretty much identified, an extension of the American faith in the energy and rationality of man.

Attitude Toward Women.—Recent students of our culture have found a good deal to say about American attitudes toward women. American men, it is claimed, tend to spoil their women, idealize them, assign them superior cultural and spiritual attributes, and at the same time permit them to exert no little tyranny in the home. The idealizing tendency finds its most extreme expression in the sentimental rhapsodies of Mother's Day. The acceptance of petticoat rule can be discerned in the cartoonist's stock figures of dominant wife and hen-pecked husband, a family pattern which contrasts sharply with most European cultures.

Hale's attitude clearly varies from this pattern. There is evidence that he experienced its impact: toward those girls who served as idealized mother images he felt for some time shy and inhibited. In the main, however, he exhibits not the slightest tendency to spoil

[4] Commager, *op. cit.*, p. 410.
[5] Erikson, E. H., *Childhood and Society*, New York, W. W. Norton & Co., 1950, p. 274.

women, idealize them, or submit to their domination. At the best, he treats them as equals and companions with whom pleasures can be shared; at the worst, as inferiors who can be ignored or made the targets of angry criticism. The family circle of his childhood did not favor the development of the more common American pattern. Both parents had intellectual and artistic interests, and the forthright father could on crucial occasions make good his claim to final authority. Hale himself achieved a forceful rebellion against maternal dominance and thus early laid the basis for his present attitudes toward women.

Conformity.—For more than a century, foreign visitors have accused Americans of excessive conformity in matters of speech, dress, manners, behavior, and ideas. The ideal of equality, however imperfectly realized in practice, has acted to produce what is sometimes called "the cult of the average man." The values associated with conformity are not fully consistent with competitive enterprise, and this conflict is a definite source of strain in our culture. Nevertheless, conformity exerts a pervasive influence in many departments of life. It is part of the American tradition to snipe at those who have achieved success and eminence, even though they may be greatly envied. The same attitude extends to eccentrics, long-haired poets, absent-minded professors, people who do things differently, and people who come from unfamiliar backgrounds. Sinclair Lewis described with memorable vividness in *Main Street* the difficulty of bringing innovations into a small American community. Most Americans, in spite of their interest in getting ahead and reaching the top, are loath to stick out from the crowd and prefer to think that they are doing things in ways of which everyone approves.

Many social scientists believe that the tendency toward conformity is on the increase in America, and one observer, Riesman, maintains that it is well on the way toward displacing competitive enterprise and becoming the predominant characteristic of our culture. With the decrease in those dramatic opportunities for individual success that were so common in the last century, there has occurred an important shift, Riesman maintains, from values of achievement to values of social adjustment. "Increasingly," he says, "other people are the problem, not the material environment," and this has the effect of training each person to guide his conduct by paying close attention to the signals of approval and disapproval that emanate from others.[6] The high value placed upon conformity and the anxiety that is experienced when one feels conspicuous are particularly obvious in the adolescent groups that constitute the American youth culture, but Riesman maintains that a similar outlook has invaded many spheres of adult concern.

If Riesman's observations are sound, then Hartley Hale again varies sharply from the culturally favored pattern. He is not particularly sensitive to signals from others, he does not object to being conspicuous, and he is predominantly guided by ideals of professional achievement rather than by goals of smooth social participation. No one would choose him as an example of the alleged American tendency toward a leveling of individuality.

Our sampling of American cultural characteristics has shown three instances in which Hale's personality follows a strongly favored pattern, two instances in which it varies from such a pattern. He exemplifies the cultural ideals of competitive enterprise, faith in material progress, optimism with respect to the energy and rationality of man. His attitude toward women, however, and his resistance to a leveling conformity represent variations from the patterns that predominate in the culture as a whole. When we seek to explain these variations we are obliged to take account of other influences which contribute to the shaping of personality. Hale's occupation, for example, which has strongly affected his development, is highly specialized and far from typical of American conditions as a whole. The frontier spirit is still appropriate in medical research, where vast regions of ignorance remain to be conquered by hard work and inventive genius. His family pattern, moreover, varied from the most common American type, and his personal development took a course that heightened his competitive assertiveness at the expense of conformist trends. The general influence of the culture is only a general influence, leaving wide scope for the many other shaping forces to which each individual is exposed. The culture encourages certain patterns of behavior and expectation without prohibiting a considerable range of variations from the norm. Hale varies in some ways from cultural norms, but if we consider his personality as a whole we are justified in calling him a very American young man. There are many cultures in which such a pattern of personality simply could not have developed. Per-

---

[6] Riesman, D., *The Lonely Crowd: A Study of the Changing American Character*, New Haven, Yale University Press, 1950, p. 18.

haps only in America would it have received substantial encouragement.

THE EFFECTS OF SOCIAL STATUS

It is a well established fact that American society is highly stratified. The cultural ideal of democratic equality and "the cult of the common man" have not prevented the appearance of marked social stratification based largely, though not entirely, on differences in wealth. In recent years social scientists have invaded a number of representative communities and remained there long enough to become thoroughly familiar with the status hierarchy. Information is derived chiefly from the residents of the community, who seem to experience little difficulty in ranking their fellow citizens with regard to social status. Questions about the relative importance of people in the community draw from most informants a ready assignment of all the people they know to definite social positions, and there is surprising agreement among the assignments made by different informants.

Agreement is smaller when it comes to grouping the people of the community into social classes. Though riddled with status differences, American society has not on the whole developed rigidly fixed class boundaries. It is far from being a caste system except with respect to the Negroes in the South. The democratic ideal is preserved in the notion that status can be improved by individual effort, and the motive of upward mobility proves to be strong and pervasive in American life. It is actually no easy matter, however, for a person to improve the status to which he was born. Social obstacles, sometimes expressed with open cruelty but more often taking the form of quiet firm exclusions, serve in fact to restrict mobility and perpetuate the existing stratification.

The seriousness of these restrictions is well shown in a study by Hollingshead, which concentrates particularly on class structure as it affects young people of high school age.[7] The social status of parents was found to exert a powerful influence on the formation of those groups which are so important in the lives of American adolescents. The "crowds" or "bunches" to which one might belong were almost wholly restricted according to class status, the lines being maintained by firm and often cruel attitudes of exclusion.

[7] Hollingshead, A. B. *Elmtown's Youth: The Impact of Social Classes on Adolescents*, New York, John Wiley & Sons, 1949.

Sometimes this rigidity of groupings even defeated the efforts of teachers to organize classless recreations at the school. The teachers themselves, however, were not exonerated of class prejudice. Mostly of middle-class origin, they were found to favor the upper parts of the social scale and to discriminate against lower-class pupils whom they considered crude and unpromising. Feeling this rejection both by teachers and fellow-students, lower-class young people withdrew as early as possible from school, took unskilled jobs, and thus perpetuated the stratification. Studies of intelligence and school achievement can hardly be adequate without taking into account the pervasive effects of social class on motivation to succeed in school.

The study of individual lives stands to benefit in several ways from this knowledge of social stratification. Upward social mobility is a motive often disguised and denied, but we are now in a much better position to look for it between the lines. We are also in a better position to estimate the strength of the social barriers with which an individual is confronted, a necessary step in building up his picture of the world and explaining the channels taken by his own strivings. The most important benefit, however, comes from realizing that the conditions under which personality develops are not at all the same at different levels of society. The simple circumstance of the mother going out to work, for example, greatly changes the character of the home as an agent in shaping the child's personality. Values and ideals, moreover, vary widely with social status. Stratification breaks the society down into a series of sub-cultures which may vary considerably from the overall cultural pattern.

It has been shown by Davis that the influences operating in lower-class homes contrast sharply with those at work in the middle class.[8] The family circle tends to be unstable, the father having often enough departed for good, the mother going out to work every day. Children begin early to play in the streets and roam the neighborhood. Under such circumstances parental standards, whatever their character, act in an erratic and often feeble manner. Much of what the child does is known only to his contemporaries and receives its valuation from a jury of his peers. The impact of parental standards is further weakened by the lack of rewards which may be given or withheld as a means of securing obedience. If these family

[8] Davis, A., in Barker, R. G., Kounin, J., & Wright, H. W., *Child Behavior and Development*, New York, McGraw-Hill Book Co., 1943, ch. 34.

circumstances combine with what Shaw and his associates call a *disorganized area,* one in which neighbors, often of different language and background, are apt to change every few months, then adult supervision is reduced to a very minimum.[9] In more stable communities each child and each family is known in the neighborhood; standards receive a reinforcement that extends beyond the home. Given an unstable family circle in a disorganized area, a child is thrown heavily on his own resources and those of the most available gang. He learns early to take care of himself, to swear and fight, very likely to smash and steal, and his social development takes place in an atmosphere of opposition to the standards of the main society, as represented especially by the police. In such an environment the code of the street-corner gang may offer greater stability than anything that emanates from the home. The pattern of delinquency may represent an individually healthy combination of adventuresomeness and submission to group standards. Certainly it has an entirely different psychological meaning at this social level from what it has in a stable and well-ordered middle-class neighborhood.

In his account of the middle class, Davis emphasizes the relative stability and permanence of the family group. The impact of family standards tends to be steady and continuous. The child is rather closely supervised even during his hours of play; his friends are to some degree selected for him. He is often reminded of his obligations to the family, and his lapses from parental standards receive discouragements which range all the way from the denial of pleasures and privileges to the withholding of love. Ideals of cleanliness, goodness, and decency are held before him, strengthened by visions of an ultimate success which will more than repay present sacrifices. The stress on upward mobility leads to the placing of high value on education, special skills, and personal presentability. Home, neighborhood, school, and church combine to maintain a united front of standards against which an open rebellion is decidedly hazardous.

In applying these findings about social status to the study of individual cases, it is first necessary to establish the status of the subject's family. Although we do not have a community study of the

[9] A convenient summary of Shaw's work is given by R. E. L. Faris in Hunt, J. McV., ed., *Personality and the Behavior Disorders, op. cit.,* Vol. 2, pp. 741-746.

midwestern city in which Hartley Hale was born, we shall probably not go far astray if we consider it similar to Jonesville, which
has recently been investigated in great detail.[10] Jonesville is not as
large, but it is located in the same section of the country and has
much the same economic structure. The investigators of Jonesville
find it convenient to speak of five social classes. At the top is Class I,
a small local aristocracy of inherited wealth such as is found in a
great many American industrial communities. Class II consists of
families more recently prosperous: the husbands are professional
men, salaried executives in large firms, or owners and operators of
moderate-sized enterprises. In Class III are to be found the small
businessmen and farm owners together with many who derive their
income from wages and salaries. The people of Class IV are typically wage earners on the farms and in the mills and shops, people
referred to by the higher classes as "poor but honest, hard workers,
who pay their taxes, raise their children properly, but never seem to
get ahead financially." [11] Class V is looked upon with contempt even
by Class IV, its members being considered shiftless, coarse, and of
doubtful morals. The men are unskilled or semi-skilled workers,
and more than half of the women go out to work in menial capacities.

Application to the Case of Hale.—The evidence contained in our
interviews places the Hale family rather definitely in Class II. The
father did not inherit wealth, although he did have the opportunity
to work his way to the top in the moderate-sized business started by
the grandfather. He was college-educated and had started out as a
teacher before entering the business. He sent both of his children
through college, helped pay his son's expenses at medical school, and
lived on the income of invested capital after liquidating his business.
The Hales lived in a good residential neighborhood. Like many
Class II members they occupied a large house of older type, which
contrasted with the smaller, more standardized homes usually favored by Class III.

Hartley was distinctly aware of a class above his own as well as of

---

[10] Warner, W. L. & associates, *Democracy in Jonesville: A Study in Quality
and Inequality,* New York, Harper & Bros., 1949; Hollingshead, A. B., *Elm-
town's Youth: The Impact of Social Classes on Adolescents, op. cit.,* 1949;
Havighurst, R. J. & Taba, H., *Adolescent Character and Personality,* New York,
John Wiley & Sons, 1949. In spite of the different names used—Jonesville,
Elmtown, Prairie City—all three studies were made in the same community.

[11] Hollingshead, *op. cit.,* p. 103.

lower classes in the neighborhood that began a block to the east.
Asked in an oral questionnaire during the undergraduate study
whether he would marry a girl from "the top ranks of society," he
said that he would do so only if she were able to "break through her
artificial life" and accept his own social position. When put the
same question with regard to a girl "of lower social position" he replied that he would marry such a girl if her status were lower only
for financial reasons but not if there were any "hereditary reasons."
In this last reservation he partly accepted what Hollingshead has
shown to be a common belief of all classes except the lowest,
namely, that the people below them have remained in lower status
because of innate inferiority.[12]

In many respects the Hale family can be understood as a typical
product of its class status in a somewhat industrialized midwestern
community. There was little suggestion of the ease and leisure characteristic of Class I, but there was also little of the striving for recognition, the hectic attempt to keep up a front, that is prominent in
Class III. The mother's cleanliness and energetic housekeeping, her
advocacy of art and music lessons, and her attempts to keep Hartley
from fighting and fraternizing with boys of lower status, all fit
neatly into the pattern of ideals found to prevail in Class II at
Jonesville. Typical also was the particularly high value placed on
education. In Jonesville the members of Class I, having a secure
position, were found to be on the whole less educated and less
interested in education that the people of Class II, who perceived
education as "the prime requisite to success."

In estimating the effect of social status, however, we must be careful not to overlook those points at which a family may diverge from
the expected pattern. The Hales showed one rather marked divergence which brings up an important problem in the use of the class
concept. They showed very little of the drive toward civic leadership that was found characteristic of Class II in Jonesville. Although
Hartley's father was in business he seems to have felt small interest
in the Chamber of Commerce, Rotary Club, and other power-
wielding organizations which generally attract the energies of Class
II businessmen.

When we seek the reasons for this divergence we are brought face
to face with a fact rather slighted in the community studies referred to, which utilize chiefly external marks of status such as neigh-

[12] Hollingshead, *op. cit.*, ch. 5.

borhood, type of house, and source of income. It becomes necessary to consider the individual's own sense of class membership, to detect the social groups and the social status with which he feels identified. This sense of identification is psychologically so important that one student of the subject, Richard Centers, has proposed using it as the main basis for defining a social class.[13] One should not assert, according to Centers, that the five classes in Jonesville are really classes unless one can demonstrate that the members feel some sense of belongingness and common interest. In the absence of such a feeling it would be preferable to speak merely of social status or position, not of social class.

This distinction proves to be a significant one in the case of the Hales. With considerable justification they felt themselves to represent more than an economic status. They stood for cultural values —for scholarship, literature, art and music—and their identification was with professional and artistic people rather than with the world of business. They did not, to be sure, feel separated from business, and they supported Hartley's first choice of advertising as a life work, but they conceived business to be a means of making a good enough living so that one could enjoy the higher things of life. This outlook weakened considerably the interest in upward mobility that might otherwise be expected in members of Class II. To some extent, people who identify themselves with intellectual and cultural values do not feel that there is any class above them. They are not likely to be wholly immune to the charms of wealth, power, and prestige in the business and political spheres, but they are less vulnerable than people who are working only for such goals without fully attaining them. The Hales could afford to have a certain contempt for mere business success.

The force of Hartley Hale's rebellion against his mother caused him to make havoc of his youthful social status. He rejected the playmates she chose for him and exhibited downward social mobility in finding companions more to his taste. His ability to play a manful part was seriously challenged by the gangs from the east; he was not satisfied until he could match these lower-class boys in fights and athletics, thus winning their recognition and acceptance. He thus used a lower social status as a place to develop and assert those masculine qualities which seemed threatened by his mother's philos-

[13] Centers, R., *The Psychology of Social Classes*, Princeton University Press, 1949.

ophy of cleanliness and caution. In retrospect he valued these experiences, as he valued his summer jobs, for the insight they gave him into the outlook and problems of ordinary people. Traces of these democratic contacts could still be found in his otherwise somewhat rightist political views. With the passing of the need for rebellion against his mother, however, and with his moving away to college, he swung back again to the social status of his origin. His wife came from approximately the same social position, his home was established in the best residential section he could afford, and in his daydreams the "ultimate" dwelling began to assume the proportions of an ample country estate.

It may seem paradoxical, especially in view of the fancied country estate, to suggest that upward social mobility is not a very important motive in Hale's current life. He certainly is competitive, he certainly wants to rise to the top; he seeks power, prestige, and an income that would permit a little conspicuous spending. But it would represent a serious failure to analyze the facts if we set this all down to upward social mobility in any precise sense of the term. Hale is a doctor and a scientific investigator. His wife came from a doctor's family, his suburban home is in a neighborhood much favored by young doctors, his country estate would be a place where he could entertain fellow doctors when not too busy fishing or building scientific apparatus in his shop. To describe his upward mobility as social would imply that he cares a great deal about the social hierarchy, wanting to frequent the best circles, join the best clubs, be invited to the best houses. Hale does not care about these things. His profession almost automatically gives him social status, but his interest in social life lies in having a good time under informal circumstances, not in achieving an upward climb. The motive which is really strong in him can best be characterized as *upward mobility in his profession.* He wants to be outstanding as a surgeon and scientist; insofar as his country estate is to be a symbol, it is to signify that he has reached the professional top. Hale is an example of a man whose energies have been poured almost entirely into the channels of a profession. At the age of thirty-three he has been moulded more by his occupational role than by his position in the general hierarchy of social status.

SOCIAL INTERACTION AND MEMBERSHIP IN GROUPS

Social scientists have found it useful to distinguish between primary and secondary groups. According to Cooley, who was the first to emphasize the importance of this distinction, a group qualifies as primary when it is "characterized by intimate face-to-face association and cooperation." [14] For a young child the family constitutes the most important primary group, but neighborhood playmates and school groups soon start to make their impact upon his social development. Secondary groups, in contrast, are organized according to special interests of one kind or another, and they do not depend either upon propinquity or upon more than occasional face-to-face association. Political parties, religious bodies, school systems, labor unions, medical associations can all be used as examples of secondary groups. Memberships in such groups are an important feature of adult life, but it is the primary groups that play the crucial part in the early shaping of personality. Within the circle of his family and within the orbit of his playmates and school companions the child receives his direct training as a member of society. It is here that he learns, often without realizing it, the general prescriptions of the culture and the expectations associated with his social status. It is here also that he builds up his social habits and attitudes, his ideas of moral conduct, and his conception of himself as a social being.

Learning Through Social Interaction.—At the outset, learning through social interaction is in no way different from learning about the properties of the physical world. The child has to learn what to expect from everything that surrounds him, what it will do in response to his own action, how he can influence it in favor of his desires. Dependent as he is, however, upon the ministrations of others, he soon learns to take a special interest in the people who provide for his wants and produce beneficent changes in his environment. He becomes especially concerned with what he can expect from his mother. Thus his earliest experience of social interaction is surcharged with the pressure of his basic needs; a great deal of his feeling of security becomes attached to predicting and controlling what will happen in his immediate human environment. For a time, at least, he is the smallest and most helpless member of the

[14] Cooley, C. H. *Social Organization*, New York, Chas. Scribners' Sons, 1909, p. 23.

family circle; the human environment consists of people much larger, stronger, more mobile than himself. Later in life he will learn to interact with younger people and with people of his own age, but his first social experience is not of this character. Social learning begins in the relationship of the infant to his providers.

In the course of time the child learns the peculiar properties of human beings. In one sense they can be more readily influenced than physical objects: cries, gestures, and words can sometimes control them in dramatic fashion. But they are less predictable than inanimate objects; they prove to have wills of their own, and their attention is sometimes found straying to other human beings. One of the most difficult steps in social learning comes with the child's discovery that the members of his family are interested in each other, not simply and solely in him. Social interaction cannot be confined to single channels; there are cross currents of affection and devotion, of jealousy and hate, and there are unaccountable changes in the attitudes of the several characters as a result of their interaction with one another. Very early in life the child thus begins to operate as a member of a group, the primary group that is his family. His first training in group membership occurs within the walls of his home.

It is likely that some of the emotional undercurrents which disturb group activities in adult life spring from the circumstances of this first training. The situation is unavoidably one-sided and autocratic. No matter how earnestly the parents attempt to create a democratic atmosphere in the home, they cannot cancel the fact of their child's immaturity and dependence, nor can they set aside the obligations that are theirs by virtue of superior knowledge and experience. They can create an atmosphere that will minimize rivalry among brothers and sisters and keep down the jealousies of the Oedipus triangle, but they cannot prevent the child from having the primitive passions and anxieties that are appropriate to his age. They can make their constraints as reasonable as possible, but they cannot force their child to a grasp of reasonableness that is beyond his years. Thus the first group experience is bound to take place in a situation characterized by tremendously high emotional stakes and by a sharply outlined hierarchy of age, competence, and authority. In wise hands this situation, well-suited to the immature state of the junior members, results in fine basic training for membership in society, but it does not always have this happy outcome. It does

not, moreover, provide good opportunities for learning to interact with a group of one's equals.

It is among his playmates outside the family that a child carries
on the social learning that best trains him for interaction with his
peers. Here he encounters a somewhat different set of social
shaping forces. There is less emphasis on good behavior and conformity to adult standards, more on individual prowess, adventuresomeness, and willingness to share in whatever is going on. At first,
interactions are apt to be tentative and discontinuous; each meeting with any other child has somewhat the character of a new experiment. In the course of time these fragmentary contacts build up
into more lasting relationships. The child behaves with greater
consistency toward each friend, and he gradually learns to react to
more than one friend at a time. Children's groups at first lack permanence and structure, but as time goes on they become increasingly organized and increasingly important in the shaping of the individual personality. Positions as leader, right-hand man, follower,
idea man, clown, and water-boy receive sharper definition and are
occupied on longer tenure. At length the child finds himself
moving into the more fixed group structure of athletic teams and
school clubs. By the time he reaches adolescence he has been repeatedly exposed to the shaping influence of groups.

Effects of Group Membership.—Group membership affects the individual in a variety of ways. It is a little too simple to pass this off
by saying that it teaches him to give and take. There is a positive
side to membership which is scarcely implied in this stock disciplinary phrase. Under favorable circumstances participation in a
group may produce a notable increase in the sense of personal
worth and personal strength. Pooling of initiative and sharing of
responsibility enable the group to accomplish many purposes far
beyond the resources of any individual member. They enable the
group to resist pressures before which individual members would
feel helpless. If a member successfully performs his part, he receives
an income of approval and esteem which greatly surpasses anything
he would be likely to secure by playing a lone hand. The strength
that comes from group membership is strikingly illustrated in small
groups such as air combat units which develop strong cohesiveness
through exposure to major stress. It was the conclusion of psychological studies made during World War II that morale was a group
phenomenon, not an individual trait, and that loyalty to one's unit

rather than hatred for the enemy produced the truly courageous feats of arms.[15]

The formative influence of groups is all the stronger because of the benefits that go with membership. The nature of this influence can best be indicated by saying that the group teaches the individual to operate within shared norms. It visits approval on what is considered loyal and good, disapproval on what is rated disloyal and bad. Furthermore, the group helps the individual to sort out the particular roles that it is practicable for him to play. It rewards with approval those roles which the person can play well and which at the same time forward the harmony and purposes of the group, but it pours contempt and ridicule on attempts to play disruptive, incompetent, or presumptuous roles. A young person needs this help in choosing among the many roles, the many pretensions and dreams of glory, that are likely to flood his hopeful fancy. In social interaction he learns what it is possible for him to become and what it is necessary for him to discard. He may withdraw from a group which affords him no gratifying roles, and he may show persistence in clinging to roles of his own imagining, but somewhere he will require the ratifications that come only from other members of society.

The shaping of individual behavior by group memberships is particularly well illustrated in street-corner gangs.[16] These spontaneous groups are little influenced by tradition, parental standards, or the dictates of the larger society, with which they are often enough at odds. Nevertheless, they are extremely effective in upholding group norms and shaping the behavior of individual members in the direction of appropriate roles. Participant observers can usually work out the status of each member with respect to all the others, and it is clear that individual behavior is sharply affected by the expectations of the rest of the group.

One of the corner gangs studied by Whyte went in heavily for bowling. It was apparent that a man's bowling performance, especially in stressful moments of the game, was considerably influenced by how well his team mates expected him to do. One man, who occupied a status close to the leaders of the group, had a reputation

[15] Grinker, R. R., & Spiegel, J. P. *Men Under Stress,* Philadelphia, P. Blakiston Co., 1945, esp. Chs. 2, 3, 6, 8, 15.
[16] Whyte, W. F. *Street Corner Society,* Chicago, University of Chicago Press, 1943.

for dependable good bowling; another, located low in the status hierarchy, could occasionally make the highest score of anyone, but was considered certain to go to pieces under stress. These judgments were doubtless based on real initial differences, but in the course of time they acted with increasing social compulsion. The erratic man could often beat the steady man when they played alone, but at the Saturday night matches, with the whole group present, the dependable bowler always turned in the higher score. Bowling scores were significantly affected by a man's social position in his group.[17]

The manner in which an individual will be affected by membership depends somewhat on the character and structure of the group. Lewin, Lippitt and White's well-known experiments with democratic and autocratic group atmospheres show that this is true even under temporary experimental conditions.[18] Their democratic groups provided members with more numerous and more significant roles, allowing them to display initiative, make plans, and find preferred ways of getting the work done. In contrast, the autocratic groups favored passive acquiescence and did little to encourage the development of spontaneous differentiated roles. When studying individual lives, it is often difficult to ascertain the character and precise shaping influence of past groups. When it is possible to study a child's group activities by direct observation, however, there can be no doubt that the course of development is markedly affected by the character of his important group memberships.

The differences between group pressures at home and those encountered on the playground and at school are important in the child's social education. At home he finds one set of norms and plays one set of roles; outside he meets a different set of norms and finds opportunity to play a different set of roles. Parents can often scarcely believe that their child, a very devil in the home, rates as a helpful and responsible citizen at school, or, conversely, that their well-trained model child has been caught by the police stealing fruit and breaking windows. As a child's memberships multiply, he be-

[17] This incident is used by T. M. Newcomb, *Social Psychology*, New York, Dryden Press, 1950, Ch. 14, to introduce an excellent survey of the effects upon individuals of memberships in groups. See also, with special reference to the various studies of gangs, M. Sherif & H. Cantril, *The Psychology of Ego-Involvements*, New York, John Wiley & Sons, 1947, Ch. 10.

[18] For a brief description see Lewin, K., Lippitt, R., & White, R. K., Patterns of Aggressive Behavior in Experimentally Created "Social Climates," *Journal of Social Psychology*, 1939, Vol. 10, pp. 279-300.

gins to discover that different groups take different attitudes toward him; he begins to realize that he himself behaves and feels differently as he moves from one company to another. This type of experience is crucial for more complex social learning. Through it the child arrives at a relativity of perspectives, realizing how widely people differ in outlook and interest. Such insight is an essential ingredient of mature social behavior and a mature moral code.[19] It is a necessary step in learning about the properties of human beings.

Concept of the Self.—Social interaction and the varied pressures of different groups tend thus to diversify a person's understanding both of other people and of himself. The concept of *self* is extremely important in the theory of personality. It is an integrative concept, needed to account for the fact that unity is preserved even under the most diversifying social influences. The unity of the organism is inescapable. The self-image has its point of reference in one body, one consciousness, one continuous series of personal memories; it cannot be separated from our enduring sense of personal identity. Differently as someone may behave on different occasions, flexibly as he may respond to social atmospheres, he remains always to some extent the same person, the same self. Although the concept of self is rooted in biological fact, it is from social scientists such as Cooley and Mead that we have learned how the concept must be elaborated.[20]

These writers, devoted to the social view of man, considered that the self achieved its development through social interaction. They were dealing, of course, not with the self as active ego but with the person's idea of himself; as Mead put it, not with the agent called "I" but with the object called "me." A person builds up his conception of himself out of the ideas he perceives other people to have about him. This perception is grounded in how they act toward him. Through social experience he has to learn whether he is brave or cowardly, handsome or homely, quick-witted or deliberate, likeable or surly, leader or follower, prophet or clown. In childhood the process often works in a fairly open fashion: children are not backward in calling each other names and classifying each other's

[19] Lerner, E. The Problem of Perspective in Moral Reasoning, *American Journal of Sociology*, 1937, Vol. 43, pp. 249-269.
[20] Cooley, C. H., *Human Nature and the Social Order*, New York, Chas. Scribners' Sons, 1902; Mead, G. H., *Mind, Self, and Society*, Chicago, University of Chicago Press, 1934.

behavior. Later the judgments of others are more apt to be inferred, but they still operate to retouch in various ways the picture one has of himself. Thus even the concept of self, central and integrative in personality, cannot be formulated without reference to social interaction and membership in groups.

Social Learning in the Case of Hale.—The case of Hartley Hale exemplifies many of these general ideas. While it is impossible to reconstruct an adequate history of his social participations, there can be little doubt about the importance of group memberships in his development. This was particularly true in later childhood, when parental quarrels increasingly made the home atmosphere intolerable and when the evolution of self-esteem required recognition as a "he-man" capable of boldness, confidence, and athletic success. Because of his stuttering Hale was constantly exposed to ridicule; we can assume that group pressure had a good deal to do with assigning him the roles of stage manager and behind-the-scenes editor during his high school years. But when we carefully consider his case we become aware that Hale was far from being a passive recipient of the social impress. We should not misunderstand the proposition advanced by Cooley and Mead—that the self arises in social interaction—to mean that a person takes no active part in the forming of his self-picture.

Hale did not accept all the judgments made about him by others. He did not accept as final, for example, the judgment that he was cocky and rude, knowing that he could be very different in what seemed to him the important relationships with adults. Moreover, he refused to accept what seemed like the clear fact that he was a stutterer. Unlike the erratic bowler of the street corner gang, whose score was adversely affected by group expectations, he clung to the ideal image of himself as one who would not stutter, and eventually, by hard struggle, he turned this image into a true fact. What people thought of him, how they reacted to him at any one time, contributed to his perception of himself but did not prevent him from working for an improved self-picture in the future.

Further light on the concept of the self can be gained by recalling that Hale sometimes rejected as too favorable the opinions held of him by others. Referring to the admiration expressed by some of his patients and colleagues, he said: "I never am quite as good as they think I am." Again, he deplored the vagueness of his mind and fuzziness of his memory, qualities which certainly did not figure in the judgments made of him by other people. It was clear in this case that he was comparing himself to his clear-minded and decisive father, that he was using an ideal standard created by identification with an important admired figure, and that he was thus to a considerable extent impervious to the picture of him held by others in his environment.

These illustrations serve to show that the development of the self-picture does not take place through a simple averaging of the evaluations that are sensed to proceed from other people. It is necessary to consider the relative importance of these other people. Nor must we forget that a person has inner information for evaluating himself. He may know full well that he was nervous even when he kept up an outer appearance of self-possession. He may know that a piece of work was done in careless haste even though his friends call it as good as his best. Similarly, he may know that an act took great inner courage and sacrifice even though others suppose it was done quite easily. The development of the self-concept is no doubt highly dependent on social interaction, but it is also a product of internal selection and organization, and it includes ideas not only of what the person has become today but of what he may become tomorrow.

When we study in the next chapter the personality of Joseph Kidd, it will be instructive to contrast him with Hale in regard to the self-concept. Hale developed a fairly firm conception of himself which seems to have evolved without sharp breaks or periods of confusion. Kidd's experience was disastrously different. As we shall see, circumstances conspired to undermine and blacken the self-picture developed during childhood, so that as a college undergraduate he was forced to attempt a major task of reconstruction. For a while he exhibited the kind of random role-playing that is characteristic of young children who are still seeking to secure a definition of themselves from the reactions of those around them. It took him several years to find out what he could become, what elements of a possible self-picture he could truly realize as his own. His crisis will serve to extend the understanding of the self-concept which we have gained from our study of Hartley Hale.

OCCUPATIONS AND OCCUPATIONAL ROLES

It is a matter of common belief that people are influenced by their occupations. We are all familiar with such stereotypes as the crabbed hairsplitting lawyer, the dry precise bookkeeper, the vague absent-minded professor, the blunt outspoken army officer, the bossy rule-bound school-mistress, the erratic but colorful actress. The force of these linkages between occupation and personality can be demonstrated by trying to rearrange them. An erratic but colorful bookkeeper, a vague absent-minded army officer, a crabbed hairsplitting actress certainly strike us as unlikely if not impossible types. For the most part the familiar linkages are not arrived at by direct observation of the people who hold different jobs. Such observation would surely reveal a considerable variety of personalities within each occupation. There would undoubtedly be erratic but colorful lawyers, blunt outspoken lawyers, perhaps even absent-minded law-yers, as well as lawyers who are crabbed and hairsplitting. The linkages are based rather on a kind of analysis of the job as generally conceived, and on the further belief that the requirements of a job forcibly shape the personality of its holder. Bookkeeping calls for dry and precise figuring; therefore the person who daily performs the job of bookkeeper must necessarily become dry and precise.

These stereotypes ascribe to occupations a greater shaping force than they actually possess. Occupation certainly does a great deal to shape a person's life, determining where and how he will spend his time, what sorts of skills he will employ, what kinds of contacts he will have with other people. Often a man's occupation exerts a decisive influence on his political philosophy. But the fact that a person's *life* is strongly moulded by occupation does not necessarily imply that his *personality* is deeply affected. When we talk about occupations and occupational roles we are referring to general requirements which affect anyone who enters the occupation. When we talk about personality we are referring to something that is unique in each individual. In Allport's definition, personality is "the dynamic organization within the individual of those psycho-physical systems that determine his unique adjustments to his environment.[21] This organization is already fairly well established by the time a person enters his life work.

Occupation does not, like the general cultural atmosphere or like social status, influence the individual during the most formative part of his development. We must therefore conceive somewhat differently the shaping effect of occupations and occupational roles.

[21] Allport, G. W., *Personality: A Psychological Interpretation*, New York, Henry Holt & Co., 1937, p. 48.

There is, in the first place, a certain amount of selection whereby occupations attract to their ranks people who already have an appropriate personality structure. The requirements of the job and its associated role then act to reinforce certain characteristics while more or less suppressing others. To a considerable extent people fall out of the occupation if their personal qualities prove inappropriate, or if they find it difficult to endure the expected roles. In most occupations, however, there is room for individual variation; the job can be done in several different ways. All these points must be taken into account when we study the action of occupational roles and search for the processes whereby their influence is exerted.

Our interest at this point is particularly in *occupational roles*, but these are only one class of the many *social roles* which exist in an organized society. Different roles are associated with being male or female, with being young or old, with the statuses of husband, father, wife, and mother, with the positions of friend, neighbor, and associate in work or play. Each position or status in the social system calls for the performance of certain functions, while at the same time conferring certain privileges. A role is a socially prescribed way of behaving, representing what a person is supposed to do because of the fact that he occupies a given position. Society expects a mother, for example, to keep her children washed and clothed and fed, to give them protection and training, to care for them when they are sick. It does not expect a father to attend directly to these matters unless the mother is absent or ill; he is expected to earn the money, however, and to keep the house heated and in repair. A mother is more readily excused than a father if she lets the furnace fire go out, but society gives fathers greater leeway with respect to keeping the children washed. Social roles, and the social expectations that give them shape, are thus by no means confined to the sphere of occupation.

An occupational role can be defined as the way society expects a person to behave by virtue of his membership in a given occupation. A physician is expected to possess certain kinds of knowledge and skill, to accept certain responsibilities, to be guided by a certain set of ideals; and it would indeed be confusing if physicians departed too widely from these social expectations. Each individual medical student finds the role of physician already defined for him; he must substantially fulfil the expected pattern or else run grave risk of losing his membership in the profession. We should not conclude, however, that occupational roles can never be changed. It is only necessary to recall the role of the physician a century ago, or two centuries ago, to realize how rapidly social expectations can change as the result of technical progress. Role expectations evolve with each generation of players. If roles exist apart from individuals, individuals also exist apart from roles, and a shaping influence may proceed in either direction.

Among occupational roles none are more highly organized than those represented by the professions. A profession is entered only through a long course of training which is designed to equip the candidate with the knowledge and skill requisite for subsequent practice. As Hughes points out, however, "the training carries with it as a by-product assimilation of the candidate to a set of professional attitudes and controls, a professional conscience and solidarity. The profession claims and aims to become a moral unit." [22] The law student, for example, not only learns the theory and technique of law but also acquires, through contact with teachers and fellow law students, a sense of membership in a professional group having its own ideals and ethical constraints. In this respect the professions contrast somewhat with trades, crafts, and business enterprises, still more with the large realm of more or less unskilled jobs. Except in rare circumstances the professional man is in his occupation for life. He must submit to its obligations, but at the same time he can usually expect to find within it the opportunity to use his full capacities in building up a satisfying career. He can often find a large part of his happiness in his work. In sharp contrast is the wage earner who grinds away at a tiresome task, or flits from one job to another, looking for happiness only when the day's work is done. Occupational role exerts a far stronger shaping force on the professional man that it does on the unskilled wage earner.

The Role of Physician.—The socially expected role of the physician is on the whole very clearly defined. It is based on his specific competence, acquired through long and difficult training, to understand and to alleviate sickness. He is not supposed to be a general wise man or sage, or an expert on political and economic affairs. His competence is specifically that of healing the sick, and his technique for discharging this duty is that of applying scientific knowl-

[22] Hughes, E. C., Personality Types and the Division of Labor, *American Journal of Sociology*, 1928, Vol. 33, pp. 754-768.

edge. He is expected therefore to perform his work in a relatively impersonal fashion, not involving himself in deep emotional relationships with his patients. Even when he practices psychotherapy, in which the doctor-patient relationship becomes the central part of the cure, he performs as a trained expert who points out the patient's emotional reactions, not as an ordinary person who becomes blindly involved in them. A striking feature of the role is its emphasis on service. The patient's health is supposed to be given regular precedence over the interests and comfort of the physician. The specifications of the role are thus clear, requiring the doctor to apply in faithful but strictly rational fashion the scientific knowledge that is at his disposal.

Inherent in the situation of curing disease, however, are many irrational elements. As Parsons has pointed out, it is hard for the doctor in actual fact to function simply as an impersonal applied scientist.[23] Often his knowledge is insufficient and uncertain; at other times he recognizes with certainty that there is nothing he can do for the patient. When thus helpless in a situation where life itself is often at stake, he is placed under the strain of not being able to meet the high hopes and tense expectations placed on him by patients and their relatives. He is also subject to irrational pressures because of the intimate nature of his work. He has the right to discuss very personal matters and to see and examine the patient's naked body. Doctors are pretty well accustomed to exert these privileges with impersonal detachment, but the patients are not similarly trained and may react with a variety of fears, resistances, sexual fantasies, and other personal feelings which interfere with the businesslike pursuit of diagnosis and treatment. The doctor's job might become incredibly involved and entangled if his occupational role were not sharply and strongly formulated. He can do his work properly only because of the protection he receives from his well-understood professional role. Both his own behavior and that of his patients are defined and controlled by this role.

It is important to notice that the role of physician does not derive its whole force from law or from the professional code of ethics. There are legal safeguards to the practice of medicine, and there is a strong professional code, but these institutionalized controls are invoked only on rare occasions. Informal controls, based on strongly felt social expectations both inside and outside the profes-

[23] Parsons, T., *The Social System*, Glencoe, Ill., The Free Press, 1951, ch. 10.

sion, actually maintain for medical practice its current high repute. The surgeon's decision to operate may be taken as a case in point. Few decisions are more crucial, yet this one is typically reached by the surgeon and ratified by patient and relatives without appeal to state authorities or professional committees. Medical men argue among themselves about "unnecessary operations." One school of thought believes that surgical intervention tends to be made too promptly, without sufficient regard for spontaneous recuperation. We know that Hartley Hale took the opposite stand, and that he did so on the highest moral grounds, believing that the decision to operate was often postponed through the physician's timidity and selfishness. Whatever the merits of this controversy, it is remarkable that the public is content to leave it in the hands of the profession. Nothing could testify more eloquently to the silent force and effectiveness of the physician's occupational role.

The role of physician contrasts in many respects with that of the businessman. Perhaps the most central difference lies in the attitude toward personal profit. The businessman is expected to make a profit for his company and for himself. He is expected to consider the likelihood of profit when he undertakes a new enterprise, and he is not supposed to get mixed up with poor credit risks. The physician is allowed to make generous charges to rich patients, but he is not permitted to refuse a patient on the ground of poor credit risk, nor may he bargain beforehand over fees. Advertising is closed to him except for a sign at his door and a modest card in the paper which merely announces where and when his services may be obtained. "The general picture is sharp segregation from the market and price practices of the business world, in ways which for the most part cut off the physician from many immediate opportunities for financial gain which are treated as legitimately open to the business man." [24] Some return for this restriction comes from the fact that the role of patient is conceived quite differently from the role of businessman's client. A patient is not expected to act like a person buying a new car. He must not shop around among different doctors, secretly comparing what they have to say about his treatment and trying to decide which doctor will give him the most for his money. He is expected to have confidence in his own doctor, and unless he decides to shift outright to another practitioner he may

[24] Parsons, *op. cit.*, p. 464.

seek additional advice only by asking his own doctor to invite a colleague for consultation.

Occupational Role in the Case of Hale.—This contrast between the occupational roles of physician and businessman has particular interest in the case of Hartley Hale, who at one point in his career deliberately chose between them. He was at first strongly drawn to the advertising business, but he shifted to medicine when shown by a persuasive friend how well he fitted the requirements of the profession. As we saw in the last chapter, both occupations genuinely attracted him, though they appealed to somewhat different aspects of his personality. Both appealed to his love of activity, excitement, and competition; both offered an opportunity to rise to the top. The special attraction in advertising was the chance it would give him to utilize his writing and drawing skills and to gratify his somewhat cynical delight in influencing people. But medicine seemed to him a more important service, and it drew fully on his absorbing passion for the biological sciences. More clearly than most undergraduates he foresaw what was involved in occupations and made his choice on the basis of genuine preference. Hale thus exemplifies the process whereby occupations draw to their ranks individuals whose pattern of personality is already appropriate for the fulfillment of the occupational role. The selective process continued even after he had entered medicine. His urge for decisive action drew him to surgery; his liking and capacity for independence contributed to his success in research. His preference for a mechanistic outlook and his lack of empathic responsiveness to others doubtless aided these decisions and certainly steered him far away from psychiatry.

The influence of the medical role in Hale's case can best be appreciated by trying to contrast what might have happened to him in advertising with what did happen in medicine. We saw that he approached advertising in an ethical spirit, hoping to accept business only when convinced of the genuine superiority of the products. It is hard to believe that this self-imposed limitation would not have brought serious conflict with his strong desire for competitive success. In an occupational role in which profits and a flourishing business are the marks of success he would soon have been forced to clip either his conscience or his ambitious wings. In medicine he was not pushed into any such position. Here the conditions for success were skill, eagerness, hard work, and devotion; little could be gained by anything that smacked of sharp practice or cynical deception. Another contrast can be drawn with respect to his relative neglect of wife and home. No doubt Hale would have gotten himself overworked and absorbed in any occupation, but when the job is at a hospital and forms part of the physician's role of dedication to sick people it can be used to justify a much greater neglect of other obligations. It seems likely that Hale's personality has been definitely influenced by his profession and that certain of his traits would have developed toward a different ultimate pattern if he had gone into advertising.

It would be a mistake, however, to contrast too sharply the medical and business roles. A hospital resembles a business firm in many respects, even though its purpose is quite different. As chief surgical resident Hale acted in part as a kind of business executive. He was responsible for planning, for equipment and supplies, and for a complicated series of relationships with personnel in superior and inferior statuses. It is therefore pertinent to examine his personality in connection with Henry's recent study of successful business executives. [25] According to Henry, successful executives in a large business organization show a series of traits which taken as a whole distinguish them from other occupational groups. It is surprising to see how many of these qualities are strongly developed in Hale.

Business executives display a high drive for achievement, receiving great stimulation from even small daily accomplishments. They are strongly mobile, feeling a need for constant progress in achievement and status. When faced by alternative courses of action they are capable of reaching definite decisions and sticking to them. They have a strong sense of self-identity: "they know what they are and what they want, and they have well-developed techniques for getting what they want." Their lives are active, assertive, and strongly oriented toward external reality. At the same time there exists, as "an integral part of this constellation and part of its dilemma," a pervasive fear of failure. "There is always some place to go, but no defined place at which to stop." Active as he is, the successful executive tends to be haunted by the fear of losing ground and ceasing to be a success. In relation to his superiors he feels a strong personal attachment and a considerable identification. They represent what he wants to become. Toward subordinates, in

[25] Henry, W. E., The Business Executive: The Psychodynamics of a Social Role, *American Journal of Sociology*, 1949, Vol. 54, pp. 286-291.

contrast, his attitude is usually detached, emphasizing their useful-
ness and effectiveness without any real interest in them as people.
They represent what he has outgrown and left behind. The successful executive is largely free from dependent ties to his parents. If
the father is felt as a helpful but not restraining figure there may be
a residual tie to him, but "those men who still feel a strong emotional
tie to the mother have systematically had difficulty in the business
situation." The successful executive must be essentially "a man who
has left home."

So nearly does Hale fit these specifications that we might begin
to wonder whether we are not dealing with a misplaced business executive. In only one trait does he deviate widely from the pattern
described by Henry. The successful business executive possesses in
high degree the ability to organize unstructured situations; he
even carries this virtue to a fault by imposing a preconceived
or familiar organization upon new situations with insufficient regard
for their novel features. In contrast, organization has always been
difficult for Hale. He procrastinates, allows things to pile up,
then belatedly orders his behavior by writing lists of what must be
accomplished. Though he usually achieves organization in the end,
he does so with struggle and discomfort rather than with easy efficiency. A similar comment might be made with regard to his apparent decisiveness. His exhaustive preparation for difficult pieces
of surgery ends in decisive action, but it certainly does not show the
bold assurance and sometimes blundering self-confidence that char-
acterizes successful business executives.

In general it seems likely that Hale's assurance and firmness of
character have been won at greater cost than is the case with the
executives. His effectiveness represents a triumph over large emotional obstacles which still have their residues in his personality.
Perhaps he is in consequence a better surgeon and scientist—more
cautious, more open to doubt, more willing to suspend judgment
until all the evidence has been considered. But there is another feature of Hale's personality, one that is not at all strongly developed
in business executives, which especially fits him for his present career. He is intensely curious, and his interest in finding out how
things work has been strongly channeled into the biological sciences.
Possibly Hale is not inherently more intelligent than the average
successful executive, but his intellect has certainly become a more
refined, subtle and inventive instrument. It is doubtful whether he

could have closed off his richly developed scientific interests in order to give his full attention to business.

CONCLUSION

In considering the shaping of lives by social forces we have made no attempt to reach systematic completeness. Our procedure has been rather to sample a few outstanding types of influence and to give them vividness by tracing their effect in the case of Hartley Hale. We have examined selected characteristics of the American culture: its emphasis on competitive enterprise, its optimistic faith in material progress, its hopes in the energy and rationality of man, its attitude toward women, its perhaps increasing tendency toward conformity. We have looked into the problem of social status and considered some of the psychological consequences of social stratification. We have given attention to the effects on development of social interaction and membership in groups. Then we have considered the action of social roles, especially those that are derived from occupational status.

If it seems confusing to have covered so much ground in a single chapter, we can reflect that much more would have to be covered in order to represent the full impact of social forces in shaping human lives. Our account of social roles, for example, falls far short of reproducing the actual complexity of roles in which each individual becomes involved. "The same individual," writes Linton, "can and does occupy simultaneously a series of statuses each of which derives from one of the systems of organization in which he participates. He not only occupies these statuses, but he also knows the roles pertaining to them. However, he can never exercise all these roles simultaneously; he operates sometimes in terms of one status and its role, sometimes in those of another." [26] Linton then illustrates this proposition by describing a day in the life of a store clerk, who acts the role of clerk while behind the counter, that of fellow employee in the rest room, that of young man (age-sex status) when he gives up his seat to a woman in the trolley car, that of father of the family when he reaches home, and that of high official when he goes to the evening lodge meeting.

These considerations bring us face to face with one of the most difficult problems in the understanding of personality. Let us call it

[26] Linton, R., *The Cultural Background of Personality,* New York, D. Appleton-Century Co., 1945, p. 78.

for the moment the problem of complexity. Each person is acted upon by a great number of social forces. Serious violence is done to the facts if we try to reduce this total impact to a few simple relationships of cause and effect. Our understanding of Hartley Hale would certainly be poor if we confined ourselves to the culture concept, to social status, or to the effects of occupational role. It would certainly be poor if we dumped his ambitious motives into the category of upward social mobility without discriminating the particular professional ladder which it is his purpose to climb. A multitude of shaping forces plays on the individual, and the action of each force is restricted by the other forces. With this plurality the literary man can readily deal, but for the scientist it is a constant source of embarrassment. The search for lawful relationships, the need for valid general propositions that can be used to formulate new research and to increase prediction and control, are hampered and blocked by the presence of too many interacting processes. The faithful student of personality must often postpone the satisfaction of discovering laws. Above all, he must avoid the pitfall of waving complexity aside, as if it were merely a surface illusion that would ultimately dissolve into a few clear-cut principles. Complexity is inherent in personality. It is no surface illusion; it is a stubborn and inescapable fact. When we forget this fact we embark upon one of those foolish ventures in oversimplification which end by impeding the understanding of human nature.

We are not yet prepared, however, to pursue this theme to its conclusions. In this chapter we have taken only the social view of man, leaving aside the biological and psychodynamic conceptions. Our attention will next turn to the biological view, but not until we have studied in detail another life in progress. The value of case studies is much increased when comparative analysis is added to individual analysis.

SUGGESTIONS FOR FURTHER READING

The pattern of American culture is allotted a chapter in each of two recent books by anthropologists: Clyde Kluckhohn's *Mirror for Man: The Relation of Anthropology to Modern Life* (New York & London, McGraw-Hill Book Co., 1949), ch. 9, and R. S. Lynd's *Knowledge for What?* (Princeton, N. J., Princeton University Press, 1948), ch. 3. A more extended but not technical treatment will be found in Margaret Mead's book, *And Keep Your Powder Dry: An Anthropologist Looks at America* (New York, William Morrow & Co., 1942). Suggestive observations are made in Erik H. Erikson's *Childhood and Society* (New York, W. W. Norton & Co., 1950), chs. 8–10, where the German and Russian cultures are compared with the American. Somewhat different approaches are made by the historian H. S. Commager in *The American Mind: An Interpretation of American Thought and Character Since the 1880's,* and by the political scientist David Riesman in *The Lonely Crowd: A Study of the Changing American Character.* Both books were published at New Haven, Conn., by the Yale University Press in 1950.

The effects of social class are well described by W. Lloyd Warner and associates in *Democracy in Jonesville* (New York, Harper & Bros., 1949) and by A. B. Hollingshead in *Elmtown's Youth: The Impact of Social Classes on Adolescents* (New York, John Wiley & Sons, 1949). These are studies of a whole community; for the effects of social class position in individual cases one should turn to *Children of Bondage* by A. Davis & J. Dollard (New York, American Council on Education, 1940). Two papers reprinted in *Personality in Nature, Culture and Society* (C. Kluckhohn & H. A. Murray, eds., New York, Alfred A. Knopf, 1948) are illuminating with respect to class differences in child-rearing practices: A. Davis & R. J. Havighurst, "Social Class and Color Differences in Child-Rearing," pp. 252–264, and A. Davis, "American Status Systems and the Socialization of the Child," pp. 459–468. The subjective aspect of class status—the feeling of common interest and belongingness—is emphasized in the book by Richard Centers entitled *The Psychology of Social Classes* (Princeton, N. J., Princeton University Press, 1949).

A good introduction to the developmental effects of social interaction and group memberships is to be found in T. M. Newcomb's *Social Psychology* (New York, Dryden Press, 1950), especially ch. 14. The concept of the self is developed by D. C. McClelland in *Personality* (New York, William Sloane Associates, 1951), ch. 14.

The study of occupations forms part of the larger study of the effect of social roles on personality. This topic is discussed in Newcomb's *Social Psychology,* chs. 9 and 13. For a sociological analysis of the medical profession consult T. Parsons, *The Social System* (Glencoe, Ill., The Free Press, 1952), ch. 10.

5. Joseph Kidd, Business Assistant

> It dawned on me after a while that I was knowing
> what I wanted. I was able to make up my mind.
>
> JOSEPH KIDD

Joseph Kidd was eighteen years old when he became a paid subject in the studies of personality. In contrast to the well-poised Hartley Hale, he was passing through a difficult adolescent crisis in the development of self-determination and self-respect. At his lowest point he suffered from acute and lasting distress in social contacts. He was troubled by severe self-consciousness, painful uncertainty as to his standing in the opinion of others, and an irresistible submissiveness designed to win everybody's favor. He felt that he had no personality of his own, and he therefore lacked any stable object on which to focus self-respect. The turmoil of his emotions made it impossible for him to concentrate upon his studies. He fell further and further behind, so that the college authorities required him to withdraw temporarily, his return being made conditional upon a good job record for twelve months and successful course grades in the ensuing summer session.

Kidd met these conditions and returned not only to college but to the interrupted studies of personality. It was possible to repeat several tests after an interval of three years, so that the study became, even in this first period, an examination of development over the course of time. He went from college into four years of military service, then returned to the family home to become for the time being his father's business assistant. He was still thus employed when we asked him, just eleven years after his first visit, to return for yet another extensive study. [1]

[1] A full report on the earlier studies was published several years ago: White, R. W., The Personality of Joseph Kidd, *Character & Personality*, 1943, Vol. 11, pp. 183-208, 318-360. The first part of this chapter is largely reprinted from that report, by kind permission of Dr. Karl Zener, editor, and the Duke University Press. Certain changes have been made in order to accommodate new information brought out in the second study.

Part One: THROUGH COLLEGE

The initial autobiography was submitted very soon after the first meeting, an encouraging sign that Kidd was interested in his duties as a psychological subject. It was written with considerable feeling, unusual frankness, and marked self-depreciation; plainly, its author was baffled by his own nature and welcomed the chance to share with a trained observer the results of his intense self-scrutiny. The opening paragraph, to be sure, had something of the propriety and exaggeration of an obituary notice, but it was not long before he related his social misfortunes, his trials over masturbation, his growing feelings of worthlessness, and his wish that he could live the last six wasted years over again. If there was self-deception in this document, it took the form of too harsh an indictment against himself.

THE KIDD FAMILY

Following an outline given him for guidance, Kidd began his autobiography with a description of his parents:

> My parents for as long as I have known them have been the most ideal couple I've ever seen. They have never to my knowledge had an argument, bitter or small; their differences are none; their respect for each other has always been the greatest. Their educations, likes, dislikes, habits, desires and emotions always coincided.

We need not assume that these lines were written for decency's sake alone. Later material shows plenty of conflict between parents and son and plenty of ambivalence in the latter's attitude, but everything indicates that the parents had reached a good working adjustment and that the home life offered many satisfactions.

The mother was born in Ireland, went to school through six grades, and came to America at the age of sixteen. Until her marriage a few years later she was a domestic servant; her son, as if to give her vicarious social status, named two prominent Worcester families by whom she had been employed. The father, also of Irish descent, was born in Worcester, and went through the second year of high school. Trained for no particular line of work, he held a meagerly paid office job with a large wholesale florist at the time of his marriage. He established his modest home in a fairly crowded but respectable Irish Catholic neighborhood in the city of Worcester.

When he was thirty-five his financial fortunes turned sharply up-ward with the arrival of a modest inheritance. This wholly unex-pected windfall came from an uncle who had emigrated from Ire-land to Australia, prospered there, and was a widower with no children at the time of his death. With this money Mr. Kidd bought out the business of an elderly German florist who had built up a considerable reputation as a floral decorator, and whom Mr. Kidd had known through his work at the wholesale house. This man was often engaged on a contract basis to take full charge of the flower arrangements at big weddings, dances and banquets. He thus considered himself something more than a retailer and referred to his shop as a flower studio. Kidd told us that his mother was largely responsible for the purchase of this business, encouraging the father to make the bold plunge. The business presently yielded such a substantial income that a college education and professional training could be planned for all five children. These plans were also the mother's work, although the father gave willing assent to her ambitious designs. It was decided that the four boys should be, respectively, a lawyer, a doctor, a banker, and a priest.

In describing his parents, Kidd placed special emphasis on the ideals for which they stood. After mentioning his mother's educa-tion and employment, he continued as follows:

As long as I can remember she has held religion primary with education secondary. She is extraordinarily religious and has kept her family so, and never tolerates any deviations of any sort from our faith, which is Roman Catholic, in any detail. She isn't fanatic about it but just staunch. My father is just as if not more staunch than she, and both try to attend mass every day. As for education it is almost secondary religion to her in that she'd sacrifice her all that her children might all become pinnacles of knowledge for her to look up to.

So far there is no hint of resentment against this staunch regime, but the adjectives chosen in describing the father suggested that it may more than once have proved irksome.

He is as obstinate as my mother concerning religion and edu-cation, but he reaches extremes sometimes and holds these as the only two factors in early life with life itself beginning at twenty-five. He is positively fanatic on the subject of liquor; never having taken a drop himself, he has stated on various occasions, "I'd rather see you dead than touch it sociably or otherwise." This is mainly because of the city environment which displays only too often the results of indulgence.

The topic of family discipline seemed to throw Kidd into a sharply ambivalent state, if the testimony of the following disjunctive sentences can be accepted:

> Their discipline is strict and spankings and such aren't uncommon; by strict discipline I mean that their rules, though few, are just ordinary but forceful. I haven't stressed the fact that freedom is extensive to a certain degree as long as we're doing what's right.

In a later interview he discussed the question more coherently. Parental discipline was based on the precept that "father runs the family," his punishments being more dreaded, more effective, more harsh and less reasonable than those of the mother. The father used spanking, denial of pleasures, and withholding of affection as his principal weapons, while the mother, always "exceptionally just," maintained her standards by reasoning, scolding, denying affection, and making the culprit feel that he had fallen short of what was expected of him. It was the denial of affection that exerted the strongest pressure, for when asked how he reacted to disciplinary measures, Kidd declared, "I tried to punish them back by denying them affection, not eating my supper, and so forth, but it didn't much work; I couldn't keep it up." Parental discipline evidently carried considerable weight in the Kidd family, the psychological weapons being particularly effective.

Since his venture into floral decorating, Joseph Kidd's father had been an unusually good provider with rising aspirations for his children. These aspirations emerged in Joseph's description of the family:

> Our family consists of five children besides the two parents, four boys and one girl. The family income is rather good, but because my father tries to give us the best besides education our surplus is usually low. I am the second oldest of the family; the oldest is a student at Wesleyan, Michael. Younger than I is Tom (17), and Mary (15), who are in High School, then Peter (12), who is in grammar school. And my father hopes to send each to college, Tom to business school and Peter to the priesthood. There is no direct discord in this family, just normal, each independent of the other pursuing his or her own likes and dislikes.

Our family life was always rather close, and cooperative till about five years ago when suddenly independence spread to each member rather suddenly much to my regret, leaving the home just an overnight stop almost.

The closeness of family ties was heightened by the parents' attitude outside their home. They were "cold" to other people; the mother especially did not build up a circle of friends, while the father was at ease in groups only when playing the piano and singing. The family group provided a sufficient outlet for their feelings and interests.

The mother was described as an easygoing, overloving, generous person with nothing nervous or erratic in her nature. When the children were small, she used to give them candy to take to school, and Joseph thought that he could still get "a thousand dollars out of her" if he asked for it. Mingled with this devotion and kindness there was a marked streak of dominance in Mrs. Kidd, and this was sometimes a source of annoyance to her children. "She would rather not have us independent," said Joseph; "sometimes I could slight her for not leaving me alone and stop butting into my affairs and opening my mail." When he was a freshman in college a girl called up to ask him to a dance; Mrs. Kidd, answering the telephone, "flew off the handle and said he don't go out with girls, he don't dance." Even when Joseph began to live at college his mother wanted to go on providing things, had to know all about his roommate, and was very much afraid "some waitress" might snatch him. Since the mother was herself a waitress before marriage, her anxiety on this score is an impressive sign of her interest in upward social mobility. Michael and Joseph learned to introduce all their girl friends as Radcliffe or Smith girls, a ruse which was temporarily successful because their mother, shy with strangers and not sure but what they might really be college girls, tried at once to make the best possible impression. Mrs. Kidd adapted herself unwillingly to the growing independence of her children. She painfully learned to reseal their letters after reading them, to refrain from voicing her suspicions about the use of alcohol, and to joke about their friends without inquiring too closely.

The father's personality was somewhat less smoothly organized. "One minute," said his son, "he'd give you the shirt off his back and the next he'll start ranting up and down." There were times when he did not like to be interrupted and would urge Joseph to look out for himself, but these outbursts gave him feelings of guilt so that the next day he would take his son to a show. On the whole, like the mother, he expected devoted submission and resisted the growing up of his children. "He puts no stock," Joseph complained, "in my judgment or ideas." No less than the mother, he was pre-occupied with the children, especially the three older boys, and above all Joseph, who resembled his side of the family. So deep was his interest that signs of independence genuinely hurt him and aroused his resentment in a way that was highly important, as we shall see, in his second son's psychological development. Joseph used the word "senile" to describe his father's condition at forty-five; this seemed to refer to a contractive tendency in his father, who had "a limited mind as far as holding many things is concerned" and who, as if disgruntled at the growing up of his boys, became "more and more retiring." Mrs. Kidd "treated him rather like a baby" and recognized that he would rather "live and take his pleasures and leave everything else to her." At times she even advised her sons as to the best way to get money out of him. In spite of his theoretical position as the one who ran the family, the father seemed to have been all along pretty much guided and dominated by his wife, and the tendency was steadily increasing.

For a time Joseph Kidd was perfectly happy in the affectionate devotion of his parents. He was clearly the favorite of both parents, a more beautiful and more responsive child than either of his nearer brothers. Yet there was enough competition for parental favor and enough transient loss of it through his own misbehavior so that he never accepted it as a matter of course. "I'd feel rottenly guilty," he said, "when I did certain things"; and again, "I have a great fear of hurting my parents; my life is guided by what they want, not what I want." The steadier devotion of his mother made him like her better than his father, his love for the latter being mingled with fear and tempered by a willingness to deceive: "I don't dare cross him directly, I'd rather out-trick him; I'd say I needed six dollars for books instead of four dollars."

Although both parents were brought up in poverty, both came into considerable contact with the upper class. Education became their second religion because it was associated with upward social mobility. Neither parent was familiar with college studies, but the people for whom they worked were college graduates, and it was easy to believe that education and money were responsible for the splendid lives that these employers appeared to live. Later on, Joseph complained that his parents cared nothing for what was going on inside him; they thought only of degrees and other outward symbols. This complaint was probably just, for the goals of upward social striving are defined by external marks such as the people with whom one associates and the signs of wealth one is able to display. The Kidd parents were devoted to their children, sacrificed much for them, and earnestly wanted them to have a good life. But their vision of a good life was contaminated by their idea of how it could be attained, with the result that the social acceptability of the children obtruded itself in their minds at the expense of subjective values. Their eyes were fixed on passports to the upper class.

MEMORIES OF THE FIRST FIVE YEARS: A
CENTER OF ATTENTION

In his autobiography Kidd accounts for the first five years in a single paragraph, but he amplified this considerably in an interview devoted to early memories.

> I was born eighteen years ago in the West Avenue Hospital in Worcester. As far as I know, everything about my early life was normal such as birth, weaning, teething, growth, etc. I had no physical or mental defects. I know I was always exceptionally intelligent (not conceit but fact) though I was handicapped to make the most of it. Being second son, I was pampered and petted a little and always was on my father's side since I resembled him a lot. He favored me more than the others always till about five years ago. My brother and I were close and were given everything. I had long golden curls and was prized. A recollection of that "adorable" age of about one and a half is clear to me and is supplemented by my mother and father. It was that I was able to pedal a bike and I can still picture myself pedaling it along, still with curls, and many people watching me and patting me on the head. My early life was a very happy one, I was always treated well by my parents and continually pushed along.

In the interview on early memories the bicycle scene was again the first thing that came to Kidd's mind. He now dated it somewhere in the third year and added the following details:

> Father was standing beside me outside our yard. My feet couldn't reach the pedals. He got a kick out of my trying to

ride. Some remarks were made that I was very good to be able to ride so young.

Later in the interview he mentioned that he "was always called very smart and very intelligent." The first son, Mike, was considered a homely boy, and the parents were frankly and audibly elated at the attractiveness of their second child, an attitude which he did not fail to register.

During the winter when Kidd was two-and-a-half, his mother took him to the school principal and tried to get him admitted to kindergarten. "He'll be three pretty soon," the mother argued, but the principal refused to waive the usual rule, and Kidd's school life did not begin until after his third birthday. In retrospect, and probably at the time, he reacted to his mother's educational zeal with mixed feelings. "At the rate she had children," he remarked, "she had to get rid of one as fast as she could to make room for another one." With entrance into kindergarten the stream of memories began to widen.

> One time I sat in the middle of a ring of children while the teacher was out. I was showing off: I took off my shoe and threw it around the room. I remember lots of faces at kindergarten, how the girls were dressed and how the boys were dressed. On the day of promotion to the first grade we were lined up and taken to the floor above. It was that day my mother dressed me in a velvet suit with lace collar. The teacher stood me up on a desk in front of the class so everybody could see it.

Probably during the fifth year belongs the memory of a Hallowe'en party where he ducked for apples which contained "nickels and cents."

> I got very tired and fell asleep at the end. I was dressed in a Buster Brown collar and a blue serge suit. The collar propped my head up when I fell asleep.

He recalled also the blue overalls with red cuffs that he and Mike wore when playing in the yard.

The most noteworthy feature of these memories is the repeated mention of clothes and, what is probably more important, the recurrence of the situation of being seen and admired, whether for prowess in riding or for beauty as the possessor of golden curls and fine garments. We are entitled to be surprised that a young man's

early childhood memories should be so loaded with items of adorn-
ment and scenes of exhibition. Kidd's interest in clothing appeared
not only in his memories but also in his imaginative trends. Twelve
responses in the Rorschach test had to do with costume, and one of
the Thematic Apperception stories turned on the almost magical
importance of good clothes. In this story Kidd described a haggard
young transient, willing to work but so unpresentable that nobody cares to employ him; one day he accidentally finds a good
suit of clothes, and his immediate success teaches him that "it is
clothes that make the man."

Kidd was a beautiful and clever child who delighted his parents.
They praised him, dressed him up, showed him off, and tried to advance him in school. He was given what may be described as a high
esteem-income, the payments coming at moments when he was the
center of attention. He was clearly favored in this respect over his
less attractive brothers Mike and Tom. It is important to notice
that he seems to have been praised more for gratuities than for accomplishments—for beauty and cleverness unaccountably possessed
more by himself than by his brothers. In the story just mentioned,
the hero's willingness to work counts for nothing until he is granted
the gratuity of fine clothes. Perhaps Kidd was thus predisposed to
feel both *helpless* and *self-conscious* when during adolescence his
esteem-income suffered a sharp decline.

Further memories amplified the statement that "my brother and
I were close." Joseph remembered asking Mike "if mouses grew into
cats, cats into dogs, dogs into horses, and horses into elephants," and
being amazed at the wisdom of the reply. Evidently the two boys
were much together, so that at five Joseph felt very badly when
Mike alone was asked to a party; Joseph walked down the street
with his brother and sadly watched him disappear into the house.
This incident was one of two memories which involved depriva-
tion; the small number confirms the statement that Kidd had a
happy and well-provided childhood. The other occasion was a
party given by the teachers for the parents. The parents were given
crackers and cream cheese, and Kidd remembered "sitting there
and not being given any." He seems to have enjoyed parties and
felt injured when for some reason they did not include him.

The memories of kindergarten did not include acts of aggression.
One of the older boys once kicked the teacher in the shins, but
Kidd looked upon this act as "very, very bad." He recalled various

scenes of boys being given the rattan, scenes which appear to have impressed him strongly. By the time he reached the first grade, however, he had begun to show the belligerent tendencies which flowered in his childhood; he had a fight at the back of the classroom and was kept after school for it.

CHILDHOOD: A PERIOD OF FORCED ADVANCEMENT

Introducing his childhood with statements suggested by the outline, Kidd enumerated his illnesses and accidents, then passed directly to an event which he considered of major importance in his life: a double promotion in school.

> I've had all the illnesses of a child such as whooping cough, measles, mumps, and scarlet fever. I was struck by an auto when I was about six and received a fractured leg; that is the only accident I've ever had. I received a double promotion from the fourth to the sixth grades in grammar school and though it seemed marvelous then I now consider it the biggest mistake my parents made. They too thought it grand, still do, that I'm so young in my third year of college. Right now I'd rather be back in my last year in High School, with fellows my own age. At any rate this double promotion put me in the same class as my brother and such didn't appeal any too well with him.

Kidd blamed many of his later troubles on the double promotion which made him younger than his classmates. The circumstances surrounding this event give us a new insight into the forces at work in his family. The fourth and fifth grades occupied the same room; and Kidd, finishing up his fourth grade lessons quickly, would sit watching the fifth graders until the teacher allowed him to move over and take part in their lessons. This proved embarrassing because one of his classmates coveted his seat and he had to keep moving back to claim it. The teacher, however, was a friend of his mother's, so that the news of his mental promise reached home and generated a parental striving. Neither Kidd nor the teacher wanted a double promotion, but the mother began to exert such a persistent pressure upon both that the child became "more and more thrilled with the idea" and the teacher consented to the step. Since education was the mother's "secondary religion," it is not hard to understand her zeal, but in the matter of double promotions this was quickened by rivalry with her husband's sister, whose only child, a boy of Mike's age, had recently skipped a grade in the same school.

At all events, during the following year Joseph was in the sixth grade with Mike, a situation which, he said, "inflated my ego so that I acted like a baby, very spoiled." Whereas Mike was quiet and reserved, Joseph "always acted wild" and often won the condemnation of the teacher.

> Once the teacher said if anyone dropped a pencil he would get three slaps. I dropped mine three times, by accident, and got nine slaps."

The evil effects of the promotion, however, did not fully show themselves for several years to come. Joseph and Mike were still close friends, and a congenial group of boys played and roamed together.

> Our "click" still held together and we played all sports together. We fellows never had a thing to do with girls in any way; all were bashful except me and I used to chase after them in my spare time and as a result had a flock of them following me (not conceit but fact).

Was it perhaps easier to win the admiration of a female audience? Kidd's interest in female company was certainly stronger than that of his boy companions, but it was a minor theme in the affairs of childhood.

> My marks were very good, and the difference in age between my classmates and I never bothered me, I always had my brother beside to help me. I was sensitive, very sensitive, ignorant of sex, mischievous, exceptionally so and was always getting in trouble while my brothers were very quiet. I was very fond of movies and sports and was very healthy. I had very many friends and close ones; as boys we stuck together. I never had any future desires as for occupation, nor hero-worship to speak of. I wasn't timid but very straight-forward and aggressive. Sports then were our only interest and amusement. And I never liked to see any of our fellows with others or others to try and get in our "click."

On the whole, it seems clear that during the childhood period Kidd was energetic, happy, sociable, and aggressive. It is worthwhile to stress these traits because they were all soon to disappear. At the time when the study began he seemed passive and even sluggish, distinctly unhappy, socially withdrawn, and anything but aggressive. By contrast, his early childhood history includes a record of some ten fights, seven or eight of which he won. According to his own account he was "always rarin' for a fight" and could completely lose his head in one, although there were instances when he backed out because he was afraid of his opponent. Curiously enough, the only fight he recalled in detail during the interview on early memories was a defeat rather than a victory. His brother Tom came over to the third-grade yard to report that a fellow had said he could lick Joseph. Kidd accepted the challenge, the fellow being no older than himself; he did well while they fought with fists, but when it turned into wrestling he was finally downed. However, even after the double promotion, when he began to associate with boys a little older, he does not seem to have been at any serious physical disadvantage. From then until adolescence he was an active member of a congenial, closely knit gang which spent most of its time at sports. The breaking up of this gang was a severe disappointment to him.

ADOLESCENCE: A PERIOD OF GROWING FRUSTRATION

Early adolescence was a crucial and painful period for Joseph Kidd. The gang started to break up: "We spread to different parts of the town as our hangouts." This process began when the two eldest Kidd boys were sent to a somewhat distant high school, and it continued rapidly when Mike, now fourteen, "started to leave the 'click' we grew up with for dances, parties, girls, and a wilder bunch."

> My brother (14) and I (12) were sent to Central High School. The first year we were together; I studied hard and got better marks and then he became independent and indifferent towards me because he wanted different associations and I suppose jealousy was beginning to get him. By this time I had begun to note and be affected by the marked differences between the ages of my classmates and I yielded, becoming childish in my actions and bragging about my age. I had acquired masturbation by this time and practiced it excessively since I studied hard, but I didn't have the slightest idea of what I was doing. I kept this up throughout High School excessively and have only stopped over a year ago. Because of this my high school marks were very low and I managed to get out of there by the skin of my teeth. Because of this I began to give up my friends, sports, and everything and used to stay in the house all day listening to the radio and studying. I became soft—soft as a banana.

This was a rather striking change of behavior, and Kidd was not entirely wrong when he traced it back to the double promotion. Being in the same grade with his brother, he had come to depend upon him for companionship, initiative, and even defense. When sexual maturity carried the brother into a new circle of activities, Kidd felt deserted and helpless; he was faced by the new task of making his own way, a task for which his being more than a year younger than the group was at this age a serious handicap. His accustomed social attitudes were now revealed as wholly unsuitable. He described as follows his junior year, when he was fourteen:

> I fooled away my time in school, and acted like a young kid of about eight, laughing, being childish and all, till all the fellows looked down on me and all the teachers especially. . . . I gave up everything, friends, sports and all the outside world. I stuck to my home and my studies. Meanwhile my brothers were out and around and I was becoming sissylike.

In a later interview, discussing fears, he mentioned a fear of losing friends and a "terrific fear of teachers; that came from Central High School":

> I was ultra-dependent, and felt more inferior toward teachers than any fellow in the classroom. Anyone whom I'm under, any authority like a teacher, I'm very submissive.

The Latin teacher earned his respect along with fear; he required that things be written out hundreds of times and "pounded it into" the pupils, a pressure to which Kidd responded by winning a prize in Latin. The English teacher, on the other hand, "a very refined fellow," stormed and threatened capriciously.

> He hated my guts because I raised cain and was silly. He called me the kid and threatened me with high heaven. He told me I was foolish to go on to Harvard. My dislike of English was fostered by that teacher.

During his senior year, now fifteen years old, Kidd was "more childish and silly than ever."

> I had all my teachers reporting me till they were blue in the face. They all banded together once and censured me for throwing milk bottles down the ventilator; but much to their regret they couldn't throw me out. I was pretty much of a stooge for them and they got a big kick out of me at my ex-

pense. During my senior year even my brothers looked down on me but didn't make it evident.

Bored by his studies, Kidd worked erratically at them and barely passed his college entrance examinations. He was not quite sixteen when he graduated from high school, and he had to lie about his age in order to get a job in the post office for the summer. He was the only boy from his school to enter Harvard College in the fall. He chose medicine for his life work "because it's always appealed to me and I'd prefer it to any other profession"; we know, however, that it was his father's choice for him and favorite among the professions. His adviser suggested that he concentrate in biology, and thus his field of concentration was chosen, though without much enthusiasm since his poorest grades were in that subject. Outside of his field he took a lot of sociology courses because "they were easy and seemed interesting." He frankly admitted that he did almost no studying in college, which was enough to destroy his liking for any course. Before examinations he "crammed," frequented tutoring schools, used borrowed notes, and even handed in copied term papers. A course in anthropology momentarily aroused his interest because it presented the theory of evolution and distinguished the provinces of science and religion on this theme, thus touching a question disputed in the Kidd family. He became more deeply interested in embryology, which held an unexplained fascination for him. On the whole, however, the intellectual side of the college experience meant almost nothing to him, and the chief lesson he learned was how to get along without working.

Although he blamed the double promotion for part of his troubles during high school, Kidd felt that his history centered around his developing sex life. He masturbated "excessively" from twelve to sixteen and believed that on this account his school work suffered and his social life practically ended. Evidently there was a great deal of shame, much more than we can attribute to a strict church or family attitude, since his brothers were not similarly affected. Because he discovered the pleasures of masturbation while lying on his back and continued to practice it in that position, he did not at first fully identify it with sex and thought that he had stumbled upon a vice peculiar to himself. It is clear, however, that he believed it injured his masculinity, for he used expressions such as "soft" and "sissy-like" to describe its effects. He was surprisingly upset when the true

facts about sex came to his attention. At the end of his sophomore
year at high school he worked at a camp for the summer.

Here I *was* shocked because up until that time I still
thought that the stork brought the babies to the hospital and
mothers went there and got them and stayed a while. I really
couldn't believe all I learned down there at once, because everything came to me like a bolt and I was dazed. Even though I
was *fourteen* I just learned down there all at once all about sex
even to menstruation.

I associated with a fellow who was about three years older
than me; he told me all about the many aspects of intercourse,
till it seemed to me something extremely pleasurable and only
that. What the church said against it only went in one ear and
out the other. He twisted and warped my mind tremendously.
Girls seemed to me nothing but a lust and none of them any
good because what these fellows would say as conversation
would affect me, and I'd absorb it and think about it.

Why did Kidd feel so strongly about masturbation? It seems
likely that there were three contributing causes that strengthened
the ordinary guilt feelings: (1) his self-consciousness, (2) feelings
of inferiority connected with enuresis, and (3) his submissiveness.
(1) In early childhood he was trained to feel the importance of
appearing well before the eyes of others; the idea of being looked
at was connected with the highest gratifications. This heightened
consciousness of an audience made it difficult for him to conceive
of a secret vice; he felt almost as much disgraced by masturbating
as if he had done it in public. A little later he was an easy victim
of the notion that masturbation leaves visible signs on the genital
organ. For a while he shunned the locker room and swimming pool
and did his best to avoid being seen undressed. When asked in one
of our tests to complete a story about a boy suffering from an inferiority complex, Kidd gave an explicit elaboration of this theme.
The complex, he declared, came from "a physical defect caused by
masturbation"; the hero endured much joking, avoided the swimming pool, "ran if anybody said anything to him," and felt that
"everyone was talking about him" wherever he went. Self-respect
was regained only when the hero stopped the habit and learned to
"kid the other fellows back." (2) Feelings of inferiority had been
slowly mounting for some years on account of his failure to control

bedwetting. His parents tried to take this problem calmly, and his father offered the supposedly comforting thought that he himself had wet the bed at a like age and beyond. Mike and Tom, however, were often merciless and occasionally reduced their brother to tears. Enuresis probably predisposed Kidd to perceive in masturbation another sign of genital inferiority and childishness. (3) Further difficulty arose on account of his submissive attitude toward boys and men, an attitude which was strongly encouraged when the double promotion made him the youngest member in all his groups. As puberty approached, situations began to arise which made him feel uneasy in the presence of his fellows. He remarked in an interview that "all through school the bigger fellows seemed to want to put their arm around me." He was not aware of any answering erotic feeling, and he found nothing attractive in the more open homosexual advances to which he was occasionally exposed. Nevertheless, he acknowledged "a lot of effeminacy" in his nature, attested by his preference for female company even in the year or two before puberty. Masturbation was sensed as a blow to his still unproved masculinity.

Thus Kidd's self-consciousness and submissiveness conspired to make masturbation a deeply humiliating experience which propelled him to withdraw from social activity and to some extent from athletics. He was all the more profoundly shocked but at the same time fascinated when his older friend instructed him in a crude and somewhat sadistic conception of male sexuality. It took another year to muster up the courage to kiss a girl, and for a time he "didn't have the guts" to go beyond "necking," but shortly after he was sixteen he picked up a "blonde derelict" known to be amenable to suggestion, took her down a dark alley, and successfully asserted his manhood. This was the beginning of a series of closely spaced episodes; influenced by the way his college companions talked, he thought that sex was the main thing in life and the "epitome of social success."

Several weeks before the adventure in the alley Kidd had fallen in love. Shortly before he enrolled at college, he was introduced "very sudden like" to Mildred, who lived not far away from his home, and he began to take her out. This was "the best possible thing," he said, "to save me from softening." He described Mildred as "just the opposite" from himself, "clean, good humored, sweet

personality, and extremely popular." In a later interview he characterized her by the following expressions:

> There is a real smile on her face all the time. She has a laugh
> that's real. There's a lot of life to her; she's very energetic. She
> is not backward in school but only slow; she didn't want to
> study. She suffers under no complexes. She will talk to anyone.
> She is not forward. She has an air of shyness but it doesn't
> cloud her personality, which is the same everywhere.

In further conversation he mentioned the strong likeness between
the girl and his mother and remarked that he told her all his troubles in the first few days of their acquaintance.

He was soon deeply in love with Mildred, and this relationship
worked a profound and not altogether constructive effect on his personality. The first effects, however, seemed to be beneficial.

> By meeting this girl, I suddenly realized the condition I was
> in mentally and physically. I began to see life as it really was,
> from which I'd been hiding the past four years. I began to look
> up to this girl, and to respect and admire her; though this may
> sound dramatic, it's still the truth.

> Since meeting this girl I've changed. I've tried to make the
> most of my school life by acting the age of my classmates in
> associating with them. I've lied about my age considerably since
> entering college. I am in reality ashamed of it, I don't want to
> be called a "kid" any more; on jobs, in conversation, at work
> or at play, I try to keep on a par with a twenty year old boy.
> I've lied about my age till I'm blue in the face, until now I
> almost believe myself that I'm over twenty since I've been tell-
> ing people that day in and day out. Since meeting this girl
> I've lived for her and tried to make her look up to me. I've
> been in love with her for two years and I know she feels the
> same about me. I've never touched her and never will illegiti-
> mately.

Kidd plainly adhered to the idea that there are two kinds of
women, the nice and the derelict, the former untouchable, the latter
made for man's pleasure. Of sexual intercourse he wrote:

> I think it should be respected to a certain degree and I think
> a fellow should be capable of making his own moral limits con-
> cerning girls. I dislike to have it referred to vulgarly. My atti-

tude toward marriage is that it shouldn't be contemplated as anything but a sacrament. I personally wouldn't care much to marry anyone but a virgin girl.

In the meantime, events at home were beginning to take a difficult course for Kidd. He was fast losing his position as the favorite child. His father, who had but lately enjoyed taking him around and saying to people, "This is Joe, he's only fifteen but he's through high school," began to shift his interest to the other boys. Kidd became increasingly aware of his father's shortcomings: his laziness, his lack of self-assertion, his unwillingness to use his mind, his avoidance of responsibilities. When the mother, entering the menopause, began to have crying spells, Mr. Kidd would stalk out of the house, leaving Joseph to utter words of comfort. Yet Joseph's relation to his mother also took a turn for the worse, largely because of his own feeling. "I can't take her affection any more," he said, "it did too much harm." Life no longer seemed bright to him. Surpassed in social accomplishments by his older brother Mike, outdistanced in athletic achievement by his younger brother Tom, rejected by his father, unwilling to be babied by his mother, bored with his college studies, he turned with unnatural intensity to sex and to his love for Mildred.

The parents' moral attitudes were essentially hostile to adolescence. Kidd's father believed that the first twenty-five years should be a period of studious and obedient preparation, while his mother feared that a waitress might step in and thus spoil the plans for upward social mobility. The parents, moreover, could appreciate only what they understood, and this did not include the intellectual interests of a university. When Mike went around with the right people and when Tom won a place on the football team they were prepared to give their affectionate esteem, but when Joseph brought home the theory of evolution they angrily announced that the church did not accept such a doctrine. At sixteen Kidd suddenly reached a point where nothing in his conduct commended itself to his parents, yet he was quite unable to dispense with their interest and support. In his story completions two years later he made his heroes take the most roundabout courses rather than hurt or disappoint their parents.

THE LOWEST POINT: A PERSON WITHOUT A PERSONALITY

Our study began in the course of Kidd's junior year at college when he was eighteen years old. This was a peculiarly bad period in his life. In a supplement to his autobiography he described the situation as follows:

> About the beginning of school I began to think a lot about myself and my place in society. I've worried and fretted a lot since. It so happened that during the football season I became extremely upset over my past. This was due to the fact that my younger brother Tom, only a junior in high school, was making some headway in football, was gathering friends (who would call for him), was going to dances, and was becoming an all around swell fellow. But he began to rather ignore me than look up to me as I did with my older brother and I also began to look at myself and say "why." He began to become independent and express his own desires about his future. He seemed so independent "why wasn't I." He was a man, "why wasn't I." He was popular, "why wasn't I, his older brother." I began to look at the past to see what made me what I was and how. I was silly, childish, sexy, moody, temperamental, unpopular, considered conceited and had no independence or personality. For the love of my girl I wouldn't have cared a hang about the whole world. I would have lived just for her and in fact I was. But she also was becoming ashamed of me in a modified way because I was not popular or at least a regular fellow since I was too much "for" her, not independent enough, too weak-kneed, and acted too much like a spoiled child, crying for my own way with threats that she realized would not be carried out.

> She could see when we went to dances just how I fitted with the world: I couldn't mix, I couldn't have fun, I just couldn't stand other people around her. I was very jealous. She began to become bored with me and threw a sink-or-swim attitude at me unconsciously.

This was the last straw. Even his girl, on whom he had been leaning for emotional support, demanded that he grow up and behave like a man with a will of his own. Good looks and pleasing ways were no longer sufficient; he had to make himself worthy of love and respect. The role of the kid was completely played out, but he did not know just what to do next.

> I began trying to fit a personality to my make-up. I began "acting" out personalities and tried observing people and copying them, but I realized what I was doing and so carried that "how'm I doing attitude," that is, continually looking at and thinking about what I'd said or done, what impression I had made. But these personalities were all short-lived because they pleased some and not others and because they didn't produce that underlying purpose of making people like me; and every time unconsciously I would resort to my childish attitude to make myself noticeable. Examples of these "personalities" are independence (but I couldn't keep it up); arrogance (but people were only arrogant back at me); big shot in sex (but people weren't so much in love with it as I thought); hatefulness (people paid no attention to me); extreme niceness (people took advantage of it, kidded me about it because I did it to an ultra degree); humorous nature (but I was only being childish, silly); quiet and studious (but people were only passing me by and I kept feeling I was missing something). I became a daydreamer so intensively that up to the present I find I'm daydreaming almost all the time. I became conscious of a person's approach and would become fluttered, flustered, would try to make a friend of him no matter who he was but I overdid it.

It would be hard to improve upon this description of an intense need for love and attention. Kidd tried to make dramatic identifications with independent, assertive people, but he was everywhere betrayed by his need to be praised and admired. There seemed to be no core to his personality, no residue of pride or self-respect now that people no longer thought well of him. The sight of football players made him remember "how I spent my time masturbating while they were out forming a personality and building themselves up." Unwillingly he forced himself to go out with the fellows around him. Compulsively he stuck to his girl, "my only contact with the outside world"; without her he would have "retreated into a hide-away, to a hermit's life, to my mother's affection"; still more compulsively he sought derelicts.

> A fellow around school had a car, I'd provide the girls (tramps) and we'd go out once or twice a week with these different derelicts. I used this sex as a personal appeasement and also tried to flaunt it in front of fellows as if I was achiev-

ing success, but I found out quite a bit later that they were thinking less of me for it.

Between worrying about himself, worrying about his girl, debauching, studying feverishly for examinations, and "smoking an awful lot," he got quite worn out and retired to the infirmary with an attack of pneumonia.

I was very sick for about a week and lost in all close to thirty pounds. This made matters worse because while in the hospital I was on my back all the time and could do nothing but think and all the time I fretted and worried myself sick. I became bitter, moody, and forceful in my determination to hurt people and make them sorry. At times I became so disgusted with all that I thought about suicide; this I can't deny as it was very true. I was very unhappy.

Emerging from the hospital four weeks later, he determined to throw himself into sports as a means of building up a personality. Four days after leaving the hospital he was playing hockey in sub-zero weather.

Just after Christmas came a real blow when I found out that Mildred had gone to a prom with another fellow and had been playing around with him while I was in the hospital. This knocked me flat, and coupled with my disgust of the whole world in general, my family and all, I determined to pack up and leave. I wrote to everyone I knew outside the state asking for a job. My mind was aching and my nerves felt ready to snap; God only knows what kept me from hopping a freight when I couldn't find a job. I was desperate. But I fought my way through midyears and came through with passing grades.

This put me at ease a little, but then the old routine continued. I made up with my girl, began going out, wasting time, thinking, daydreaming, and worrying.

And so matters rested at the end of his junior year. Kidd was to himself a man without a personality, helplessly pushed around by the strongest impressions of the moment. He experienced no stable governing forces in himself which might become the object of self-respect, and in consequence his mind was full of distressing tensions. Our knowledge of his more acute discomforts came from a supplementary autobiography written for us the following autumn.

He was then feeling considerably better, so that an offer of thera-peutic assistance, which would certainly have been appropriate the previous spring, no longer seemed indicated. In retrospect it is easy to see that Kidd's very interest in the study, his frankness, and what we might describe as his determination to put his worst foot foremost, gave evidence of a desire for help. The initial situation had not been defined, however, as one in which help was available; as a consequence he always gave us the story of his distresses in the past tense, as things he had suffered but now felt to lie safely be-hind him. In point of fact the chief interviewer responded to his need to the extent of discussing some of his problems with him, of-fering sympathy and encouragement, and being helpful with practi-cal issues especially in relation to the college authorities. Neverthe-less, the relationship hardly qualified as planned psychotherapy; Kidd's further development must be laid largely to events and to his own efforts.

ANALYSIS OF IMAGINATIVE PRODUCTIONS

Before we attempt to gather the threads of Kidd's story into a fully intelligible pattern, it will be profitable to examine his im-aginative productions as represented by the stories he told in the Thematic Apperception Test. As noted before, this test is one in which the subject is asked to make up stories, prompted by a series of pictures usually susceptible to several interpretations. In per-forming such a task the story-teller draws on whatever resources he may possess, including stories he has heard and events in his own life, but the special value of the method lies in its power to reveal tendencies which are barely or not at all conscious and which could not otherwise be discovered except by long and searching analysis. A noticeable repetition of themes in the stories usually indicates some persistent emotional problem in the teller, and further infer-ences can be drawn from the behavior and competence of his he-roes, the attitudes displayed toward parent-figures and love-objects, and the way the plots are brought to an outcome.

Three themes appeared so insistently in Kidd's fantasies that we can accept them as clues to important latent strivings. The first theme centers around the longing and loneliness engendered by loss of a loved person. There are five occurrences of this situation in the course of the twenty stories. Given a picture of an elderly woman peering from the threshold of a half-opened door, Kidd related the following unusual story:

> This picture, to me, depicts an old woman, about seventy years old, peering with longing in her eyes. She is alone in this house in which she lives, and has been alone there for the past ten years since her husband left—died, I mean. They were a devoted couple and loved each other dearly. His death shocked her and since they were childless, she was left positively alone. The past ten years haven't at all worn off his absence. At times the sense of loneliness so greatly overcomes her that she begins searching the house for him believing he is still there, sitting and reading. This idea which she holds that he is still alive and present in the house so overwhelms her as years go on, that eventually, one night, she imagines seeing him in a chair and goes over and speaks to him. The next morning some neighbors, missing her, search the house and find her seated in a chair very comfortably opposite an empty chair. She had died of a heart attack during the night.

In another story a young husband "by his constant nagging, jealousy and sureness of himself" kills his wife's love and drives her to leave him and marry again. He soon discovers, however, that he cannot bear her loss; he becomes "an outcast because of his eccentricities" and finally commits suicide. Here it is recognized that the hero, if such he may be called, by his selfishness sacrificed the treasure of love, but the value of this treasure in the storyteller's estimation seems all the greater from the tragic events that follow.

These stories, a sufficient sample of the five that turn on lost love and longing, give evidence that Kidd has experienced a deep feeling of bereavement. Since the chief characters in his life history were all still alive, this feeling probably came from the steady decline of his esteem-income, especially the gradual moderation of his parents' love and the growing indifference of Mildred. It is important that he several times made his heroes to blame for injuring a love-relation, just as he blamed himself for having alienated Mildred's affections. In any event, the repetition of this theme in the stories gives evidence of an unusually intense craving for love, a craving that seems to contain strong elements of dependence.

The second outstanding theme occurred virtually unchanged in three of the twenty stories and with variations in four more. Perhaps the clearest expression was given in response to a picture which showed a gray-haired man looking at a young man who is sullenly staring into space. The younger man, according to Kidd, was a surgeon whose wealthy upbringing had given him an inhuman attitude.

>His operations were rash and sometimes without sympathy. Rather than spend precious time mending a mangled member he would take the easy way out and amputate. He sometimes unnecessarily operated because it was always quicker to learn the trouble that way than slowly studying the symptoms and this caused many of his patients to die. His career was on the brink of downfall when a kind old physician took him in hand, and for a whole year showed him the other side of life with its millions of people; its poverty; its sorrows; its love. The surgeon explained not from a lecture hall, but from an intimate standpoint, his duties toward these people. What arms or legs meant to them and what life and death meant to them, which must be included in our education towards profession. This, of course, caused this young doctor to realize he was dealing with people and not running a business, and then with this advice he succeeded.

The young man in this story is spoiled, thoughtless, cruel, and, judging from the phrase "running a business," greedy. These traits begin to spell disaster for his career, but he is taken in hand by an older man who is obviously interested in his success and who forwards it by educating him in kindness. The underlying theme of this story can be expressed as follows: *transformation of cruelty and greed by the sympathetic interest of an older man.* This theme occurred in another story with much less help from the picture, which showed only the silhouette of a man's figure against a bright window. Kidd told of a poet who had a grudge against the world and wrote spiteful poetry which nobody bought. When he was on the brink of starvation, an old man who had read all his work told him to climb a certain tower and find great wealth. Expecting to find money, he obeyed, but instead he encountered a vision of light and human happiness which set him on a successful literary career. The third occurrence of the theme was in response to a picture showing the dejected form of a boy huddled against a couch. Kidd saw a lad who had become vengeful "against his religion and his people" because of the death of his father. A priest, however, realized his frame of mind and comforted him so that he "braces up and goes ahead." All three of these stories make it clear that the principal character (the identification figure) is activated by hate, and two mention greed. The kindly intervention of the older man is completely successful in effecting a reformation and in setting the hero's feet on the road to success.

By "variations on the theme" we mean stories in which the hero is impelled by the same destructive motives but in which no older man comes to the rescue. In one such story aggression and acquisition reigned unchecked, so that the chief character committed what amounted to murder and was left in an agony of fear and horror before a punishment that fitted the crime. In another, an inventor used his ingenuity to get rich from the sale of explosive chemicals; he reformed and devoted himself to medical science only after an accidental explosion killed his beloved wife. From such stories we can infer that Kidd felt a profound helplessness to control the forces in himself. His villainous heroes, the victims of circumstance, were pushed on by destructive impulses only to be severely punished for the consequences. Only once did the hero try to change himself, influenced by love for a beautiful girl, and here he "finds the struggle hard" and was "tortured constantly by evil temptations," although he conquered in the end. In the main, Kidd did not borrow much strength from women. Perhaps they were too closely bound up with his aggressive problem to save him from it: two women were killed and a third alienated in his stories. His formula for strength was the affectionate interest of an older man, who alone could transform and socialize his impulses and save him from feelings of remorse. We learn from this how highly Kidd valued his father's love and how deep a loss he sustained by its withdrawal just as he reached an age when independence was expected of him and when father-substitutes were not easy to find.

The two themes so far discussed do not put us in possession of entirely new information. To say that Kidd longed for love, that he felt helpless to control his impulses, and that he craved the affectionate interest and guidance of older men, is not to point out wholly unsuspected latent strivings; indeed, Kidd showed all of these tendencies in his manifest behavior. But the repetition of such themes in fantasy is not without great significance. Fantasy is a realm of freedom where wishes are horses and beggars may ride. Kidd, however, proved quite unable to use this freedom to create a better world where love and succor are provided and where heroes lay hold of their destinies, conquer their weaknesses, and claim the captaincy of their souls. From this we discern no new qualities, but we discover that certain strivings are backed by very large reserves of energy, so large that they repeatedly polarize the field of fantasy.

Kidd's third theme, on the other hand, pointed to tendencies that were not overtly expressed. Several of his heroes betrayed deep feelings of bitterness and hate; they bore grudges against the world and seemed to feel that everyone was against them. Furthermore, Kidd seemed almost to enjoy enlarging on their cruel behavior and equally cruel punishments. A slum boy with a stolen car, for example, ran down the mother of seven children and was thereupon forced to view the mangled body. The inventor was gripped by a "lust for money and power" which included a willingness to blow up most of mankind and which actually resulted in the death of his beloved wife. The young surgeon used the scalpel with callous brutality. Most striking was a story about "the cruelest man in the Roman Empire" who constantly thought up new tortures for enemies of the state and who "loved to see them squirm, plead for mercy, and then slowly, very slowly, die in the worst possibly way." Here we seem to be touching a deep well of resentment, a primitive desire to hurt and destroy, urges which Kidd never brought to expression in the submissive contacts of everyday life. In the safe realm of fiction he opened the gates to the bitterness engendered by his progressive deprivations of love and esteem. Perhaps the mother of seven children was killed because his own mother had hastened him into kindergarten in order to make room for younger siblings. Perhaps the grudges against life were expressions of feeling toward the playmates who deserted him, the father who lost interest in him, the girl who made impossible demands on his maturity. At all events Kidd's tendency to revel in aggressive scenes gives us insight into his tension and feelings of desperation. His dependence on parents and friends, and the strong feelings of guilt described in the autobiography, prevented him from working off the resentment he kept feeling as his frustrations increased. He could only seethe with feelings he hardly dared recognize as fury.

INTERPRETIVE SUMMARY

From all that we can gather, Joseph Kidd started life with many assets: good looks, vigor, cleverness, and the admiring devotion of his parents. His early childhood, both at home and among his playmates, was healthy and happy. Something went wrong, however, so that by the time he reached his junior year in college hardly a vestige remained of his early promise. In order to understand him we must try to work out the reasons both for his earlier success and for his later failure. In explaining the failure we must be careful not to overdraw the picture, for it will presently be our task to understand his more or less spontaneous recovery.

Kidd's parents staunchly upheld two ideals, religion and education. Religion provided for the moral and spiritual side of life, while education opened the way for upward social mobility, an aspiration to which the parents were singularly drawn through their contact with the upper class. When Joseph, their second son, proved to be an unusually attractive and clever child, their delight knew no bounds and they could not resist the temptation to shower him with praise, show him off to their neighbors, and push him ahead in school. He was early accustomed to be the center of attention, and his economy of happiness was founded upon a very large income of loving admiration and acclaim. This childhood situation undoubtedly conferred an initial sense of security and well-being. But it may well have slowed his progress toward independence, and there seems little doubt that it enhanced self-display and self-consciousness, encouraging him to value himself as others visibly and audibly valued him.

At the outset Kidd had no difficulty in mingling with the neighborhood children. With his brother Mike he belonged to a group of some fifteen or sixteen boys who regularly played and roamed together. Kidd recalled four who were his special companions, but none of these early friends stood out sharply as individuals. He emphasized their availability and familiarity when he described them as "just handy, well-known, healthy individuals." Group activities included a certain amount of vandalism, but Kidd emphasized the "goodness" of his particular crowd in contrast to others in the vicinity. Although they "hit the trash barrels" and occasionally broke windows, they made good use of the city playgrounds, where one summer Kidd was captain of a very successful softball team. They also showed themselves to be relatively stable elements in juvenile society by having paper routes and working on Saturdays in grocery stores. Kidd recalled that his earliest role in the group was "pretty active." He was capable of getting his way and convincing the others, and for a while was "pretty notorious" for vandalism.

The last-named tendency was, he reported, "whipped out of me by the old man," and in later years he became a milder and less prominent group member. Group activity was a decidedly satisfying part of his childhood. "Life seemed cleaner and more enjoyable then that it does now," he said in retrospect; "we certainly were active and on the track I'd like to have stayed on." Apparently he achieved an excellent balance between home and playmates. Energies frustrated at home, including resentments, could be taken out in group activity, where he seems to have made good beginnings in the development of self-respect.

The zeal of the mother presently led to a double promotion in school, which put Joseph in the same class as his older brother. This started a very significant development in the younger boy's personality. Thrust into prominence because of his brightness, he began to experience the inevitable conflict between the role of bright child and the role of good fellow in the group. Even after his promotion he was brighter than the other members of the class, though at least a year younger. "I kind of lost the common bond," he commented, "which should exist between kids in the same class." It seems clear that Kidd yielded extensively to the temptations inherent in the role of bright scholar. Accustomed to praise and prominence at home, he could little resist their charm at school. Only gradually did he realize that his enjoyment of distinction was alienating him from his fellows. Even more slowly did he realize that their jealousy and hostility were responses to an attitude of superiority on his own part. Circumstances had placed him in two incompatible roles, and it was hard to learn that he could not have the benefits of both.

The difficulty increased when Kidd and his brother went to the distantly located Central High School. Few of their immediate neighbors were headed for college, and this step marked the final collapse of the local groups. For Kidd, twelve-years-old in a class where the average age was fourteen, the question of social membership took an acute turn. He had formerly been able to win respect by fighting or feats of strength, but now his only available role was to please and amuse his older companions by becoming a "clown" and a "stooge." As they all grew older, Kidd's attitude progressively failed in its purpose of winning esteem. He described this development in one of his story completions: the hero, good-natured and humorous, overhears one day a conversation from which he learns that "what he thought was being a good sport other people considered being a clown"; finding that he cannot "regain good standing with his friends by trying to be serious," he becomes discouraged and leaves school. This story runs closely parallel to its author's own experience. He gradually learned that the smiles of his comrades were counterfeit coin heavily alloyed with sneers at his "clinging vine nature," as he later learned to call it. In consequence he turned more and more to the home.

He turned to the home, where he studied hard and went out scarcely at all. Now that Mike was definitely going with older boys and taking an interest in girls, Joseph had but one companion, the cousin whose double promotion had been one of the causes of his own double promotion. Kidd did not really like his bookish cousin and went around with him only as an alternative to loneliness. He spent more time with his father, hoping for a feeling of support in his role of bright boy on the way to college. This hope was not wholly unjustified, but we can judge that Kidd needed much more from his father at this point than the latter was able to give. The role of bright child is one that can be sustained only by strong parental support, especially if the child has at some point greatly enjoyed the company of other children and then experienced the loss of that company. Such a role is most readily played by only children, or by the only boy, to whom the parents can give concentrated support. It is favored by physical frailty and by parental values which sustain the child in an attitude of contempt for mere athletic and social prowess. This situation did not prevail in the Kidd family. The parents could not support Joseph in the role because they had no real interest or understanding of it themselves, except as a route to higher social status. Clearly they expected Joseph to be not only an outstanding scholar but also a brilliant social and athletic success. These things they understood better, and they were badly disappointed when Joseph failed in accomplishments which seemed to come easily to less talented Mike and Tom.

Kidd was thus not really satisfying parental expectations, yet now that he had lost his hold on companions of his own age his main motive had become to follow the path laid out by his parents. His mother, constantly busy running a "continuous kitchen" for her large family, satisfied his dependent tendencies yet disturbed him with a pressure toward achievements beyond her own understanding. His father was proud of him and gave him praise, but himself displayed none of the energy and application that he expected of his favorite son. Joseph had the distinct impression that his father did not want his own indolent routine and simple pleasures disturbed too often by a boy who should be looking out for himself. It is not surprising that Kidd felt starved when he tried to draw his whole emotional support from his home. The result was a growing anger, a growing rebellion, which he dared not express at home and which therefore broke forth in the form of silliness and mischief at school. He did not dare to stop studying, but he could no longer take an interest in that hated obligation.

It was at this point that puberty multiplied his difficulties. His pangs of shame over masturbation were sharpened by the habitual self-consciousness which made him feel that everybody knew what he was doing. Furthermore, he believed that his irresistable urge to masturbate came from studying too hard, thus being a miserable consequence of the very thing his parents were demanding of him, and he was sure that it interfered with his masculinity and put him at an additional disadvantage with boys of his own age. This was the frame of mind in which he received his sexual enlightenment from the older friend at camp. It is of interest that he perceived sexual conquests as a possible means of regaining not only self-respect but also the respect of his fellows. He was disappointed when he later found out that his college friends, in spite of their talk, had little admiration for a boastful "big shot in sex."

Kidd was floundering in all these difficulties when he met and fell in love with Mildred. He made it quite clear to us what he wanted in this relationship and how he constantly tended to spoil it. He wanted someone who would provide for him and love him as an ideal mother would love an only child. He wanted someone who would praise him and give him his own way. So strong were these cravings that he fell in love quickly and blindly, without much reference to Mildred's actual characteristics. Probably she too fell in love, impressed by the handsome neighborhood boy who seemed destined for a glamorous career. But Kidd soon found himself once more the object of demands. He felt that Mildred wanted him to be an heroic figure, whereas in fact he was shy and submissive with other boys. She grew tired of his dependence and was not inclined to restrict her interest entirely to him. Instead of contributing to his esteem-income, Mildred became an additional cause of bankruptcy.

One of the stories told by Kidd in the second Thematic Apperception Test, given three years after the first, surprisingly illuminates certain features of his development. The picture showed a young man lying face downward on a bed.

> The story of a youth who throughout life considered himself persecuted and unhappy because of others' attitude toward him. He never quite understood why people did not like him, taking any attitude people had towards him as being one of hate. And thus finally he turned away from outside activities altogether, remaining aloof from people whom he had come to fear, having no friends, living only by himself. He developed an attitude of animosity toward his fellow men and wanted to become a greater success so that he could in this way dominate and as a result satisfy his persecutory complexes. He never realized that perhaps the fault lay in himself. The people's attitude toward him depended on himself, not on other people, but for years he struggled under the impression that the trouble was on the outside, not that anything he would do was wrong; until the day he came to the realization, having met a girl he loved, that the world was right and he was wrong, that all his trouble, unhappiness, general lethargy was a result of his own imagination, and in an attempt to get on a normal footing with the outside world for the sake of this girl, he found it was too late—the little part of his life had come and gone, and that to start out again he would have to revert to a second childhood, and could in no way adjust his feelings of animosity to the outside world, with the final result being that it only led to greater introversion. The more he tried the more secluded became his life until he desperately committed suicide.

In this story Kidd gave a perfect account of a sequence of psychological events which is often found in cases of serious social maladjustment.[2] The hero unwittingly displayed certain attitudes which caused others to lower their esteem. Angered by this loss, yet unwilling to perceive his own part in provoking it, he magnified the difficulty by ascribing more and more hostility to others. This could only result in his feeling weaker and more uncomfortable in their presence. Having thus through his own resentment poisoned his social relationships, he withdrew to solitude but built compensatory fantasies of power and success. Kidd even included the therapeutic process whereby insight is gained into the self-defeating character of

[2] Horney, K., *The Neurotic Personality of Our Time*, New York, W. W. Norton & Co., 1937, esp. ch. 4.

one's own strivings, though this insight came too late to save the hero from despair. Kidd's story helps us to understand his own social difficulties during adolescence. There were plenty of external obstacles, but he revealed here the internal forces which helped push a previously active, friendly, energetic youngster completely out of athletic and social circulation.

Kidd told another story in the same test which perfectly illustrated his feelings about esteem and self-respect. He described the plight of an "intelligent, humble, and ambitious" man who could not raise himself above a hand-to-mouth existence in "the stages of lowest labor" because of the economic depression.

> Gradually he began to realize that the greater difficulty between himself and success lay primarily in his appearance. So over a period of time having saved a small amount of money, he one day appeared in a small town in good clothes. . . . Very soon after, with the appearance of a well-to-do man of profession, he gradually became the center of attention and was smart enough to hold it and earn the esteem of the people. By his own imagination he built up a past life comparable to what people would expect; by a gradual self-suggestion won himself over to this position; and in a short time had established himself successfully in an enterprise in the city and lived the rest of his life in extreme comfort and security, showing that it is not what you *have been* but what you *are*.

Here we are given the pattern of success, from which we can infer the pattern of frustrations that would lead to failure. To make a good appearance, to have good clothes, to become a center of attention, to enjoy a high esteem-income, these are the conditions upon which success and happiness are founded and upon which depends the power to transform and ennoble oneself by autosuggestion. When Kidd was denied these gratuities of his early childhood, he gradually passed into the fatal cycle of resentment and its suppression which he so well described in the other story. The interruption of this cycle could be accomplished only by restoring an income of esteem.

Where was Kidd to look for a new source of esteem-income? His high hopes in Mildred were not altogether relinquished, but more often than not his companionship with her left him with an almost unendurable feeling of inferiority. He had a fleeting fancy that his younger brother Tom would look up to him and take him as a model, but Tom followed straight in Mike's footsteps. Both Mildred and his biological studies at college dammed the flow of parental esteem, and he arrived at a state of complete emotional bankruptcy. The word that he chose most often to describe the state was "self-consciousness." He represented himself as being painfully aware of other people's actions or words toward him and intensely concerned with their favor. Whereas in childhood, he said, "their eyes were on me all the time," in adolescence he began to have a desperate fear "of being insignificant, of being unknown, unheard." "I want people to talk about me," he continued, "whether bad or good. I'd just as soon have a bad reputation as a good one." In spite of this last defiance, it was doubtless true in the beginning that he wanted only good opinion. He was always acutely aware of what people thought about him, but this did not turn into a problem until he realized, particularly through the actions of his parents, his brothers, and his girl, that people were no longer inclined to think well of him. When this lesson was persistently pounded into him from all sides, he could see no value in life and even thought of suicide. But he was not really ready to give up the search for coveted esteem-income, even if at first he found no better plan than a frantic attempt to act out impossible roles.

AVAILABLE CAPACITIES AND EXISTING LIMITATIONS

Physical Traits.—Kidd's physique was strong and solid, well-adapted for energetic and strenuous activity yet entirely free from strain and tenseness. His shoulders and chest were broad, his hips narrow, and the muscles of arms and legs large and well-developed. Considering the social value attached to strength and energy in childhood, Kidd seems to have had a fortunate physical endowment. We have seen that he won the greater part of his fights, and he told us that his arm muscles were always especially good so that he was "able to beat the best of fellows in wrist contests." He took part successfully in numerous sports: football, baseball, hockey, tennis, and cross-country running. Kidd's physique was such as to be felt as an asset and reason for self-respect, the more so because his face and coloring caused him to be esteemed first as a pretty child and later as a good-looking young man.

In spite of his excellent build, however, Kidd spoke of a "sluggish, lethargic" feeling and pronounced himself less inclined toward athletics than the others of his school group. He may have misjudged his energy by comparing himself mostly with older playfellows, especially his brother, who was always a little taller, leaner, and more rugged. It is also possible that his motivation became sluggish and lethargic when, as the youngest of his group, he found it difficult to excel in sports.

Affective Qualities.—In striking contrast to Hartley Hale, Kidd was unhappy most of the time he was in college. Sometimes he merely felt discouraged and depressed; at other times he experienced great inner tension and a feeling of desperation. Success and elation had hardly come his way for a number of years. Although he could enjoy sports and especially a friendly and humorous social gathering, for the most part his happiest moments were characterized by relief from tension rather than by great joy. Even his sexual adventures, necessary as they were to his self-respect, yielded only a momentary satisfaction. Occurring mostly in the dark in the back of a car, they were quickly accomplished: "I just want to go ahead and get through with it," he told us; "I usually feel a little disgust afterwards anyway."

In an interview on the various emotions and their control Kidd represented himself as extremely impulsive. "I lose my temper easily," he said, "and do nothing to stop it." Arguing and being angry he found pleasant, but control of temper proved almost impossible. In spite of his general submissiveness he often lost his temper quite violently with his friends and fellow students. It seemed that he had small power of control and could stop impulses only when he was truly afraid of their consequences. He declared that his feelings were easily aroused, that he gave them full vent when stirred, and that he often acted on the spur of the moment without stopping to think. Consistent with this were his self-ratings on a questionnaire, where he revealed himself as a changeable and disorganized person, unstable in his sentiments, erratic in his habits and in the pursuit of his goals. He gave himself a high rating on the statement, "I find that my likes and dislikes change quite frequently," but he dropped to a low mark when it came to the item, "I find that a well-ordered mode of life with regular hours and established routine is congenial to my temperament." For the statement, "I am on time for my appointments," he selected the lowest rating, a fair warning, one might say, of the long series of tardily kept or entirely forgotten appointments which marked his relation to the study. He also denied himself any efficiency in the matter of studying or in the matter of making his daily life run smoothly. All in all, he professed a degree of disorganization that seriously interfered with adaptation to the college world.

Intellectual Characteristics.—In the Wechsler-Bellevue Adult Intelligence Test, Kidd scored an I.Q. of 118, putting him in the 90 percentile of the general population. He was much better on the verbal scale (I.Q. 126, 97 percentile) than on the performance tests (I.Q. 107, 68 percentile). Immediate recall was particularly good, and he spoke of good retention in everyday life, saying that "any situation is vividly pictured" even when he was not concentrating upon it. Although he loved arithmetic in grammar school and was successful with geometry in high school, the tests showed no great signs of mathematical ability. Reasoning and associative thinking were comparatively poor, a finding that was fortified by his inability to discuss general ideas clearly. He claimed deep thinking on philosophical subjects, believing that he could "stay in an argument with any priest" on the theme that man is only an animal, but from his exposition of this theme one got the impression of a ruminating pictorial mind rather than one that made its way actively to clear concepts and rational synthesis.

Kidd's showing on the Wechsler-Bellevue Test would suggest that he might have some difficulty with his college studies, but another test (the Wells Alpha Examination) found him at the 99 percentile in the verbal exercises and at the 98 percentile on the performance items. Both scores were higher than the average for Harvard College students. On the other hand, he fell far below his college mates on the Scholastic Aptitude Test of the College Entrance Examination Board, so low that there was at first some question whether he would be able to succeed with college work. Events proved that he could usually earn a passing grade by working hard at the last moment, thus utilizing to the fullest his good immediate recall. His college record, however, was a dreary succession of just-passing and just-not-passing grades, so that he was on probation most of the time.

Although Kidd seemed restricted in his grasp of general ideas and abstractions, he was not without gifts of imagination. He told stories of better than average originality in the Thematic Apperception Test. His use of language was frequently crude and awkward, but narrative seemed to bring out his best power of organization, as was shown by his reasonably conjunctive stories and especially by his account of his own life where the motive for understanding was intense. Such organization, however, seemed to be the spontaneous product of passive brooding rather than an active mastery of experience. Kidd rated himself as less than average as regards being logical and coherent in his thinking and admitted that he had spent little time trying to formulate his ideas clearly for communication. Outside of college work his reading was limited to newspapers and weekly news magazines.

Special Abilities.—Kidd proved to stand fairly high in two tests of manual dexterity. In the matter of fine motor coordination he claimed unusual excellence. According to his own account he made the best dissection of the dogfish brain that his instructor in biology had ever seen. Another manifestation of this skill was his ability at picking locks; at camp, he opened four trunks, the owners of which had forgotten their keys. Although he disclaimed mechanical insight, he had a good record in the rapid mastery of such skills as driving a car and running a motor boat. Kidd did not seem to be handicapped with respect to mechanical mastery, but he showed none of the interest in this subject that was so characteristic of Hartley Hale. One might almost have thought that he had been brought up in a different world, so small was his concern for mechanical objects and desire to construct material things.

In artistic appreciation he rated himself quite low, a judgment from which we could not dissent in view of his remarks:

> I don't know one color from another. I can't tell a good piece of poetry from a bad. I can't see yet why they rave over Shakespeare. As for painting, I just see whether a picture looks natural. I have a good appreciation of music: classical, probably something soft and mellow.

Poetry and painting had scarcely appeared on his horizon, music was something he heard on the radio, and Shakespeare was one of the lessons he was obliged to study in school. He had received little encouragement for that flair for story-telling which appeared in the Thematic Apperception Test. His father played the piano, mostly for the purpose of accompanying songs at social gatherings, but while Kidd admired this piece of social skill he had received no encouragement to emulate it.

Social Skills and Attitudes.—In most of his social relationships Kidd was essentially passive and submissive. Occasionally he could be angry and argumentative; he told us that he was often irritable and impulsively critical, that his friends did not consider him compliant, and that he liked to carry on a verbal battle to the bitter end. It seemed likely that his submissiveness was the stronger of the two attitudes and that he tried to counteract it at times by putting up a bold argumentative front. When questioned about his leading and governing ability Kidd almost desperately disclaimed any such talent. "I can't have anyone depending on me to show them," he said, "I really can't, and I can't take the initiative at a supper table." He also questioned his capacity for friendship. Influenced perhaps by unfavorable comparisons with a very affiliative acquaintance, he found himself "not really interested" in friends, "not very dependable or trustworthy," and quite unable to keep confidences.

In view of the prominent place occupied by exhibition in his early memories, it is of interest to scrutinize the pattern of Kidd's self-ratings on this tendency. He gave himself high marks on all items that had to do with saying humorous things, acting the clown, talking about himself, boasting, showing off, and telling tales with dramatic exaggeration. These marks seemed to refer to what he did in congenial and familiar surroundings; under more exacting circumstances, especially when he was called upon to perform before a group, his behavior received a much lower rating, and he never took the lead in enlivening a dull evening. He very much liked to have people watch him do something that he did well, but with equal vehemence he disliked to feel that they were just looking at him or that their eyes were upon him. The need for exhibition appeared to be exceedingly strong, but it was associated with such a low frustration-tolerance that he did not always dare to express it openly. Deep preoccupation with the impression made on others was indicated by his maximal self-ratings on the following five items:

I often think about how I look and what impression I am making upon others; my feelings are easily hurt by ridicule or by the slighting remarks of others; when I enter a room I often become self-conscious and feel that the eyes of others are upon me; I often interpret the remarks of others in a personal way; I pay a good deal of attention to my appearance: clothes, hats, shoes, neckties.

This preoccupation with himself and with the esteem of others doubtless prevented Kidd from utilizing his social potentialities. It

was clear, for example, that he was capable of strong empathic feelings and of understanding the inner life of other people. Highly sensitive to inner problems and distresses, he was yet so bound up in
his own sorrows that he almost never took action in behalf of others.
His powers of sympathy, love, and lasting friendship seemed held
in check by the more pressing urgency of finding himself and securing a stable basis for self-esteem.

FROM EIGHTEEN TO TWENTY-ONE

In April of his junior year Kidd had just recovered from the
shock of learning that Mildred had another boy-friend. After a
quarrel with her he made peace again and quickly slipped back
into the unsatisfactory routine of the autumn term. His attempt to
establish a place for himself among his college acquaintances by
joining an intramural baseball team proved desultory, leaving him
with the impression that he "just couldn't mix." His plans began to
disintegrate.

> Just after midyears I began losing desire to go to medical
> school and I began looking around for easy prospects, business,
> teaching, but I couldn't put my heart into anything, it was all
> in this girl. I did nothing but work and plan for this girl and
> tried to make myself better for her. I was a terrific dreamer but
> wasn't much of an architect. My family was still rather looking
> askance at me for my actions, the way I was spending money.

As the term progressed, he became more and more bored with his
school work. Aside from his evenings with Mildred his only interest
was the lively company of a friend at college with whom he often
went out in search of "derelicts." Presently his friend began to study
for general examinations and another source of interest was cut off,
for Kidd never made these expeditions alone.

With the approach of final examinations he became so upset that
he passed only two of his courses.

> I had lost all ability to concentrate, remember, think, and
> correlate. I just couldn't study because when I did I became
> all nerved up and jumpy. I'd work, go out, go to a show, any-
> thing rather than open a book. I tried making up my mind to
> study but even this didn't help; I tried threatening myself and
> forecasting a wicked future in the event I failed at school, but
> my mind was continually going like a house on fire, nothing
> made sense.

During the summer he was employed as chauffeur at a summer estate in the Berkshires. He began to get a better hold on himself, but his work was not supervised and he found himself dodging unpleasant tasks and doing things that he himself considered wrong. He daydreamed a lot and would occasionally "sit on a log and look into space for hours." It bothered him that he could not manage to make a positive impression on his employer. His brother Mike, he felt sure, would have used the opportunity to get himself a permanent job in the employer's business.

Nevertheless, he returned for his senior year feeling a good deal better. He was more calm, more on the alert "for interests and a future," more able to "get out and act like a man." One more blow was in store for him, however, before a permanent improvement could take place. In September, Mildred took a position as a maid in Shrewsbury. Here she fell in with what Kidd described as a "fast crowd," threw him over in favor of new boy-friends, and fortified her rejection by having her employers forbid him to come to the house. Kidd was desperate. Night after night he could not sleep; day after day, secluding himself from others, he tried to reason his way out of a vicious circle of emotions. He could not help masturbating a great deal, and his imagination ran riot over Mildred's escapades with her new companions. It will be remembered that Kidd had never put Mildred in the class of girls with whom sexual intercourse was permitted; he maintained a celibate relation even when after a session of "heavy petting" his own inhibitions were the only obstacle. Now that she had rejected him and transferred herself to the class of "bad" girls he felt a burning desire for intercourse with her and for personal revenge, motives which do not seem to have been clearly distinguished in his mind. "I almost committed some pretty dastardly incidents," he wrote; "only an overwhelming fear deeply imbedded since early days kept me settled. At one time I came very close, but my inability to obtain a car at the last minute thwarted me."

It is important to work out the pattern of Kidd's conscience insofar as it bore on sexual matters. Sexuality as a whole lay somewhat under a cloud of guilt, but within the shaded area there were two distinct degrees of darkness. With "bad" girls, who in losing their virginity had sacrificed their claim to respect, sexual intercourse was allowable. Kidd held such girls in contempt not unmixed with fear. In one interview he announced that "society should nail bad girls to the cross," and he admitted that he never went out with them alone, not wanting to take the responsibility for "conducting the situation." Apparently by leaving the initiative in the hands of another boy he reduced his own anxiety connected with these escapades. All this, however, was very different from the clear pronouncements of his conscience on sexuality with Mildred. Before her fall she was a good girl, a virgin, a future wife who reminded him of his mother; with her, erotic activity must never be consummated. From another incident we learn more of what Kidd's conscience demanded. He met a "bad" girl in the Berkshires, but he "couldn't touch her" and even found her "repulsive" because she was three years older than he. His conscience drew its line so that good girls, regardless of age, and older girls, regardless of virtue, were both strictly prohibited.

The departure of Mildred, however painful at the time, marked the turning point in Joseph Kidd's life. A few weeks later he met Grace, with whom he formed a very close friendship.

> We talked for hours on end and had quite a few good times together. She was very mature, of good broad character, the deepest sincerity. I've never met anyone quite like her. But our interpersonal feelings were far apart and had no emotional ties, at least I hadn't. She had money and a car and with me was very free with these assets. She in no way interfered with my time and tried to do a lot for my school work—she was always "on call."

During the autumn and winter Grace and her car were sources of much comfort and entertainment. With other girls and fellows they went out several times a week, driving far and wide. Kidd was particularly gratified that the girls, who had jobs, contributed their share of the expenses.

At about the same time Kidd moved into one of the college dormitories. In order to save money he had been living in a dingy rooming house, but now he determined to do better for himself. This move made him feel much better, for he "met a fine crowd of fellows" and began to have a really good time at college. When seen at about the first of January he reported that he was much better able "to tell Joseph Kidd what to do." It was too late, however, to save his college record. He was still unable to study: when he sat down with a book he spent most of the time looking out of the window. He went to "few if any labs and less lectures," could not even hold part-time jobs successfully, and prepared for each examination by one night of study. He had long since given up hope of a degree without summer courses, but his record was so bad that he was expelled from the university at midyears.

> When I received the news from Harvard it didn't bother me very much. That which hurt me was my parents' disturbance: it broke their hearts. I left home for three or four days and lived with a friend. When I returned, nothing harsh was said. My father became rather easy about it and began to offer me an opportunity to go to some other college. But this I refused to consider and just said I'd rather take care of things myself.

Kidd's half year was a failure, but it was not without its encouraging signs: he had left home, he preferred to direct his own life regardless of his parents, and he was finding new companions and new sources of satisfaction in their company. Above all, he was beginning to seize the helm that steered his own behavior.

Presently he found an agreeable position as a clerk in a Worcester business office.

> It was clean work and very interesting. . . . On the job one met a lot of people and since we had no responsible supervisor the job was comparatively easy. During my fourteen months in this position there were four other college undergraduates with us. When our nominal supervisor left in September I was given the position with a raise in salary.

> On the whole I found my sojourn pretty amusing as to the people I met, the contacts I made, and the good times involved. It was a wonderful insight into business living routine and with me time seemed to pass very rapidly. It seems like yesterday that I began to work there. All employed in our department, above our job which was only considered as a part-time job, were college fellows and of the "regular" type.

It can be seen from this account that Kidd put emphasis on two features of the job not directly connected with the work itself: its easiness and its social status. Nevertheless, he did the work successfully and was promoted; furthermore, his job, imposing a certain order on his life as well as yielding an appreciable esteem-income, set in motion three more constructive strivings.

From the first of the year on I began to read quite a bit and began to take piano instruction at a downtown studio. I joined the YMCA around that time and began to take a different physical interest in myself. I struggled with the piano but found it hard to return to a routine. I kept it up until summer school opened. I gained something from time and money spent and would really like to return to it when the opportunity permits. . . .

I've gone in for exercise in rather a strenuous fashion, something which I never did before. Throughout the summer I did quite a bit of sculling and have lately been doing some running to improve my hockey. I also improved, through much practice, my tennis and swimming and have started to throw off smoking for financial reasons and otherwise. My athletics were always of a slack calibre but this I've modified by taking an active interest.

Meanwhile his erotic life began to fall into new patterns. The friendship with Grace gradually moved into physical intimacy, and for the first time in his life he was able to combine sex with respect and sincere feeling. This development was probably easier because his emotions were not deeply involved and because Grace offered encouragement: "it never could have been any more than friendship on my part and I talked her out of a crush on me." He admitted a little coolly that Grace was not good-looking and that he did not often take her out in public. Still he had broken down one of the barriers that blocked his capacity to love, and he had even encroached a little on the rules regarding age: Grace was six weeks older than Kidd.

Parallel with this development came a change in his activities with the "bad" girls. For a while after meeting Grace these continued with their usual frequency. He spoke of "five or ten" acquaintances and mentioned with a touch of pride "one young girl continually calling me and asking me to force her from her virtuous bonds—this I finally did."

But the more I engaged in it the less satisfied I was and when it did occur the reaction was one of disappointment shortly afterwards; for it didn't seem as though this was exactly what I wanted. In other words I judge it to have been another escape mechanism or shunt for my drives.

He began to rub out the line between good and bad girls; he came to like one of the latter, and treated her with something approaching a lover's tenderness. At last a situation arose, following Grace's departure for a distant job, in which all the old distinctions were obliterated. He met a "married girl," two years older than himself, whose husband was on the point of departing.

> She had a car and money to burn and wanted to fire it all on someone who would keep her emotions tepid. I took up with her at this point and with this girl my sex ambitions were satiated and really subsided. I spent a week with her down in Connecticut on our vacations. My relations with her were many and wholesome and from her I learned about all there was.

There was real friendship in this relation; in fact, the girl began to ask Kidd what he would do if she divorced her husband, to which he replied defensively, "Nothing; sit at home and listen to the radio." He took her to his home on one occasion, introducing her as a college girl and using only her first name. His mother was delighted and invited her to a family party. In spite of the coolness with which he gave these descriptions, Kidd felt a genuine interest in the "married girl" and could have imagined marrying her under circumstances less at odds with his parents' moral scruples.

As he began to bring sex and love closer together, he lost interest in sex without love. He was at last able to "quit browsing around," which made him feel a great deal better. As his energies were drawn away from the preoccupation with sex, he was able to distribute them into a more balanced array of interests. It was no doubt a matter of great importance that his later girl-friends valued him so highly and took the initiative in declaring their interest. If Mildred took the last props from under his self-respect, Grace and the "married girl" put back a substantial foundation.

Kidd's year as a business clerk was on the whole a contented one. When he returned to repeat his senior year at college he was far more poised and self-possessed than we had ever seen him. His problems seemed to have reduced themselves to two. (1) Studying was still extremely difficult. "My mind," he said, "seemed to close up when I opened a book; I seemed to have formed some aversion to it." (2) He was still uneasy about his social relationships. Too submissive toward boys, too dependent on girls, too vain about

himself, he continued to fall short of his own specifications for masculinity, especially in the matter of being respected by his own sex.
He still missed in himself certain assertive, dominant qualities
which he would have liked to find there. In spite of these unwelcome
traces of the past, however, Kidd's general condition was greatly improved. He closed his supplementary autobiography with the following words:

> That's the story up to date just as it has come to me. . . . I
> took things rather easily and allowed certain relations to sink
> in. I have striven to get away from over-worrying about my-
> self and adjust myself so as to form my own way of living or
> personality as it is called. I am grateful for the opportunities
> afforded me but now it seems that everybody's dreams or am-
> bitions are about to be interfered with. A lot of worrying and
> thinking about myself I am going to be able to do behind the
> butt of a gun. This sort of realization sort of snaps one out of
> it. At any rate here's to a successful future.

SUMMARY OF CHANGES DURING THREE YEARS

At the age of eighteen Joseph Kidd reached a point of esteem-
bankruptcy. His credit with his parents, his brothers, his school and
college companions, and his girl Mildred had steadily fallen away,
and in the college environment he could not seem to find new
sources of esteem-income. At twenty-one we found him back at a
subsistence level of esteem, his behavior more orderly, his plans
more structured, and his mood more hopeful. The main changes
can be summarized as follows.

1. Kidd managed to achieve a somewhat better relation to his
parents. He dared to express his annoyance at parental supervision,
and he learned to live independently, supporting himself and
making his own vocational decisions. His parents, for their part,
accommodated themselves to this independence and lightened their
pressure for impossible achievements. Kidd's expulsion from college brought the relation to its inevitable crisis, forcing him to
assert his autonomy and his parents to relinquish their control.
When he found and successfully held a business position his parents
were distinctly pleased. In consequence, his own resentment declined, and he became better able to accept his father as a figure for
identification. The piano lessons seemed clearly designed to equip
him with his father's chief social accomplishment. His aspirations,

which included "a comfortable future" and "enough means to send my children to college," began to represent a less momentous leap above the status in which he had been reared. He was learning to resist the ambitious pressure which had previously made his home life so uncomfortable.

2. Kidd made progress in bringing about a fusion between sex and love. Preliminary to this advance was his escape from Mildred, who incited him to behave like a grown-up man yet put him on a diminishing ration of love so that he was left unsustained in his struggle for improvement. Good fortune then came to him in the shape of Grace, who met his high demands for esteem, and who taught him that respect could be compatible with sex. Further progress resulted from his relationship with the "married girl." The gap was certainly not closed; having once been burned, Kidd was cautiously shunning the flame of passionate devotion. Nevertheless, he had learned to make more of these relationships than a mere exhibition of sexual potency, and he had become able to dispense with frequent intercourse as a "shunt for his drives"—a momentary anodyne for the tensions and inferiorities that had previously kept him in torment. Little esteem could be won or self-respect accumulated by those episodes in the back of a car, but his power to command the love of Grace and the "married girl" gave him something, at least, on which to build a more satisfactory image of Joseph Kidd.

3. Although he returned to college for a last desperate attempt to get a degree, Kidd began to scale down his vocational aspirations. His business position, however small, met his expectations in the way of social status without imposing demands that were painful to meet. He found a happy environment in the office and could see for himself, even without the ratification that came when he was promoted, that he was fully equal to the job. During the period when he was not obliged to study he found new sources of interest; he even did a little reading, thus occupying some of the time formerly consumed by unhappy rumination and daydreams. Here again the gains were not securely won, for he returned to college and did not renounce medical school, even though his inner resistance to the old parental program continued to express itself in a violent distaste for studying. He had made a distinct advance, nevertheless, over his earlier outlook which contained no middle points between being a doctor and being a total failure.

Part Two: FROM 21 TO 29

Our contacts with Joseph Kidd during the next eight years consisted of two exchanges of letters, one when he was overseas and one when he returned at the end of the war. When we proposed the second study, he responded with immediate willingness. Upon his arrival we were struck by his gain in confidence and maturity. Workers who met him for the first time thought that he looked young for his twenty-nine years, but he certainly looked much older than the round-faced, curly-haired, hesitant youth we had known before the war. One of the most marked changes was in his tone of voice. The soft, sometimes barely audible, speech of his college years had given place to a voice of normal firmness and assurance.

FOUR YEARS OF MILITARY SERVICE

Some time after graduation Kidd applied for the Army Air Corps. He was attracted by the prospect of flying and also by the fact that "the money seemed good." This application failed, but with the approach of the draft he announced himself in favor of "getting everything you can while the getting is good, especially if you know someone or have the means to get it; they're all looking for something cozy." These sentiments seemed to guarantee that Kidd, whatever else might happen, would certainly not suffer from a shattering of fragile romantic ideals. His second application for the Air Corps was successful, but his training was not scheduled to begin for more than a year. He worked for several months in a war-connected job, but soon found himself feeling extremely restless and impatient. Accordingly he secured release from the Air Corps and was inducted into service as a private. For some time he was signed up for the specialized training program in medicine, but when this failed to materialize he volunteered for a health survey unit. While he was in training for this work, a personnel officer, who took an interest in him and hated to see a man wasting his college education, encouraged him to apply for admittance to a medical school. Kidd's grades, however, had not been good and the application was rejected. In due time he went overseas with a unit consisting of fifteen men and a commanding officer. He sailed "with a laugh," completely carefree, feeling that he had found exactly what he wanted. His parents and brothers were sensitive to rank and commissions, but he himself felt wholly satisfied with his humble status in a small unit.

Throughout his years in military service Kidd found himself repeatedly selected for special attention. "Every place I went," he said, "I found older men or men better off than myself who seemed to become interested in me." The commanding officer of his unit had already singled him out for special jobs and special study. Kidd judged that this officer "had a lot of faith in me, lacked faith in himself, and needed somebody on whom to depend." Kidd found it extremely irksome to be singled out in this way, and he refused to become a model soldier. When the unit disembarked he led the men on an escapade; they were AWOL for twenty-four hours, a thing which both infuriated the commanding officer and badly hurt his feelings. This incident was typical of many in which Kidd took a prominent part in raising Cain and dealing lightly with military regulations. After about a year of service with the health survey unit, however, his work was deemed satisfactory enough to warrant a commission, and he was transferred to a larger post. At once the colonel took a liking to him, invited him to table, spoke to him in mess hall, and tried to get special favors for him. "That I didn't like at all," Kidd related. "Perhaps he needed to depend on me, too. It was a bad deal, to be in with the boss and out with the outfit." Less than three months elapsed before the colonel, purely as "a personal thing," appointed Kidd detachment commander in charge of some eighty men recuperating at a convalescent hospital.

Elevated to this new post, Kidd was completely miserable. He had just been "getting in fine with the junior officers," but now he found them jealous and resentful, and the enlisted men furious. In particular he lost the friendship of a former college football star, "a rugged, good-looking fellow," who was the logical choice for the appointment. Kidd had several violent scenes with a sergeant who hated him and created every possible difficulty. He was able to hold his own in these scenes, but he found intolerable his duties of disciplining the men. The position really called for an older man, he believed, upon whom the enlisted men could legitimately look as a father.

> He would have to be hard, stiff. I never felt so bad as when sitting in judgment on some drunk, probably having a hangover myself, or on some man who had been caught with a native woman, as I had done myself. Sitting in judgment is

what disturbed me. I had to mete out punishment, I had to be
severe . . . I like to be *with* other fellows, not *over* them.

When the colonel was transferred to another command his successor
lost no time in summoning Kidd, telling him that he was a misfit as
detachment commander, and transferring him back to health survey work. If Kidd was unhappy at his demotion, this feeling was
more than compensated by his enormous sense of relief. "I tried to
fail," he said, and he was now free to resume work which he found interesting and which required little initiative.

In spite of his failure in leadership, Kidd looked back on his years
in the Army as the happiest time in his life. "I enjoyed the experience," he said; "I'll remember it all my life." He used the word
"freedom" to describe one of the chief benefits of Army life, then
mentioned the provision that was made for one's comfort: three
square meals a day, money in the pocket, only a few hours of work.
Alcohol flowed freely, nurses provided feminine companionship,
and there were occasional opportunities to take hunting trips and
see the country. "It was a great life for a lot of people," he remarked; "when I came back I had a good deal of what I wanted
under my belt." In another interview he attributed his contentment to "the fact that I got away from home, from school, got in
with people, became less of an individual, more a part of a group."
He contrasted himself with more settled men, generally married
and with families, who wrote letters and wanted to get home. "I
wanted to get up and go," he said; "I wanted to live, I wanted to
get out with the guys," and there were enough men similarly disposed so that he did not feel out of place in having such feelings.
He obtained some satisfaction out of having a commission to take
home, but while he remained in the service he was content to
remain in a subordinate position. Yet it was not entirely for
its good times that Kidd looked back with satisfaction on his years
in military service. Even more important was the gradual but permanent change that had taken place in his personality.

Kidd's own words were as usual very helpful in understanding
this crucial development. In an hour devoted to free association he
spoke as follows:

I think I want to stay among people as much as possible because I understand them, I think I do, I can operate with people. I learned that very rapidly in the Army, very quickly, and

took to it very well, being able to work on people for what you want, bring them around to your way of thinking, but mainly to get what you want from them. That's what we call 'corning' in the Army.

He then described a small business which he and another soldier had set up for personal profit. Materials for the business, and knowledge of how to use them, were obtained from suggestible men in charge of stores, on representation that they were needed for the regular duties of the unit. This minor racket was interrupted when Kidd received his commission. His associations continued in the following vein:

> I wasn't wholly successful in the Army, I didn't make a lot of friends, I didn't accomplish too much. I just feel as though I learned a lot of very useful things, and I think I got rid of a lot of the errors in my system where certain things have to be learned by trial and error, which is dealing with people. I made an awful lot of mistakes with people and lost their friendship or lost their respect, and the like of that, but I don't mind thinking about that today because I accomplished something. With every experience I derived something of advantage to myself, put it away where it would do me some good in the future.

If Kidd's sentiments on getting what you want seem somewhat crudely self-centered, they nevertheless represent a certain progress over the blocked self-assertion and the whining demandingness which he displayed as an undergraduate. One might say that in the Army he had found belated opportunity to take up the thread of development broken off when he lost his contact with group life at the age of twelve. He returned at last to the track on which he would have liked to stay, that of group activity and group respect. In the Army he raised Cain as he had formerly done on the streets of Worcester, never carrying it quite far enough, however, to draw severe discipline. He restored his feeling of belongingness with companions of his own age, and he rejected the kind of ideals for which his parents had stood. Thus he cancelled that surrender to parental ambitions which had only led him into deeper and deeper distress. Regaining contact with impulses more truly his own, he began to build a nucleus of self-confidence and self-respect by learning to get what he wanted through his own efforts. The pursuit of this necessary development required that he be placed *with* other fellows, not *over* them. To be competent among equals was more important than to be in a position of authority. Thus he felt as threats the attempts that were made to give him prominence and advancement— the very things that had ruined his life in school. No doubt he enjoyed the flattering attention of officers, but he had been too badly burned in that fire to let it come near him again. Perhaps the dependence he attributed to these officers was an externalization of dependent feelings which he did not want to experience in himself. At all events he "tried to fail" whenever he was pushed forward, and he refused to be deflected from a developmental task which at last began to feel right and natural.

RETURN TO THE FAMILY HOME

In view of the nature of his development in the Army, Kidd's return to the home of his parents was nothing short of a crucial test. Would he feel once more the old familiar pressure, would he succumb to it, or would he find it possible to continue his growth toward independence and self-respect? In a letter Kidd likened separation from the service to a jump without a parachute. The "sorely missed heroes," he reported, had hardly more than walked through the door than they were "handed aprons and paint brushes." By this time Mike and Tom were married and were in their own homes, but Joseph had nowhere else to go. At first it looked as if he might succumb. He put out new applications to medical schools and enrolled in a summer session where he found a chemistry course painfully difficult. "The first year I was home," he said, "I didn't like it too well, didn't stay home much, didn't take any interest in it." In a desultory way he tried to help with his father's business while awaiting decisions on his applications to medical schools, but on the whole his life threatened to resume the disorganized pattern that had characterized it before he entered the service.

Before long, however, he discovered an opportunity for development right at home. His father's prosperous business began to decline. For years the business had been operated in the dingy old-fashioned shop originally purchased from the German floral decorator. In the meantime, rivals had come into the field, and Mr. Kidd found himself rapidly losing business to competitors equipped with air-conditioning, cooled show cases, and fluorescent lighting. It was clear that he needed to invest in a new establishment, but he showed no disposition to undertake such an enterprise. He wanted to continue in the old familiar way, especially now that his youngest boy Peter, handicapped in health and never successful in school, had joined him in the business and took some of the drudgery off his hands. Mrs. Kidd was again the chief source of initiative. As each of the older boys returned home she made him the object of a persistent campaign to secure a new flower studio. She poured forth her financial worries, her suspicion that the father was giving money to his improvident sisters, her despair because he kept no systematic accounts of his income and expenses.

Kidd rejected an interviewer's suggestion that his mother nagged the boys; he described her method as "harping," which seemed to him "a little bit different, but still just as disagreeable." "She'll stay on a subject," he said; "it becomes almost a maniacal fixation to her. She won't ask you to do something, but she'll stay on the subject of what's wrong, and of course you know the only logical solution." Again, "she's very jumpy and neurotic now; she complains and looks for sympathy, and she has a very clever way of playing one against the other." Her urgency was irritating, but Kidd judged her to be right, and he clearly saw the difficulty of forcing his indolent father to take the necessary steps.

Michael and Tom were busy with their own occupations, one being a lawyer, the other a clerk in a bank. Joseph alone had time at his disposal. With no help from his father, who resolutely turned his back on the whole enterprise, but with the strong support of his mother and the agreeable willingness of his brother Peter, he set out to reorganize the business and build the new shop. Mrs. Kidd, he said, was "wholly on my side, she leaned heavily on me to get done what she wanted done." Yet he did not feel driven by her pressure. He saw through her technique of "harping," kidded her continually for her irrational and stubborn ways, and criticized her with no little severity for her slurring remarks about her husband and his money. He confided to an interviewer that his mother had a very "dirty tongue," by which he meant that she tended to tell tales about people and knife them behind their backs. He considered this "the worst possible crime," and told his mother so.

Having taken on the project of rescuing the family business, Kidd began by trying to get an idea of his father's financial position. This was not easy, because his father often cashed large checks or made them over directly to creditors without keeping any record of the transaction. Kidd collected several bills which his father had long given up. He then offered to make out the income tax and was able to reduce it substantially by claiming deductions which his father had overlooked. Mr. Kidd expressed neither gratitude nor amazement; nevertheless, he was sufficiently impressed to allow Joseph to set up his books in such a way that all transactions appeared in the checking account. It was a moment of triumph when his father confided the combination of his safe, even though the contents proved to be of no great value. Kidd seemed to glow with pleasure when he related this symbol of paternal faith. But the father balked when it came to being involved in the new building; he gave his consent only on condition that he be not bothered by any of the details. This project therefore devolved almost wholly on Joseph, who had to secure the property that was to be rebuilt, engage the architect, contractor, and decorator, decide upon details as the work proceeded, investigate heating and ventilating systems, and procure enormous amounts of information for the family conferences at which vital decisions were made. After a year of work the new flower studio was ready for use. It won immediate acclaim, evoking spontaneous compliments from nearly everyone who saw it, and Kidd derived tremendous satisfaction from his achievement.

In making the many contacts with people that were required to carry out this project, Kidd was much helped by his experiences in the Army. He was no longer a novice in getting what he wanted out of people, and he now had a chance to turn his training to good account. He was far from at ease, however, in his new and responsible role. He felt that everything in the studio had to be the latest and best of its kind. When ventilation had to be considered, for instance, he investigated every brand of equipment and collected stores of information about it. People told him he worried too much.

> I was very, very upset during that period. I smoked a lot, I moved around an awful lot, I talked excitedly to people, especially those from whom I was trying to get the information which would stop me from getting concerned and worried. And I would feel very, very relieved when I got the information authoritatively. I think it pays off to feel that way because you will tend to do more, you will tend to assure yourself you're right.

He had undertaken to do something for his family which involved expense and risk, something to which his father was opposed, something for which he himself lacked technical training. Obviously he had a high stake in being right.

Kidd mentioned in many interviews the satisfaction he derived from the success of the flower studio. He even intimated that he would have been loath to return for our second study if he had not had this solid accomplishment behind him. In an hour devoted to free association he kept returning to the theme. He said that he felt "a keen obligation" toward his parents and that "the purpose of repaying them was accomplished" by the project. This made him feel much better about leaving home and seeking out a life of his own. He knew that he had let his parents down—"turned their sacrifices for me into a joke, into a terrific loss"—by failing at college and by spending money running around with girls. "They were not only unhappy about it, they were very displeased." Certain of his associations suggested a feeling that the debt was even yet not fully paid. The business was on its feet again, but what if its apparent recovery proved only temporary? What if something happened to none-too-rugged Peter? Nevertheless Kidd's predominant feeling was one of tremendous satisfaction. "I gained peace of mind," he said; "I didn't have it when I came back." He also gained a real feeling of knowing what he wanted.

> I'm very happy because I accomplished that. I'm not getting all the credit at home, but it doesn't bother me. In myself I am very happy and satisfied. . . .

> I found myself becoming more definite on things, which I'd never been before. There were things I wanted a certain way; I was damned if they weren't going to be that way. I knew they were right and I wanted them done. And I don't remember ever having been so definite on anything before. It dawned on me after a while that I was knowing what I wanted. I was able to make up my mind.

These statements deserve comparison with his remark at the age of twenty-one: "I can't make a decision on my own and back it up; it's always guided by some factor outside my own intellect." Belatedly he was learning to respect himself and daring to act upon his own judgments.

The nature of the pressure which Kidd felt at home becomes clear from this chapter of his history. His failure to justify his parents' sacrifices and fulfil their high expectations had left him with a heavy burden of guilt. He had to repay them in some way and show them that he was good for something. When the Army forcibly took him away from home, he was justified in postponing this obligation and leading his life as he really desired. On his return, however, he resumed his attempt to carry out the parental plan of going to medical school. Having found contentment in the comradeship and irresponsibility of military life, and having experienced again the old boredom and blocking when he tried to refresh his chemistry, he must have known that he was never going into medicine. But he could not announce this as a decision. He had to wait until the final failure of his last application made it clear to his parents that he could not take the course they had originally planned for him. Although this released him from a burdensome obligation, it did not set him free. But in the meantime he had begun to work off his debt by building the new flower shop. The project had to be a complete success in order to pay so vast a debt and prove him at last a worthy son; hence his anxiety while the work was in progress. When it *was* a complete success he was rewarded by "peace of mind"—relief from guilt—and a feeling that he was at last free to go away and seek life on his own terms.

Kidd had done more, however, than pay a debt and cancel his feelings of guilt. He had also caused his parents to respect him. Even if they did not acknowledge it, he knew that he had done a good job and earned the right to their respect. He had also found a way of rivaling, if not surpassing, his brothers. In contrast to Michael, who was receiving practically all of his law practice from his father's friends, he had carried through a successful project without paternal blessing. In contrast to Tom, the bank clerk, who had drawn plans which the contractor found impossible, he had taken pains to learn what he was about and to secure advice when it was needed. He had clearly shown himself to be a better man than his father, who was now highly dependent upon him. Strengthened by all these demonstrations of his own adequacy, Kidd could at last feel real affection for his father, recognizing all his severe limitations yet enjoying his humor, his piano-playing, and his ability to create hilarious good times. In a way the relation between father and son became reversed, the son setting standards of initiative and business efficiency which the father was scarcely able to emulate. Certainly Kidd no longer felt constrained to live his life according to patterns emanating from his father.

Kidd's relation to his mother remained somewhat more complex. It revealed certain undertones which had barely been suggested in the earlier studies. All the Kidd boys had learned to tease and gently reprove their mother for monotonous harping and persistent curiosity. Joseph, as we saw, had taken her to task for slanderous gossip and had learned not to expect rational discussion on subjects close to her heart. Yet it was evident that he had great respect for his mother, whose drive and ambition had been solely responsible for the family's economic and social success. When first married she had wanted to take a job herself, and she was contemptuous of her "lazy Irish" neighbors who had no thought of rising in the world. If she had actually remained somewhat like them, gossiping over her tea and never using her mind for serious thinking, it was because she had sacrificed her own life for her children. Kidd's attitude was compounded of respect, tolerance, and occasional outspoken criticism, but there was another element in the relationship. Somewhere along the way he had acquired a profound resentment which came to expression mostly through indirect channels. Perhaps the original cause lay in her having other babies in close succession; perhaps it was her continual dominance and harping.

When Kidd was asked to associate to the phrase, *the worst crime,* he arrived finally at the subject of hit-and-run driving, which he characterized as "pretty cruel and heartless," a thing it would be impossible to forgive. It will be recalled that in an early story for the Thematic Apperception Test he caused a selfish and degraded young man to run down and kill the mother of seven children and to suffer torments of remorse afterwards. The earlier plot and the later associations began to seem like threads in a pattern when we observed the course of his thoughts upon being given the phrase, *what frightens me.* He spoke in part as follows:

> It doesn't bring anything to mind right off the bat. Very little frightens me. Ah. . . . (long pause) . . . I couldn't say what outside of. . . . ah. . . . physical violence doesn't bother me. . . . ah . . . perhaps anything happening to my mother. That doesn't frighten me, but that's always in my mind for fear that she'll step off the sidewalk to cross the street. Perhaps I fear a little bit that she might do it and get hit and killed some time.

There are a lot of clowns driving in hopped-up junk-boxes. They likewise don't look or think where they are going. That's probably the only thing I fear, is her out on the street, is fear that she might be accidentally killed.

If she should die a natural death tomorrow, I would feel bad but not so very broken up, but I think I would be very, very broken up if she were killed.

This curious fear that the mother would be accidentally run down by careless "clowns in junk-boxes" has several earmarks of an anxiety derived from early childhood. It can be interpreted as representing a hostile wish with respect to the mother, coupled with a fear that the wish might become a reality. If such a wish and its attached fear was still active enough in Kidd to create a definite uneasiness, we can see added reason for his feelings of guilt toward the family, his gratification at having maternal support, and his joy in the successful payment of his debt. We have now to consider whether a parallel problem has beset him in his relationships with women in general.

RELATIONS WITH WOMEN: UNEASY BACHELOR

Great was our surprise to learn that Kidd's relation to Mildred had not ended during his twentieth year. He was quite sincere when he told us that it was over and done with, but he had not allowed for the possibility that Mildred would resume her interest in him and that he would find this interest irresistable. Shortly after the close of our earlier series of interviews he met Mildred at a party. He learned that she had sought an invitation because she knew he would be there. They began going out again together, but the relation was a stormy and tormenting one. Kidd was greatly bothered by Mildred's continuing interest in other fellows, and he felt that she was but little concerned with him personally; she never remembered, for instance, what he was doing in college or what medical school he might be hoping to attend. At Christmas he took her a present, only to find her receiving a call from another young man. One night he went to her house when quite drunk, thus losing the esteem he had enjoyed from her parents. Yet in spite of all these difficulties Kidd felt that Mildred fulfilled his ideals, and he became increasingly sure that he wanted to marry her. He believed that his impatience to enter military service came partly from a desire to break through her coldness and draw expressions of her regret and affection. While he was in training he thought about her a great deal. On a three-day pass he saw her and had a nice time, but felt that something was on her mind. He mentioned his feelings to Mildred's mother, saying that he wanted to give her daughter a ring, and it was his impression that the mother acted disturbed and unhappy at this news.

Presently Kidd had a furlough, which led to a new development in the relationship. He and Mildred went to a bar together and drank more heavily than usual. Then they drove to a secluded lake where Kidd undertook to end the long-standing taboo on sexual intercourse with Mildred. "After all those years I went right ahead," he said, "took off almost all her clothes, and tried to have sexual relations with her," but although "she was cooperative, I couldn't have an erection; that was from the drinking. After all those years of wanting it, I couldn't have it." Some remarks made during this episode convinced him that Mildred was pregnant. Nevertheless Kidd dated her the following evening for the movies. The situation was awkward: "I felt guilty," he said, "and she felt pretty foolish about the whole thing." Kidd told us later that he had occasionally been impotent when extremely drunk; otherwise, he was a stranger to the experience.

They did not meet again before Kidd went overseas. Months later Mildred wrote that she was unhappy for him. He wrote back, saying that he loved her and wanted to marry her, but her subsequent letters were filled with news items and never touched a really serious note. Although after a time she stopped writing, he returned full of hope that she might be waiting for him. He learned, however, that she was engaged; she was married a few weeks later. "The day came and went," Kidd reported; "it didn't bother me too much. I don't like to talk about it." Sympathetic murmurings from the interviewer did not prevent him from continuing:

> I wouldn't want to meet her husband. I'm glad I didn't do anything rash or ridiculous like dashing off and getting married or going to California. If it had happened before the war I think I'd have gone out of my mind. . . . If her husband died, I might play cat and mouse with her, but I wouldn't get involved again. It's a killer of romance when a girl has children by someone else. That should close the gate.

Kidd may not have perceived all the possible difficulties in his relationship with Mildred, but in retrospect he put his finger on one of the most central problems. He was entirely sincere in wanting marriage, he told an interviewer, yet there were times when he was visited by doubt.

> Sometimes when we made up and got together again I wasn't satisfied. I don't know, I wasn't at ease. I thought I was very sure it was what I wanted, but a great many times I doubted what I wanted. I guess I didn't have myself, so I wanted her. I wanted her life; I didn't have my own life.

He had met Mildred when he was at low depths of unhappiness and disorganization. His strong attraction to her was heavily mixed with dependence and a hunger for esteem. Mildred's coolness, her demands upon him, her faithlessness did not wholly destroy feelings that were rooted in such urgent needs. It is doubtful whether Kidd could ever have cleared the relationship of these elements so inimical to a strong free partnership, and it was probably best for his future development, however painful the period of suffering, that he did not become permanently entangled in his first love. If he met Mildred today for the first time, it would be a different Joseph Kidd who met her: one more capable of knowing what he wanted.

In the meantime Kidd had continued to keep his eye open for sexual opportunities. His experiences in the service carried forward the development that had already begun after his first separation from Mildred. His most frequent companions were nurses, "older girls" whom he could not consider "bad." "I found that the woman cared for me when she did it," he reported, "so why should I think ill of her?" Sex became a natural as well as a pleasurable thing. He recognized that his earlier "hit-and-run affairs" had been heavily motivated by ideas of conquest and achievement. "When it was a question of going steady with a girl and sleeping with her, that was a new challenge. That gave me an entirely different outlook on women in general." When he returned from the service he lost no time in establishing similar friendships. For more than a year he frequented the apartment of a "divorced girl," often taking supper there and joining a congenial group of unmarried young people for whom the apartment served as a sort of social center. But he did not fall in love and he did not move closer to marriage, even though he began to feel embarrassingly conspicuous as a bachelor nearing thirty.

Kidd told us that he wanted to find an attractive, agreeable, intelligent girl with definite interests of her own. He wanted her to be distinctly different from his mother in respect to this matter of interests. The main function of the interests would be to prevent the girl from becoming dependent on him and interfering with his time. Kidd deplored the unfortunate state of one of his golfing companions whose wife always seemed jealous about the golf games. "There's nothing worse than an idle woman," he said. He believed that a wife should "put up with what a man might do to annoy her" and "make very little demand on his time," not requiring to know "where he's going, what he's going to do, and the like of that." In one of his stories for the Thematic Apperception Test he represented a girl as "trying every means to hold" her man, "trying every ruse, every method to catch him. Most of these methods are pressure methods, wearing down, constantly chasing." Besides his fear of losing the freedom of his spare time Kidd greatly dreaded being trapped in a monotonous job with no prospects. He cited the grim plight of one of his friends as a warning example. This man frankly hated his job, but with a wife and children on his hands he dared not sacrifice such security as it offered.

It was clear from his remarks that Kidd was not ready, even at twenty-nine, to settle down in marriage. He still needed to go ahead with a process of development generally accomplished earlier: testing out his own proclivities, becoming sure of himself, finding a vocation. Emotional difficulties had long hampered him in taking these developmental steps, but now that he was on the way he was acutely aware that he needed freedom. But there was more to the problem. He did not seem to fall in love with any girl. "I don't know, I don't love them," he said, and then, making a revealing slip of the tongue, "I think to get married *again* I would like to love somebody." Asked by the interviewer if Mildred had been the only girl he ever loved, he said: "That's right, I mean felt so deeply, but I wouldn't want that same strength of love, I mean something so overpowering and so overwhelming as to cut you off from all you . . . from all the range of living."

This is a real dilemma. He wants deep love, but not the same kind of deep love that previously made him suffer and that seriously blocked his development. It is hard for him to feel this new deep love, free and self-respecting, because he still is not sure of himself, still becomes betrayed by dependence, and still, in consequence, experiences the hostility that went with his dependent love for his mother and for Mildred. He described as "cold and sarcastic" his general attitude toward women. He kids them a lot, as his father kids his mother. "I like to treat women," he said, " as a very odd class of individuals. I think it's for the sake of humor, but I guess at times I can get a little too sarcastic, a little too embittered, and with women who like me I am very cold." He was aware that he kept women "at arm's length," and for the time being he did not really want to do otherwise.

RELATIONS WITH MEN: WILLING LISTENER

Kidd's self-consciousness and submissiveness in the presence of men continued to bother him when he entered military service. He still found it difficult not to "act like a son or kid brother" if a man showed him friendship. But he began to find a solution to this problem.

> During the service it began to disappear more or less. I found that in getting occupied, staying occupied, things worked out better. If I drove a truck all day, eight hours a day, I felt better that night. I wasn't thinking about myself, everything seemed to disappear, I could get out of the truck and talk to these fellows without suffering any complexes. That all seemed to disappear, and I just went ahead with what I had to do and what I had to say. It was plain work, it was activity, just keeping the mind occupied.

Work and the suppression of self-conscious thoughts made it possible for him to feel more like a man among men. As we have seen, his self-confidence and power of assertion increased rapidly while he was in the Army, though he remained unable to accept the responsibilities of leadership.

Strengthened by these experiences, he became able, on his return, to improve his relation to his older brother Mike. He still perceived a wide difference between them—himself too sensitive and too fearful of giving offense, Mike too blunt, assertive, and inconsiderate—but he no longer judged this difference to be wholly in Mike's favor. With two men friends he and Mike made a foursome at golf nearby every Saturday morning, and Joseph played a basically better game than his brother, though he sometimes envied Mike's relaxed slam-bang methods. Joseph began to realize that Mike held him in real respect, asking his advice, suggesting that they might go into business together, expressing disappointment at Joseph's plans to go elsewhere in search of his fortunes. A considerable burden of inferiority feelings was lifted from Joseph's shoulders by this development of the fraternal relation. His grief was painful and enduring when his brother's career was cut short by a fatal illness.

Alcohol was of some importance in helping Kidd's social adjustment. When he was in the service it played a part not unlike activity and hard work; it freed him from self-consciousness and allowed him to feel on equal terms with the other men. After the war he met alcohol wherever he went, and he often drank more than he wanted simply because everyone else was doing so. Although alcohol had contributed to his poise and self-confidence he viewed it as a possible danger. People told him that he drank too much, and he was sufficiently impressed to make a test of his power to restrict his drinking. He was pleased to discover that he could control it, that he was by no means in the grip of alcohol, but there remains a certain conflict between his desire to go along with any crowd and his desire to curtail alcohol "very definitely and, if possible, finally."

Kidd's relationships with men have begun to assume a characteristic pattern more rewarding than the old confused submissiveness. It is his particular pleasure to get them to talk, and he has developed no little skill in the role of encouraging listener. He prefers to make them talk about their work, so that he can learn more about life without entering controversial realms. If political questions come up, he takes part in the discussion, though he doubts whether people are much open to conviction on politics. He finds it difficult to express and support consecutive opinions of his own. His technique of argument consists rather in drawing out the opinions of others and then picking them to pieces. What he likes best, however, came to expression when he was asked to associate to the phrase, *I admire:*

> I admire intelligent people who can talk about their field, most especially if they are in a field involving people. I like to sit down and talk with somebody about their business, question them on it from different points of view and find out anything and everything I can.

Kidd then described a man in his middle thirties, a confirmed alcoholic, whom he sometimes met at the apartment of the "divorced girl."

I never enjoyed talking to anybody so much in my life, in spite of the fact that he was always somewhat under the influence. He was always very intelligent. He knows and understands people, a very effective talker. Nobody else down there liked him too well, but I would invite him in if he walked by the apartment and offer him a drink and then talk to him. He wasn't interested in talking to me too much; he was interested in the liquor and the food. He was a very smart fellow, very enjoyable, worldly-wise. He had been around.

Further light was shed on this type of relationship by his associations to the phrase, *when people meet me:*

I still have a tendency to a very small extent to exhibit some of those traits of embarrassment or feeling of inferiority which plagued me for as long as I can remember . . . I used to be very uneasy, then less and less as time went on, and today I'm probably one-tenth as uneasy as I was.

Asked if he experienced the uneasiness with any particular type of person he said:

People I would probably like to be, probably a well-built, good-looking, clean-cut fellow, very personable and very easy . . . Probably the easier he is with people in general, the uneasier I would feel . . . If he was sympathetic and kindly towards me, then I felt very much easier and could get along with him. But it was lacking probably the traits which I definitely lacked and saw in him that made me uneasy, over-anxious, or something like that.

In these excerpts Kidd makes it clear that he is working on the problem of identification. He wants to be like these admired figures, to have their good looks and masculine self-confidence. The core of his difficulty in their presence lies in the feeling that he compares unfavorably with them. By getting them to relate their exploits and exhibit their "know-how," he possibly feels a certain sharing of their strength, and he is constantly storing up images of how he himself would like to behave in future situations. Kidd's ideal image of himself still has the earmarks of an overcompensation for past inferiorities. In his actual behavior—his willing listening—he seems inclined to settle for vicarious satisfaction rather than copying his models. We know that he has become much more capable of assertion than he used to be, and it is therefore legitimate to assume that his present relationship with men—a compromise between an ideal image and his actual preference for easy-going agreeableness—represents a stage of adjustment that is not incompatible with growth.

PRESENT SITUATION AND PLANS FOR THE FUTURE

Kidd's present life is easy but dull. For the most part, there is little to do in the morning. Almost every day he can sit down after breakfast to read the newspaper, or he can practice golf strokes or do setting-up exercises. He has resumed his piano lessons at a popular studio, and he spends several hours a day at the piano, partly practicing, mostly picking out tunes. His duties as business assistant are often discharged by half-an-hour's work when the mail comes in, though sometimes he shares with Peter the more time-consuming work of preparing floral decorations for an important occasion. He no longer feels under pressure at home, but he gets bored with that small world and generally leaves in the afternoon, taking his evening meal outside in the company of friends.

This routine is by no means satisfactory to him. "I don't like this life," he said, "I don't like it because it's too comfortable a racket. I hope I'll be able to do a day's work when I go out and get another job, which I plan to do in the very near future." He expressed the fear that if he did not get out soon he might never take that step. He does not in the least like the business.

> I think there's just too much sham connected with this business . . . The money is good, the hours are good. Another thing about it is that it calls for no ability and very little initiative, and you accomplish very little. You do a job, you make money. You've got nothing to show for it when the job is done. Your work is thrown away the next day.

He wants to prove that he can work and make his own way rather than living off his father's business, but he has also developed, chiefly through the building of the flower studio, a need to exercise his growing power to deal with people and to have his efforts issue in substantial accomplishments.

At the time of our interviews Kidd had reached a definite decision to leave home within a few weeks. He thought he would start by taking any available job, but as soon as possible he would try to find the kind of thing he really wanted to pursue as a vocation. The thing that appealed to him most was the idea of owning and operating a public golf course. Although capital for the investment was lacking, he knew that certain ventures of this kind had proved profitable, and he liked the idea of building up a golf course into a "big, beautiful place, as much a credit to myself as it would be a money-making enterprise." His visits to golf courses had given him ideas about improvements which he was eager to embody in a course of his own. He was impatient to set forth in search of his vocation, but at the same time he was prey to certain misgivings. Repeatedly in the interviews he returned to the subject, and we could see that it awakened deep conflict.

One element in this conflict is a hesitation to give up the pleasures and comforts that go with his present life. "I would always want to be able to enjoy life," he told us. "If I couldn't be more than a street-sweeper or laborer, where eight hours of your waking day is spent only in making money, I think I would go on the road as a hobo so as to enjoy life." He likes golf, bowling, playing the piano; he would someday "like to take up sketching and probably painting." "Those things are time-consuming," he well knows, "but I hope that I will always have the time." In the hour devoted to free association he discussed his music and golf as follows:

> I want to be able to play the piano well both because I enjoy it and I know what a useful social factor it is. But I do enjoy it myself, I can spend hours alone with it; some people may call it a waste of time, but it's an achievement, something I get my mind occupied with, doing something progressive.

> Golf is the first sport that I . . . first time I remember wanting to do well, to go out of my own way to achieve a knack, a degree of success, and I like the game. I can go out and play it by the hour, by myself, and I also know that it is a good and a useful social medium, and I would like to achieve a certain reputation. I would like to succeed in becoming a good golfer, putting a lot of time in it, and a lot of money in it, and a lot of patience in it. I want to continue that, too.

As business assistant to his father, making a comfortable living by working ten or twelve hours a week, he has plenty of time to pursue these interests. The privileges of his present life thus offer stiff competition to his desire for independent achievement in a vocation of his own.

The difficulty of Kidd's decision was shown in the fact that he talked about it in almost every interview. It also appeared rather plainly in his imaginative productions. Two of his stories in the Thematic Apperception Test dealt symbolically with determinism and freedom, handled in such a way as to suggest that determinism meant the expectations of others, freedom the urges within himself. In both cases freedom was triumphant. One hero, for example, stood on a hill looking back on the foggy, dirty mills from which he had escaped. "He is free from a rigidly patterned, heavily pressured existence, where gradually his daily routine is more and more taken up by what he is required to do; all those demands on his time and physical and mental processes." The source of this imagery would seem to be Kidd's conflict with family ideals: on the one hand, the pressure to spend all his time studying so that he might fulfil parental aspirations; on the other, the freedom he felt with the neighborhood boys before puberty and with his comrades in military service. The mills mean home, school, home-work; the hilltop means escape from the home. Yet in the present situation his images have to be almost reversed. Staying at home guarantees an extraordinary amount of freedom, whereas setting out to find a career carries grave risk of having to go down into the mills and submit to demands on his time and thought.

Equally confusing is the reversal that has taken place with respect to moral degeneration, a theme common in his earlier stories and not absent from the current set. One story, for example, told of a man going down hill to moral abandonment because he chose friends and performed acts "very much against what he had been taught, what he had been given, and what he was capable of." Reacting against these imposed ideals, "he wound up a drunkard, a criminal, and eventually died a very sick and broken man." This is the old familiar theme that we previously guessed to be a reflection of Kidd's inner struggle during the high school and college years, when his urge toward freedom became so entangled with hostile and sexual fantasies that he experienced it as dangerously degenerate. At present, however, the danger of degeneracy lies in remaining at home, where his evening rovings expose him too often to the temptations of alcohol. Kidd's present conflict cannot be solved, it can only be confused, by reviving the imagery of his earlier ones.

The truth of the matter would seem to be that Kidd, belatedly rejecting the pressure of parental aspirations, has begun to develop along two lines and has reached a point where the lines necessarily diverge. He has developed along the line of doing pleasant things, such as music, bowling, and golf, thus restoring contact with his own inclinations and following paths of natural interest. He has also developed along the line of assertiveness, gaining a certain assurance in knowing what he wants and getting what he wants from others. With the latter trait is associated an increased sense of the satisfaction to be derived from accomplishment and the leaving of creditable monuments. The pleasant side of life can best be served by remaining where he is, business assistant in an exceptionally easy and lucrative occupation. The goals of assertion and achievement can only be reached by breaking away, which means taking chances, courting anxieties, and possibly not getting anywhere in the end. Kidd is unwilling to settle for the easier way without at least attempting the steeper path. This is partly because he has tasted the satisfaction of independent effort and achievement. It is partly for another reason: he cannot wholly abandon the hope that he will some day justify his early promise and prove to be the outstanding member of his family. The character of this motive is well displayed in one of his associative sequences. When asked to associate to the phrase, *I secretly,* he responded with a candor that was exceptional even for him:

> I kind of secretly wish to be a renowned success. Probably more renowned than successful; in other words much like a movie star or politician or some other public figure whose reasons for renown aren't very concrete. I wish that perhaps to . . . well, to show the girl that I once loved and who since left me and married somebody else . . . try to make her regret . . . and perhaps to show the people and the public in my past that I am what they thought I was. . . . It's more of a revengeful success rather than a . . . a . . . so that they might say, I'm sorry, I'm sorry for what I did to him or . . . and I probably would like to see them regret very much what they did or what they said.

In this astonishing piece of insight we are shown an added reason for the importance of Kidd's present conflict. No doubt the motive of revengeful success urges him forward; there has been much pain and humiliation which it would be pleasant to assuage. Perhaps this motive also adds to his misgivings: only a quite dramatic success could truly accomplish the purpose. We must bear in mind that this "secret" fantasy of revengeful success is not unconscious. Kidd told us about it. That it holds him in an irrational grip would be a decidedly arbitrary conclusion. It is one of the elements, nevertheless, in a very difficult conflict.

OPINIONS ABOUT PUBLIC EVENTS

When we knew Kidd as an undergraduate, he was not in the least interested in public events. If pressed for an opinion he was likely to respond with a borrowed verbal sentiment which often sounded strangely at odds with his actual behavior. Being at that time rebellious against religion, he nevertheless trotted out with approval all the conventional moral and religious precepts of his parents. He declared himself in favor of severe legal restrictions on the sexual behavior of unmarried people, and he opposed the idea that young people should have a knowledge of contraceptives. His mildly liberal views on the social order gave equal evidence of borrowing. He was clearly still working out his problems in a personal sphere and was unprepared to transform felt values into attitudes on public questions.

When we sought his opinions at the age of twenty-nine, we found them still less clearly formulated than was the case, for example, with Hartley Hale. Kidd continued to exhibit mental traits not highly favorable to building up a consistent political philosophy. Although good at detailed observation, he shied away from general ideas and preferred to operate in a factual, concrete fashion. He did not enjoy being questioned about his views. It was hard, he protested, to come right out cold with what you believed on a subject; he preferred to get the other person talking, reaching his own views in the form of criticisms as the conversation proceeded. Although he regularly read a paper and a weekly news magazine he seemed to have little knowledge that was quickly available for use in discussion.

Kidd's failure to reach consistent opinions was exemplified in his discussion of birth-control. The state ballot in the last election had carried a referendum on this issue, and it was certain that he must have heard many hot arguments, yet his exposition was so full of contradictions that he himself finally admitted: "I haven't formulated any definite ideas on that subject." It became clear that he believed in the right of the Church to take an active stand on birth-control. This enabled him to present several of the Church's arguments with respect to the referendum. What he had not worked out was his own relation to the Church; he therefore could not decide whether he stood ready to defend these arguments. Living at home, he sometimes went to Mass to please his parents, but he did not count himself a good Catholic. "I don't believe in the Church's strictest measures," he said; "I'm one of those guys who thinks that they don't apply to me but they should apply to certain other groups in society." A little later he declared flatly: "I don't believe in the commands of the Catholic Church." Yet his rejection of the Church had not inspired him to formulate an alternative philosophy.

> I don't have many set principles that I live by. I mean I'm not too ethical in any morality or in regard to finances. I think that if I saw the chance to beat somebody for a large amount of money I probably would do it. I think if I found a wallet in the street, I doubt if I would return the money. I certainly believe in living and let live. I mean, I believe in the truth. I wouldn't perjure myself. Right now I wouldn't anyway perjure myself in order to obtain anything. I can't say what I don't mean. I find it a little difficult to sell somebody something which I don't believe in myself, no matter what the game might be.

Neither community activities nor politics hold any appeal for Kidd. "I don't think the average fellow gives a darn about community activities," he said, and he expressed sharp distaste for the community in which he was living. His sole venture into politics consisted of helping the campaign of a man he considered dishonest, a man for whom he refused to vote when it came to marking his own secret ballot. This man held a city position which allowed him to dispense the favor of engaging Mr. Kidd as floral decorator for public banquets, and it thus qualified as good business to support his election campaign. "I've been hanging around politics enough to know it and appreciate it," said Kidd, "and I don't think I like it."

His views on wider political questions seemed to have swung in a conservative direction since the earlier studies. "I've become a staunch Republican," he said; "the Democratic Party in power today has garnered most of its backing from Labor, and is very partial to anything Socialistic." One of his most stable opinions proved to be a violent antipathy toward labor unions, which he perceived as exploiting the economy without performing any genuine services. He was also against business monopolies, and thus emerged as the champion of the small independent business man—the person he would like to become. For the next Republican Party platform he proposed "definitely less government spending, and decrease in the income tax." He would hesitate to cut the Social Security Program even though "many lazy, improvident derelicts" benefited by its provisions, but otherwise he favored the smallest possible government interference with free individual enterprise. In the international sphere he perceived Communism as the outstanding evil. He had once read a Communist book and found some of the doctrine appealing, but he felt that this doctrine was now being used as a cynical cover for power politics. Recognizing the need for "more teeth" in the United Nations, he balked at the thought of our surrendering more sovereignty. He also rejected the idea of building up India, a course which could only result in competition for markets and a lowering of our standards of living.

In his opinions Kidd thus stood a little to the right of Hartley Hale. His political views were heavily dominated by an imagery of exploitation. The groups he opposed were always characterized as exploiting the average citizen, the small independent business man, for the sake of profit and power. Why has Kidd been so impressed by this particular image? Why does he tolerate so readily his own exploitative tendencies? We could hazard the beginnings of an answer by pointing out that he certainly felt exploited by his parents' aspirations. These aspirations, however, carry us at once into the social setting of the Kidd family and thus back to the shaping of lives by social forces. Before we leave Joseph Kidd it will be instructive to compare him with Hartley Hale, especially with respect to these forces.

COMPARISON WITH HARTLEY HALE

We have studied the lives of two men who are products of the American culture. Both have been exposed to the same overall influences, such as the emphasis on competitive success and the faith in material progress through individual enterprise. If we were comparing these two men with the Chinese, for example, we would certainly find them more American than Chinese, and we would probably be impressed by similarities between them. They are alike in their basic faith in individual enterprise, their materialism, their rejection of ancient religious dogma, their lack of respect for the wisdom of the elders. Even in their attitudes toward women they are more like each other than they are like the Chinese. But the moment we try to compare them as individuals we are obliged to sharpen our analysis and look for the specific pattern of cultural influences that came to bear on each man. It is only in the most general sense that Hale and Kidd grew up in the same culture. The worlds of their childhood were actually very different.

It is probably of small importance that Hale was brought up in a medium-sized midwestern city and Kidd in a large eastern city. The significant differences lie rather in social status and in the ideals and values that prevailed in family and neighborhood. Kidd grew up in a neighborhood of Irish Catholics most of whom were not more than a generation removed from peasant life in the old country. His own parents were typical: the mother an immigrant, the father a child of immigrants. The neighborhood was not a disorganized one, by no means a slum, but it was more self-contained and less oriented toward upward mobility than would be the case in the average middle-class community. The ambitions that prevailed in the Kidd family thus set them off from their neighbors; not one family in a hundred tried to send its children to college. Kidd described, almost in traditional stereotypes, the "lazy Irish" of his neighborhood, the women gossiping over their tea, the men content with a day's pay and a corncob pipe. Cohesiveness was provided by the common ethnic background, the common religion, and the fact of a virtual control of local politics. Everyone had a friend in the city government, and everyone expected that the bonds of friendship would be cemented by financial favors. Kidd's father by no means held himself aloof from this kind of activity. The outspoken theme of exploitation and easy money in Kidd's philosophy was not a personal invention. It came straight from that segment of the culture in which he was reared.

Kidd grew up in a more crowded neighborhood than that inhabited by the Hales. The space for play was limited to streets and playgrounds. The emphasis of his early training was social. At home or in the streets he was surrounded by children, doing things in groups, with the accent on what all could do—sports and mischief—rather than on the patient mastery of individual skills. One of Hale's outstanding characteristics was his interest in mechanical objects and his urge to master and construct them. For all we know, Kidd may have had nascent proclivities in the same direction, but they certainly received a minimum of encouragement. His parents could provide few toys and materials for making things, his brothers were always ready to invade his privacy, his friends constantly pulled toward group activity, and his schools placed no emphasis on practical constructiveness. Hale built radios; Kidd merely listened to them. Social and economic circumstances encouraged this difference, whatever other roots it may have had.

The effect of differences in social status can best be brought out by considering the reasons for the presence of Kidd and Hale at Harvard College. For Hale, going to a well-known college meant doing the same thing that his scholarly father had done. It meant going to a place where he could advantageously study some of the things in which he had become greatly interested. It soon came to mean a pathway to the profession he independently chose for himself. It was also his temporary home and social world, and it was a world in which he had no special reason to feel out of place. Very different was the situation of the young man from Worcester, who came to Harvard because his parents wanted him to rise in the social world. Going to college meant doing something that his father had never done, that neither of his parents understood, and that appealed to no spontaneous scholastic interests in himself. It meant continuing an obligation which had already proved miserably irksome. When he was at home he felt estranged from the young men of the neighborhood. He was supposed to sit studying while his father wandered off for an evening of companionship and singing. He was almost equally estranged from his college companions, whom he saw for the most part only between classes during the day. Hale's adjustment to college life was not automatic; he worked hard to make his way. But he did not have to bridge such yawning chasms as lay in Kidd's path. The mental indolence and rigidity of Kidd's home provided no preparation for the intellectual side of college, while for its social side the street-corner life of an Irish neighborhood in Worcester gave him anything but the proper schooling.

When we turn from social status to occupational role, we are again confronted by highly significant differences. Hale and Kidd were both premedical students when we first made their acquaintance, but they were already being differently shaped by their anticipated occupations. Hale had a clear conception of the doctor's life. He wanted to get there, he expected it to be exciting and re-warding, and he found the intervening steps, especially his work in biology, fascinating in their own right. He submitted willingly to the discipline of difficult courses and of research, organizing his life so that he could build firmly these foundations for his future. Of Kidd we may say that he perhaps never really wanted to be a doc-tor; certainly he found little but frustration in the studies that would have carried him toward that goal. His life was not organized by his anticipated profession; it was, rather, disorganized by his un-derlying rebellion against the parental pressure which included that profession. This rebellion continued to haunt him in the Army, where he "tried to fail" in the military hierarchy, a striking contrast to Hale's zestful rise in the medical hierarchy. If Hale's case taught us much about the shaping effect of an occupational role, Kidd shows us what can happen when such a role is deeply uncon-genial.

Some of the outstanding differences between the two men today spring from the fact that Kidd does not yet have a stable occupa-tional role. Most people would probably agree that Hale is more mature than Kidd, but what does such a statement mean when ap-plied to men of thirty? Maturity is achieved by living, and for most men of thirty the pattern of living is strongly influenced by the roles of husband, father, and member of an occupation. Hale has had a lot to grow on. Kidd, in contrast, not having succeeded in the choice of a wife or of an occupation, has remained in the somewhat amorphous state more characteristic of the early twenties, and has simply not made the crucial commitments that challenge maturity and stimulate its increase. Hale finds happiness in the pursuit of his profession. He sees the meaning of his life in the services he can render as a doctor and in the knowledge he can discover by scien-tific research. Kidd still does not know what his life is going to mean or where he is going to find enduring happiness. If we want to call Kidd less mature, we should bear in mind that we are making a very complex statement that includes the situation as well as the person. Maturity is not a simple quality.

The contrasts between Hale and Kidd are much illuminated by considering the differences in the social forces which have shaped their lives. It is evident, however, that we cannot explain every-thing in this way. Their personal histories show an intricate series of differences which do not depend entirely on social forces. Furthermore, they are not alike with respect to appearance, physique, temperament, intelligence, or special skills, and some of these differences may be based on natural endowment. With two fully studied cases for comparison, we are in a good position to investigate current thinking about the biological roots of personality.

6. The Biological Roots of Personality

> Our theme is Nature and man as part of Nature.
>   C. S. SHERRINGTON

Up to this point we have made no attempt to relate the study of lives to any basic theory of behavior. We have considered our cases as people rather than as organisms, which means that we have studied them in the complexities of everyday human life without trying to reduce their behavior to fundamental mechanisms. In this chapter it will be our purpose to bring personality into line with the *biological view of man*. We tried in the fourth chapter to see what could be learned from the social sciences; here we shall examine some of the leading ideas that come from research in biology and physiological psychology. The first impression will probably be that we have jumped to an entirely different realm of discourse. We were talking about lives; now we suddenly shift to the elementary mechanisms of behavior, abstracted from all those personal patterns which characterize human beings as we know them in daily life. If the climate seems to change, however, it is all the more important to trace the route by which the two realms are connected. Basic mechanisms somehow produce the behavior of physicians or business men, and it is one of our most vital tasks to understand how such things come about.

Central to any fundamental theory of behavior are the concepts of drive and of learning. The first concept is used for the active or energetic characteristics of an organism, the second for its plasticity in meeting the environment. These concepts carry us straight into the question of innate endowment. Individual variations in the strength of different drives suggest themselves as possible roots for later differences in motive and purpose. Learning implies a capacity to learn, and differences in this capacity seem to be strongly related to inborn endowment. The biological view of man thus requires us to think about the essential structure and equipment with which each individual embarks upon his career of learning. It bids us consider that individuality arises not only from a unique history but also from the starting attributes of the person who lives that history. And when we take this point of view we cannot arbitrarily stop with drives and the capacity to learn. Other qualities, such as energy-level, mood, and temperament, play an important part in human life and require consideration as possible elements in natural endowment.

THE PROBLEM OF INNATE ENDOWMENTS

It is a misfortune that the discussion of endowments has often strayed from the open fields of science and lost itself in the brambles of politics. Human nature has been made the scapegoat for many a program of exploitation. A martial instinct has been invented by those who wanted war. Competition and the profit motive have been declared inescapable human traits by the interested advocates of a cut-throat economy. The inherent stupidity of the average man has been used to justify seizure of power by dictators and cheap propaganda by demagogues. Innate racial inferiorities have been invoked to cloak political oppression and economic discrimination. In the nature-nurture controversy there has been a tendency for nature to keep bad company, while nurture has more often walked with those whose sentiments were humanitarian, democratic, and optimistic. The misuse of ideas about heredity has sometimes been so fantastic and savage that it is hard not to reject the whole notion with angry contempt, taking one's stand for a purely environmental theory and raising the flag for a doctrine of absolute innate equality.

It is our business here to draw the nature-nurture controversy firmly back into the realm of scientific discussion, where the taking of stands and raising of flags give precedence to a careful scrutiny of the facts. Our task is to examine the evidence for the existence of innate variations. The true humanitarian spirit need have no anxiety over the outcome of such an investigation. On the contrary, it will welcome the facts, whatever they may be; for if such variations really exist, it is neither wise nor kind to disregard them. If there are real differences of intellectual ability, for example, it would be both wasteful and cruel to force everyone to the same level of achievement, relentlessly pushing the poorly endowed

while holding back the better endowed. If differences in temperament have a true innate basis, it would be dictatorial to expect
everyone to develop along the same lines. The democratic ideal is
in no sense violated by a finding that people are not born in all
respects equally endowed. A democratic society is better equipped
than any other form of social organization to maintain respect for
the individual, to help each member make the most of his endowments, to provide scope for different patterns of life, and thus to
make beneficent and constructive use of human variation.

From what is known today about the mechanisms of heredity we
would expect to find each individual uniquely endowed. When
the germ cells of two parents unite, only a part of each parent's
potentialities can be utilized in forming the new individual. The
forty-eight chromosomes initially contained in each germ cell become reduced by half, so that the new life receives only twenty-four
from each side of the family. The selection depends on biochemical
conditions still refractory to research and probably very complex
in character. There is scarcely a chance, however, that the resulting
individual will be precisely like any individual who has ever before
existed. The mechanism of heredity provides for a reshuffling of
genes on each new occasion, and thus creates a degree of novelty
every time a new life is begun. Two children of the same parents are apt to be more alike than two children of different parents,
but they are never quite alike and often seem remarkably different even from the moment of birth. The babies in a maternity
ward might be taken to the wrong mother if an inattentive nurse
shuffled the tags, but they would rarely be mixed because of a difficulty in telling them apart. Only identical twins enjoy the distinction of being hard to tell apart.

The ubiquity of individual variation is increased by the complex
way in which genes are related to discernible traits. There are but
few instances in which a unitary trait is determined by a single gene
and transmitted predictably according to the Mendelian principles
of dominance and recessiveness. Most of these traits, moreover, are
too restricted in character, like eye color, to be of major significance
in the study of personality. More typically, observable traits are determined by many genes in a fashion too complex to be unraveled.
This seems to be true, for instance, of certain traits in animals
which have been sharpened by selective breeding. Representative of
such experiments is that of Tryon, who selected the faster-learning

and slower-learning rats in a maze experiment and bred them in separate strains until he had produced two very different groups of "bright" and "dull" rats.[1] Similar experiments have produced breeds of active and passive rats, jittery and placid rats, wild and tame mice, friendly and shy dogs.[2] Such studies constitute impressive evidence for the importance of heredity, but they do not indicate much likelihood that the traits in question are determined by single genes. Before the selective breeding begins, differences are more or less normally distributed among the animals, and several generations of inbreeding are necessary to produce sharply differentiated groups. According to Murphy, "this means not a single gene, acting on an all-or-none basis, but a multiplicity of genes. Very few single-gene factors related to personality have been found."[3] Traits such as activity and passivity look elementary to an outside observer, but in the gene world they are the outcome of a highly complex interaction.

The mechanisms of heredity thus seem designed to produce unique individuals. Each person has his own profile of variations, some small and some great, from general averages. The next thing we would like to know is the precise nature and extent of these variations. Are they important enough to influence the course of individual development and to limit significantly the impact of environmental forces? Aware as we are today of the vast importance of learning, sensitized as we are to the subtle influence of psychodynamic processes and of social forces, we have to approach this question with a wholly new sophistication. We have to search for native endowments and interpret their possible influence without sacrificing what we know about the multitudinous effects of learning. The gap between an innate trait and an attribute of the adult personality cannot possibly be bridged by a verbal gossamer thread of direct cause-and-effect. What is required is a solidly supported conceptualization which can specify the effects of any general trait on the lifelong process of learning. If innate peculiarities are important, it

[1] Tryon, R. C. Genetic Differences in Maze Learning Ability in Rats, *Yearbook of the National Society for Studies in Education*, 1940, vol. 39, pp. 111-119.

[2] These experiments and their genetic meaning are discussed by Murphy, G., *Personality: A Biosocial Approach to Origins and Structure*, New York, Harper & Bros., 1947, pp. 57-62; and by Cattell, R. B., *Personality: A Systematic Theoretical and Factual Study*, New York, McGraw-Hill Book Co., 1950, pp. 139-141.

[3] Murphy, *op. cit.*, p. 58.

is because they consistently color the individual's responses to his environment and thus produce significant slants in his life history. The understanding of such effects can start from no better point than the study of individual lives.

TEMPERAMENTAL TRAITS

The word *temperament* refers roughly to qualities of a quite general nature which manifest themselves in many aspects of behavior. Three customary meanings are distinguished by MacKinnon: (1) characteristic emotional experiences (strength, depth, and speed of emotional arousal, changes of mood, etc.); (2) assumed physiological bases for such experiences (glandular differences, for example); and (3) kinetic characteristics (energy and control of motor responses, expressive movements, etc.).[4] It seems a reasonable assumption that emotional and kinetic traits are correlated with qualities of the nervous system and with the biochemistry of the internal environment within which that system operates. Certainly the relationship is clear enough in extreme cases of glandular disorder. Excessive thyroid activity, for instance, is associated with high-strung and overactive behavior, while thyroid deficiency produces a dull and apathetic state. When thyroid deficiency is compensated by artificial preparations, there is often a fairly prompt change in the direction of contentment and alertness. Such examples give reason to suppose that the secrets of temperament lie hidden in the biochemistry of bodily tissues.

This is a realm in which it is easy for secrets to remain hidden. There are hundreds of ways in which biochemical processes and their products might be measured, but we badly lack insight into the patterning of these processes, into their effect on the functioning of nervous tissue, hence into their possible relation to significant basic traits. It is well-nigh impossible at present to select the right physiological variables for an understanding of temperament. Some progress has recently been made with respect to the autonomic nervous system, which is closely related to emotional experience. Measures of pulse, blood pressure, respiration patterns, salivation rate, and other autonomic functions show that siblings are less alike than identical twins but more alike than unrelated children,

---

[4] MacKinnon, D. W., The Structure of Personality, Ch. 1 in Hunt, J. McV. (ed.), *Personality and the Behavior Disorders,* New York, The Ronald Press Co., 1944, Vol. 1, pp. 8-9.

thus suggesting a sort of "autonomic constitution" which is at least partially inherited.[5] Considerable study has been devoted to the balance of activity between the sympathetic and parasympathetic divisions of the autonomic system, a balance which seems to differ with some consistency from one individual to another.[6] Promising as are these leads, however, we are still a long way from being able to pin down the physiological dimensions most likely to be important in the development of personality.

The whole problem can be approached in the opposite direction, so to speak, by looking for consistent differences in behavior, postponing for later study the correlation of these differences with bodily conditions. A formidable difficulty in this approach lies in distinguishing between innate consistencies and those produced by a consistent environment. The studies of development made over many years by Gesell and his associates, for instance, certainly suggest individual consistency with respect to energy output, social responsiveness, talkativeness, and a variety of other traits, yet in certain children these traits changed a good deal, and it was never possible to disentangle innate and environmental elements with satisfactory finality.[7] More crucial are continuous studies of children starting from the time of birth. This method has revealed highly consistent early differences in such traits as activity level and the tendency to smile and laugh.[8] Yet again we find ourselves confronted by promising leads without any real decisions as to the clustering of the differences.

Physique and Temperament.—It is impossible here for us to make an exhaustive survey. Instead we shall concentrate on one particular problem which happens to lead us to hypotheses that can be examined in the cases of Hartley Hale and Joseph Kidd. It has long been observed that the majority of mentally sick people--

[5] Jost, H., & Sontag, L. W., The Genetic Factor in Autonomic Nervous System Function, *Psychosomatic Medicine*, 1944, Vol. 6, pp. 308-310.

[6] Darling, R. B. Autonomic Action in Relation to Personality Traits of Children, *Journal of Abnormal and Social Psychology*, 1940, Vol. 35, pp. 246-260; see also Cattell, R., *op. cit.*, pp. 277-282.

[7] See especially Gesell, A., et al., *Biographies of Child Development*, New York, Paul B. Hoeber, 1939, which includes reports of carefully studied infants who were examined again in adolescence.

[8] Shirley, M. *The First Two Years: A Study of Twenty-Five Babies*, Minneapolis, University of Minnesota Press, 1933, Vol. 3; Washburn, R. W., A Study of the Smiling and Laughing of Infants in the First Year of Life, *Genetic Psychology Monographs*, 1929, Vol. 6, pp. 397-537.

though by no means all—fall into the two categories of schizophrenia and manic-depressive (or "cyclical") psychosis. The schizophrenic syndrome seems to be most generally characterized by a lack of mental and affective contact with other people, so that intellectual processes become disorderly and fantastic while emotions appear curiously inappropriate. Manic-depressive patients, in contrast, seem to be drawn from the ranks of highly sociable people, and come to grief rather through powerful dislocations of mood, ranging in the extreme cases from wildly buoyant hilarity to deep self-reproachful despair. That something more than unfortunate life circumstances is involved in these two mental disorders first came to light in evidence that they tend to run in families, evidence which continues to multiply and which cannot be wholly explained away by environmental conditions.[9] Then came the important observation by Kretschmer that schizophrenic patients tend to be of rather slender and fragile physique while manic-depressive patients are mostly of solid and well-rounded build.[10] Similar specimens of physique are found, of course, among healthy people, but Kretschmer speculated that the slender, fragile healthy people would exhibit *schizothymic* traits (shyness, sensitivity, independence, etc.) while the well-rounded ones would show a *cyclothymic* pattern (gregarious, open, but subject to ups-and-downs of mood), and he presented a series of impressionistic studies in support of this contention. The association he claimed between mental-disease type and body form seems to have been roughly confirmed by further research, but his wider propositions about physique and personality remain in a controversial stage.[11] Nevertheless, Cattell showed, through factor analysis of personality ratings, that a substantial fraction of the individual differences among college students could be attributed to an underlying variable ranging from schizothymia to cyclothymia.[12] Whatever its relation to a constitutional basis, this particular dimension seems to be very important in describing the differences in human behavior.

[9] Thorpe, L. P. & Katz, B., *The Psychology of Abnormal Behavior,* New York, The Ronald Press Co., 1948, ch. 6.

[10] Kretschmer, E., *Physique and Character,* trans. by W. J. H. Sprott, London, Kegan Paul, 1925, Ch. 2.

[11] Klineberg, O., Asch, S. E., & Block, H., An Experimental Study of Constitutional Types, *Genetic Psychology Monographs,* 1934, Vol. 16, pp. 145-221.

[12] Cattell, R. B., *Personality, op. cit.,* esp. pp. 56-59.

The possible relation between physique and temperamental qualities has been pursued further in a long series of studies by Sheldon.[13] Using exact measurements of body build made from standard photographs, Sheldon reached the conclusion that there are three main components of physique: the soft and round (endomorphy), the square and strong (mesomorphy), and the slim and light (ectomorphy). Each individual physique is a combination of these three components, but the proportions may differ greatly. To investigate temperament Sheldon used extensive individual interviews designed to bring out consistent preferences and peculiarities along such lines as posture and movement, exercise, relaxation, eating and sleeping habits, reactions to stress and to alcohol, adventurousness, sensitivity and general attitude toward other people. The findings again lent themselves to an hypothesis of three components. These seemed to be closely correlated with the components of physique, and Sheldon accordingly called them *viscerotonia, somatotonia,* and *cerebrotonia.* When *endomorphy* predominates in the physique, the digestive viscera are massive relative to other structures, and the body form is softly rounded, though not necessarily fat; with this goes the viscerotonic syndrome which includes relaxation, love of comfort, conviviality, and sociability. In predominant *mesomorphy* the somatic structures—bone, muscle, and connective tissue— have the first place, the body being firm, strong, and somewhat rectangular in outline; with this goes *somatotonia,* characterized by vigorous assertiveness, a preference for action, and a dominating but somewhat insensitive attitude toward other people. When *ectomorphy* predominates, the body is fragile, linear, and delicate in structure, the arms and hands, for instance, being slender and poorly muscled and the chest rather flat; with this goes *cerebrotonia,* of which the marks are tenseness, overvigilance, sensitiveness, a tendency for action to be inhibited, and a certain ineptitude in social situations.

Sheldon's evidence for these relationships was fairly strong, though not absolutely conclusive, and further research has tended to give

[13] A brief account of this work is given by Sheldon in Hunt, J. McV., *Personality and the Behavior Disorders, op. cit.,* Vol. 1, Ch. 17. The original references are Sheldon, W. H., Stevens, S. S., & Tucker, W. B., *The Varieties of Human Physique,* New York, Harper & Bros., 1940, and Sheldon, W. H., & Stevens, S. S., *The Varieties of Temperament,* New York, Harper & Bros., 1942.

them support.[14] One would expect in any event to find correlations between physique and some of the traits which Sheldon calls temperamental: between soft roundedness and love of comfort, for instance, or between powerful musculature and a delight in exercise and activity. The challenging part of his theory lies in the claim that bodily constitution is an effective determinant of consistent individual differences in such traits as assertiveness, self-confidence, sensitivity, attitudes toward people, and even the preferred philosophy of life. These are qualities upon which the environment obviously makes a tremendous impact. Temperamental endowments must indeed be important if they can leave a consistent imprint on characteristics so open to learning.

We must be careful to bear in mind the difficulty of demonstrating an innate factor under such circumstances. If the relation between mesomorphic physique and social assertiveness, for example, is really an innate one, this must be because of a central determinant which contributes both to a strong development of somatic structures and to an energetic functioning, let us say, of the nervous system. But we cannot assume that physique and social assertiveness are related only through this innate central factor. Our measure of their relation cannot be a pure measure of something innate. This is because physique enters into the development of personality by another route, that of the responses which other people make to it. For boys growing up in American high schools, the possession of an athletic physique is a great social asset. It opens avenues to the distinction that comes from athletic success, and it forms an important element in popularity with girls. A correlation between mesomorphy and social assertiveness, therefore, does not constitute conclusive evidence that the social behavior is linked to an innate trait. It might be merely the cumulative consequence of success and popularity. One must admit, however, that the claimed correlation between soft rounded people and sociability, or between slender fragile people and social aloofness, cannot so readily be attributed to life experiences.

Application to Cases.—Let us now see what sense can be made of

[14] Seltzer, C. C., Wells, F. L., & McTerman, E. B., A Relationship Between Sheldonian Somatotype and Psychotype, *Journal of Personality*, 1948, Vol. 16, pp. 431-436; Morris, C., in Kluckhohn, C., & Murray, H. A., eds., *Personality in Nature, Society, and Culture*, New York, Alfred A. Knopf, 1948, Ch. 11.

this puzzling problem by turning to the two young men whose lives we have already studied. Sheldon's measures of the components of physique are expressed on a 7-point scale in which 1 represents the weakest possible development of the component, 4 an average amount, and 7 the strongest possible development; the resulting three scores are called the *somatotype*. Hartley Hale's somatotype is 2-5-3½ (2 in endomorphy, 5 in mesomorphy, 3½ in ectomorphy); Joseph Kidd's is 4-5-1½. From the fact that both are most strongly endowed with the mesomorphic component we would expect, according to Sheldon's findings, a considerable similarity of temperamental traits, but Kidd's greater strength of the soft rounded component and decided lack of the slender fragile tendency would be expected to produce differences. Both men should be predominantly active, energetic, and assertive, but Kidd's display of these qualities should be tempered by a certain easy-going amiability and pleasure in human contact, while Hale's energy should be more nervously restless and intense. To what extent do the two men in actual fact fulfil these expectations?

In Hale's case there is very little departure from the expected pattern. He is indeed energetic, favors activity, and flawlessly fits several other traits listed by Sheldon as defining somatotonia: love of risk and chance, bold directness of manner, physical courage for combat, competitive aggressiveness, need for action when troubled. He also displays a good deal of the love for domination and power, the freedom from squeamishness, and the insensitivity to the feelings of others which constitute further items in the temperament scale. In short, Hale behaves in a manner that could be pretty well predicted from his somatotype, according to the findings of Sheldon's research. We have seen, however, that precisely in such cases the social aspects of the behavior, at least, might well result not from a temperamental proclivity but from the flattering social rewards yielded by a good physique and athletic success. Certainly Hale's physique was a crucial item in the dramatic "backbone incident," which set him on his way to self-confidence in physical competition. From this point onward he "grew stronger," as he himself put it, winning respect as a neighborhood athlete, finding bold friends whose example helped him conquer his anxieties, strengthening his social confidence by alliance with an ever-widening circle of acquaintances. Without athletic prowess he would probably not have become the most popular member of his high school class.

Hale's physique is thus clearly related to his social assertiveness through direct channels of learning.

There has been much glibness in attributing behavior to innate endowments, but we must at this point beware of an equal glibness in setting it all down to learning. If temperamental traits made a contribution to Hale's development, we would expect this contribution to show itself in the form of certain far-reaching consistencies in behavior. Analyzing Hale's career from this point of view, we discover that he has repeatedly shown a cluster of traits consisting of *high activity level, zestful interest,* and *power to control disruptive emotions.* The first two traits contributed to his social success, particularly in high school where his activities as an editor, stage manager, and general entertainer were at least as important as his athletic prowess. The trait of control appeared consistently throughout the stressful events of his life. In the "backbone incident" he learned not only that he could win a fight but also that he could force himself back to the battleground, preserve a brave front, "bore in with verve," use his fists effectively; in short, that he could control the inroads of anxiety. Earlier he had managed to control the guilt feelings that marked his rebellion against maternal interference. Later he was able to overcome his fears of moths and of water. He controlled the emotions engendered by parental quarrels without becoming a model child. Almost always he controlled his anxiety before athletic contests and turned in a first-rate performance. Today he can control intense anxiety when a difficult piece of surgery threatens to go wrong, continuing to work with fine motor coordination and mental alertness. Hale is a man who does not easily go to pieces; neither motor nor mental control is readily disrupted by emotional stress.

The traits of high activity, zestful interest, and control of disruptive emotions are not manifested by Hale merely in social situations. They show themselves equally in his dealings with the material environment: his photographic laboratory, his apparatus, the absorbing problems of his research. He seems to have shown them early in life, though time has strengthened especially his power of control. These are traits of a quite general character, the sort of thing we might hope to relate ultimately to properties of nervous tissue and its biochemical environment. Perhaps they, or something like them, form the real core of the larger cluster of twenty traits which Sheldon uses to define somatotonia. At all events it is not hard to see how they might extend their influence into a person's social behavior if the environment did not respond in a manner too discouraging. High activity would usually result in greater frequency of social contacts, a wider range of acquaintances, and more dominant behavior in face-to-face situations. Zestful interest would make the person more interesting to others, more colorful and stimulating as a companion. The power to function effectively under stress, to be "on the ball" in competitive situations, would favor the building up of a history of successes very beneficial to self-confidence. The traits in question must be regarded, of course, simply as proclivities which favor but do not determine a certain pattern of social development; as Murphy expresses it, they "have no clear destiny of their own." [15] In Hale's case the favored pattern became an actuality.

When we turn to Joseph Kidd we find a very different situation. Our search for possible temperamental consistencies must here take account of the fact that the whole coloring of his behavior changed between early childhood and adolescence. In adult life his level of activity has been moderate, his zest low, his interests restricted, his control of disruptive emotions not sufficient to give him much peace of mind. Yet in elementary school, before he began to feel the effects of his unfortunate double promotion, he could disturb the classroom by wild behavior, and with his playmates he was often ready to show himself a capable fighter, a notorious vandal, and a leader in adventurous enterprises. Kidd seems to have displayed in these early years a pattern of traits not unlike Hartley Hale's, a pattern that roughly fits the concept of somatotonia and that is therefore consistent with Sheldon's views concerning the mesomorphic component of physique. But this pattern did not survive the miserable social situations and emotional problems in which Kidd became involved during later childhood and early adolescence. Today he can be called somatotonic only with respect to his love of exercise, his eating habits, and certain other traits very directly related to bodily constitution. No imprint of somatotonic traits can be discerned in his unassertive human relationships, his shunning of power and leadership, his continuing uneasiness in the presence of people. The assertiveness of his early years failed to color the ultimate course of his social development.

Further search for temperamental consistencies in Kidd's behavior

[15] Murphy, *op. cit.*, p. 54.

is hampered by the almost exclusively social character of his interests and his problems. We have to search in the very spot where his social history has left an overwhelming imprint. The strongest thread of consistency seems to be a certain passivity in human relationships. Kidd seems generally ready to let the other person fix the character of the relationship. He does not usually try to dominate the situation and make of it what he wants; rather, he hopes that the other person will create a pleasant relationship. And he can easily become miserable when, as in the case of Mildred, this hope is not fulfilled. Counteracting this tendency and learning to get what he wants from other people has been for Kidd a belated and difficult development. But does this consistency yield evidence for a temperamental endowment of passivity? Was there in Kidd's refusal of leadership a kind of biological protest against a social role for which he felt temperamentally unsuited? It is a pity that we can only ask this question, not answer it, because a sound understanding of such problems would be immensely useful in vocational guidance. Inasmuch as Kidd has moderate strength in the endomorphic component of physique, and displays quite a number of viscerotonic traits, it would be possible to make a case for some temperamental passivity, though we would certainly have to admit that the environment had subdued somatotonia and over-developed a secondary endowment. Such an assumption, however, is scarcely compelling in view of the evidence that social situations became linked with anxiety, a linkage which could well paralyze any form of social assertiveness. Perhaps Kidd is inherently more passive than we would guess from his physical endowment or judge from his early behavior, but the weight of evidence seems to lie with an environmental explanation.

Better understanding of temperamental traits calls for more careful analysis of their nature. It also calls for substantial progress in anchoring them to biochemical and neurological variations. Only when such progress has been made will it be possible to assess the suitability of somatotypes as measures of temperamental traits. Our two case studies do not help us in solving this problem, which obviously requires a large scale investigation. They do acquaint us, however, with the kind of individual study which must be made of every case if temperamental differences are to be properly discerned amid the effects of experience. It is not enough to make a cross-section of current behavior, a profile of present traits. One must view the person in the perspective of his life history, finding out, if possible, what he started out to be like in early life, searching for enduring consistencies, and seeking to grasp the effects of learning throughout the whole course of his development.

ABILITIES

Intelligence.—Of all human abilities intelligence is the most carefully studied. Unlike temperamental traits, which are essentially diffuse in their effects, intelligence can be brought to a focus in problem situations and subjected to fairly precise measurement. The measuring of intelligence has been a major concern of psychology ever since the publication of Binet's first scale in 1905. Mental tests were originally devised to sort out school children who could not keep up with their classes. It was an obvious step from this to the sorting out of both duller and brighter men in military selection and assignment. The Army group tests, developed in the United States during World War I and given to more than two million men, provided tremendous impetus for the further study of intelligence. At first it was supposed that intelligence was a unitary trait, so that a person could be assigned an overall score without further remark about individual peculiarities. Now it has become routine procedure for examiners to report the qualitative characteristics of each person's performance as well as the overall score. Each person uses his mind in a somewhat individual fashion. Why he does so sets a challenging problem for the student of lives.

The measurement of intelligence yields a very wide range of individual differences. To a limited extent these differences depend upon environmental influence. It is not easy to free intelligence tests from cultural influences and specific effects of schooling. Neglect of this fact has sometimes led to unjustified conclusions about differences between ethnic groups or between social classes. Allowance must also be made for motivation with respect to tests and for the disruption of performance by anxiety. There is, nevertheless, an overwhelming weight of evidence that individual differences in intelligence spring largely from innate endowment. On the whole there is little change in a person's overall test performances even when measurement is repeated after a great many years. Age may bring wisdom; it may bring seasoned judgment, habits of disciplined thinking, and an impressive accumulation of knowledge; but it does not, after some point between the fifteenth and twentieth years, produce an increase in the efficiency of basic mental operations. Investigations designed to increase the intelligence ratings of children through special teaching or through exposure to a stimulating environment do in fact show an increase, but it is never a large one. Identical twins reared in contrasting environments remain remarkably similar in intellectual performance. Attempts to raise the attainments of mentally retarded children suggest only that one is pushing against inexorable upper limits of endowment. There are undoubtedly many things that prevent full use of innate intelligence, but genetic endowment is primarily responsible for existing individual differences.

We have still no clue as to the neurological conditions with which intelligence is correlated. In cases of severe retardation there is sometimes a real deficiency of brain tissue and a greater simplicity of cortical structure. Brain injury in the course of life sometimes produces a significant reduction of mental capacity. Certain biochemical disorders, such as thyroid deficiency, may slow down mental functioning, but if the disorders are corrected the original mental level is promptly restored. Certain drugs have produced a marked improvement in mentally dull children, but the effect peters out after a few months and does not constitute a lasting major change. Beyond these very general evidences that the brain must be structurally sound and must have a favorable biochemical environment, we know nothing about the neurological determinants of difference. We have no idea what it could be that differentiates the brain of a person with an I.Q. of 140 from that of a person with an I.Q. of 110. We can measure performance, but we cannot measure its biological roots.

It is interesting to compare people of more or less equal intelligence and to notice how differently they use their minds. Some people do picture puzzles with effortless speed, while others simply do not seem to see the shapes that will fit together. Many a gifted mental worker cannot replace a burned-out fuse or drive a car with real skill. Sometimes a person who readily grasps the complexities of party government will balk at fairly simple arithmetic, while an expert in mathematical physics will lapse into confusion when confronted by political issues. Obviously interest and training have a lot to do with these qualitative differences, but it would be arbitrary to assume that they have no innate basis. In point of fact it now seems probable that intelligence is not a completely unitary trait. There may be a general factor of efficiency, but in all likelihood there are also several more special components in which, as in the components of physique, each person is differentially endowed. It is repeatedly found, for example, that some people score much higher, others much lower, in the *verbal* part of an intelligence test as compared with the *performance* part. There is a similar tendency toward independent variation between the *verbal* items and the *numerical* items.

Factor analysis of extensive test batteries has suggested a number of primary abilities which in different proportions make up each individual's endowment.[16] It is thus probable that the slanting of one person's interest toward mathematics, another's toward literature, another's toward architecture, and so forth, results in some measure from innate proclivities. In cases of unhappy vocational adjustment one often gets the impression that external considerations, such as entering the family business or aiming for an uncrowded vocation, have worked at odds with strong innate proclivities. There are many young people who have responded to the appeal of a career in medicine only to find that their minds, excellent in other directions, fumbled hopelessly with the peculiar intricacies of organic chemistry.

Individual Patterns of Intelligence.—Our understanding of these problems can be deepened by again consulting Hartley Hale and Joseph Kidd. Both men were given the Wechsler-Bellevue Adult Intelligence Test; Hale's I.Q. was 130, Kidd's 118. Closer inspection shows that Hale's advantage was largely in the performance part of the scale. His I.Q. on performance subtests was 126, compared to Kidd's 107, whereas his I.Q. on verbal items was 133, as against Kidd's 126. It is interesting to note that Hale's near equality between verbal and performance scores is more typical of engineers than of medical men, who on the average display a greater verbal predominance. He is, of course, something of an engineer—his attic workshop and his research testify to that—and he cares little for psychiatry with its predominantly verbal tools. His total score, however, is not out of line with his successful academic career and with his marked attainments in his profession. The Wechsler-Bellevue Test has been found to yield lower scores than other tests at the upper levels of intelligence. Hale's score places him in the

---

[16] For a brief discussion of these problems see Stoddard, G. D., *The Meaning of Intelligence,* New York, The Macmillan Co., 1943, Ch. 6.

top one per cent of the general population and does not suggest that he will be greatly troubled by intellectual limitations.

Kidd's score on the Wechsler-Bellevue Test raises more difficult problems. It suggests a level of ability that would make his college career a hard one, and it is thus consistent with his actual performance in college. But when we gave him the Wells Alpha Examination, a test better suited to discriminate at the upper levels of intelligence, he came out with scores that were higher than the average for Harvard College students. Which result is to be believed? Generally in such cases one credits the better performance; if the subject can do it at all he must have the capacity to do it. One would certainly assume from the Wells Alpha score that Kidd would be able to make a good record in college. We know, of course, about the emotional problems that stood in his way, that probably interfered grievously with his use of intellectual capacity, and that might even tend to depress some of his scores on tests of mental ability. But we have not yet fully explored the qualitative aspects of the two men's use of their minds. This leads to some very interesting discoveries.

As an example of qualitative differences we shall first examine performance in the Vigotsky Test. In this test the subject is offered a variety of small blocks and required to divide them into four consistent categories. The problem cannot be solved by using the more obvious principles; there are too many colors, for instance, and too many sizes and shapes for a fourfold classification. The correct solution is much more complex, and it is generally reached by college subjects only after much trial and error and a certain amount of prompting by the examiner.

Hale found the solution a little more quickly than Kidd, but our interest lies particularly in the way the two men worked at the problem. Requested to think aloud as he worked, Hale verbalized a series of clearly formulated hypotheses. Some of these he rejected merely by inspection; others he tried out by working with the blocks. His procedure can be described as *conceptual* in that he formulated principles and tested them out mentally before trying any random experiments with the blocks. Kidd's approach was very different. He seldom worked with a well-defined idea; rather, he placed the blocks in tentative arrangements, as if he felt that by fully exposing himself to their perceivable properties he would eventually see the solution. This procedure can be called *percep-*

tual. Although it sounds less efficient, the perceptual approach is just about as good as the conceptual in solving the Vigotsky problem, as it is in many of the problems of everyday life. Too stubborn an attempt to conceptualize, too little account of the properties of the blocks, can easily lead to failure in the test. Kidd reached the correct solution, but it is of interest that even when he did so he experienced great difficulty in formulating the general principle behind his classification. He described the four groups but fumbled badly when it came to stating the higher abstraction. Many subjects prefer the perceptual approach but can easily conceptualize the result once they have achieved it. Kidd found real difficulty in taking this final step.

The difference shown in the Vigotsky Test is consistent with results from other procedures. Kidd's scores were well below Hale's in those subtests of the Wechsler-Bellevue which are most conceptual in character. The same difference is apparent in everyday life. In a political discussion, for example, Hale's views are clearly formulated, more or less fixed in advance, and pronounced confidently with little regard for what his listeners may feel or know. Kidd starts with no opinions, and he prefers to make other people talk so that he can reach his own conclusions from the material they put before him. Again, in procuring mechanical apparatus Hale decides what he wants and goes out to get it, if not to make it, while Kidd collects information from everyone and then decides what he wants. But the moment we start to follow this difference through its ramifications in everyday life, we become aware of its striking resemblance to the consistent trait difference which we examined in the previous section. Kidd's intellectual approach to things is marked by a much greater passivity. He tends to open himself fully to the promptings of the material but hesitates to exert himself in the direction of active mastery through conceptualization and logic. Hale attempts from the start to dominate the material, trying to align it with preconceived ideas, highly conscious of the organization he is seeking to impose. But the very phrases we use to characterize intellectual procedure serve also to characterize the social procedure of the two men. Kidd's use of his mind reflects his more general trait of passivity; Hale's thinking shows the assertiveness that colors all the rest of his behavior.

Our examination of qualitative differences leads us to conclude that intelligence cannot be altogether separated from the rest of personality. Intellectual operations are part of the organic whole and show the properties that are characteristic of the whole. This does not mean that a person's mental qualities are no more than extensions of his general personality traits. As we have seen, intelligence ranks as a special kind of ability based on a special innate endowment. It seems likely, moreover, that within this endowment there are further innate specializations which make one person excel in verbal operations, another in performance tests, another with numerical problems, and so forth. In the case of certain aptitudes, notably musical genius and the mathematical gifts of the "lightning calculator," special endowment seems to be minimally related to other traits of personality. Both of these aptitudes sometimes appear precociously and sometimes exist in a person otherwise quite poorly developed. But these are extreme cases; our findings with Hale and Kidd are more typical of the overlap that is to be expected between mental traits and more general traits.

Other Types of Ability.—The contribution of endowment is clearer in the case of intelligence than it is in most forms of ability. Often it is well-nigh impossible to disentangle innate elements from the cumulative effects of practice and learning. Take manual dexterity as an example. Probably there are potential differences in the facility with which this asset is acquired, but the process of acquisition is an exceedingly long one. It starts with the baby's manipulation of the objects within his reach. It receives practice in the nursery-school child's cutting with scissors and in the elementary-school activities of writing and drawing. Increasingly it becomes caught up in larger patterns of interest or of disinterest. Joseph Kidd did pretty well on dexterity tests, and his history showed isolated instances of skill such as picking the trunk locks at camp and making good drawings in biology courses, but manual dexterity had very little significance in the main interests of his life. For Hartley Hale, in contrast, this kind of skill became increasingly important with the passage of time. He needed it for his mechanical interests, for building radio sets, for wiring the lights in school plays, then more and more in his biology courses and experimental work, until finally it became an essential element in his career as a surgeon. Hale constantly used his hands in finely coordinated work; a huge history of practice lies behind today's manual dexterity.

Even more complex is an attribute such as mechanical ability. Perhaps Hale had natural gifts for this kind of thing, but we have also noticed that he received, in contrast to Kidd, considerable encouragement during early childhood. When he started to build radios it was in the company of similar-minded friends; an overlap began between mechanical and social interests. This overlap increased during his career as a stage manager in high school. In the course of time mechanical ability became an integral part of his special attainments, his claim to distinction, and his ideal image of himself. It was inextricably caught up in his central interests and values. Meanwhile he had accumulated a tremendous amount of useful related information. He possessed a seasoned knowledge of electricity, for instance, long before he needed to use complex electrical devices in his medical research.

Most adult abilities, then, have to be conceived as the end product of several conditions which have influenced the history of learnings. At the start there must be sufficient innate facility with the needed activities, and early circumstances must be such as to encourage them. Very important is the extent to which the activities then become incorporated in a larger pattern of ongoing interests. When their importance to the person becomes enhanced by such an association, they are almost certain to receive more than average further practice and to bring about the accumulation of stores of relevant knowledge. It is this end product of developed skill, interest, and "know-how" that constitutes the contemporary ability, whatever its biological roots in tissue endowment.

DRIVES AND MOTIVES

The chief driving forces in man are no longer called instincts, no longer conceived as elaborate patterns of unlearned behavior such as exist at other levels of the animal kingdom. Drives are looked upon rather as tensions mobilized by certain definite conditions in the tissues of the body but directed, prior to learning, only in a quite diffuse fashion. When the body tissues need nutriment, for instance, a chain of events occurs which makes for restless and more or less random activity, directed toward a goal only in the sense that the taking of food is the specific thing that will reduce the tension. All the intervening steps between being hungry and finding food must be filled in by learning. The concepts of drive and learning are fundamental to any understanding of human behavior. Drives create a restlessness that stimulates learning, while learning produces swifter and more efficient ways of reducing the tension of drives.

Visceral Drives.—The concept of drive seems particularly clear when it is possible to specify the tissue conditions and neural mechanisms which produce the marked heightening of activity. Precise specification can be most nearly achieved with certain strong visceral drives in which the tension is focalized in a restricted group of tissues. Such is the case with hunger and thirst, sex and lactation, the need for oxygen, eliminative needs, and the avoiding of pain and extremes of temperature.[17] It would lead to a tidy theory if we could suppose that these identifiable visceral needs constituted the whole basis of human motivation. We know from Freud's work, if from nothing else, that the sex drive can play a versatile and tortuous part in behavior, often heavily disguised by rationalizations and other defensive devices. If we extend the kind of ruthless analysis that has so often revealed erotic strivings beneath the surface of behavior, we might be able to disclose simple visceral urges at the root of every act. Such seems to be the contention of Masserman, for example, who unmasks as follows the motives of students reading his book on psychiatry:

> Why is the student reading this book? To gain, or at any rate seek, knowledge. To what end? To be a more capable—or at least a more widely read—psychologist, physician, social worker or whatever. But why be one? Here the replies may consist of protestations, more or less vehement or sincere, that the reader wants to prepare himself for future research, enlighten the current darkness of his chosen field, serve suffering humanity, and so on. But further and franker introspection will reveal that beneath such rationalizations lie somewhat more mundane, though still quite complex, strivings. These may be actuated by desires for prestige, financial gain, opportunities for marriage, a favorable environment for a future family, and other quite realistic—and withal quite human—motivations. Finally, even these "social" strivings, however displaced, rationalized or sublimated, can be traced to more nearly elemental sexual or parental drives, and, lastly, needs for sustenance, shelter, protection from injury and other such physiologic deter-

[17] An exposition of current theories about basic drives is to be found in Symonds, P. M., *The Dynamics of Human Adjustment*, New York, D. Appleton-Century Co., 1946, Ch. 2.

minants as emerge when the core of our living is stripped of its multiple-faceted social adaptations and verbal embellishments.[18]

This is certainly an uncompromising piece of reductive analysis. Does a person seek knowledge only to become a more capable professional worker? Does a person elect to serve suffering humanity only to assure himself of a good living? One gets the impression that important human strivings may have been jettisoned, along with the "social adaptations and verbal embellishments," by a skipper over-eager to bring his ship into a safe conceptual harbor. But it is not so much the voyage as the harbor itself that demands more careful scrutiny. The quotation from Masserman reflects a much too simple idea about the physiological drives that constitute the core of our living.

Close inspection reveals that none of the visceral drives are as simple and unitary as they seem. Hunger has a specific focus in tissue needs for nutriment and in contractions of the stomach, but hunger proves to be capable of subtle variations depending on the precise character of the nutritional deficit. A specific salt deficit, for example, drives animals to leave other kinds of food and travel many miles in order to reach salt licks. Vitamin deficiencies sometimes provoke an appetite for specific foods containing the needed elements, even in animals who can know nothing about vitamins. Tissue needs are much more varied than we imply when we speak of hunger; the tensions they create are much more complex than is suggested by referring to a hunger drive. But the moment we try to consider what it is that tissues really need, we find ourselves propelled far beyond the original conception of visceral drives. All the tissues of the body are alive, which means that they are not perfectly stable and that any of them can become the seat of tension. In particular the nervous system and the muscles are living tissues, not inert wires and mechanical levers which are content to rest forever unless someone pulls them. Shall we assume that the human nervous system, so vast a structural advance over that of even the primates, contains no requirements of its own and serves only the business of the viscera? More likely a system of tissues so delicately poised for action actually needs action; sense organs crave stimulation, muscles demand motion, the whole person wants to be doing something.

[18] Masserman, J. H. *Principles of Dynamic Psychiatry*, Philadelphia, W. B. Saunders Co., 1946, p. 106.

We do not have to reject the concepts of drive and tension, but we are certainly not on sound biological ground if we insist that a few neatly packaged visceral drives provide all the motivation in human life. The roots of behavior are more diversified than that.[19]

Complex Nature of Adult Motivation.—Much is gained by thus broadening the concept of drive. Active exploration, curiosity, play, aesthetic interests, the enjoyment of thinking, and many other characteristic human concerns take an intelligible place in the biological view of man. Even so, drive remains a somewhat individualistic concept and does not afford all the help we need in understanding social behavior. In order to fill this gap, social motives have often been approached in the opposite direction: not by inference from basic drives but by generalization from observed social behavior. Thomas once offered the suggestion that all human beings manifest four wishes or cravings: for security, for new experience, for recognition or status, and for emotional response from others.[20] This suggestion has been variously criticized, amended, and expanded; no one seems inclined to deny it important elements of truth, though perhaps few are satisfied with the specific formulation. A more searching attempt to gather social motives into a consistent scheme was made by Murray, who included, in addition to physiological needs, a variety of needs primarily social in orientation, such as affiliation, recognition, dominance, nurturance, exhibition, deference, and abasement.[21] It is obviously impossible to correlate needs of this kind with specific tissue conditions. They are generalizations from social behavior, classifications of possible goals. Without such concepts it would be difficult to give an adequate generalized description of behavior at its more social and highly integrated levels. But if we want to work out the developmental history of such needs, if we want to know how they arise and grow, we must start not from generalizations but from motive patterns as they appear in individual lives.

When we try to describe an individual case and understand what is "really there"—what effective forces are actually operating in one particular personality—it proves necessary to specify motives in

[19] This general view of motivation is expounded by Murphy, G., *Personality, op. cit.,* Chs. 5, 6.

[20] Thomas, W. I. *The Unadjusted Girl,* Boston, Little Brown & Co., 1923, ch. 1.

[21] Murray, H. A., *Explorations in Personality,* New York, Oxford University Press, 1938, Ch. 2.

very great detail. True as it may be that Hartley Hale and Joseph Kidd are both striving for recognition, and that Hale is striving the harder of the two, we cannot properly understand the history of this striving or its present mode of operation until we describe the specific interests through which it seeks outlet. Hale is not striving for recognition for his athletic ability, as Kidd would like to be recognized for his golf; he does not seek an audience for his singing, as Kidd would like to have one for his piano-playing. Hale specifically strives for recognition as a physician and scientist, and he wants that recognition to come from fellow-physicians and fellow-scientists. Whatever spread his need for recognition may enjoy in fantasy, it gives a strong push to behavior only along specific lines. The main stream of Kidd's need is less channeled, for he perceives no opportunity to continue building flower studios, but he favors some line along which he could leave objective monuments to his credit.

This specifying of individual motives leads us to important insights. In the course of life, urges become increasingly channeled into particular kinds of action and interest. As these channels develop, energy is withdrawn from other kinds of action and interest which originally seemed perhaps equally alluring. An analogy can be suggested to what happens when water is poured on sloping sandy ground: small streams push out in several directions, but when one of these finds the best downward route its channel is quickly deepened and the water drains out of the other streamlets. But this process of finding and discarding channels is not the only thing that happens. Simultaneously there is a gathering of different motives into more inclusive spheres of action and interest. Almost all important human concerns represent an integration of numerous motives, which come to a focus on a specific interest or work together in an available social role.

Kidd's interest in operating a public golf course can be taken as a case in point. It is a way of making money. It is a "white-collar" job, or, more accurately, a "sports-shirt" job, which fits his status aspirations. It makes room for his interest in playing golf and attaining distinction along that line. It allows relative freedom with his time. It provides opportunities for pleasant sociability and for the willing listening which he finds so satisfactory. In picturing such an occupation Kidd senses that it would provide channels not for one main motive but for nearly all of his important strivings. Needs become channeled in the course of development, but they also become absorbed in larger patterns of on-going interest and concern. Hale's professional career has become virtually the sole channel of his desire for recognition, but his career has also become the main channel for a variety of other needs, including his dominance, his curiosity, and his pleasure in mastering mechanisms.

These ideas about motives do not make for simplicity of conceptualization. The constant criss-crossing of drives, interests, and sentiments has suggested to Cattell the concept of a *dynamic lattice*. [22] Probably nothing less simple can be of any assistance in studying motivation as it occurs in the individual case. We shall not, however, pursue this concept in detail; rather, we shall turn attention to our two cases with a view to finding out what difference it makes to conceive of drives as being involved in a dynamic lattice.

Analysis of Sexual Motivation.—For illustration we can use the sex drive. Is it useful to suppose that Hale and Kidd differed in the strength and quality of their respective sex drives? They certainly differed a great deal in their overt sexual behavior. Hale told us in his student days that he enjoyed an occasional erotic adventure, but it was clear that his deeply satisfying sexual experiences occurred in the setting of an enduring relationship marked by affection, tenderness, and mutual esteem. Kidd, on the contrary, felt a strong barrier to sexual gratification with the object of his affections, but was powerfully driven to find casual partners for hit-and-run escapades. A generation ago Kidd would probably have been described as oversexed, but he himself held a less naive theory. When he called sex a "shunt for my drives" he was recognizing, in principle, that his evening hunting was a focal point in a dynamic lattice. He was saying that much more than the sex drive was involved in his sexual behavior. He felt the necessity to prove his adventurous masculinity, to demonstrate that he could be a fearless cave man, and thus to shore up his tottering self-esteem. We can infer that the desire to escape from irksome school work, from family pressure, and from the difficulties of social adjustment added to the charm of these evening adventures. One might even ask, paradoxically, how much the sex drive itself was involved. Kidd later learned to enjoy sex in a far more profound way than was possible in the awkward and rapid consummations that occurred in the back of a car. To say that he was oversexed is meaningless. He was using sex to

[22] Cattell, R. B., *Personality, op. cit.*, pp. 157-162.

prove his worth, to buck up a frustrating daily life, and probably to anaesthetize the very real anxieties with which he was beset. Hale's anxieties were not channeled into the sphere of sexuality nor into his relationships with girls. The dynamic lattice was constructed on another pattern.

To some extent the sex drive feeds into homosexual channels as well as heterosexual ones. The cultural taboo on homosexual behavior is a strong one, but the reports of Kinsey and his associates show that it is not infrequently violated, while the psychoanalytic study of the neuroses makes it clear that homosexual feelings can have important and subtle ramifications behind the scenes even when the taboo is outwardly effective. In Hale's case there is only one point—his deference toward certain older men who took an interest in him—which plausibly suggests homosexual feeling. In all these instances, however, the older man displayed interest specifically in Hale's intellectual productiveness and proved willing to take a chance on his powers of achievement. If the sex drive was involved at all, it certainly stood in a subordinate relation to Hale's ambition and scientific interests, motives which played, as we have seen, a vital part in his development.

In Kidd's case the situation is rather different. A great deal of his adolescent behavior lends itself to interpretation as an expression of passive homosexual inclinations and of defenses against such inclinations. His masturbation at puberty seems to have begun with a passive attitude of both body and mind, and he did not at once associate this pleasure with an active sex role. He told us that older boys sometimes liked to put their arms around him; reciprocally, he felt a strong admiration for clean-cut, good-looking fellows, and he was particularly likely to become flustered, uneasy, and self-conscious in their presence. We noted also that he was really none too confident with derelict girls; his adventures with them showed decided elements of overcoming anxiety and proving masculinity. It is a legitimate hypothesis that during adolescence Kidd's sex drive flowed considerably into homosexual channels; legitimate also to conceive that some dim awareness of this fact contributed greatly to his difficulty in achieving satisfactory human relationships and building a basis for self-esteem.

This is a legitimate hypothesis, but is it a true one? Kidd was aware of no erotic interest in boys or men, and he viewed with mild distaste, yet with no apparent anxiety, the homosexual advances that occasionally came his way. Thus he was not homosexual in any ordinary meaning of the word, nor was he so in any biological sense. The Sheldon somatotype photographs permit a rating on what Seltzer calls the *masculine component* in physique, but Kidd rated high on this component and exhibited few of the traits, except specifically social ones, which Seltzer found to be correlated with a weak masculine component.[23] It is therefore more profitable to assume that Kidd's adolescent behavior formed part of a dynamic lattice of social motives. From earliest years he was shown off for his good looks, encouraged to enjoy admiration. This doubtless predisposed him to take particular pleasure in finding himself from time to time an object of interest to older boys. During childhood he had a strong need for the companionship and esteem afforded by play groups, but his advancement in school and constant association with older boys forced him into the roles of "clown" and "stooge" and made him constantly uneasy about his standing with others. Kidd's submissiveness to other boys was a product much more of social anxiety than of sexual inclination. It was a consequence of his hunger for esteem. And it has declined as his need for esteem grew less clamorous. Recent years have witnessed a growth toward less submissive, more assertive attitudes. The earlier obstacles were not sufficient to prevent the occurrence of natural growth.

THE CENTRAL POSITION OF LEARNING

When we studied the shaping of lives by social forces, we found ourselves obliged to face complexities that seemed anything but conducive to clear thinking. We constantly found it necessary to reject simple categories and simple relationships. It was misleading, for example, to place Hale's ambitions under the concept of upward social mobility, just as it was misleading to identify his parents' values with those of Class II in the status hierarchy. Further specification of details, further individuation, proved always necessary in order to make general ideas fit the case before us, and we were constantly impressed by the interaction of forces, by the plurality of processes that conspired in one way or another to influence the individual life pattern.

In the present chapter the facts have forced us in a similar direction. We have met difficulties in isolating basic, uncomplicated

---

[23] Seltzer, C. C. The Relationship Between the Masculine Component and Personality, *American Journal of Physical Anthropology*, 1945, Vol. 3, pp. 33-47.

temperamental traits, in specifying the inherent dimensions of ability, and in breaking down motives into a series of underlying drives. We cannot start our thinking with a neat set of biologically rooted concepts, and in any event what we observe in behavior seems never to represent the action of single elements. Even generalizations of a higher order, such as mechanical ability or a need for recognition, do not suit the individual case unless we specify the channels of expression and the relationship to larger patterns of interest. The metaphor of a dynamic lattice sometimes seems too simple, and one begins to wonder whether it would not be more appropriate to speak of a tangled impenetrable jungle.

The chief villain in all this complexity is *learning*. The root of our trouble in understanding personality is that each person lives through a more or less unique series of events and learns something from practically all of them. This fact is obvious, but its full significance is often not appreciated. There are certain things, of course, like the multiplication table, that are learned once and for all, and there are certain other things, like compulsive attitudes and defenses against childhood anxieties, that are learned with such rigidity as to repeat themselves with little change in subsequent situations. For the most part, however, cumulative learning is constantly taking place, modifying old forms of behavior, channeling motives in new directions, building up new skills and competences, reshaping patterns of interest, giving a new specification to purposes and goals.

The trouble with having a nice set of universal variables to describe personality is that experience does not let things alone. Temperament gets mixed up with ability, intelligence overlaps with motivation, visceral drives mingle their energy with social needs, aptitudes become involved with social rewards and larger patterns of concern. We said before that complexity was inherent in personality, not a surface illusion but a stubborn and inescapable fact. If this seemed true when we considered the impact of social forces, it is still more striking when we contemplate the criss-crossing lines and the hierarchy of patterns that learning imposes on the biological materials of human nature.

It is well to remember at this point that the study of individual lives is not the only interest we have in human nature. Generalities that apply to groups of people, or to people as a whole, are for many purposes tremendously important. Great progress has been made in industrial relations, for example, by recognizing that employees on the whole need to have a feeling of status and significance as well as economic security. Perhaps status and significance would not characterize accurately the desires of any one worker; case studies would reveal a highly individual series of motive patterns. Correct generalizations are crucial, however, when a problem has to be solved not by individual measures but by general policy. The rise of the Nazi Party in Germany could have been infinitely better understood, and its consequences better anticipated, through a grasp of certain general wishes engendered in the German people as psychological consequences of military defeat and economic restriction. Perhaps no two Germans wished exactly alike, but there was enough commonality in their wishing to make it a powerful political force. When our goal is to understand group behavior, it is misleading to insist on the highly personal variations that confront us in the individual case. But when our practical goal is to deal with individuals one at a time, as in guidance or in psychotherapy, then it is often the generalities that are misleading. And when, as in this book, we are concerned with understanding the natural growth of personality, we must keep our eyes fastened on what happens in the course of individual lives.

There is one important respect in which we can simplify our thinking without sacrificing its utility in case studies. If learning is our central concept, then innate endowments must all be understood as having a relation to the learning process. The older constitutional and instinct psychologies fell into disrepute because they failed to bridge the gap between presumed innate traits and observed behavior, blithely assuming that the traits contained everything that was necessary to produce the behavior. Only a radical application of the idea of learning can remedy this defect and lead us to understand the true significance of innate endowments. As we said at the outset of this chapter, innate traits are important because of the effects they have on the learning process: because of the consistencies they bring about in the individual's responses to his environment and the significant slants they produce in his life history. They are important, in short, because of the encouragement they give to certain kinds of learning and the limits they set upon other kinds.

Let us now see whether or not this idea can be applied to the diverse kinds of endowment—drive, ability, temperament—which we have studied in this chapter. Individual differences in the strengths of different drives obviously fit the formula without protest. *Drive* and learning are inseparable concepts, and the effect of a drive is to favor a certain direction of learning. We do not know whether differences in the innate strength of drives have much importance in personality; our study of Hale's and Kidd's sexual behavior gave us rather the opposite impression. It would be premature, however, to dismiss the possibility, and the relation to the learning process offers no theoretical obstacle. When we turn to *abilities* it is at once apparent that intelligence has always fitted our formula. It has always been defined in some such way as the speed and efficiency of learning, and it has always been measured either by the products of past learning or by performance in new learning situations. Verbal ability, numerical ability, musical aptitude, even manual dexterity, can all be most readily conceived as facilities in certain more specific directions of learning. *Temperamental traits* fit the formula less obviously, but it is a fair contention that they, too, can only be understood as relative facilities or infacilities of a more general kind.

In Hale's case we discovered far-reaching consistencies which seemed best described as high activity level, zestful interest, and power to control disruptive emotions. Such qualities are important not as static possessions but as constant influences upon the learning process. They do not magically create assertive traits, but they increase the frequency of behavior that is likely to build up, under average circumstances, the habitual patterns of attitude and skill called dominance, self-respect, and leadership. Hale enjoyed a certain natural facility in learning assertive behavior; correspondingly, he was handicapped and slow in learning to become a relaxed and convivial companion. Such a difference is the same in principle as a differential readiness to learn verbal as compared with numerical materials.

Innate endowment can thus be conceived as the individual pattern of facilities and infacilities in different kinds of learning. We can think of it as a series of preferences with regard to different lines of development, preferences which may or may not be encouraged by the environment. It is possible for small initial differences to widen greatly in the course of experience. Thus if a child learns to talk a little early but to walk a little late, and if he receives gratification and praise for his verbal prowess but feels

slow on his feet, his development may receive a slant which culmi-
nates in his becoming a skilled linguist with a vast sense of inferiority in athletic activities. He presses forward along the line of his
excellence, maximizing his competence and building it into his
main interests, meanwhile neglecting his physical activities, with the
result that a difference innately small becomes a difference actually enormous. Similarly, a child with a good imagination but a
touch of social awkwardness may specialize so whole-heartedly in
the better of his two functions that he becomes an aloof schizothyme
who makes his living by literary work.

It is also possible for innate differentials to be reversed by strong
environmental pressure. Talents can be crushed if their signs bring
ridicule and contempt. A person of artistic inclinations may be
obliged by cultural pressure or economic circumstances to become
a third-rate business man, or a person with a great gift for practical affairs may be steered into an academic ivory tower. Natural
endowment is presumably often powerless to leave its favored imprint on the life history when environmental forces have a different conception of what the person should become.

By giving learning the central place we have been able to simplify a little our understanding of the biological roots of personality. Even so, our knowledge is regrettably incomplete. There are
still grave difficulties in answering the kind of question that plagues
people who feel discontented with what they are doing. Are they
discontented because they have been deflected from the pathways
preferred by their natural endowment and forced to function
against their own grain? When the environment forbids the exercise
of a strong gift such as musical talent, or when, conversely, it in-
sists that a tone-deaf child take music lessons, we can say with fair
confidence that the resulting discontent comes partly from misuse
of natural proclivities. For the most part, however, we cannot make
confident judgments about this kind of thing. Except when facilities or infacilities are extreme, we cannot unscramble the contribution of inborn inclinations from the effects of social pressure and
emotional involvement. We found it impossible to decide, for instance, whether or not Joseph Kidd possessed the intellectual aptitude needed for success in medical school. The whole subject of
school work was so buried in emotional entanglements that we could
obtain no clear view of his inherent capacity. Kidd's case bears
striking testimony to the importance of psychodynamic analysis in

this as in other problems of development. We shall presently examine and attempt to evaluate the psychodynamic view of man, but first it will be well to broaden the base of our factual knowledge by carefully studying a third life history.

SUGGESTIONS FOR FURTHER READING

The biological roots of personality are discussed in Part Four of *Personality and the Behavior Disorders* (J. McV. Hunt, ed., New York, The Ronald Press Co., 1944, Vol. 1.) Ch. 16, by Penrose, is on heredity; ch. 17, by Sheldon, surveys the constitutional factors in personality; ch. 18, by Cobb, examines the behavioral consequences of lesions of the brain; and ch. 19, by Shock, describes a variety of physiological influences on behavior. Similar ground is covered by R. B. Cattell in *Personality: A Systematic Theoretical and Factual Study* (New York & London, McGraw-Hill Book Co., 1950) in chs. 5, 10 and 11.

The testing of intelligence is well described by Ann Magaret in her chapter in *An Introduction to Clinical Psychology* (L. A. Pennington & I. A. Berg, eds., New York, The Ronald Press Co., 1948), ch. 15. Jean Piaget's brilliant essay on the nature of intelligence has recently been translated: *The Psychology of Intelligence* (New York, Harcourt, Brace & Co., 1950).

Recent research on the subject of drives and motives is reviewed by C. T. Morgan & E. Stellar in *Physiological Psychology* (2nd ed., New York & London, McGraw-Hill Book Co., 1950), chs. 18–20. A searching inquiry into the nature of human motivation will be found in H. A. Murray's *Explorations in Personality* (New York & London, Oxford University Press, 1938), ch. 2.

For a broad survey of the problems of learning consult E. R. Hilgard, *Theories of Learning* (New York & London, Appleton-Century-Crofts, 1948).

7. Joyce Kingsley, Housewife and Social Worker

> I have been very lucky to have the kind of family
> I have. They have given me a good foundation, and
> now it's up to me.
>
> JOYCE KINGSLEY

Joyce Kingsley was first studied when she was a senior in college. She was one of several students who were invited to take part in a study designed to bring out some of the relationships between opinions and other aspects of personality. Invitations were issued in such a way as to secure a group which represented a diversity of opinions; beyond this, selection was determined by the subject's willingness to give the time, at a fee based on current rates for student employment. Joyce responded to the invitation with enthusiasm. She needed spending money, she was interested in social problems, and she enjoyed the prospect of possibly contributing to research in a field closely related to her own. No doubt she was also interested in what she might learn about herself, but at no point did she give signs of desiring our guidance or advice. She took her duties seriously, doing her best to provide whatever information we seemed to require. Like many subjects, she clearly enjoyed being the object of so much personal interest by so many workers, and this bonus seems to have increased her willingness to tell everything she could about herself.

Five years later Joyce, by this time married and living in a midwestern city, came to Boston for a brief visit to her parents. This visit was made the occasion for our second study.

Part One: THROUGH COLLEGE

FAMILY BACKGROUND

The Kingsley grandparents, beneficiaries of a fairly successful business venture in the previous generation, lived comfortably

240

and sent their children to college, but their granddaughter was firm in placing them well down in the middle class. In spirit, she declared, they preserved the smugness and narrow interests of their New England small-town forebears. The grandmother, still living, annoyed Joyce by attempting to pry into her affairs, by gossiping, and by having no serious interests in life beyond disposing of personal effects. The family fortunes had long since dwindled, but the grandmother was still able to maintain, with occasional help from Joyce's father, her own small separate establishment. Joyce more than hinted that her constant presence in her son's household would not have been welcome.

Joyce's father had been destined for business, but after completing four years at a college of business administration he rebelled against the parental design and, much against his father's wishes, entered the ministry. After three years in a nearby theological school he made what his daughter referred to as "the big break" by accepting the call of a parish in Indiana and establishing there his first independent home. Subsequent calls took him to larger parishes, first in Michigan, then in New Jersey. He became known especially for his success with administration, so that after twelve years as a pastor he was summoned to a full-time executive post in the regional organization of his denomination, with headquarters in Boston. He still occupied this post at the time of the second study.

The Kingsley grandparents expressed the hope that their son would marry a "nice Boston girl," but again he kicked over the traces by choosing a wife who came from the West. Joyce's mother was a college graduate and a teacher. She had attained this status largely by individual effort, receiving neither help nor understanding from her parents, whose resources were limited and whose marriage eventually disintegrated. Joyce was not very well acquainted with her maternal grandparents. The grandmother suffered a "mental snap" in middle life; on the single occasion after this when Joyce saw her she appeared "old, frail, bewildered by the noise of the family," and her thoughts were constantly occupied by spiritualism. Joyce had not seen her grandfather since she was six, but he, too, had left an unpleasant impression: he was anxious to be affectionate, and Joyce did not care to be fondled. The maternal grandparents were assigned definitely lower middle-class status by their sociologically educated grandchild. They had both been brought up in German-speaking immigrant homes and had only partly assimilated American middle-class values. Joyce mentioned an incident to illustrate their lack of proper standards. As a year-and-a-half-old baby she had been left with them for the evening while her father and mother attended a meeting. They wanted to be nice to her, so they took her to the movies. "Mother was furious at such poor judgment," said Joyce, adding that she never went to the movies again until she was at least nine or ten.

Joyce's mother, fighting her way up the educational ladder, had clearly rejected her parents and their social status. There was little contact between her and her parents even when, during the Michigan years, the two families lived no great distance apart. Mrs. Kingsley's rebellion extended into the sphere of political opinions; her study of American history had given her a "terrific reaction" against the staunch Republicanism of her childhood home. Her religious affiliation was also of her own choosing, and it was in consequence of this act of independence that she met her future husband. That the friendship progressed to marriage may have been partly due to a sense of alliance in the common cause of achieving independence. Both the young theological student and his future wife had rejected the materialism, the narrow interests, the cultural barrenness, and the unreflective political conservatism of their childhood homes. Both had turned to religion as an integral part of the quest for a better and nobler way of life.

In determining the social status of Joyce Kingsley's family it is necessary to specify quite a number of details. In the first place, both parents had become professional people in their own right; therefore, as we saw in studying the family of Hartley Hale, they occupied a curious position somewhat to one side of that central status ladder which is determined largely by wealth. Joyce was fully aware of this dilemma. "We have to entertain and make a small salary stretch," she said; "we have many obligations to fill;" and this placed the family and kept it definitely in middle-class financial status. On the other hand, many of the social contacts were upper-class or were with other professional families. In discussing status, Joyce made the common professional distinction between two kinds of upperness. She said:

> This distinguishes the upper and lower: using your mind to the greatest possible extent. My family is upper in this sense. Money is a side issue; in that sense I have no particular ambition toward the upper.

It must also be mentioned that the social status of a minister has to be defined somewhat differently from that of other professionals whose contact with their clients is more restricted and less personal. In carrying out the duties of his office a parish minister is expected to enter even the wealthiest homes and to be treated at least as an equal. His uppermost social status is thus in a sense determined by the range that is represented in his parish. Mr. Kingsley's parishes included members who were upper-class in the social-financial sense, so that when his daughter disclaimed an interest in that kind of status it was not because of a feeling of hopeless exclusion.

In Joyce's case we can perceive with peculiar sharpness the collision between democratic ideals and the subtle directives of social class. During her later childhood, in a crowded New Jersey industrial city, she was not allowed to play indiscriminately with the neighboring children. When the family moved to Boston, sacrifices were made so that she could attend a private college-preparatory school and seek her friendships among her schoolmates. Earlier she had gone to public school, and when questioned about her contacts with lower-class children she said, "I wasn't part of it, but not an outsider either or a snob." Then she added, "My ambition is to put people at their ease, including those below you socially." Yet Joyce's considered values were based on the Christian democratic ideal, and her response to class and ethnic differences had indeed been much softened by her parents' explicit attitudes toward these questions. The Children of Israel figured as very wonderful people in her early education, and when in New Jersey she first saw mysterious Yiddish signs and was told that this was the neighborhood of the Children of Israel she felt at once that it must be a "most special" place. Occasionally the family had a Negro maid, who was always treated with respectful consideration. She remembered being furiously indignant at tales of injustice and cruelty weepingly related by one of these helpers. Joyce's convictions with regard to ethnic groups were entirely free from prejudice, and she was prepared to act according to her convictions. But she had been exposed to so much status conditioning that her feelings did not always keep in step with the equalitarian ideal. Often the best that she could attain was a condescending tolerance. Speaking of Negro classmates at college, she said, "I'm not overly close, but I talk to them when I get a chance." We must count it to her credit that she then added, "That sounds smug, doesn't it? I don't mean it to be."

If the social status of the Kingsley family cannot be written off with a single phrase, the same is true for Mr. Kingsley's occupational role. We must be careful to avoid stereotypes in understanding this particular member of the ministerial profession. Contemporary life histories show many cases of rebellion against the spiritual claims of religion in favor of an occupation at once more materialistic and considered to be more practical. In view of this trend we become inclined to think of ministers as being also ministers' sons and as continuing, perhaps rather unadventurously, to tread in paternal footsteps. The idea of a courageous young man flouting the materialism of his parents and going into the Christian ministry with a chip on his shoulder, so to speak, does not fit with our common preconceptions. Yet Mr. Kingsley had to defy his parents in order to become a minister; in the beginning, at least, there was a rebellious freshness in his desire to exert a spiritual influence and to create a happy, cooperative, Christian home. Let us now consider how his life enterprise appeared to the eyes of his daughter after it had been going on for twenty-three years.

THE KINGSLEY FAMILY

When Joyce handed in her autobiography we found that she had elected to give a title to the story of her life. She called it *Joyous Adventure*. She had not had time to complete the proffered list of topics, promising to supply the rest at a later date. The break came between *major positive experiences* (defined in our outline as "events accompanied by great elation: success and joy") and *major negative experiences* ("events accompanied by great depression and discomfort: frights, humiliations, failures, transgressions"). At the end of the interviews we reminded her that the written autobiography was incomplete. In due time we received a detailed account of what she considered to be her major negative experience, together with a full discussion of the remaining topics in the outline.

Joyce's positive and negative experiences are highly significant in understanding her personality, but we must revert for the present to the earlier part of *Joyous Adventure* in order to appreciate the formative influence of the family circle. Of her father Joyce wrote as follows:

> He is a very remarkable man. Some people think of him as always smiling, others talk of the kind and thoughtful things he is always doing; no one has ever seen him get angry, and

almost everyone thinks of him as a very busy man (and he is). . . Wherever Daddy has gone he has been particularly successful in the administration end of Church work. He devotes most of his time, of course, to the Church. He has been particularly active in Sunday School work. He is also very much interested in the cooperative movement and is an active member here in Boston. He is very skillful at doing many things—I think he would make a competent gardener, plumber, cook, or carpenter, or almost anything else you could think of. He is very observant. I imagine that's why he can do so many and varied things.

Joyce's praise is unqualified, but we are entitled to wonder how she felt about this admirable figure when she was younger and could not appreciate his public importance and service to the community. She has drawn us her father in profile, intent on the many things he can do so well, rather than as a person bending his gaze upon herself. Although she mentions repeatedly the happy atmosphere of the home and the many things they all enjoyed doing together, there is an undertone of frustration that her relationship with her father was not more warm and demonstrative. She remembered that at the age of five, during a time when her mother was away, she was greatly grieved because her father left her for the evening with her godmother. Another memory, presumably a little later, was introduced with the remark: "Neither of my parents was overly affectionate; Daddy was busy, but we had tremendous fun with him." Then followed this recollection: "I loved going into Daddy's study and tracing writings. I went there after I was supposed to go to bed, turned on the light and traced writings." When we examine the stories Joyce told for the Thematic Apperception Test we find that she has portrayed two kinds of fathers. One is quite cold and authoritative; he "dominates his children to such an extent that he expects them to feel just as he does," and he is further characterized as "self-conscious," "self-righteous," "crabbed," "priggish," "thrusting all emotion aside." In describing this character Joyce was reminded of Father Barrett in *The Barretts of Wimpole Street,* an identification that leaves room for considerable hidden emotional interest in a talented daughter. The other kind of father appears in two stories, both involving the circumstance that the mother is dead. This father is devoted to his daughter, around whom his life revolves; he grieves deeply in the story in which she is killed in an accident, and he yields gracefully in the tale that ends with her meeting and being wooed by a handsome young artist. But we need not rely on inference, for in a later interview Joyce told us how she felt. Asked what she considered to be bad or missing in her upbringing, she replied:

> I only regret that—well, it goes back to Dad's childhood when he wasn't close to his father, and his mother didn't help him to get close to his father. Dad is helpful but he is not very close. He hasn't many close friends. I take after him. I didn't have any close contacts with friends, that is, family close friends.

In the autobiography Joyce characterized her mother as follows:

> Mother's interests have been many and varied. She is an excellent teacher. When we were little she had a nursery school. Later on, when I was in college-preparatory school, she taught seventh and eighth grades. She has a very eager and logical mind and has turned it to many uses. Everything from writing Sunday School lessons to devising quick and efficient methods of cooking and doing dishes has benefited from her logical approach. She has remarkable insight into human situations, and has helped many people to solve their problems through her kind and understanding approach.

Again Joyce has used the profile method, and again we must look further if we are to discover the mother's role in the daughter's emotional development. The mother's influence was so constant that Joyce could not separate it out into particular incidents. Mother read to the children, she taught them the Bible, she took them on trips, she participated in some of their games, but from none of this can we gather much about the daughter's feelings. When we look at the Thematic Apperception Test stories we find Joyce prone to eliminate the mother: the heroine's mother was dead in four stories, and older women in the pictures were sometimes made into aunts or foster parents rather than mothers. It appears that the heroines achieved greater freedom of action through this handling of mother figures. In one remarkable story we were told that as a little girl the pictured heroine was dominated by the pictured old woman: "I'm not sure if it was her mother or if this woman is an entirely different critter." At all events the old woman, a gossipy and scheming person, still continued her attempt at domination, while the heroine successfully asserted her own personality

and rejected the interference. This struggle, Joyce predicted, is destined to continue, and the heroine's efforts will not be quite fully
successful because "she's tied to the woman in some way— it isn't
a case where she can get away from her even if she goes to the far
ends of the earth." The full import of this story will become clearer
when we examine Joyce's account of her moral training. It is clear,
however, that the mother's influence was strong and pervasive, that
it was somehow sensed to be an interference, but that outright
resistance could not be openly contemplated. Moreover, it seems
justifiable to assume that Joyce found the bargain of submission a
hard one, insufficiently rewarded by maternal appreciation. She said
in a later interview, "I minded Mother's being taken up with
work perhaps more than I should have minded it."

Joyce was the eldest child and only daughter of the family. She
was followed within two years by Albert, then a few years later by
Henry. "I adore both my brothers," Joyce told us, and in the autobiography she did their profiles as follows:

> Albert, who is 18, is already an expert on everything con-
> cerning electricity; Henry, who is 14, has a lively sense of
> humor and a keen mind which he can turn to anything.

These profiles were considerably amplified in later interviews, and
it is important to examine the effects of the two brothers on Joyce's
development.

Her earliest memory has to do with Albert. The episode is given
as follows in *Joyous Adventure:*

> I have faint memories of a party given there. I think it was
> a children's party and I'm pretty sure it was a birthday party
> given for me. Albert was old enough to sit in a high chair and
> to know very much that he wanted to come to that party. I
> remember that he screamed and had to be taken out into the
> other room, and that he sat in his high chair howling away be-
> cause he wasn't included in the festivities.

This incident sets the theme for everything she had to say about
Albert. It seems that Albert was "bad"; at least he always had a
"bad temper." He got into a great deal of mischief, such as locking
his sister and himself in the bathroom so that firemen had to be
called to the rescue. Joyce recollects that he tried to climb into her
crib, a thing that her mother says could not have happened. But
Albert's badness was especially remembered in situations like that

of the birthday party, when he was excluded from something that
Joyce was allowed to do. Thus when the Kingsleys went next door
to inspect a radio, leaving him behind because he was too small, he
was found on their return to have swallowed a quantity of pills
from the medicine cabinet. Again, when he was still too young for
church, which Joyce in her best frock was allowed to attend with her
mother, he appeared suddenly in the chancel, unkempt and dirty,
while his father was conducting the service. Joyce confessed to having "violent disagreements" with Albert, though in retrospect she
called them "very childish and remote." His badness did not preclude "wonderful times" together, and lately she has come to consider him a "wonderful guy." In an interview she said:

> We have had lovely times together. We're not really close;
> there's no demonstrative affection, it's just esteem for each
> other. He sort of idealizes me and is proud of me. He expects
> girls to be like me. But he considers me dumb on things scien-
> tific.

Albert's badness seems to have had a drastic effect on the course of
Joyce's early development. His behavior was a shock to his parents. Joyce noted that she herself always "followed the baby books,"
was "docile and willing," and "never did anything to offend mother
or father." After this happy introduction to parenthood the Kingsleys
were utterly unprepared for Albert's rambunctious ways. In many
a drastic scene "mother and father didn't know what to do"; indeed, they were so upset that they asked their friends for advice, and
at one point Mrs. Kingsley retired for several weeks to a rest home.
It can be sensed that to a certain extent Joyce admired and envied
her brother's rebellious assertiveness, but the effect of his actions on
the parents must have strengthened her inclination to play the well-
behaved part she had begun in her days as an only child. Being good
now acquired the meaning of a strategy in the competitive struggle
for parental favor. The only trouble was that the parents seemed unable to give Albert the punishments he deserved. There was danger
that they would play the game unfairly by failing to make him a
proper outcast. Joyce told us that at some point in these early
years she developed a fantasy of an imaginary companion. Far
from being a playmate, this companion, Myra, was a woman who
had had a great many children and who therefore knew exactly how
to deal with them.

I objected to going to bed one night and I discussed it with Myra. She was on my side; it was not right for me to have to go to bed. I must have doubted that Mother and Daddy were right. Perhaps I sensed their hesitation in knowing what to do with Albert.

We judge that Myra was both more appreciative of the wishes of a good child and more severe in punishing a bad one.

Brother Henry exerted a less marked effect on Joyce's development. "We welcomed him when he was born," she oddly remarked; "we were excited about him." Like Albert he passed through a stage when he "couldn't be even remotely civilized" without discipline, but if she is sometimes still angry at his noise and disorderliness she has come to admire his brilliant mind and his practical skills. "He's such a good cook," she wrote, "that he can make substitutions in recipes and have his things turn out to be delicious, whereas I'm still at the follow-the-directions-very-carefully stage." Henry's health is not of the best, so that he is sometimes moody and difficult. This causes Joyce to feel concern about him, and she sometimes wonders whether her mother is not taking his troubles too lightly in calling them just a phase of growth. She even wonders on occasion whether Henry is not punished unfairly, but although she has once or twice expressed this thought she usually checks it with the reflection that her mother is tired. There are times when she and Henry become real pals, though for the most part she is "pretty much an older sister." It is evident that Joyce's attitude toward Henry changes under different circumstances. She can be annoyed and somewhat punitive, but she can also sympathize when he seems unhappy and misunderstood.

Joyce Kingsley's history exhibits with unusual clarity the effect of the family group on later social development and group memberships. It also shows, more explicitly than our two previous cases, the impact of moral constraints and the internal evolution of conscience. We are therefore justified in examining at considerable length what Joyce wrote about the family atmosphere.

Our home has always been a very happy one. **Our** family has been quite close together—in our own kind of way. It's not a family where there is a great deal of affection shown overtly, but we do have strong ties and mutual interests and enjoy doing things together. No one of us had a lot of attention as an individual—so that none of us feel that we, or any of the

others, are the "favorite" with our parents. I guess I have
never been much of a worry to Mother and Daddy. Neither of
them is dominating or possessive but they are fond of all of us.
I can't quite describe their attitude: they leave us pretty free,
but they are always concerned with the way things are going
for us. Perhaps it can be summed up by saying that they realize
that we aren't possessions of theirs, but they are nevertheless
vitally interested in our welfare. This means that they can be
quite close to us and very fond of us, but not use that feeling
in a way that would be harmful for our development. Our family responsibilities as well as our privileges as members of the
family have always been made important. I, as the oldest, and
a girl, have perhaps had quite a large share in the responsibilities, but I do not feel that it has been a disproportionately
large share. Our servants have been few and far between, but
I think they were all fond of me.

It is odd that Joyce selected this particular point to remember
about the servants. Perhaps her wondering about love should be
taken as referring unintentionally to the whole preceding paragraph. An undemonstrative regime, no matter how fair and devoted,
can create an air of uncertainty about love, especially when more
than one child is involved. Again we feel that Joyce is a little dubious about the bargain of conformity: was she asked for too much,
was she given too many responsibilities, in return for a restrained
and evenly divided show of parental affection? The heart is not always satisfied by what the head considers fair. But Joyce was not
prepared to object, and she still does not openly object, as we see
from her remarks on discipline.

Looking back, it doesn't seem as if we've ever had much discipline. Or maybe I'd better say that I never had much. It isn't
a case of always having done everything I should do, but
rather one of being punished more by the conscience pangs I
have afterwards than by Mother and Daddy. Punishment,
whenever it has been given to any of us, has been perfectly
fair—which is perhaps why I don't remember it. This situation
makes me completely unable to determine just what our most
serious offense could have been (or is). I think that perhaps
it's obstructing the family harmony and progress by putting
considerations of ourselves before those of the welfare of the
whole group when they have not deserved that importance.

The last sentence reminds us that Mr. Kingsley was interested in

the cooperative movement and makes it plain that cooperation occupied a high and explicit place in the moral code of the Kingsley
household. Cooperation is a mature concept the essence of which is
not easily grasped by young children. Indeed it is scarcely possible
to create a domestic cooperative movement: inevitably the parents
function as final arbiters when it comes to deciding what obstructs
"family harmony and progress." We should not be surprised that the
glad cooperation desired by the parents sometimes felt like an irksome yoke to the daughter. It is clear from the following paragraph,
however, that the cooperative ideal was applied for the most part
to understandable necessities, and that the Kingsley parents played
with their children and shared happy times as well as requiring contributions.

> I have already spoken of the amount of work around the
> house which the family has done together. This has been true
> ever since we have been old enough to help. It has never been
> more than we could handle. When Al and I were five or six
> years old we had duties like setting the table for breakfast or
> drying the supper dishes, and we did these for our weekly
> allowance of five cents. By the time Henry was two he had re-
> quested to stand up on a high stool and wash the dishes!
> Mother and Daddy used to play games with us and they also
> read aloud to us. We all planted gardens together and did
> things like raking leaves and shingling and painting floors, too.
> One summer we fixed up a car trailer and took our tents and
> supplies and camped west as far as Montana. During the last
> few summers we have all worked hard on a cottage at the
> beach. We have had a lot of fun doing things together, and
> planning things together.

Returning to the question of moral training, we find that Joyce
characterized it as "largely unspoken."

> By that I mean that Mother and Daddy have not been pri-
> marily concerned with it—or, rather, they have never given us
> "lectures" on the subject of our morals. We have always talked
> to them freely about our impressions of what is going on
> around us, and I think we have benefited from those discus-
> sions in that our moral education has not been imposed on us,
> as it were, but has gradually and normally developed as we
> were ready for it. In the last year or two Mother has been
> utterly amazed to find that Albert and I, in talking to her, have
> voiced almost identical opinions about subjects which we have

never discussed before. We feel very strongly about some things. The only possible source of our moral training seems to be in what Mother and Daddy have lived, and in what we have done together as a family. I ask myself how this can possibly be. And my answer is that I don't know. It really doesn't seem logical that indirect influence could be so strong. Our conduct at home has had to measure up to certain stand- ards, but it has never been a case of "you do this, or else . . ." Mother and Daddy have been consistent in their own behavior. I imagine that there has been strength for us in that very con- sistency—for if we ever doubted the rightness of anything we did, that certainty was there anyway, acting as a sort of sup- port to us. Our religious training has not been so indirect. I imagine that it is quite possible that much of our moral training has come from this . . . Here again, Mother and Daddy were always consistent in living their religious principles. This was a far more effective teacher than all the spoken words, whether meaningful or unmeaningful to us, could ever have been.

Joyce's description of the way in which moral values got into her behavior must be accounted quite a classic of its kind. The Kingsley parents evidently took seriously their obligation to exemplify, as well as to preach, high standards of Christian conduct. They did not argue or quarrel, they did not criticize people, they were contained and long-suffering when a disaffected faction in the regional organ- ization of their church placed them under sharp criticism. They also stood for the cooperation and the personal freedom that formed part of the ideals of their church. As Joyce paradoxically put it, they had "a sense of leading people to freedom of choice"; they even tried to "do this with each other." It is clear that Joyce early adopted the path of conformity. She became a firm ally of her parents and their values, as one can see from her constant use of "we" in talking about her family. When younger brothers began to compete for parental love she became all the more firmly cast in the role of doc- ile, responsible child. Unquestionably there was strain, but Joyce sustained her alliance through all the vicissitudes of childhood and adolescence, reaffirming it on the final page of her autobiography with the words, "I have been very lucky to have the kind of home and family I have." If it had been hard to live up to her responsi- bilities, she had never openly rebelled against them, and as she reached her twenty-first birthday her life was firmly established on the religious and moral values of her home. One can guess that Albert and Henry, never able to equal Joyce in her chosen role, experienced greater difficulty in becoming cooperative members of the family group. Albert, in particular, found the role of rebel more rewarding. At eighteen he had definitely broken with the church, and he was more or less constantly at odds with the family. There were in fact several points of serious friction developing in the Kingsley household, but of these we did not learn until the second study.

CHILDHOOD: GOLDEN YEARS

Joyce was puzzled about the paucity of her memories. "I don't know why my memory is so hazy about my early experiences," she wrote; "I just remember little snatches of events, and all my memories are happy ones."

Actually her early memories were about as numerous as those of other subjects, and they were not always completely happy. We begin to sense that Joyce has quite a stake in believing that her life's adventure has been a joyous one, unmarred by major negative experiences. Yet what she recalled about childhood, especially what she recalled about the years in Michigan where she lived until the age of seven, suggested many grounds for happy contentment. The minister's daughter was considered a charming and lovely child— "Sweet Joyce," she was called—so that she was the recipient of much attention and many gifts. She remembered the bread houses made by one friend of the family, the flower wreaths often presented by another. She took a great interest in flowers, recalling the time at Michigan as one long brightly colored summer. Christmas pageants, Easter hunts, birthday parties crowded her recollections. There were a good many animals: dogs, rabbits, chickens, and a cat, the latter having to live under the porch because Mrs. Kingsley did not like cats in the house. Joyce was also fascinated by wild birds, thrilled when she saw a "special" bird like a bluebird or noticed a robin perching on the window sill. She was fond of dolls. For a while all dolls, regardless of sex, were named Samuel because she was so fascinated by the Biblical story of the boy who was called by the voice of God. There was a time—a short time—when with Albert's help she sometimes gave a doll rough treatment, but soon people began to give her dolls with nice clothes, and in the end she had about twenty-five dolls, mostly too nice to be played with. Joyce seems to have been from the start sensitive to beautiful things, responding with real joy to colors and sounds, to nature and to lovely objects, and her childhood environment seems to have provided her richly with these sources of pleasure.

A favorite playtime activity, shared with Albert, was a game called "waterworks." The children often made their mother take them to see the town waterworks; afterwards they would build models with blocks, realistically continuing to wear their rubber boots in the play room. One game was played by Joyce alone. "I early aspired to be a lexicographer," she wrote; "I remember copying lists of words in the back of primers, and trying to include all the words I knew, arranged alphabetically, almost as soon as I could write." But most games were shared: with Albert she played store and church, with the boys of the neighborhood she hunted for "very special" marbles and buried tin boxes containing "very special" treasures to be dug up again later. When she began to go to school, at the age of five, her circle of acquaintances enlarged and included, for the first time, girls as well as boys. She wrote: "There were quite a few other children and I enjoyed them." As far as she could recall, her social behavior was always "cooperative," her disposition "sunny and cheerful," her reception by others uniformly friendly. "I wasn't much interested in competition," she said; "perhaps I never needed to be."

However much Joyce may have forgotten unpleasant happenings, the tone of her early childhood seems to have been predominantly happy. The strongest evidence for this judgment lies in the pained astonishment she recalled having felt when suddenly confronted by evil. With regard to Albert's swallowing of the pills she remembered being "quite astonished that he would do that." She described with similar words how she felt when her kindly-meant attempt to pat a strange rabbit resulted in her being bitten: "I was shocked that he would do that; I was angry at first, but then I reasoned that he didn't know I was going to pat him." The most dramatic instance was the occasion when she was stung by a bee. This event occurred on the steps of the school, and its import was probably heightened by the fact that her mother was busy helping one of the teachers who had cut her hand on some glass. At all events Joyce, who had come on roller skates, fell down and landed on the bee. "It stung me," she said; "that was a bitter blow, I didn't expect to be treated that way."

Joyce herself recognized that her cooperation abruptly vanished on the occasion when she went to the hospital. She was six years old and was suffering from a mastoid infection. Resisting all the blandishments of the doctor and nurses, she refused to eat, drink, take medicine, or submit to examination unless her mother were present. It finally became necessary to provide a cot bed so that her mother could stay at the hospital practically all the time. The child's anxiety is sufficiently explained by circumstances, but it is perhaps not without significance that conformity and cooperation should be the things that collapsed when she was sent away from the family circle. One is led to infer that at this period Joyce's conformity was sustained by a feeling that she stood closer to her mother than did the outrageous Albert.

While the family remained in Michigan, Joyce's education was in the hands of her mother, who ran a school for her daughter and a few neighborhood children. This venture seems to have sprung from the mother's desire to be active rather than from any disapproval of the local schools. When Mr. Kingsley was called to a city parish in New Jersey, Joyce entered the second grade in the public school. "It was very different from the kind of school I had known," she commented; "I didn't really get well settled until I was in the third grade, but from then on I was very much a part of things that went on." She remembered her teachers quite clearly, almost always with affection. Along with three or four other pupils she was regularly accused of being the teacher's pet. One teacher, an elderly woman whose hands were tremulous, appointed Joyce to write for her on the blackboard. Another encouraged the children to write letters and send presents to Joyce when she was at home with an illness. It was during this period in the New Jersey public school that Joyce decided to make teaching her life work. But in spite of her tendency to identify with her teachers and to become the object of their special interest she took an active part in the affairs of her contemporaries. In addition to the more organized activities, such as dramatics, Girl Scouts, and young people's groups at the church, she was a member of a couple of clubs in the sixth and seventh grades which degenerated pleasantly into "rowdy clubs."

PREPARATORY SCHOOL: ADVENTURES IN SELF-DISCOVERY

When the Kingsleys moved to Boston, Joyce was entered at the Walter School, a small private school for girls. She was "bewildered at first," but soon she became acquainted with her new schoolmates and found herself "getting adjusted again." It was not long before she emerged in the eyes of the teachers as a well-behaved, reliable girl who worked hard and did well in her studies. Joyce touched lightly on the effort she had to make in order to win her way at Walter, but a period of uneasy strain is suggested by the fact that she had occasional attacks of daytime enuresis during her "early teens," her first years in the new environment.

> I got it under control in after years. I've often wondered about what it was. Being with older and younger people a lot and being a little silly, I would laugh very hard about things and then I'd have a little trouble controlling my bladder. I rather imagine I took things a little more foolishly than they were meant. When I was with older people there was pressure to measure up to their standards. To live up to them meant being noisy about things and laughing a lot.

As she achieved a happier and more secure position Joyce began to learn things about herself in relation to other people. She began to be troubled by the difficulty of managing different roles with different groups. She also began to feel a marked conflict between family ideals and the values of her adolescent friends. In *Joyous Adventure* she discussed these problems as follows:

> I have always had a great many friends, but most of the friendships have been quite casual. Usually I can "handle" only two or three good friends at once. My friends are not all the same kind of people, and I sometimes find it difficult to mix those who are interested in music, for instance, with those who will have nothing to do with music. I haven't had quarrels with any of them. I have usually been a leader in groups, but have often felt not as much a part of the gang as I would have liked. This has been partly, I think, because I don't share most girls' attitudes toward boys . . . I do not feel that I have been left out of groups, although I do not feel that I have been an integral part of some groups with which I have associated. . . .
>
> I have usually been regarded as quite an idealistic person, although possibly that's because I have had ideas and ideals and have not been hesitant about expressing them.

It is easy to see that Joyce, strongly identified with parental values and inclined to extend the identification so as to include teachers and school authorities, would have difficulty with adolescent peer groups. She was soon typed as a minister's daughter, a Victorian, and a goody-goody in her own right. "I hated it," she said; "they don't know the half of it." She kept holding class offices, but this only caused her to be "regarded more as a class officer than as an individual." She found this "hard to take," yet her efforts to break down the reputation were often not successful, leaving a barrier between her and girls whose affection she desired. "Can you be a member and leader at the same time?" she asked.

Joyce was unaccustomed to rejection. Just as she had been shocked by the rabbit that bit her and the bee that stung her, so now she was upset to find that her well-intentioned goodness and idealism made her the object of criticism. It was impossible for her to go over suddenly to the rebellious independence of adolescence, yet this meant that she could not meet the demands for conformity which are so imperious within adolescent groups. She could not move all the way from the family culture to the youth culture, and she was at a point where compromise between them was well-nigh impossible. At times she was extremely unhappy. When she wrote her autobiography, these particular troubles were four of five years past, but they had been sufficiently grave to alter her vocational plans. She wrote as follows:

> For the last several years I have realized more and more that I do not want to teach, although I am intensely interested in education. I want very much some day to make it possible for people to enjoy their schooling and their lives more than many of them do now. I have known some very unhappy people. Usually I have not been in a position to make them really happy (they really have to do it for themselves, anyway). But they may benefit by having some "tools" which will help them to become more happy, and thus to be more useful and productive members of society. The ambition to do something about this has been growing for the last four or five years. The best approach would probably be through schools. Many people go through school being perfectly miserable because they had some problem which they could not solve for themselves, and so often they wanted help but didn't know where to turn for it. One or another form of this ambition has existed during the last few years, and it has always seemed perfectly attainable, although I do not know yet just what I am going to be able to do about it.

Two of the events which Joyce rated as her major positive experiences took place during her last year at Walter School. The first of these, which she considered "most major," was meeting Rennie. The occasion was a young people's convention sponsored by the church, and Rennie was one of the delegates from Indianapolis. Joyce told us that she had always enjoyed boys as playmates, but when she came to Boston and entered a school where the emphasis was on "men for dances and for dates" she felt at first decidedly lost. Before long she was being dated, and she enjoyed especially boys who could "discuss things, especially politics, economics, social problems, religion, and philosophical problems." "I really enjoy them as *people*," she wrote, but she soon found that she did not enjoy them as cave men. Holding hands and kissing did not please her; as for necking, "that was the surest way for a boy to get himself vetoed." Rennie, however, did not hastily insist on these prerogatives, and Joyce soon began to discover in herself a whole new range of emotions. During the convention she and Rennie had wonderful times together, including planning "the farm we both wanted to have some day." Separated again, they "kept the mailman very busy," and occasionally Rennie came for a weekend.

> As we grew older we grew more and more certain that we were the people for each other. It's hard to be objective in telling what kind of a person Rennie is. He has had as happy a childhood as I have. He is much the same kind of person I am, only he is more gentle and kind and understanding. He has been a leader all through school, too, and he has been more of a success scholastically than I. We share the same interests, except that he is intensely interested in group sports, especially in baseball.

Evidently Joyce took comfort in the similarities of background and interests, the sharing of religious and other basic values. With fundamental solidarity assured, she felt no threat in their disagreement on politics: they could "get quite heated" when she espoused Roosevelt and the New Deal against his "midwestern Republicanism." In due time they considered themselves engaged, and a public announcement to this effect was made during Joyce's senior year at college, a little more than four years after their first meeting.

In writing about Rennie, Joyce told us how she felt without reference to the particular time when she felt it. It is probably safe to assume, however, that both the joy and the idealism expressed in the following paragraphs were active elements in the relationship from the very beginning.

> We are both looking forward to being married, although we are not sure yet when we can be. We want to create the kind of home we have longed for, and we want especially to do many things together which we have not been able to do before. Here again our ideals are pretty high. We believe that there is just one person created for everyone, and we do not regard marriage as a thing to be tried and abandoned if things don't go smoothly. We think that things can go smoothly if we consider each other.

> Through Rennie and with him I have found more satisfaction and joy than I have ever found in any other way. The most wonderful thing about it is that it continually grows and develops and I sometimes wonder if I can hold any more without bursting.

The second major event in Joyce's last year at the Walter School was her election as president of the Student Government Association. This association had only just been started; its organization and its policies all had to be built up as new creations. Joyce proved to be a hard-driving president. She wrote as follows about the year's accomplishment:

> I expected quite a bit from the girls in building it up, and I got a good deal of it. The major part of the experience was working with them—and working with the teachers. At the end of the year the organization was really established and the girls had a good deal of power to run their own affairs, and although the faculty was included in making decisions they seldom gave any advice unless we asked for it.

Let us pause to examine these two major events: student government and Rennie. Why were they major? Why do they stand out as landmarks in Joyce's history? When we undertake to study the natural growth of personality we are committed to explaining the positive developments, the forward strides, as well as the problems and frustrations and defeats. We find Joyce troubled, uneasy, inwardly quite unhappy during her first years at the Walter School; then happen two major events, and she begins to function with great freedom and energy, almost bursting with happiness. Any psychotherapist would be delighted if he could produce so large a change in so short a time. We are entitled to suppose that the two events were felt to be "major" because they opened paths through an existing dilemma, gave Joyce a chance to go forward without too sharp a change in direction, and provided expanding opportunities for the expression of her main needs and interests.

Taking first her work in student government, it is clear that Joyce had solved the problem of the respected but unloved office-holder. She had cast her lot with student officialdom, and she was fully prepared to accept whatever isolation from the youth culture this might entail. Having taken this step, she was free to advance into a more dominating role than she had ever assumed before, expecting much of the girls and getting it from them. She was free to affirm her ideals, to side with law and order, to create an organization designed to govern the more unruly tendencies of the adolescent group. She could develop her identification with parental values as against the disruptive tendencies exemplified in Albert and Henry. Many of her oldest needs were thus caught up in a new pattern of constructive activity. Yet there was an important difference between her new position and the one she had occupied in the family circle. She was now the elected president, the legitimate authority, not merely the eldest daughter who was uncertain of her standing and bound to a firm code of cooperation. She could at last really run things the way she wanted them run. Furthermore, it was part of her job to make the students maximally independent of faculty control. It was easy for her to keep peace with the teachers because she shared most of their ideals, but she did not have to be their mouthpiece. She could symbolize her right to be independent of parental control without tumbling into the disruptive rebellion of the youth culture.

Thus Joyce won her way through the formidable social problem of adolescence, but how, we must ask, had she accomplished the crucial first step? How had she overcome her fear of isolation from the peer group, her seemingly urgent need for the affection and approval of the other girls? This is where her meeting with Rennie was crucial. When she returned to school for her senior year and assumed her presidential duties she had met Rennie, enjoyed his company, fantasied the future farm with all that it implied. The mailman was being kept busy. She was in love and her love was returned; though only sixteen, she had met the man she was going to marry. Thus she had jumped clean over the rating-and-dating problems of adolescence. From being the prim and backward girl who evoked the sneers of her more sophisticated companions she had gone at one bound into the position of an engaged young woman, leaving adolescence behind her. She did not need the esteem of the still-experimenting girls once she had swept past them and reached the stage toward which they were groping; all the more she did not need it from the girls when she was receiving it from Rennie. Thus she freed herself from meeting the requirements of the youth culture and regained her capacity to work for the ideals she had taken from parents and teachers, ideals upon which she and Rennie were in essential agreement.

It is not to be assumed, of course, that Joyce's development really advanced at a magical pace. Her love for Rennie was at first undoubtedly that of a starry-eyed schoolgirl. Subjectively, however, her relationship to Rennie gave her a tremendous increase of happy confidence and security, thus opening the way for further development in several directions. She could even allow herself more feeling in response to boys, secure in the knowledge that she could afford to reject a boy if he insisted upon too much sex or in some other way displeased her. This was illustrated in the incident of Carlos. Joyce described Carlos as "the only other man in whom I have ever been seriously interested." He was a Latin-American who had come to Boston to study music. He was unable to find a place to live, and when his plight came to the ears of the ever-helpful Mr. Kingsley, he was promptly installed in the Kingsley household. Almost as promptly Carlos began to take an interest in his host's 17-year-old daughter. Joyce described what happened as follows:

> As I have said, I am very interested in music, and was especially much interested at that time (when I was a senior in preparatory school). Carlos knew of no other relation to have with a girl except an amorous one. I regarded him as an interesting person who danced well, and with whom I could play duets. I was so interested in Rennie that I didn't think of Carlos as anything but a friend, as so many other boys had been. He had always gone around with rather "fast" girls whom I didn't enjoy. Naturally I saw a lot of him and became more and more fond of him. For a while he convinced me that I was in love with him. It didn't last very long, because I soon realized what kind of a person he really was. Carlos is really very sweet, and very dependent on other people. He's lively and gay, and I especially fell for his good dancing. But he can (usually) wheedle

anything he wants out of people, and he isn't honest with himself or with others. So that put an end to that.

Carlos was not classified as a major positive event, but in spite of his indignant dismissal he seems to have had a considerable influence on Joyce. She experienced a quickening and deepening of her aesthetic interests, which thenceforth occupied an increasingly important position in her economy of happiness.

COLLEGE YEARS: LIVING WITH ENTHUSIASM

It was during her first year at college that Joyce encountered her major negative experience. Perhaps under no circumstances could her recent happiness have continued at its exalted level, but the actual situation let her down with a bad bump. "I look back on it as a perfect nightmare," she wrote; then, becoming scientifically analytical, she considered under five headings the "several forces" that produced her misery. Her first two paragraphs described the difficulties so commonly met in making the transition from a small school to a large college:

(1) I had come from a school situation where I was one of the 'big shots.' I don't think that ever went to my head, but I was used to being in the middle of things, having the lead often, and having people look up to me and respect what I said (sometimes). I had also been very successful academically, never getting a mark below a 'B.'

(2) I didn't know anyone else who was going to Radcliffe, and most everyone else did. I was living at home, and that made getting acquainted even harder.

Joyce's next point is given a coloring somewhat more peculiar to herself. Having lost her distinguished position, she found it more difficult to dispense with the approval of her age-peers.

(3) At school I had always stood out against the mores of the crowd. I wouldn't chase after boys at the dances, nor would I discuss my dates as much as the other girls did. I found that this approach didn't work as well at college; not that one had to broadcast dates, but several times after I had taken very attractive boys to dances and had had good times with them I was rather automatically 'admitted' to friendship with many girls. In prep school I would have scorned those people, but I soon learned that I should not in college.

In her next point she returned to a common complaint of freshmen, especially those who cannot live at college.

> (4) Also I think I was unaware of much that was going on around me. I had to study hard and help at home and didn't get to Forum or the League for Democracy or the Outing Club meetings I would have liked to have gone to sometimes. I was timid about talking to professors and instructors. In other words I wasn't outgoing enough.

Joyce did not weight her "several forces," but it is probably justifiable to assume that the fifth one was the most shattering of all. The keystone seemed about to drop from the arch.

> (5) And to make matters worse, I went down to Princeton for the first time to visit Rennie in November. Rennie was going through a time when he wanted to be very much 'one of the gang.' He had a roommate who was facing the same difficulty and who couldn't understand anyone who wasn't just like him (and I wasn't). I was thoroughly bewildered at college, and looked to Rennie for help. I didn't hear from him for three months or so after that visit. I didn't know what had happened. And that just added to my bewilderment.

Rennie was young, too; he was disappointed when Joyce, deep in the throes of her other problems, seemed unresponsive to a weekend of jollity. It began to look as if the idealistic romance would not survive the college years.

After a while Rennie broke his silence, but Joyce was no longer so confident about the future. Her pattern of life began to change:

> Toward the end of the year I began going out a lot, got more into things, made many friends, and stopped worrying about my marks. I decided to go to school that summer, and became thoroughly adjusted to the whole situation more or less automatically, so it all turned out all right after that.

She made herself more "outgoing," even to the extent of having two or three dates a week. Joyce was pretty and lively; it was not her fate to be a wallflower. She enjoyed going out, especially with boys who could talk about serious things, and it was doubtless reassuring to her to find that she need not be without partners. Her new friendships were not, however, marked by "serious interest," even of the sort evoked by Carlos, much less of the kind she had felt, and still felt, toward Rennie. They were also not marked by any forward steps in sexual experimentation. (She had decided that this realm should be explored only after marriage. Even in an interview with the woman who had earlier been her tutor, for whom she felt warm admiration, she dealt with the topic of sex in somewhat distant fashion. "I regard sex as a sacred thing," she said; "I've always objected to anything else." And she confessed to a "sort of repulsion against the dirty side of it, as it were." Joyce had experienced "no tendency" toward masturbation, which she felt would probably disturb her.) She was not accustomed to discuss sex with her friends; such knowledge as she possessed came from her mother, largely in answer to questions, and from courses in biology and psychology. Her store of information she considered rather limited, but about this she was cheerfully unconcerned. "I think I know the things I need to know," she said; "if there are more things that I need to know I will know them, by finding out or by intuition."

Joyce's real feeling remained attached to Rennie, and before long her affection was again reciprocated. Within a year of the ill-starred trip to Princeton they became secretly engaged. The reason for secrecy can be inferred from the reaction of Joyce's parents when, nearly two years later, she consulted them with a view to announcing the engagement. They both approved highly of Rennie, and were probably not startled at the news, but they were reluctant to believe that the time for marriage had really arrived. Although they agreed to issue the announcement, they counseled that the engagement should be a long one so that both youngsters would have time to become more settled and mature.

Once her engagement became a fact, even though a secret one, Joyce found herself again released from dependence on the approval of her girl friends. She began to resume her role as an official. Several elective offices came her way, including a rather prominent one in which she felt that she was able to make an important contribution. The "feeling of separation" that had characterized her freshman year was replaced by a welcome sense of belongingness.) In an interview she listed "having a great many friends" as one of the three best things in life, "being ostracized" as one of the worst. She learned that office-holding at college did not entail the same estrangement from the group that accompanied it during her school-girl years. She took increasing pleasure in meeting people and talking with them, sharing enthusiasms and serious interests. "I love to talk and discuss public affairs," she told us, and although she did not choose friends on this basis she found particular pleasure in the company of those who shared her interest in public events.

With regard to closer friendships, however, she remained unsatisfied. No longer fearful of rejection as a teacher's pet and "goodygoody," she still felt that her relationships lacked intimacy and depth. She noted that her best friends were either older or younger, that she tended—like her father—to be somewhat distant, and that she didn't know how to set about deepening a friendship. Replying to a question about her intuitive ability, she said that her intuition was "pretty good, mostly in the sense of understanding rather than in the sense of being empathic." Clearly she craved intimate friendship, but it was difficult for her to experience the feelings that nourish such a relationship. It was difficult to give confidences and to exhibit the quality of sincerity which she several times mentioned as the essence of true friendship. Joyce's problem is not the less interesting for being extremely common among college students and for exemplifying a marked characteristic of the American culture. Diffuse sociability and close personal friendships are two very different things. Our contemporary culture encourages the former but strews various obstacles in the way of the latter. Before we analyze this problem in Joyce, however, it will be well to complete our description of her college years.

A wide range of interests and enthusiasms kept her happily busy during her last two years at college. There was never enough time for all the things she wanted to do. Discussing politics, meeting people, taking part in student activities took up part of her energies, but she was also interested in pottery, sewing, and cooking. Her early fascination by flowers and birds continued, exposing her to a bad annual attack of spring fever, and she was often "ecstatic" over beautiful views and glorious sunsets. She loved the colorful, the cheerful, and the gay in objects as well as in people. Positions of special importance in her life were occupied by music and dancing. She loved the music that went with dancing, but she also loved choral music and experienced some of her deepest rapture in connection with the great religious choral works. Starting at nine, she had taken piano lessons for several years and had become fairly proficient in reading music at sight. The system used by her piano teacher did not emphasize sight-reading, but Joyce shunned the difficult exercises, "never practiced properly," and developed her piano technique more or less in her own way. She found in sight-reading not only musical pleasure but also a challenge to work the piece out, similar to the challenge of solving a problem in mathematics. She considered music the greatest of her enjoyments.

Joyce's use of her mind in intellectual pursuits afforded an interesting comparison with Hale and Kidd. Even in artificial test situations there were fundamental differences. With the Rorschach inkblots, for instance, she showed none of Hale's precision or preference for mechanical objects, nor did she display Kidd's laborious search for details and leaning toward drab interpretations. She was inclined to take in the whole blot at a glance, giving it an overall interpretation that made up in enthusiasm for what it lacked in point of detail. Her main responses suggested a proclivity for vague, rosy-hued philosophizing, and something of this sort could be detected in her approach to serious intellectual problems. In conversation her ideas flowed forth with fluent ease, but they took the form of generalities sometimes none too well backed by detailed information; her arguments proceeded not so much by strict logic as by an almost aesthetic combination of concrete examples and strongly affirmed values. In the Vigotsky experiment her classifying of the blocks was almost entirely a perceptual process, in contrast to the highly logical Hale. Like Kidd she manipulated the blocks as if waiting for them to announce their properties, but she did not have Kidd's difficulty in formulating the principle once she had discovered the correct solution. Logic was available to her, but she preferred to work in a more colorful, aesthetic fashion.

In spite of this quality in her thinking, Joyce's general ideas were formed into a working philosophy which in a very real sense acted as a guide to behavior. She was far more explicit concerning values than either Hale or Kidd. This was because she was heir to her parents' explicit system of values, an inheritance which she showed no disposition to reject. Both parents, it will be recalled, had rebelled against rigidly Republican backgrounds and sought the position of independents in politics. On the national scene they supported the New Deal and were warm admirers of President Roosevelt. Locally they often cast their votes for Republicans, partly because they considered certain candidates abler, partly in protest against certain candidates whom they believed to be dishonest with public funds. When Joyce was asked for her own views with regard to people who had recently run for office, she came out with precisely the same slate that had been favored by her parents. "It's irrational to vote for a party regardless of who's up," she explained; "I try to be open-minded." It was noteworthy that when she discussed political figures she often reported that "we" feel thus-and-so, "we" think this-and-that, as if opinions were a matter of unanimous decision around the Kingsley dining table. "We admire Mr. and Mrs. Roosevelt greatly," she said in an interview; then she called attention to a parallel "greatness" in the way the Roosevelts and her parents had taken public criticism.

It goes without saying that Joyce was religious. "Religion has been a life-long thing for me," she wrote; she accepted it because "it has the most plausible explanations of how the world came to be and why man is what he is." We were not vouchsafed an account of the more personal side of her religion. "The religious experiences I have had are too intensely personal to write or to relate." But it was plain that religion was the cornerstone of her thinking about social problems. "I don't believe that men will ever be completely happy," she wrote, "until their lives are on a religious basis; by that I mean they will acknowledge God as the Supreme Being and the source of their lives and proceed to try to live up to that." She recognized that such a development could not be forced; it must come about as a slow growth through education in the broadest sense of the word. Essentially she held the view that social betterment comes about by improving the quality of individual lives. Her own role was "to live as well as I can, to build the characteristics I say others should have in myself, and to try to help my children to have them also."

It is interesting to note that Joyce's personal philosophy was a shade more individualistic than that of her father, who was, as we have seen, deeply interested in the cooperative movement. The following excerpt, given in answer to a question about cooperation, is hardly a model of clarity, but its confusion becomes meaningful when we recall her position as eldest daughter in a cooperative home, pledged not to put personal interests ahead of those of the group.

> Cooperation is a wonderful thing, but for its strength it depends on people realizing their own value. It's important, but I value my own privacy a lot; so I'm not sure that it's valuable in all fields. But cooperation in any economic endeavor is the

best thing; potentially every man has a chance. Though it often takes a long time. We're tied down by the past. If it were left that each individual were left in freedom to the greatest extent and could still fulfill his obligations, it would be a good thing. When one is tied to a thing like that you have to do it all day and all night, and it suppresses individual wishes— which might be a good thing. But anyhow it would be difficult.

Joyce herself recognized in these remarks a lapse from her usual standard of coherence. "Oh, I guess I'm rambling," she said, "but I do get so enthusiastic and excited!" She probably did not recognize, however, the precise nature of the personal problem that was here invading her public sentiment. Privacy and independence had suffered a bit in her development; service to the group figured as a somewhat bleak duty, in contrast to the lively enthusiasm that characterized most of her behavior.

The story of Joyce's last two years at college would be incomplete without mention of her baby cousin Philip. In fact, Joyce listed Philip, along with Rennie and her presidency of student government, as one of the three major positive events in her life. Philip came to live with the Kingsleys because his mother became mentally deranged shortly after his birth. He was soon "the center of everything," and his mother's continued ill health made it seem not unlikely that he would be a permanent member of the family. Joyce wrote:

> He is now a year and a half old, and one of the most delightful babies there has ever been. I have had a grand time taking care of him and playing with him. He is quite cooperative most of the time, and a joy to be with.

Elsewhere, comparing him with her two brothers, she made the remark, "I'm freer to shower my affection on Philip." Apparently she found in Philip a sudden, unexpected, welcome outlet for a flood of tender cherishing that had previously been impounded within her. Her maternal feelings found a channel agreeably free from obstacles. With characteristic enthusiasm she took on the mothering of her parents' "adopted" child.

Writing about her plans for the immediate future Joyce gave her chief aim as that of finding a job on the West Coast. Rennie's training in the sciences placed him in a highly specialized section of the military program, and he expected to stay on the West Coast for the duration of the war. She continued:

Another chief aim is to be married. I think that emotionally we're ready to be married now. We have other problems to face, though: mostly finances, and parents who think we should see more of the 'big wide world' first. The parents can and will take care of themselves when the time comes, but the finances aren't as easy as all that. There just plain aren't any at this point. I have enough money to take me to the West Coast and hold me over until pay checks start coming in. Rennie has a private's pay, most of which he puts into war bonds. We think now that it will be better to wait a while for these reasons. But that doesn't stop us from planning and working hard toward this, our main aspiration, all the time.

Joyce was stepping forth into a troubled world and an uncertain future, but she was doing so without dismay. She looked forward with cheerful confidence to whatever might happen next in life's joyous adventure.

BENEATH THE SURFACE: ANALYSIS OF FREE ASSOCIATIONS

It should not be laid down as a dogma that no one can have a happy childhood. We have reason to believe that Joyce's childhood was, in the main, a happy one, and that her adolescence was in a good many respects a joyous adventure. Yet we were led to suspect that she had a special interest in painting a sunny picture of her life, as if her emotional economy somehow depended upon seeing things in their most cheerful light. Her own surprise that her early memories were so uniformly happy can be taken as evidence of a dim sense of incompleteness. Furthermore, it became increasingly apparent that certain tendencies—independence, rebelliousness, aggression—played almost no part in her self-picture but betrayed their presence in side remarks or in statements quickly dismissed as of no importance. Was she fully satisfied that her duties as eldest child and only daughter were no more than fair? Was she content when she came to recognize the silent infiltration of parental moral values? Had she been able to accept without rebellion the whole high code which her parents preached and sought to exemplify? Did she resent the tie to her mother? Did she herself have certain qualities which defeated her search for close friends? On all these points there were scraps of evidence suggesting that beneath the surface Joyce was not without her resentments and aggressions. Her psychological development had not been as easy as she seemed inclined to believe.

It will be remembered that Joyce characterized Rennie as "more gentle, kind, and understanding" than herself. Interesting in this connection is a story she told in the Thematic Apperception Test. A young couple was happily married, but the wife destroyed the initial happiness by "making selfish demands" on the husband, stubbornly persisting even when she saw that he did not like it. When the husband was called to military service, she weepingly realized her loneliness and loss, and during the three years of his absence "just concentrated in everything she did on overcoming interest in herself and making herself more and more outgoing and thoughtful of other people." Because of this strenuous moral development on the part of the heroine the story came to a happy ending. It may well be that this tale recapitulated her own temporary estrangement from Rennie; at all events, it suggests that Joyce was to some extent aware of a streak in herself that was very different from her professed ideals, a streak of selfish demandingness and resentment that could be subdued only with a definite struggle. It is not surprising that if being "thoughtful of other people" required such formidable self-discipline it would not be readily available in the spontaneous form needed for intimate friendship. We can think of Joyce as one who, because of a need for alliance with parents against brothers, had tried to be too good too soon. She had tried to suppress her selfish needs faster than they could really be suppressed, especially in view of occasional doubt about the sufficiency of parental rewards. As a result her selfish needs had given her a real tussle, and she was still made uneasy by their undercover activity.

Our clearest insight into how Joyce carried on the battle for goodness came from an hour devoted to free association. The session was conducted by a woman graduate student who put questions only when Joyce fell spontaneously silent. As often happens in free association, Joyce chose her first topic by looking around the room, but almost at once she arrived at an emotionally charged problem—her mother.

> The first thing that comes to my mind is seeing the curtains. I like to plan dresses and things. I like to sew. I'm thinking, worrying—no, thinking of dresses I need. I want to try to make some block prints to put on the bottom of a skirt. Pretty little birds with crowns on their heads. Mother thinks that maybe flowers would be good. Big spring flowers. Umm. (Pause) This

> is difficult. I don't feel like thinking any particular thing at this point.

Pages could be spent analyzing this utterance, so simple and banal yet thematically so rich. The most significant item is the decorations on the dress. Will it be birds or flowers? Will it be what Joyce wants or what Mother thinks is good? Here the associations block and the outcome is enigmatic. The outcome of this conflict is also enigmatic in the Thematic Apperception Test. The story has already been mentioned in which a young woman finds herself bound by a mysterious and inescapable tie to an older one. In contrast, there are two stories in which the heroine rebels against parental expectations and successfully goes her own way. The first story finds her leaving the farm with its round of domestic duties in order to become a music teacher. In the second story a girl of eighteen falls violently in love, and there is nothing her mother can do to prevent her from going ahead with marriage. It is interesting, however, that Joyce gave a certain distance to these two plots: she specified that the farm parents were European immigrants preserving foreign ideals, and that the love-smitten girl of eighteen was only the adopted child of the worried mother. Thus both in her stories and in her initial free association Joyce avoided a definitive decision on the mother-daughter problem.

Pursuing the free associations further, we find that Joyce devoted a substantial part of the hour to thinking about the Parkins family. Mr. Parkins was a close friend of the family, and the one child, an adopted daughter Mabel, was one of Joyce's friends and schoolmates. Joyce had been talking about her brother Henry, incidentally criticizing her mother's insufficient concern about the boy's health; then came a long silence which was broken as follows:

> I can't help wondering about Mabel. Her mother seems to be awfully happy about letting her go away. I wonder if Mabel can sustain that and pull through it without getting sick. She doesn't know how to cook and isn't interested in learning. It's most cruel to children to protect them like that, to indulge them in everything and give them what they want— whether they're adopted children or not. After all, in later life they are not going to have such privileges. Lack of discrimination in buying things and . . . I think Mabel would be much happier if her mother hadn't let her dress up so in

school . . . with high heels, carrying a big load of books, all stoop-shouldered. It was unnatural. She's never been very happy. She's always had to think how her mother would react. She seems to have had the right approach, though. She just lets things ride and her mother comes around, like she did about Fritz.

Then followed some remarks about Fritz, Mabel's fiance, a foreign-born young man with various undesirable traits which, however, Joyce was inclined to excuse on the ground of a difficult economic and family situation. She was soon back at Mabel.

Maybe Mabel will do a lot for him. What a situation it would be, though, to start out and not know how to cook and take care of a house. Nor to use money. Plenty of people start out knowing very little, but they are more practical than Mabel is. Maybe she has it in her and we've just never seen it. (Pause) She certainly has developed a method for getting around her mother. I wonder if it's a conscious method or Mabel just is that way.

It seemed like a change of subject when Joyce, again pausing, began to talk about Mabel's father, but she did not stray far from her underlying theme. Mr. Parkins was a saintly man, never known to criticize, but always "the prey of his wife's will." Two or three episodes were mentioned to exemplify his wife's selfish, nagging demandingness and his own distress at her behavior. Then Joyce said:

Mother said he was very embarrassed that Mrs. Parkins hadn't gone to the meeting after Mother had called her up and told her of my engagement. It was hard for her to take. She felt it very keenly that Rennie is a college graduate and Fritz isn't. It is also a little tough on her that Fritz is a foreigner and Rennie isn't. Still, I can't imagine Mabel settling down with any of the people her mother would have chosen.

It appeared that Mabel had taken no chances of incurring parental objection to her engagement. Unlike Joyce, she had made the announcement herself.

It must have been a little hard for both of them, to just suddenly have her get a ring and take it to church and show it around and let people know that way. When Mabel showed the ring herself it was as if her parents weren't backing her up. Mrs. Brown said at the time, 'Wasn't it a shame!' We were kind of flabbergasted that anyone would say that about any kind of engagement.

Possibly Joyce received a silent inner warning at this point that her sympathy for Mabel's independence needed a touch of discipline. Had not her own parents given her great benefits yet at the same time left her free?

It certainly makes you appreciate parents who are aware of things and particularly who are eager to leave you free to make your own choices and accept the responsibility you are going to take. I think if we'd been very wealthy I still would have learned to cook, sew, and so forth.

Having said this much, however, she received another prompting from a tendency not quite so docile:

I often wonder just what it is that made them the way they are. . . .

It certainly helps the parents out to have older children to accept some of the responsibility, so that they are left a little freer to take care of the others.

This was dangerous ground, and she did not tarry longer. After dealing with several other matters she went into a long discussion of memory, which eventually led her to the following observation:

Seems kind of strange when all your childhood memories are happy ones and you wonder why there aren't some unhappy ones. You don't think there would be, or the happy ones would bring them up if there were any. I wonder just how much there is to the idea of repression. Seems as if sometimes it must be exploited a bit.

And these remarks on memory, which brought the free association hour to a close, could by no means be regarded as chance driftwood on the surface of Joyce's consciousness. In the very last interview of our series, which we call the "worm turns interview" because of the encouragement that is given the subject to criticize both the procedures and the investigators, she offered as her sole serious criticism the failure of the interviewers to appreciate the importance of her having had a happy childhood.

Joyce's free associations clearly disclosed the residual tension left by her full acceptance of the parental ideals of conduct. She had been obliged to give up a little too much of her independence and the pursuit of her own desires. She had accepted a little too much of her mother's domination. Beneath the surface there was resentment and rebellion. Nevertheless, her adoption of an approved life pattern had been far from a sullen and mechanical conformity. She had thrown her whole soul into it, she had lived it with enthusiasm, and it had brought her great rewards such as her presidency of student government, her place in college activities, and Rennie. Within its requirements she had fallen in love and was planning her own home, and her life was rich with a wide variety of interests. Rebellious aggression was probably linked with childhood anxieties, but it was also out of harmony with her current self-picture and could be sensed only as a disruptive force in the program of her ongoing concerns. The free associations show how she dealt with it. She could be very critical of—not her own mother, but Mrs. Parkins, who selfishly ruled the household. She obviously envied Mabel's independence, but she could be indignant about Mabel's crudeness in announcing her engagement and about her ignorance of household duties. Throughout the free associations her comments about people were decidedly acid, and as she voiced her criticisms she did nothing to avoid the implication that her own way of doing things was morally superior. She thus gave herself constant doses of reassurance while at the same time making outlets for no small amounts of righteous aggression. Her treasonable impulses seemed well-controlled by this procedure, but at the cost of the tolerance and humility that would have helped her to make intimate friendships.

BALANCE SHEET AT COMMENCEMENT

We have now followed Joyce Kingsley's life up to the end of her senior year at college, and we are about to find out what happened during the next five years. It is of interest to pause a moment in order to consider the problems that would be involved if we attempted to predict Joyce's future. Has our understanding given us increased power to foretell how she will behave? Has the kind of information that we derived from our case study put us in a position to predict where her problems will lie, where her strengths will appear, what her chances are for a happy and productive life? Prediction is one of the surest tests of knowledge, but let us be wary about what we commit ourselves to predict concerning the future of a personality.

The outstanding obstacle to prediction lies in the fact that one person can never be considered alone and for himself. All of us are in constant interaction with circumstances and with other people. Each step of our behavior has an effect of some kind on our environment; every next step is influenced by the way the environment has just responded. In order to predict one person's course of life we would have to be able, strictly speaking, to predict the behavior of everyone with whom he came in contact, and we would have to be able to specify in advance the circumstances in which he would become involved. We cannot predict the outcome of Joyce's marriage when we do not have a full case study of Rennie. We can, of course, make the guess that Joyce will experience difficulty with the sexual side of marriage, but the extent of this difficulty cannot be fully gauged without knowing how Rennie is going to behave as a sexual partner. We might venture to predict that Joyce will be troubled by "selfish demandingness" in relation to her husband, but we certainly cannot extend this prediction very far without knowing how Rennie will respond to demands and what expectations he has about married life. We sense that Joyce may want to exert a certain power over her husband, making him conform to the images that are in her mind, but we can scarcely foretell the course of this tendency without knowing what images Rennie has in his mind and how he will respond to the pressure of dominance. We infer that Joyce will be enthusiastically fond of her children and that their welfare will be quite a central value in her life, but we cannot predict such important considerations as the number and sexes of her children and whether they will be "cooperative" like Philip, sweet and docile like Joyce herself, unruly and rebellious like Albert and Henry. We assume that Joyce will have some difficulty with the parental tie, especially the tie to her mother, but we cannot fully guess what will happen without knowing how much actual contact she will have with the parental home and how the parents themselves will behave.

What can we say about her social relationships and her need for intimate friends? Much depends on the human environment into which she moves. In a group that prided itself on bohemian freedom and post-Freudian sophistication she would quickly and scornfully be labeled "Victorian." This would probably bring back the feelings that troubled her during her first years at the Walter School. On the other hand she might land among people much concerned with community service who would label her "public-spirited" and give her an appreciated place in their affairs. To what extent do we expect Joyce's idealism to be shattered by contact with the seamy side of life? Certainly this depends on the seaminess of her environment and on the suddenness and directness with which she is exposed to conditions from which she has thus far been shielded. We know that she cares a great deal not only about religion in general but also about her particular denomination. Will the balance of her personality be seriously upset if she lands in a community where her denomination is not represented? A person and his environment are in constant interaction, and we cannot hope to predict very far ahead when our knowledge is largely confined to the person.

It is not to be supposed, however, that this intrinsic difficulty is the only obstacle to predictions about personality. Even if we could magically foretell circumstances and the behavior of the human environment we would find the path of prediction full of pitfalls. Frequently a careful case study permits us to say that certain tendencies are present, even that some tendencies are strong and others less strong. But we have no precise measurement of the strength of these various forces nor of the conditions that set them in motion; hence we can only guess which ones will prevail in crucial situations that require decisive choices. A good example can be found in Joyce's relationship to her mother. Even if we knew how her mother were going to act, it would be hard to decide whether dependence or independence would in the end prevail. Joyce herself cannot tell us; she does not know. She gives us evidences of the conflict and clear grounds for inferring that both tendencies are at work, but we cannot be certain which of her somewhat disguised Thematic Apperception plots, for example, is most likely to become a reality. Our diagnosis of what is crucial in a person's life is still no more than a rough estimate.

There is yet another difficulty which is perhaps still more formidable. It springs from the fact that our knowledge about personality has been derived disproportionately from the study of psychologically disordered people. We are poor at understanding, even worse at predicting, the extent to which interests can substitute for one another in making up a satisfactory pattern of life. We know that

Joyce has set her heart on marrying Rennie, that several important problems seem to be solved and important needs satisfied by this course. We also know that she attaches central value to her role as a mother and that strong needs would be satisfied by having children. Here are two points at which events might not take their expected course. Rennie might be killed or might change his mind; or, if neither of these events occurred, she still might not have children. In clinical cases we find time and again that major frustrations of this kind have precipitated breakdown and psychological disorder; the personality must be slowly and painfully salvaged after its hard buffetings by fate. Joyce's own maternal grandmother, for instance, lost her grip on sanity through the tragic early death of one of her children. But major frustrations are more common than break-downs. Often it happens that a whole life pattern seems ruined, yet the person goes on and draws upon other resources in himself for the reconstruction of a happy and useful existence. When this happens we do not meet the person at the clinic or hospital, there-fore we have very small knowledge about the processes involved in such a case. We do not understand the circumstances under which one group of interests and motives can take over for another; more broadly, we do not understand how many of a person's potential interests it is necessary for him to pursue in order to feel satisfied as a whole. Prediction cannot go very far while we remain ignorant of such important matters.

Although we cannot expect to do much at present in the way of predicting the future course of a life, we should still do our best to understand any process of growth after it has taken place. Being wise after the event is not a triumph of scientific method, but it is often the only way we can proceed in attempting to become a little more wise before future events.

Part Two: FROM 21 TO 26

Immediately after graduation Joyce departed for the West Coast, where she secured a job in the large military research unit to which Rennie had been assigned. She and Rennie were married the fol-lowing spring. Rennie's educational plans after his release from military service brought them back to Boston for a two-year period, during which they occupied an apartment in the Kingsley home. Then Rennie obtained a position with a large manufacturing com-pany, and he and Joyce moved to Detroit to set up a home of their own. It was from there that they came, two years later, for the brief summer visit which gave us the opportunity to make the second study.

OUT INTO THE WORLD

Joyce was excited by what she found awaiting her on the West Coast. The scenery was enchanting, the people in the vast unit were endlessly interesting, the work kept her happily occupied; in short, it was "just the most fascinating place that anyone could possibly be in." She continued to live with enthusiasm, and she soon became aware of considerable changes taking place in herself. Questioned about these changes, she gave us the following piece of self-analysis:

> I think that getting away from home did a lot for me, as far as change goes. I think that just being away did a lot, though I'm not quite sure how. Maybe making my own decisions without any . . . oh, there hadn't been parental interference, but there were attitudes about what I did, and without those around, I think that accounts for a good deal of starting independence, my foundation for it, anyhow.

Continuing her discussion of change, Joyce reminded us that she had never had many close friends and did not know how to make them. The new situation helped her a great deal with this problem. Rennie had found a highly congenial group of friends many of whom had either wives or girl friends, so that Joyce was immersed in a pleasant social whirl. "I just sort of got a beginning there," she said; then she added, laughing at her own way of putting it, "I could see the possibilities and get some techniques for being a friend to somebody." Her relationship with Rennie "grew a great deal," and she believed that this had a lot to do "with changing attitudes and gaining independence." Joyce was not in a competitive situation as regards men, nor was she too starvingly in need of the approbation of other young people; this made it easier for her to enter on the path of establishing warmer friendships.

Joyce expressed astonishment that the strict standards under which she had been reared did not interfere with her social growth on the West Coast. She described the situation as follows:

> One thing that amazed me out there was my quick adjustment to a change of standards. As was probably evident be-

fore, standards at home were pretty high and pretty strict, in a way. And . . . Well, in the unit there were just no holds barred in conversation; anything went. And I didn't have any trouble adjusting to it, which amazed me, because I would have thought I would have. But it was the pattern, it was a completely new place, completely different, and it just came all right. Fortunately!

By way of illustration she mentioned a girl who had "*quite* a reputation" with the boys. "I discovered that she was a very charming girl and I thoroughly enjoyed her."

The theme of adjusting to different standards was developed further in another interview during which Joyce was asked what she wished had been done differently in her own upbringing. She wished that she had gone to college far away from home, feeling that she would thus have learned earlier to be more tolerant of other people and their standards. Her words fully corroborated the inferences we previously made concerning self-righteousness and its effects on friendship.

> I think that being away at college would have been awfully fine because I would have had a chance to establish myself separately and to really test what I thought I believed. As it was, I didn't have that until I went out to the West Coast, and fortunately it came smoothly then. But I had a sort of sense of being different from everybody, which isn't conducive to establishing good relationships with new people at all. I mean, I don't think it was being different in the sense of being better, although there are some implications of that in the sense of 'this is the way for me to behave; you don't behave that way'—you know. You can't help feeling that what you think is right is the best thing. But I think that the social adjustment eased a good deal when I got away from those standards. And it wasn't so much a question of not accepting the standards any longer as it was of being freer to see and understand other standards.

The last sentence in Joyce's reflections is of particular interest. Pleased as she was to find herself growing more tolerant and friendly, irked as she was by the memory of her former prudish subjugation to the parental value system, she nevertheless claimed that her new understanding had not made it impossible for her to act upon standards of her own. It is often difficult for a person to achieve independence of parental ideals without swinging to an opposite extreme and becoming an enemy of all fixed values. Joyce implied that she had avoided this swing of the pendulum. From an incident described in another connection we concluded that she might well have judged herself correctly on this point. Her job was at the young people's recreation center, and she found herself increasingly at variance with official policy. One or two of the employees seemed to her unsuitable to be in charge of adolescents, and several parents had become unwilling to have their children go to the center merely to dance, drink "cokes," play cards, and do a little necking. Joyce's desire to be a friendly person and a cooperative member of her society had not obliterated her antipathy toward the youth culture of early adolescence. She was outraged, moreover, by the failure of the recreation center to offer its young clients sufficient opportunities for the development of serious interests. Her anger was further aroused by a series of orders issued in peremptory military fashion though intended only for the civilian personnel; one such order required her to work overtime on evenings when Rennie was at liberty. She was already meditating a letter of protest when another order arrived which affected one of the few remaining serious enterprises at the center. Some strange bureaucratic whim dictated that the paper published every Wednesday by an enthusiastic group of youthful editors should thereafter be published on Friday. Joyce undertook to voice the editors' objections, only to find herself on an endless chain of official "buck-passing." So she composed her letter to the higher authorities, detailing her grievances and outlining a program of what she believed could and should be done at the recreation center; at the same time she resigned from her job. She distributed the letter widely to interested parents and to the military hierarchy, including the Commanding Officer of the post. "And something did get done," she told us:

> They used the blueprint that I'd started on as a basis for working it up again, so I think it was a useful thing to do. But, again, I think it was another step toward independence, because here I was, thinking something out completely for myself without going to talk to Mother about it, which was really something when you get right down to it. And having confidence in my ability to do it.

During her year on the West Coast Joyce thus made rapid strides toward independence. To a considerable extent she extricated herself from hitherto unquestioned parental influences and acquired the confidence to feel and act in her own right. Being away from home was a highly successful venture. At no time, however, had she really been an insecure stranger without a point of anchorage in the new community. She was engaged to Rennie, and presently she became his wife.

MARRIAGE

When Joyce first arrived at the military post she elected to live inexpensively by taking her meals at the mess hall. Soon the fare began to pall, so she started cooking the evening meal in her dormitory room and inviting Rennie to eat it with her. "It was just superb," she said; "we spent all our evenings together and went hiking practically every week-end." Rennie was due for a furlough in December, but Joyce's parents vetoed a plan to have the wedding so soon. This was disappointing, but "the winter flew by in a hurry," and by May the Kingsleys were able to have their house redecorated and their preparations made for a large wedding. "I made my own wedding gown and some of my trousseau," said Joyce, but then she added truthfully, "Mother made most of it because I didn't have very much time." After the wedding she and Rennie returned to the West Coast until his military service was completed, at which point they took a honeymoon camping trip in the mountains. Then they returned to Boston and settled down in the apartment, a more or less separate suite of rooms in the Kingsley house, which they were to occupy until Rennie completed his specialized training.

When questioned about the sexual side of marriage Joyce reported, after a little hesitation, that she had experienced some difficulty in achieving a relaxed attitude. That she was able eventually to attain orgasm and a feeling of satisfaction was due in part to her husband's understanding.

> Fortunately Renn is one of the most patient people on the face of the earth, and I think he understood how it does take a while to get to the point where you really are free and warm. Having strict standards makes it a very difficult break. I think that Renn did . . . while I don't know that he realized the problems, I think he did everything he could to make it easier. And when you're very much in love it's easier anyhow, I suppose, than when you have doubts. I think also that it's a process that goes on and on.

In response to another question Joyce said that it had taken "about a year" to reach good sexual adjustment. When the interviewer remarked that this was not an unusually long period, she said, "It seemed long to me." One can hardly escape the conclusion that for a while she experienced the sexual relationship as an irksome obligation, a frustratingly difficult task rather than a pleasure. She has made progress, but she is not unaware that learning to be "free and warm" is a process that "goes on and on."

Joyce was more concerned, however, about a problem in marital adjustment that arose where she least expected it. Shortly after the marriage Renn reached the conclusion that he no longer believed in religion. Joyce was deeply upset; "it was especially difficult for me," she said, "because I had grown up in a home where there was strong religious influence and I had expected certain elements of that to carry over into our own life together." What bothered her most was the discovery that she could not do anything to change Renn's views. At first she was much concerned about "helping him to see the light," but she soon realized that her efforts only made matters worse.

> I eventually got to the point where I saw that there wasn't anything I could do except sit back and see what happened. He sort of wanted to work things out for himself and wanted to take his own time doing it. It's sort of hard to get to the point where you can realize that the best thing for you to do is just plain not to push it. It took me a year or two to really be able to do it.

The problem was aggravated by the move to Boston, where Joyce felt that Renn "had to keep up certain appearances." She kept hoping that events would hasten his return to religious faith. When his mother died she thought, "Now maybe this will help." She encouraged herself by practicing silent psychological diagnosis: his agnosticism was part of his need to achieve independence from his parents. All of this was not very comforting, for Renn seemed to be making little progress back toward religion. When questioned, Joyce admitted that her disappointment about his religious views had hindered the process of sexual adjustment. "It made me overly critical," she said, "and I don't think it helped me in the relaxing problem."

The move out to Detroit proved helpful in reaching a compromise on the question of religion. Away from the parental atmosphere Joyce found it easier to make fewer demands. Furthermore, the minister of her church in Detroit turned out to be an uncongenial person having a different shade of views from those to which she was accustomed, and she herself preferred to attend, at least temporarily, a church of another denomination which had an active program for young married people. "There are so many other things to do on week-ends," she admitted with a laugh, "that we've become rather lax about church-going." Renn agreed to accompany Joyce to church, but she found it expedient not to press for too frequent attendance, and she decided not to insist on the custom of saying grace before meals.

There was another problem which likewise reached its height during the stay in Boston and improved after the move to Detroit. Joyce discovered that she could not help behaving somewhat like the demanding wife of her story in the earlier Thematic Apperception Test.

> I found it awfully hard to leave Renn as free as he wanted to be left, for quite a while. Of course the transition from courtship to marriage is quite something. I think that I expected some of those same attentions to hold over and found it a little difficult when at times they didn't. And I made demands on Renn which he didn't want to have made on him because of that, demands for time and attention. . . . I had sort of a picture of a glorious future when we did everything together, which is really very silly, because I don't think it does anybody that much good. You've got to have independent things so that you bring something new into the relationship all the time.

Joyce was shrewdly aware that this problem was mixed up with that of becoming independent of her mother. Renn told her that she was a different person when she was near her mother.

> I think I realized that in coming back there would be a problem, that Mother had never realized the influence she had on me, and that I knew it but didn't know what to do about it, how to handle it. She never wanted to influence her children in terms of deciding what they would do, or think, or feel, but she has a very strong personality herself and she just inevitably *does*. I don't think she can help it. And I think that I sort of depended extra much on Renn because of that, to sort of tide me over. And that's pretty difficult for a new husband to take, really.

Things began to look different when Renn received an excellent appointment in Detroit and moved his wife away from the Kingsley home. He and Joyce bought an old house very cheaply and worked together to bring it into a state of good repair. Having more of her husband's time and attention, Joyce could afford to be more tolerant of his occasional independent activities with men friends and associates at the shop. Hearing her description of Renn we were reminded of some of the things she said earlier about her father, but Renn's exploits were even more numerous than Mr. Kingsley's:

> He has great skills in mechanical things and in carpentry and in gardening and masonry, and any other direction you want to turn, practically. . . . He has great facility in ironing out human relations problems; he's just so creative in human relations. . . . And then he plays on a baseball team, the company baseball team. He's pretty terrific. Boy, can that guy hit! Golly! Wonderful! I have to go to every game. I don't have to; I go by choice. We form an active rooting group for our division team. . . . They're getting him in the Young Republican Club—over my dead body!

Joyce has learned somewhat painfully that she cannot dominate her husband nor direct the course of his life. He is no longer Rennie; he has proved to be Renn. But perhaps he has served all the better in disengaging her from her mother's influence, and perhaps she is more rather than less fond of him now than she was in the days of courtship and honeymoon. At all events she is happier. "Looking back," she told us, "I think there was never a time when I was really unhappy, and yet it seems to me that I'm so much more happy now than I was then. It quite amazes me!"

Joyce was well aware, however, that she would be still more happy if she had a baby. Thus far she had failed to conceive, and she was greatly distressed about it. She had sought medical aid and been given a clean bill of health, but the advice to "go to it" had not served to solve the problem. At first she worried too much, counting days and keeping temperature charts, but this seriously interfered with relaxing at times when conception was most likely to occur. Then her physician suggested that she forget about it and take up some line of work or study that would absorb her interests. In consequence of this advice she entered the school for social work, but when spring came she "got to one of those times when it is *very* hard not to have children" and appeared again at the physician's office. She was found to have an elevated basal metabolic rate and other evidences of tension. The school year had been strenuous, so she was advised this time to take the summer off and vegetate for a while. She was in process of vegetating at the time of the second study.

In discussing this major frustration, Joyce agreed that there were certain advantages in not having children too early in one's married life. She realized that she and Renn had had a chance to do more things together and to build a strong relationship, and she felt that he would probably be a better father and she a better mother because of having to wait for a baby. But her perception of the silver lining did not detract from her feeling about the cloud. Asked if she were using school work to keep her mind off the problem, she replied:

> You can't. I mean, it's just impossible to forget it. I wonder how anybody does, if anybody does. It's just always with you, and there are times when it's more pressing than other times, like this spring when my sister-in-law and one of my best friends both had babies at about the same time, and that was just awful. . . . You think you've gotten control of it, then whamo! You haven't after all. And it just keeps cropping up.

It is significant that Joyce here made no use of the device we suspected her of practicing when she wrote *Joyous Adventure*: that of putting things in a rosy light and repressing the disagreeable aspects of experience. She was in close touch with her maternal desires and was not in the least inclined to find anything joyous in their frustration. If she harbored repressed feelings that made her resist becoming a mother these feelings were operating in a very circumscribed channel—that of producing tension in the sexual relationship—and they were distinctly not creating a falsified picture of the blessings of childlessness.

THE KINGSLEY FAMILY REVISITED

Five years had wrought a dramatic change in the Kingsley household. The stable serenity portrayed by Joyce in the year of her graduation from college had given place to decided storm and stress. Mr. Kingsley had passed through a serious crisis with regard to his work. Mrs. Kingsley had suffered a bout of ill health from which she had emerged to resume on a larger scale her independent career as a teacher. Joyce was revisiting her parents when she came for the second study, so we chose them as a topic on which to open the new interviews. We found that we were in for some surprises.

In his position as regional executive officer for his denomination, Mr. Kingsley was under the control of a regional Board of Governors. He had always had a certain amount of trouble with the Board, but recently there had grown up a strong movement to oust him. For a time it seemed that his office might be abolished. Finally the Board decided to extend it temporarily but to give Mr. Kingsley a less flattering title. Joyce considered that the situation was not good and probably never would be. "The effect in the family," she told us, "was felt most by Mother who has had a terribly hard time adjusting to the attacks—the very vehement personal attacks— that have been made on Daddy." Mrs. Kingsley was struck down simultaneously by arthritis and colitis. Her physician told her, in effect, that she could regain and keep her health only if she broke out of the frustrations of her present way of life and embarked upon the kind of career she really wanted. This advice, based on the supposition that the physical ailments were rooted in psychological problems, proved to be thoroughly sound. Mrs. Kingsley resumed her study of education and was soon appointed to an important post in a well-known school. According to Joyce this gave her "a completely new lease on life; it's just lifted her out of all the petty little mirey sorts of things." What things did Joyce have in mind?

> It took her out of home and it gave her people whom she enjoyed to associate with. Before, she'd been rebelling like fury against associating with the traditional church-woman sort of activity where you go and sew once a week or knit. One time she was program chairman of a reading club, and she was quite ecstatic about the prospect of presenting modern poetry, Rilke and so forth. And the good ladies didn't take to that. She was just completely ill at ease in that sort of life. And going back to school just helped a great deal to give her people that she really could enjoy and intellectual stimulation for the very brilliant mind that she has.

Happy as she was over her mother's new buoyancy, Joyce could see "ways in which it isn't so good." Mrs. Kingsley was so determined to stay out of church affairs that she would not even attend a convention in which her husband was much interested. "That is going too far to extremes," Joyce declared; "people kept asking where she was, and she told me something about Daddy saying that he couldn't invent any more excuses." Mrs. Kingsley had hoped that as a consequence of the friction in the regional office her husband would leave the church altogether "so that they could go off and start afresh," and for a while Mr. Kingsley actually entertained the idea of turning to secular administrative work. But, as his daughter expressed it, "when a man has put his whole life into the church you just can't change it that way." When the worst of the clouds cleared away, Mr. Kingsley decided to stay on; he felt that his work was important, and he resisted his wife's urgings to make a break while it was still possible.

When we asked Joyce more about her father and his work we received an account that corresponded scarcely at all to the picture drawn in her earlier autobiography. Her description included the following:

> When he's really in a pinch he comes to and he pulls himself out of it. But his main trouble is that he lets himself be bogged down by a myriad of petty details, and because of that he gets so busy with them that he can't do the big things. And much of the stuff he does is really not necessary.

These general statements were given detailed support. Apparently Mr. Kingsley did many things around the office which could readily have been delegated to others. He charged himself with details that properly belonged to individual parishes and their ministers. In addition he managed his mother's finances and made out her income tax, and he did a great many things around his own home. Joyce concluded:

> I don't know how to account for the rest of it. I mean, it's just bad organization. And he's so mired down in it and has been at it for so many years that it's just come to the point where he's running himself ragged. It's crazy, but he can't get himself out of the rut apparently. He's that way and I guess you have to take him that way. It seems very silly, a lot of it, to me.

The drastic change in Joyce's attitude toward her parents, especially toward her father, deserves careful consideration. She exhibits a trend, quite common in the twenties, toward detachment and frank appraisal. We have already described a similar progression in Joseph Kidd's outlook on his parents. On the whole she is not unduly caustic, and there is certainly no little admiration for her mother's achievement in independence. The thing that is unusual in Joyce's case is not her objectivity at twenty-six but rather the gilded picture she created at twenty-one. Granting that things were better at that time, we must still ask why she needed to believe that her parents were so perfect, her home life so harmonious, as she portrayed them in the first study.

In attempting to answer this question it is necessary to bear in mind that identification with parental values played a vital part in her plan for living. It had served her in early childhood as a means of keeping Albert from crowding her out of parental favor. It had served at puberty as a weapon against the youth culture and as a platform for action and leadership. There had been little occasion to repudiate these values, which had not prevented her from finding a future husband, which shielded her from things like sex of which she was afraid, and which frustrated her only to the extent of limiting her capacity for friendship. As we saw, she had not really attempted to set up an identity of her own or to accept full responsibility for decisions and opinions. But her loyalty to home and parents cannot be fully understood as the mere persistence of a pattern previously found useful. We must also consider a special feature of Joyce's situation which exempted her from perceiving the conflict between dependence on parents and the attainment of adult autonomy. Her avenue of escape from the family, her means of effecting the transition from dependent to independent status, was guaranteed in advance by her engagement to Renn. She was like a guest at a house party who does not need to become aware that he is bored because his passage is already booked to leave on the morrow. Renn's values were not very different from those of her home, and she knew that her parents could offer no permanent obstacle to her marrying such an admirable man.

As we saw, she was much upset after marriage when Renn's religious values proved to be different, so that her own religious interests had to be the subject of compromise. She was again upset when renewed proximity to her mother reanimated the old dependence, and she then blamed Renn for failing in the function she had counted upon him to perform. In order to complete our explanation of her earlier need to canonize the home, however, we must bear in mind that she drew from it a certain comfort as she stood on the threshold ready to depart. Until she was actually out in the world, until she could prove herself and find her own identity, Joyce needed to feel that her upbringing had been perfect, that her parents had given her a "good foundation," that she would thus be equal to whatever tasks lay ahead. Once she knew that with Renn's help she could take her own stands and find the security of friends, she had little further need to lean on an idealized picture of her family.

Joyce brought us up to date concerning her brother Albert, of whose development during five years she sharply disapproved. Albert's passion for electronics had increased during military service and he had afterwards gone directly to work in an industrial laboratory without attempting to complete his education. Toward the family he was more surly and rebellious than ever. After displaying interest in a girl much admired by the Kingsleys ("We were pretty thrilled about it," said Joyce, reverting to the "we" of her undergraduate opinions), he perversely drifted off and married a girl as unkempt and careless as himself. As Joyce described it, "They both go around wearing jeans and shirts and tousled hair and practically look like twins." Joyce admitted that they "seemed pretty happy together," and she wondered if their coming baby might help them to be less rebellious. Throughout her conversation about Albert one could sense the working of her old childhood grievance. Albert was bad, but he did not receive enough punishment. He neglected his appearance and his education, he was boorish, he did just what he wanted, he did not marry the right kind of girl, and he was rewarded by having a baby which both he and his wife would probably neglect. Joyce could hardly be blamed for having a continued sense of injustice.

Among Albert's sins was his undue influence over Henry, whom he indoctrinated with rebellious and bohemian ideas. Apart from this, however, Henry was developing nicely, and Joyce found him altogether charming. But it was when we inquired about Philip, now six, that Joyce really warmed to her subject. "Oh, he's a honey," she said with a laugh; "he's just delightful." We learned that she had helped take care of Philip during the stay in Boston and that for the past two summers Philip had lived with her and Renn in Detroit while Mrs. Kingsley took summer courses. "We have a lot of fun," she said, "and so does he." Joyce rejected our suggestion that Mrs. Kingsley could not have had much time to take care of her adopted child. "Her freedom from the general situation," Joyce declared, "has not meant that she has ignored Philip in any way. I mean, he's had mothering all right. He's had more variety of people around him and it's been good for him, because he's a very social little guy." Joyce believed that the visits to Detroit had been decidedly helpful to Philip. Renn was an eager mentor in sports; he had already inducted his youthful cousin into baseball, football, and tennis. And Joyce was sure that the atmosphere of their home would make things "a good deal less confining" for Philip "than they were for Albert and me, for instance. I think it will be a lot easier for him to adjust to the general mores than it was for us."

Some of Joyce's views on child rearing emerged from an incident about which she told us with some pride. Philip was being constantly annoyed by the teasing of a girl playmate, which often drove him into a tearful rage. The little girl's mother told him to hit his tormentor as the only possible way to make her understand. Philip consulted Joyce concerning this heroic prescription.

> I presented him with another way to do it, thinking that that could very quickly get out of control. How would he know when to stop? That's expecting a good deal from a 6-year-old. I suggested that he run off and do something else interesting when he wanted to do what she was doing, and first thing he knew she'd get interested in that. He was very intrigued and found that it worked, and he could get back to the swing before she got through with the tractor, and so forth. He would pretend that he didn't even hear her when she was saying something that bothered him.

If Joyce has in some respects diverged from parental ideals, it is not in the direction of tolerating overt aggression. One wonders whether she invented the technique used on Philip or whether she merely remembered it.

It seems probable that Joyce's large share in taking care of Philip gave her a certain consolation for having no baby of her own. Philip was available, however, only in the summer time; for the rest of the year her substitute activity was to attend the school for social work.

PREPARING FOR SOCIAL WORK

When Joyce was advised by her physician to take up some work that would occupy her interest she was at first completely at a loss.

"What on earth do I want to do?" she asked herself; then, consulting her experience on the West Coast at the recreation center and her more recent girl scout work in Detroit, she decided that the greatest promise lay in social group work.

> The social work part can just go hang, as far as I'm concerned, but you have to take the other stuff along with group work. And it just seemed like practically the only thing that I was really interested in and fitted for and could get into. . . . As far as the actual work of group work goes, it's the spot for me, because it combines a very intensive understanding of the individual personality, the psychology of the individual, with a just developing understanding of what goes on in a group. . . . But getting that darned old degree is just plain drudgery. I don't know if it's worth it, I really don't.

Joyce believed that her studies at the school, and the field training that went with them, had helped her to become more tolerant of diverse standards. One feature of her family's value system carried over very nicely into social-work philosophy: the emphasis on "leaving people free to make their own choices." "That is something that falls right in with what I've always had," she reminded us; "practically a family standby, or at least a standby of our church." To illustrate her remarks she chose the subject on which she herself had previously been most intolerant.

> The place where the standards come in is the question of 'Now here's a bunch of teen-agers; what about their petting?' That sort of thing. And do I try to impose my standards on them or do I accept what they've got? And in working on something, do I work toward my standards or do I work toward something they choose? That sort of thing. And that's the only place where there has been any conflict, and that isn't conflict, really, because the emphasis in group work is on the use of the worker's personality as a tool in working with the group. And in doing that you have to generate warmth, if you haven't got it—and we hope you have—for all sorts and conditions of people, as they happen to be. And you have to accept their standards for what they are, which is part and parcel of this question of leaving a person free, really.

It is indeed difficult to effect a reconciliation between fighting for one's standards and working with people in that peculiarly tolerant and disarming fashion that is characteristic of social work. Joyce's problem at this point is more than a personal one.

It was obvious, of course, that Joyce had not entered social group work because of urgent need for a career. For the present, her whole heart was set upon having children. She had often, however, weighed the claims of homemaker and career woman, and her mother's example made it impossible for her to overlook the difficulties of a decision. "I still feel that the combination of some form of career with children is a good idea," she said, "but I don't quite know how it will work, or how to carry it out." Then she offered some wise reflections on the needs of young children and concluded that only some sort of part-time volunteer work would be compatible with these needs. Yet it was hard to make any solution retain a permanent shape. "I haven't solved for myself yet the conflict between getting educated and having children, and I don't know that I will. I keep trying. But you think you've got it under control and sometimes it just blows up in your face, and you gradually work it out again." The forces on either side of the conflict seemed too strong to remain long bound by a rational solution. But of course it was impossible for Joyce to reach a stable attitude when she did not know one of the most essential facts. She had to face the possibility that a career would be forced upon her or that the homemaker's role could be chosen only by adopting children. With this issue unsettled it is hardly surprising that she should close with the comment, "It's awfully hard to relax about the whole thing."

On the question of warmth in personal relationships Joyce did not, when pressed, make excessive claims to progress. When asked whether she had some close friends in Detroit she answered, "Yes, we do," and it required a further question to learn anything about friends whom she did not share with Renn. She then mentioned a number of people encountered at the school or in her scout work. "I feel much more able to handle relationships on my own," she said. "That took a while, I don't know just why." Speculating on the reason, she brought up the one-sidedness of the relationships that prevailed between the Kingsleys and their friends. A minister's family, in her view, must constantly play host and hostess; it is always "more on the 'give' of a relationship than on the 'take.'" "And you see yourself," she concluded, "in a different role from what is the normal role, it seems to me." Perhaps her choice of words tends here to confuse the issue. It is when one acts in a supe-

rior role, such as minister's daughter, president of student government, or leader of a scout troop, that warm response may seem
to be lacking, especially if the people toward whom one acts are
either awestruck or irritated by that role. Joyce had always found it
difficult to step out of such roles. "I used to feel," she reported,
"that if only people would come to our house everything would be
fine." Apparently at "our house" she felt protected by the atmosphere of family solidarity, an atmosphere which doubtless also had
its effect on the visitor. When she went to another person's house it
was harder to be "us"; she had to face the more formidable challenge of being only herself. In spite of her progress on the West
Coast and her gains in Detroit she still had quite a lot to learn.
"I think," she said, "that I have good hostessing skills but am just
developing the more basic make-this-a-warm-and-lasting-relation-
ship sort of skill. It is a long process, too. Got a long way to go yet."

Joyce's trouble with this problem sheds interesting light on the
psychological requisites for warm personal relationships. She exhibits a persistent need for intimate friendship and close confidences, but she is bothered by an almost equally persistent obstacle
to reaching the desired goal. Perhaps her need has been arti-
ficially strengthened by the current emphasis in social work on
personal warmth, but it clearly antedates her entrance into professional training. She has long craved greater opportunities to share
her perplexing problems, her anxieties, her most precious feelings
and cherished aspirations; to receive similar confidences from others; and thus to find support and solidarity for the inner self that
cannot be embodied in social roles. But she does not quite dare to
expose herself. She cannot give quite enough to encourage a return
of intimacy from others. We have seen that Joyce is easily capable
of being assertive, but always under the condition that she is standing for what is right, that her behavior is sanctioned by moral
standards. Under these conditions she has proved herself a worthy
fighter.

It is essential to intimacy, however, that a person should be able
to reveal what he is and what he feels regardless of its value for human betterment. He must be able to talk about what are clearly
faults, from a moral point of view; indeed, the exchanging of faults
and the comparison of anxieties is an important element in cement-
ing a real friendship. It is here that Joyce runs into trouble. She
learned long ago to suppress the kind of unruly impulses that flow-

ered so disgracefully in Albert. Through the example of her parents she learned to express no resentments and to permit overt criticism only of what was morally inferior. There is a feeling of risk about candor, a feeling that she might be punished for it, that she cannot really afford to dissociate herself from the moral pattern. Perhaps she unwittingly asks herself the same question that she raised about Philip's hitting his teasing playmate: "How would he know when to stop? That could very quickly get out of control." In Joyce's experience the control of aggression, as of other feelings, is intimately bound up with moral standards. It is no wonder that she feels hesitant about situations which must be, by definition, beyond good and evil.

As usual, however, we find Joyce facing the problem of growth. She mentioned two friends who were often outspokenly critical, toward whom in return she was sometimes critical; then she went on to say that she had found these relationships particularly satisfactory and helpful. She is thus beginning to sense one of the most important places where her defenses are in need of loosening.

8. The Psychodynamics of Development

> To be healthy means to overcome the past.
>
> W. STEKEL

To some extent the psychodynamic study of man bridges the gap between biological and social ways of thinking. On the one hand it is concerned with drives, learning, and the general process of adaptation. On the other hand it deals with the social environment, particularly that portion of it, the family circle, within which the child accomplishes his earliest learnings and first adaptations. Owing its original impetus to Freud's work with neurotic patients, it is still based largely on knowledge obtained in the course of treating maladjusted people. If this circumstance has somewhat limited the scope of the findings, it has at least served to keep the focus of interest on the individual and his development. Psychodynamic study never overlooks the personal meaning of experience. Its basic material is the pattern of urges, anxieties, defenses, and values that appears in the individual life. In describing our three cases we have necessarily utilized a considerable array of psychodynamic concepts; understanding would scarcely be possible without them. In this chapter we shall consider these ideas in a somewhat more systematic fashion. Following the plan used in the chapters on social shaping forces and biological roots, we shall select for discussion certain leading ideas derived from psychodynamic investigation, then apply them to the three lives with which we are now familiar.

THE FREUDIAN STAGES OF DEVELOPMENT

Using the techniques of free association and dream analysis, Freud was able to reconstruct some of the developments through which his neurotic patients had passed during the first five years of life. His evidence showed that neurotic disorders could often be traced to difficulties connected with the bodily functions and pleasure strivings of infancy. Studies of children have amply confirmed many of Freud's inferences concerning the importance of bodily interests. The infant's world is a small world: hunger, discomfort, and pain loom as overwhelming threats; while food, comfort, and pleasurable stimulation constitute the outstanding values. Freud therefore organized his theory of development around body pleasure, which he conceived to be successively focalized on the oral, anal, and genital zones. Going further, he conceived that the pleasure derived from these zones was basically all of one quality, related to one generalized source of energy or *libido,* so that the whole sequence could properly be described as psychosexual development.

At first there was sharp dispute over giving sexuality such an expanded meaning, but if this usage is somewhat loose it at least calls attention to important continuities in the child's pleasure-seeking experience and to the ways in which early learning can affect later more strictly sexual interests. Each stage of psychosexual development is focussed on a pleasure-giving zone with its special potentialities in the way of gratification and frustration. Each stage evokes from the parents a particular pattern of encouragements and prohibitions, thus giving rise to its own special forms of fixation or anxiety. The history of each stage, finally, leaves a characteristic imprint which predisposes the person to develop in certain ways over the years to come. The theory is thus equally relevant to normal and abnormal development.

During the *oral stage* the mouth is the outstanding sensitive zone; sucking and swallowing are the oustanding pleasures. The first psychosexual stage is thus closely allied to the process of nutrition, but sucking pleasure is to some extent independent of the need for food. Babies are frequently observed to suck their thumbs immediately after refusing to take more nourishment. The deprivations of this stage consist of not being fed promptly and not being allowed sufficient sucking pleasure. These deprivations often come to a head when the baby is weaned from breast or bottle. A further complication arises when the teeth begin to come through: biting emerges as a new source of pleasure, but proves to be an ill-chosen response when used aggressively in answer to feeding frustrations. As Erikson has indicated, the oral period is the time during which the infant establishes a basic sense of trust or mistrust, both toward the human environment and toward himself.[1] He learns how much

[1] Erikson, E. H. *Childhood and Society,* New York, W. W. Norton and Co., 1950, p. 219.

he can rely upon the environment to provide for his wants, and he learns how much he can rely on his own body as a source of comfort and pleasure.

If experience during the oral stage is generally gratifying, the child is started on his way with a sense of assurance that all will be well. He forms a first estimate of the world as a place where his wants are likely to be gratified. Yet the dependence which is a real characteristic of this period may also be carried over; the "oral character" may display even in adult years an enduring expectation that the world will take care of him and a conspicuous need for the praise and support of others in maintaining his self-esteem. When the oral stage is full of frustrations, the child becomes predisposed toward pessimism and mistrust, carrying over from this early experience a sour attitude toward life. When a time of gratification is followed by sudden frustration, perhaps through abrupt weaning, the child is likely to object aggressively, and he may continue to display in adult life an attitude of whining demandingness.

During the second and third years of life the focus of interest shifts to the anal zone. The mucous membranes of this region are sufficiently sensitive so that both the retention and expulsion of feces yield definite pleasure. The child becomes interested in the process and its products, but he is soon made aware that his parents favor a more complex attitude. The importance of the *anal stage* lies not simply in the gratifications that are involved; the process of toilet training brings on a contest of wills between child and parents, and the child passes through his first serious encounter with demands for scheduled conformity. He discovers that the parents are annoyed when he moves his bowels too soon or retains the contents too long; they are pleased when he chooses the right time and place and performs his duty promptly. Thus toilet training becomes an arena in which giving and withholding, self-control, and the issue of yielding to the demands of authority or rebelling against them, all receive a first crucial testing.

Various predispositions can result from the happenings at this stage. Freud first pointed out a pattern of three traits—orderliness, frugality, and obstinacy—which he found frequently linked in patients having obsessive-compulsive neuroses and which he traced to the anal stage.[2] Orderliness, he maintained, represented a continua-

---

[2] Freud, S. Character and Anal Eroticism, 1908, in *Collected Papers*, London, Hogarth Press, 1924, Vol. 2.

tion of obedience to parental requirements; frugality was an elaboration of the habit of not giving out the feces too readily; obstinacy stood for a kind of passive resistance to the parental authorities whom one dared not openly defy. Abraham indicated as most favorable for later development a sequence in which "the child succeeds in making a virtue out of necessity;" his anal pleasure "is replaced by gratification in his achievement, in 'being good,' in his parents' praise." [3] Failing this, however, the anal stage might produce predispositions ranging from a surly and stubborn self-sufficiency to an extremely meticulous conformity, both having subtle accompaniments of doubt and shame.

The next stage of psychosexual development reaches its height during the fourth and fifth years, when pleasurable sensations become more definitely localized in the genital organs. This childhood stage is known as the *phallic stage;* it is to be distinguished from the *genital stage* which is not reached until the advent of puberty. It comes at a time of rapid advance in locomotion and assertiveness. The focus of erotic interest lies in stimulating the genitals, exhibiting them, and perhaps engaging in mutual exploration and play with others. All of this becomes united, however, with the new capacities for taking initiative and engaging in active competition. "The danger of this stage," says Erikson, "is a sense of guilt over the goals contemplated and the acts initiated in one's exuberant enjoyment of new locomotor and mental power." [4]

The child's urges during the phallic period lead him straight into the Oedipus conflict, which becomes, according to the Freudian view, a crucial turning point in psychosexual development. If energetic assertiveness has not run into difficulties anywhere else, it is almost sure to do so in connection with the wish to be the favored parent's exclusive favorite. Neither parent can yield to this demand, and methods of rejecting it are often such as to create anxiety about sexual feelings and assertiveness in any form. The most favorable outcome of the Oedipus conflict occurs when the child can accept the frustration, identify himself with his parents and their demands, and begin to direct his energies toward mastering the world around him. The events of the phallic phase create predispositions chiefly with respect to assertiveness, love, and guilt. If

[3] Abraham, K. Contributions to the Theory of Anal Character, 1921, in *Selected Papers*, London, Hogarth Press, 1927.

[4] Erikson, *op. cit.*, p. 224.

the period is traversed with but little restraint or frustration the child may not experience enough guilt to make him an endurable member of society; assertiveness and self-love will dictate a large part of his behavior. On the other hand the burden of guilt may be so great as to crush initiative and cripple all feelings of love. Here as in the other stages a middle ground seems most favorable if the child is to go forward and overcome the past.

According to Freudian theory the phallic phase is followed by a period of latency during which sexual interests are subordinated to other concerns. It is clear from anthropological research that the latency period is a product of cultural forces rather than biological necessity. At puberty, however, the satisfaction that can be obtained from the genital organs definitely increases, thus making possible the *genital stage* of psychosexual development. If there is not too strong contamination by residues of earlier attitudes, the whole libidinal energy is now brought under the primacy of the genital zone and the person becomes capable of giving and receiving both love and sexual gratification.[5]

Let us turn at once to our three case studies to see whether or not these ideas contribute to our understanding. It will probably not have escaped notice that Joseph Kidd fits in many respects the concept of the oral character. Perhaps his interest in food, cigarettes, and alcohol suggests a quite literal residue from the oral period, but we are more concerned here with legacies of a more general sort. Kidd himself described the whining demandingness and the intense dependence that characterized his behavior toward his principal girl friend. We know that he liked girls who paid their way, provided cars, and cooked meals for him; further, that he sometimes broke out with biting, sarcastic remarks about the girls in his circle of acquaintance. He gave us a classic account of his eager attempts to please everyone and to bolster his external supplies of esteem. In considering his free associations we noted the still lively fear that his mother might be killed, and we inferred that this fear concealed an archaic anxiety-linked urge to injure the mother. Putting together all these pieces of evidence—the signs of dependence, the demandingness, and the aggressive feelings toward women—we can make an excellent case for predispositions established during the oral

---

[5] An excellent account of the Freudian stages is given by Brown, J. F., *The Psychodynamics of Abnormal Behavior*, New York, McGraw-Hill Book Co., 1940, ch. 10.

period. We can infer that, as a baby, Kidd received great oral gratifications followed by abrupt frustration. And when we bear in mind two facts, that his mother was strongly interested in her children and that his next brother was hardly more than a year younger, such a sequence seems not at all improbable.

It is interesting to compare this interpretation with one which we considered in the chapter on biological roots. In that chapter we weighed the possibility of attributing Kidd's dependence and passivity to an innate temperamental predisposition. We found the evidence unimpressive, particularly in view of his considerable activity and assertiveness during middle childhood before circumstances conspired to ruin his relationships with children of his own age. We are now dealing again with a predisposition, this time of a sort laid down by experience in early life. The evidence this time is somewhat more impressive. The alleged predisposition explains more features of behavior; it accounts for the aggression against women as well as the dependent tendency. But we must still not overlook Kidd's middle childhood, and this will serve to remind us that predispositions are not all-powerful. Any predisposition must be encouraged by the environment and elaborated through learning if it is to emerge as a distinctive characteristic of personality. Had we known Joseph Kidd when he was nine years old we would probably have judged that he exhibited few residues of the oral stage. It was only when his forward development became obstructed that he fell back on earlier attitudes and ceased to be able to overcome the past. Or, to phrase it somewhat differently, it was only when his basic demands for support and esteem were not met by the environment that he relapsed into the whining demandingness and resentments that had formed his earlier responses to oral frustration. Predisposition in the oral stage helps us considerably in understanding Kidd's personality, but we must not turn it into a sovereign principle at the expense of other discernible influences.

When we turn to the case of Hartley Hale we find traits that suggest predispositions laid down during the anal stage. We noticed the almost obsessive thoroughness with which he did much of his work, and he himself complained of being caught in the toils of procrastination, neatness, and meticulous attention to details. Hale's mother seems to have fulfilled quite closely the Freudian conception of an anal character type, and it is of particular interest that Hale himself, who for the most part rebelled against her petty tyranny, should occasionally be overtaken by compulsions toward neatness and order. It is easy to infer that toilet training was a sharp issue between this mother and son and that Hartley emerged from the struggle with predispositions which included both rebellious independence and conformity, together with distinct ingredients of shame and doubt. Independence took the lead, submissive conformity and shame were largely suppressed, but Hale still revealed at times the rest of his inheritance from the anal stage. It might be added, though this is more controversial, that psychoanalytic workers generally interpret the symptom of stuttering as a product of conflict among anal trends. To the stutterer, as Fenichel expressed it, "speaking means, first, the utterance of obscene, especially anal, words, and, second, an aggressive act directed against the listener." [6] But we need not rest our case concerning Hale on this somewhat dubious theory of stuttering.

Our understanding of Hale brings up an important problem which again emphasizes the necessity to keep one's thinking in the broadest possible perspective. For the most part this man was able to make effective use of traits which in some situations might prove hampering to freedom and happiness. His intensive study before difficult operations might suggest procrastination, doubt, and anxiety, but it made him in fact a better surgeon. The maintaining of an aseptic environment would look like an extreme compulsion for cleanliness in any other setting, but it is realistically essential in surgery. Doubt and neatness both rate as virtues in scientific research. These examples lead us to the larger generalization that many features of life in a technical civilization are organized along compulsive and obsessive lines. Rigid time schedules, complex filing systems, monotonous and repetitive jobs, the mechanization of routines, the emphasis on accumulating and retaining money, these and a hundred other characteristics of our culture tend to give utility and value to personality traits which receive their first predisposition in the anal stage. Reports on the incidence of neurotic breakdown in military service show that men with compulsive-obsessive tendencies were not particularly vulnerable.[7] Apparently they

[6] Fenichel, O. *The Psychoanalytic Theory of Neurosis,* New York, W. W. Norton and Co., 1945, p. 312.

[7] Michaels, J. J., and Porter, R. T. Psychiatric and Social Implications of Contrasts Between Psychopathic Personality and Obsessive-Compulsive Neurosis, *Journal of Nervous and Mental Diseases,* 1949, Vol. 109, pp. 122-132.

could utilize so much of their heritage from the anal stage that they were relatively free from inner stress.

Our study of Joyce Kingsley reveals material which is of interest chiefly with respect to the Oedipus conflict. A great deal of evidence can be interpreted to signify that this conflict was important in her development. She recalled that in childhood she liked to sit in her father's study and look at his books; she indirectly likened him to Elizabeth Barrett's father; she regretted that he was so undemonstrative and inaccessible; she told a story in which a girl and her father lived happily together until the ideal young lover came along; she told other stories in which mothers were dead or were identified with horrible dominating old women. The hypothesis seems in order that Joyce wanted to be her father's favorite, to be called by her father as Samuel was called by God, and that she developed an appropriate array of resentments against her mother who dominated her and stood in the way of such a goal. Her father contributed to the frustration by failing to send out a clear call, and it was perhaps from this experience that Joyce developed her special annoyance at wifely dominance over husbands as exemplified in the Parkins family. At all events, Joyce emerged from the conflict strongly identified with parental values, a position which received added benefits because of Albert's rebellion; she also identified strongly with the previously feared mother. This corresponds roughly to the so-called "normal solution" of the Oedipus conflict, although Joyce's version involved a rather severe sacrifice of rebellious and independent tendencies.

The predisposition established by Joyce's Oedipal experiences seems to have influenced in certain respects her relationship with her husband. She fell in love when she was quite young, and it appears probable that she did not fully differentiate Rennie in his own right; rather, she fell in love with someone who was like her father but whom she could have as her own. Rennie was like her father in the sense that he was active in the same church, was serious-minded and idealistic, and was certainly a man of whom her father would approve. If we are right in assuming that Joyce made this partial identification, then we would expect that it might sharpen certain problems in the marriage relationship. Two items suggest themselves as derivatives of the Oedipus conflict. In the first place, the spectre of the incest taboo may have crept in to delay Joyce's progress with sexual relaxation and enjoyment. In the second place, she was especially bothered, as we saw, when Rennie did not pay her enough attention and failed to free her from her mother's domination, just as her father had failed to free her a good many years before. Joyce's reactions to Rennie can thus be understood as containing residues of the Oedipus conflict, but we must not overlook the fact that she also responds to the real differences between husband and father. Except at certain moments she rarely fails to understand Renn in his own right.

THE INFLUENCE OF PARENTAL PERSONALITIES

It is impossible to give an account of child development without perceiving the tremendous importance of the attitudes taken by parents. The child's experiences in the early stages of development are not a function of himself alone; rather, they represent the results of continuing interaction between himself and the members of his immediate family. One might even say, recalling the psychosexual stages discussed in the previous section, that parental attitudes are of paramount importance in determining the course of development. The parents are always implicated, and it will be worth our while to consider what attempts have been made to bring their attitudes under systematic observation.

Work on this problem is hampered by the fact that reliable direct observations can rarely be made. If an observer enters a home in order to see what attitudes the parents take while interacting with their children, he will be treated to a public performance which may not in the least correspond to what was happening before he knocked on the door or to what will happen after he is out of earshot. Even the troubled mother who brings her child to a guidance center is not likely to give observers a fair sample of how she treats the child at home. For the most part our knowledge of this intricate subject is derived from the free associations of patients, from the behavior of children while being treated, from the always questionable reports given by parents, and from the shrewd but necessarily scattered intuitions of professional workers. These are indeed casual foundations on which to build a systematic structure, and we should not set our hopes very high.

An attempt to organize the problem has been made by Symonds, who suggested that parental attitudes might be classified so as to lie on two dimensions, one extending from acceptance to rejection, the other from dominance to submission.[8] *Acceptance* meant that the child was loved and that he received kind care and consideration. *Rejection* implied that the parents either overtly or covertly did not want the child and were inconsiderate of his interests. *Dominance* referred to an attitude in which authority and discipline were emphasized, the child's wishes being subordinated to patterns of conduct and goals desired by the parents. *Submission* designated the reverse of this: indulgent subordination of parental wishes to the desires and whims of the child. According to this scheme the attitudes of any given parents could be characterized by indicating their place on each of the two dimensions.

Clinical evidence shows pretty clearly that parental *rejection* has an unfavorable effect on development. If a child's first experiences in human relationships make him feel that he is not wanted, he is given little basis on which to build self-confidence or a warm feeling toward others. The training of children requires that they should be rewarded when they give up pleasures in order to adopt some more mature form of behavior. Parents who can offer affectionate interest are in a good position to make their children feel that growing up can be a source of gratification and pride. If the child wants to please them and to be like them, he can easily endure the temporary frustrations that go with relinquishing childish ways. Parents who lack affection are in a much weaker bargaining position. They can use force, but this is likely to produce either sullen compliance or evasive rebellion, if not both. They may resort to intimidation, but this produces anxiety and a deadening paralysis of the child's own urges. If they fail to enforce any discipline, they merely pass along the problem of socialization to other authorities, the teachers and church workers and police, who will be fortunate indeed if they can win the second round after the first round has been lost.

Clinical workers have been impressed by the special difficulties that arise when parental rejection is present in a covert form. It sometimes happens that parents attempt to suppress their rejective feelings by adopting overt attitudes of kindly interest and concern. It is difficult, however, to make a complete success of this manoeuver; under the constant pressure of childish demands and irritations the intended attitudes collapse and the child learns that in certain

[8] Symonds, P. M., *The Psychology of Parent-Child Relationships*, New York, D. Appleton-Century Co., 1939, pp. 18-28.

crucial respects his interests are not considered important. Karen Horney has attached great significance to this pattern in the family histories of neurotic patients. "The basic evil," according to her view, "is invariably a lack of genuine warmth and affection." [9] When a child is for the most part well-treated, when his parents tell him that they have only his interests at heart, his response to occasional evidences of rejection is apt to be peculiarly disastrous. He senses all too clearly the underlying threat to his security, but he dares not express his resentment lest he still further shake the feeble foundations of parental love. Anger and anxiety must both be controlled; self-confidence and self-respect are almost certain to suffer.

The effects of parental *dominance* are of a somewhat different nature. The child's attitudes toward authority and his power of initiative are likely to be chiefly affected. When dominance is associated with acceptance, the child is likely to become a fairly docile vehicle for parental intentions. He accepts parental values, attempts to realize parental hopes, and adapts himself to the requirements of authority in the school and in the community. The danger in this pattern of development lies in its possible effect on self-confidence. Dominated children sometimes have difficulty with new and free situations in which they must rely on what they can improvise rather than on what they have been taught. They may be unhappy on the playground, uneasy in the creative art class, bewildered by new and unfamiliar schoolwork. Parental *submission*, on the other hand, is liable to produce faults of an opposite kind. Overconfident conceit and a blithe disregard for the rights and interests of others are characteristic of the "spoiled child" whose parents have made his wishes their guides.

The differential effects of parental dominance and submission are clearly shown in Levy's well-known study of maternal overprotection.[10] The mothers selected for this study were all strongly acceptant, but they carried this to a fault by overprotecting their children. They attempted to keep their children safely at home, preventing them from developing friendships or finding independent interests on the outside. They offered help with homework, excused their children from irksome household tasks, and generally tried to

[9] Horney, K., *The Neurotic Personality of Our Time*, New York, W. W. Norton and Co., 1937, p. 80.

[10] Levy, D. M., *Maternal Overprotection*, New York, Columbia University Press, 1943.

make the home so attractive that there would be no incentive to leave. With respect to dominance and submission these mothers fell into two rather extreme groups. The dominant group had diligent, docile, neat, polite children who were hopelessly timid on the playground and awkward with other children. The submissive mothers, highly indulgent, found their children increasingly impudent, tyrannical, and violent around the house, and at school full of bossiness and self-display.

Complications in the Individual Case.—When we try to apply these ideas to the study of individual lives we are at once struck by the difficulty of making a proper diagnosis. How close can we come to placing the Hales, the Kidds, and the Kingsleys on the acceptance-rejection axis? On the whole, these three pairs of parents probably stood pretty well on the side of acceptance. Their children all had something good to say about their devotion. Yet none of our three subjects spared their parents a certain amount of criticism for failure to understand them and appreciate their needs. Kidd complained specifically about parental pushing which obstructed an appreciation of his own real wishes and problems. Hale was deeply upset when his parents appeared to forget him in the course of their quarrels. Joyce Kingsley was not satisfied with her father's distance, her mother's preoccupation with work, or the burden of household duties that fell to her lot in the name of family cooperation.

We meet here the same difficulty that has confronted us several times before. Just as we found the concepts of social class and of upward social mobility too general to provide an adequate description; just as we found drives such as sex, or motives such as affiliation and recognition, too broad to pin down the actual facts; so now we discover that a highly abstract concept such as acceptance-rejection gives us very limited help in detecting the precise impact of parental attitudes on the individual case. And we must know the precise impact if we are to achieve real understanding of the process.

The same difficulty naturally besets us with regard to dominance and submission. Both Joyce Kingsley and Joseph Kidd felt the weight of parental dominance, but there was a subtle difference in the quality of this dominance. In the Kidd household it took the form of dressing Joseph in fine clothes, showing him off, pushing him into the limelight, forcing him ahead in school, and putting pressure upon him to enter the medical profession. He was not given the chance to voice his own preferences in these matters; in fact, it took quite a little persuading to enlist his interest in what proved to be the disastrous double promotion. Kidd was hurried into activities before his own motives were fully aroused. His parents took initiative for him, with the result that they took it away from him and robbed him of the satisfaction of doing things on his own account. This encouraged a feeling of helplessness together with a kind of passive resistance which operated to prevent him from fulfilling parental expectations. The Kingsley parents, in contrast, were rather sharply aware that they should not be too directly dominant. Their religion emphasized freedom of choice; they realized that their children were not to be regarded as possessions, and they tried to encourage a proper amount of initiative. But they stood for a firm and explicit set of moral values which they did not hesitate to enforce. Joyce's mother, moreover, unintentionally dominated others simply because of high energy and positive opinions. Joyce's initiative was less injured than Joseph Kidd's, but it was not easy for her during childhood to take steps of which her parents might disapprove, and she would still rather take such steps without having them know about it.

Another difficulty in working out the effects of parental attitudes lies in the fact that two different parents and a certain number of brothers and sisters are usually involved. The Kingsley parents presented a fairly united front, but it was of great importance in Joyce's development that conformity carried the added benefit of beating out her brother Albert in the struggle for parental affection, just as it must have been important in Albert's development that he could never hope to compete with his sister in virtuous conduct. In Kidd's case the two brothers, one just a little older and the other just a little younger, obviously played a crucial part. The older boy's presence was often a support, though his jealousy could be a threat. The younger one's athletic and social success was a definite factor in precipitating Joseph's most serious crisis. Hartley Hale seems to have been somewhat the beneficiary of the differences between his parents. His mother was overprotective, telling him to wear rubbers and not to fight, but his father often forgot to wear rubbers and arranged for him to have boxing lessons. Hale exhibited practically none of the tendencies found in Levy's study of overprotected children. He rebelled against overprotection, and it is quite possible that his father's attitude gave considerable aid in this enterprise.

If it is necessary to consider the parents and siblings as constituting a total pattern of influence, it is also necessary to bear in mind that the attitudes of all members of the circle change in the course of time. When we characterize a parent as dominating we must realize that he does not necessarily dominate all the time or with respect to everything, and we must allow for the possibility that he changes as he grows older. Joyce Kingsley told us in some detail how her parents had changed in their methods of child training as a result of experience with each successive child. Sometimes parents change attitudes because of events happening in their own careers; they are not immune to wars, economic depressions, political problems, and marital crises. Often they change because of their own special reactions to different phases of the child's growth: a mother may adore her child while he is relatively helpless, for example, but react angrily when he is big enough to break things and launch out on independent adventures. Change of parental attitudes played a drastic part in Joseph Kidd's career. When he disappointed his parents and lost his position as the favorite son, he was placed under many of the pressures that are the lot of a rejected child.

There seems to be little doubt that parental personalities exert an important influence on child development. But it proves to be very difficult to isolate these influences from others which are always operating at the same time. This accounts for the lack of progress in rendering a systematic account of the topic. The effects of parental attitudes are no doubt as lawful as the weather—and just about as difficult to weigh for purposes of prediction.

THE SUPEREGO SYSTEM: CONSCIENCE AND IDEALS

It is again to Freud that we are indebted for the very useful concept of the superego. The concept was evolved in order to explain the appearance of seemingly irrational guilt feelings in the free associations of neurotic patients. It appeared that the patients were troubled not only by the wayward and perverse impulses that seethed beneath the surface of awareness, but also by a persistent tendency to feel guilty and miserable, as if someone were about to visit punishment upon them. These guilt feelings often seemed oddly foreign to the patients' conscious standards, and Freud therefore believed that they were carried over from early childhood. He traced their origin to the child's collisions with parental moral authority. After a certain number of experiences with parental displeasure the child learned to forestall punishment by inhibiting the behavior that would evoke it. Freud described this process as an introjection of parental standards, and he envisaged the superego system as governing the child, much as the parents themselves had originally done, by chidings, threatenings, and exhortations to perfection.[11]

The superego can be regarded as the child's form of conscience. As such it is subject to all the limitations of childish understanding. For the most part the meaning of rules and the purpose of prohibitions exceed the comprehension of a four- or five-year-old child. In a series of investigations on moral judgments Piaget has shown that young children think of a rule as something that simply exists, almost like a physical object; only in middle or later childhood do they grasp the idea that rules are created by men for a distinct social purpose and can be changed by mutual agreement.[12] In his early years a child is likely to assign absolute status to the rules that emanate from his parents, and his application of these rules will be literal and indiscriminate. Thus if the parents scold him for a boisterous outbreak he may conclude that all active assertiveness is bad rather than making the more precise deduction that the noise disturbed his parents. Furthermore, a child may react to a frustrating prohibition by attributing either more or less anger to the parents than they actually felt. In this way his superego may become either more violent or more lenient than the pattern from which it was copied. Clearly the young child is handicapped in grasping the implications of a moral code. It is small wonder that the action of the superego appears irrational if it continues to govern his thoughts and behavior in adult life.

Although it was discovered in the course of studying neurotic patients, the superego is an important concept for the understanding of any life history. It is upon the foundation of the superego that later moral values will be constructed. Freud was sceptical about the possibility of changing this foundation, except through the long process of psychoanalysis. He conceived that a mature moral code

[11] Freud summarized his views on the superego in *New Introductory Lectures on Psychoanalysis*, New York, W. W. Norton and Co., 1933, pp. 82-98.

[12] Piaget, J., *The Moral Judgment of the Child*, New York, Harcourt, Brace and Co., 1932.

might be reached through later experience and reflection, but he doubted whether these accretions had much effect on the original moral nucleus. This is not an easy point to prove, but we would certainly be neglecting an important insight into the development of personality if we failed to search carefully, even in a quite healthy life history, for evidences of an archaic conscience and for signs that it has not wholly surrendered its power over conduct. Many forces tend to fixate the superego, and its effects on development are by no means limited to the production of neurotic guilt feelings. It is worth noticing, moreover, that social conditions are often quite unfriendly to the outgrowing of one's childhood conscience. Few people are really encouraged to think for themselves on moral matters. For the most part society finds it easier and safer to utilize irrational guilt feelings as a means of keeping people in line.

Applications in Case Studies.—The arbitrary way in which the superego often functions is well illustrated in that curious set of rules whereby Joseph Kidd guided his sexual behavior. He was doubtless reacting to a common pattern in his local culture when he divided girls sharply into the "good" and the "bad," the untouchable and the touchable. We noticed that he was not quite at ease even with the touchable girls, which suggested that the superego might mildly disapprove of sex in any form. But there was a vast difference between this gentle chiding and the highly authoritative and absolute attitude of his superego with regard to good girls, especially Mildred with whom he was in love. Here he was sharply inhibited. He could not carry sexual play to its logical conclusion even when Mildred was clearly willing, nor could he, when years later he summoned courage to make the attempt, successfully consummate the sexual act. Furthermore, during his college years it was tremendously important that a sexual partner should not be older than he was. Good girls and older girls were alike forbidden. Only if a girl were both younger and bad was he allowed to consummate intercourse.

While it is impossible to be fully certain about the origin of this pattern, we are justified in assuming that it expressed in some way what Kidd had grasped about sex when he was quite a small child. The prohibition against good girls and older girls probably reflected the conclusions he drew when he was forbidden to express erotic feelings toward his mother. It might even be assumed that originally the prohibition was understood to apply to all women, but he became able to revise this global idea when the culture, in the person of the older camp friend, forced upon him the distinction whereby bad girls were practically eliminated from the category of womanhood. Kidd's further learning had all the earmarks of a slow but persistent attempt to push out the boundaries of safe action, to enlarge by slow degrees the zone within which he might find sexual expression without painful feelings of guilt. Gradually he found it possible to sleep with girls who were a little less young and a little less bad, until at last he was finding satisfaction with young women whom he really respected. This dogged struggle to contain the superego was motivated by his tremendous need for sexual relationships, a need which we have already discussed as something that involved much more than sex. There still remains, we infer, a skeleton force at the command of his archaic conscience. It governed the situation on the night when he took Mildred to the lake, and it may now be delaying his progress in finding a new object for deep love.

A somewhat different aspect of the superego came to light in our study of Joyce Kingsley. The effects of the superego should not be conceived simply as inhibitory. Included in the concept is the idea of identification with parental values of a positive kind. The child not only introjects prohibitions; he tries in many respects to copy his parents and to make their behavior the pattern for his own. It was possible to observe in Joyce certain inhibitions which probably dated back to the period when the superego was being formed. She was far from free with respect to sexual feelings, and it was extremely difficult for her to voice aggressive sentiments except when they represented a defense of moral standards. But the outstanding evidence for a still active superego was the strong identification with her parents and their values. She scarcely knew how these values had seeped into her life; even her mother was surprised to find them so strongly developed in her and in Albert. Inasmuch as moral training had been "largely unspoken" Joyce assumed that the origin of her conscience must have been "in what Mother and Daddy have lived, and in what we have done together as a family." To this we can agree, but it is illuminating to add Freud's proviso that the crucial learning took place around the ages of four or five. Joyce learned quite early to copy the pattern which Mother and Daddy were living. At the time of the first study she was still dwelling not unhappily in her original identification. Only later did she have occasion to question this "good foundation" and realize that not all of her moral code was suited to adult life.

Our examples show that the concept of the superego has great value in the understanding of lives. It explains the presence of irrational guilt feelings, the persistence of senseless patterns of inhibition, and the lasting power of certain moral standards which the adult self recognizes as no longer appropriate. It explains the peculiar tension that sometimes occurs when a person acts in accordance with his consciously wrought value system only to find himself feeling as if he had committed a grievous sin. It explains, in short, many obstacles that hinder the process of moral growth. When a child is lucky enough to form a superego which is not greatly at odds with a workable adult value system, his development can proceed with relatively little moral tension. But our cases reveal also that the superego may be strong and active without presenting an absolutely insuperable barrier to new growth. Joseph Kidd slowly tested the limits imposed on his sexual life and gradually pushed them fairly far back. Joyce Kingsley slowly overcame her identification with inflexible standards and learned to be more tolerant and humane in her attitude toward other people. Joyce left home with very few sentiments that were not directly borrowed from her parents; she came back five years later with a much revised set of values representing a considerable advance in utilizing her own experience. The outgrowing of the superego is a topic well worthy of more investigation.

THE EGO SYSTEM: DEFENSE AND ADJUSTMENT

Freud divided personality into three regions: id, ego, and superego. He conceived of the id as a reservoir of primitive drives with all their attendant wish-fulfilling images and fantasies. These drives maintained a more or less constant push toward action, seeking to utilize the muscular system in order to arrive at gratification. The superego represented a primitive means of controlling the waywardness of impulse, but this concept could scarcely do justice to the testing of reality, the planning, and the conscious activity which is so inescapable a part of our experience. The concept of the ego was introduced to fill this gap. In picturing the ego Freud was perhaps too strongly influenced by the hapless plight of his neurotic patients. "One might compare the relation of the ego to the id," he wrote, "with that between a rider and his horse. The horse provides the locomotive energy, and the rider has the prerogative of determining the goal and of guiding the movements of his powerful mount towards it. But all too often in the relations between the ego and the id we find a picture of the less ideal situation in which the rider is obliged to guide his horse in the direction in which it itself wants to go." This is unfortunate enough, but the poor ego has more to do than guiding an unruly horse. It has to respect the demands of the superego and it has to appraise reality before it can determine a direction for the imperious urges of the id. "It feels itself hemmed in on three sides and threatened by three kinds of danger, towards which it reacts by developing anxiety when it is too hard pressed." The gloomy situation of the ego evoked Freud's heartfelt sympathy. "Goaded on by the id, hemmed in by the superego, and rebuffed by reality, the ego struggles to cope with its economic task of reducing the forces and influences which work in it and upon it to some kind of harmony; and we may well understand how it is that we so often cannot repress the cry: 'Life is not easy.'" [13]

These picturesque remarks hardly do justice to Freud's views on the ego, but they perhaps serve to indicate the rather helpless part he assigned to this agency in his system of psychology. His interest in the ego sprang from two considerations. In the first place, he conceived that the task of psychotherapy was to strengthen the ego by teaching it to perceive and control those forces of the id and superego which had been holding it in irrational subjection. The ego was, in other words, that portion of the personality with which it was possible for the psychoanalyst to work. In the second place, Freud became increasingly interested, as his work advanced, in studying the mechanisms of defense, and these had to be understood as operations accomplished by the ego. Defense mechanisms were not conceived to be conscious acts; they were manoeuvers into which the ego was unwittingly driven in its attempts to cope with conflict and anxiety. Nevertheless, it was only through the ego that they could be observed, and their study constituted a substantial part of what Freudians presently began to call their *ego-psychology*.

Effects of Defense on Development.—The idea of *defense* is of

[13] Freud, S., *New Introductory Lectures on Psychoanalysis, op. cit.*, pp. 108-109.

great importance in the understanding of lives. Anxiety is an unavoidable feature of existence both in childhood and in adult years. It is a painful and disruptive emotion, a signal that life itself may be in danger, and it thus evokes the most strenuous efforts toward coping with the difficulty. Its disruptiveness is likely to interfere with rationality, all the more so in childhood when the child's grasp of the situation may be in any event quite inadequate. The defense mechanisms disclosed by psychoanalytic study are for the most part somewhat primitive ways of coping with danger. They are not ideal solutions; they all imply that the true state of affairs has been somewhat falsified in the interests of safety. This is most evident in what is probably the most primitive of the mechanisms: *denial*, as when a baby persistently looks away from a source of danger, an angry man declares that he is not in the least upset, or an ostrich hides his head in the sand. The situation is not much different with *repression*, which signifies the ejection from consciousness of frightening memories and of impulses in oneself that might lead to dangerous consequences. In fact all the mechanisms—projection, reaction-formation, isolation, undoing, intellectualization, and so forth—imply a certain failure to take full account of reality, whether it be the reality of the outside world or the reality of one's inner experience.[14]

The effects of anxiety and defense on development have been most fully studied in connection with the neuroses. The crucial point seems to be that defensive measures are likely to interfere with the progress of further learning. They represent ways of responding in which the person dares not take full account of reality. To the extent that they become fixed, they prevent him from making a new and more hopeful appraisal of reality. The tactics of the ostrich never permit one to find out that the danger is less great than he supposed, if this be true; and it is very often true with respect to things that seemed frightening in early childhood but could easily be dealt with a little later in life. In the neuroses it is a regular finding that the patient is still afraid of childhood threats; he still repeats defenses against them which cripple his adult behavior and which do not permit him to revise his earlier estimate of the danger. A patient feels uneasy in the presence of his employ-

---

[14] The psychoanalytic view of defense mechanisms is well set forth by Anna Freud in *The Ego and the Mechanisms of Defense*, London, Hogarth Press, 1937.

ers, for example; he tends to placate them by ingratiating submission, and this actually hinders his chances of advancement because his employers really want him to show initiative and bring new ideas into the business. It turns out that the patient behaves in this self-defeating way because he still feels the excessive fear that he used to feel when scolded and disciplined by his father. In those earlier crises he applied defenses against his own resentment, repressed his wish to assert himself in return, accomplished the reaction-formation of being extremely submissive, and thus protected himself from further anxiety; but at the cost of never again asserting himself in the presence of older men and never learning that it was safe for him to do so. Conceived in this way, neurosis is the consequence of a block in the learning process. Defense against childhood anxiety has taken so large a toll as to wall off important areas of development.[15]

We must be careful not to draw from this account of neurosis a set of false conclusions about the normal course of development. One is certainly not justified in asserting that people without neuroses are free from residues of childhood anxiety and defense. No one can get through childhood without anxiety, and no one is likely to be wholly free from the patterns of defense that served him in his early crises. It is perhaps reasonable to suppose that when childhood anxieties are less severe, the defenses will be less primitive, less indiscriminate, less likely to interfere with important directions of new learning. But a lot depends on the precise character of the original fears and the way the child happened to understand them. Furthermore, circumstances have a great deal to do with the precipitation of a later neurosis. Suppose that our man in the last paragraph had gone to work for an extremely authoritarian employer: his pattern of ingratiation might have led to his becoming his employer's right-hand man so that his business success would be assured. Case studies of relatively healthy people show that problems of anxiety and defense are part of the universal stuff of development. It has gradually become clear, moreover, that we should not think of anxiety as having only a pathological effect on development. When not aroused in catastrophic proportions it serves as a very definite incentive in the normal process of growing up. Hartley Hale is not the only subject in our experience to declare

[15] This view of neurosis is more fully described in White, R. W., *The Abnormal Personality*, New York, The Ronald Press Co., 1948, Ch. 6.

that a certain amount of anxiety gives zest to life and releases one's full capacities.

Finally, the whole conception of defense mechanisms is beginning to emerge from its earlier neurotic context. Mechanisms of defense are merely somewhat primitivized forms of the general strategies we all employ in dealing with the problems of existence. In the early years of psychoanalysis quite a lot was written about *rationalization,* which was described as a trick of making up nice-sounding reasons for behavior that was really quite impulsive in nature. This kind of rationalization, however, is merely an inept use of the very same process whereby a research scientist tries to find the logic in a confusing set of findings, seeking an hypothesis that can be subjected to further test.

Broadening the Ego Concept.—These considerations bring us back to the concept of the ego. We can no longer be contented with an ego that merely carries out defense mechanisms or that struggles wearily to ward off oppressive conflict and disintegration. Freud would have done well to include his own ego in the field of observation and choose metaphors that would do justice to his own life of persistent toil, critical self-discipline, and creative discovery.

A valuable elucidation of the concept has recently been offered by Erikson, who attaches importance to *ego identity*—the sense of being a distinct individual in one's own right within a social framework. [16] A necessary nucleus for this sense of identity is the progressive mastery of useful actions such as walking, talking, reading, or carpentry. "Ego identity gains real strength only from wholehearted and consistent recognition of real accomplishment," and this recognition must be on the part of the child himself, for he "cannot be fooled by empty praise and condescending encouragement." It is particularly important that the child should perceive his accomplishments as being relevant to adult social reality; what he does must have "meaning in the culture." He needs to have as soon as possible a sense of partnership in a larger world. One of the readiest mechanisms for furthering one's ego identity is that of *identification* with people in the environment or with historical or fictional figures. "The ego identity develops out of a gradual integration of all identifications." Large and small fragments of identification are drawn together with the sense of competence and accomplishment to form the unique synthesis which is one's own self. Erikson con-

[16] Erikson, E. H., *Childhood and Society, op. cit.,* esp. pp. 207-218, 237-243.

siders the study of identity to be "as strategic in our time as the study of sexuality was in Freud's time." It is difficult for the child to feel a sense of useful participation in the mechanized home life of the push-button age, equally difficult for him to discern his future significance in the complex impersonal life of an industrial civilization.

With Erikson's contribution in mind we can profitably institute a comparison between the concept of the *ego* and the concept of the *self* which we examined briefly in an earlier chapter. [17] Social scientists have placed great emphasis on social interaction as the chief means whereby one builds up a sense of self. We learn about ourselves from others. We find out about our own characteristics by hearing others describe us or by observing the responses they make to us. Certainly there is much truth in this way of looking at it, but the theory was never very satisfactory in explaining the selection and synthesis that occurs in forming a self-picture. Hartley Hale served to point up this difficulty. We noticed that he was sometimes unable to accept the good opinion held about him by others; he sensed within himself certain mental traits of confusion and uncertainty which he felt they did not fully appreciate. We inferred that he refused flattering opinions because of an enduring identification with his quick-thinking, decisive father, whose standard he wanted to emulate. By introducing Erikson's concept of ego identity we can resolve the difficulties left by the purely social theory. There are two ways in which a person selects among the many social "judgments" that are available for a self-picture. He selects partly through his knowledge of his own ability—his sense of the ease and confidence with which he can perform certain acts or take certain roles. He also selects on the basis of his identifications. He himself is much more interested in being one kind of person than in being another kind. By combining the social view of the self and the psychodynamic view of ego identity we come much closer to understanding the vital center in the organization of personality.

Even though the concept of the ego has been greatly expanded since Freud made his first attempt to define it, there is still some danger that the whole matter will be oversimplified. The ego is responsible for defense; it is responsible for adjustment; it is responsible for the active mastery of the environment. But how are these things accomplished? What are some of the ways in which such activities

[17] See pages 121-123.

are carried out? These questions have been challengingly raised by Murray, who describes the ego in the following words:

> The concept of ego emphasizes the determining significance of 1, conscious, freely-willed acts: making a resolution (with oneself) or a compact (with others) or dedicating oneself to a life-long vocation, all of which "bind" the personality over long periods of time; 2, the establishment of a cathected ego ideal (images of a figure one wants to become); and 3, the inhibition of drives that conflict with the above-mentioned intentions, decisions, and planned schedules of behavior.[18]

A somewhat similar direction of thought has been taken by Dollard and Miller, who believe that full understanding of the process of psychotherapy can be achieved only be taking into account the higher mental processes of reasoning and planning.[19] The ego, then, beyond serving as an umpire among the forces to which it is exposed, acts as an executive agency which sets goals, discharges obligations, makes and keeps promises; it also acts as a planning board which tries to foresee the future and guide the course of coming developments. These personified figures of speech are difficult to handle in a scientific system. But there is no doubt that people behave in these ways, and we must not overlook such facts when we are trying to take a more than colloquial view of human nature. We shall return to this topic in the final chapter.

NEUROTIC TRENDS AND NEUROTIC BREAKDOWN

The concept of *neurotic trend* was brought into prominence through the work of Karen Horney. Like Freud's ideas it was devised to explain certain features of the neurotic personality, but it involves principles that are important in any theory of development. The concept is used primarily in describing adult behavior, and its special virtue lies in pointing out the ramifications of anxiety in the fully developed personality. Implicit in Horney's idea is the concept of normal trend or normal interest. Neurotic trends do not stand alone; they reveal themselves by lending an exaggerated intensity to what would otherwise be quite ordinary

[18] Murray, H. A., *Explorations in Personality*, New York, Oxford University Press, 1938, p. 138.

[19] Dollard, J., and Miller, N. E., *Personality and Psychotherapy: An Analysis in Terms of Learning, Thinking, and Culture*, New York, McGraw-Hill Book Co., 1950, especially Part III.

forms of interest and striving. They make their possessor vulnerable to neurotic breakdown under certain conditions, but they by no means necessitate such an outcome. Horney believes, in fact, that neurotic trends are not always inconsistent with effective living and that some of them are so strongly encouraged by social conditions that they may lead to conspicuous success.

The nature of neurotic trends can best be described by making up an example. Let us say that we know a student who exhibits great sociability, spending virtually all of his time in the company of other people. So strong is his gregarious bent that he hates to study by himself and prefers to carry his books to a place where he will have people around him. Thus far his behavior does not decisively indicate a neurotic trend. We might judge it to be within the normal range of variation as regards the strength of social interest. But presently we discover that our student's sociability exhibits an indiscriminate character: he forces his company on a honeymoon couple, converses on the bus with a passenger who obviously wants to go to sleep, and generally fails to distinguish between appropriate and inappropriate moments for social interchange. We discover further that his social appetite is insatiable: he wears out his welcome by talking far into the night, as if he could not bear to tear himself away from a social occasion. Finally, we learn that he becomes extremely uneasy when he is by himself; he grows so tense and restless that he cannot possibly study or even concentrate on light reading, and he feels obliged to rush out and look for friends even if it is a time quite unsuitable for calling. These three signs— lack of discrimination, insatiability, anxiety when frustrated—are offered by Horney as criteria for diagnosing the presence of a neurotic trend. They signify that the person is not just sociable. His craving for society undoubtedly satisfies a true social need, but at the same time it rescues him from an anxiety which for some reason is set off by being alone. Neurotic trends serve two purposes: satisfaction and security. [20]

When we turn to our three cases we find what is perhaps the most instructive example of a neurotic trend in Hartley Hale. We noticed Hale's self-driving devotion to his medical career, and al-

[20] The concept of neurotic trend was introduced by Horney in *The Neurotic Personality of Our Time*, New York, W. W. Norton and Co., 1937. The most explicit discussion is in her book, *Self Analysis*, New York, W. W. Norton and Co., 1942, Chapter 2.

though we must allow that his vitality, his interest, and the natural demands of the profession could easily account for nearly all of his behavior we should not overlook the possibility of an additional security goal. Were there signs that hard work served in any sense to rescue him from inner sources of anxiety? This seemed to be the case. His long hours at the hospital and his evenings in the photographic laboratory gave us a certain justification in calling his behavior indiscriminate and insatiable, but the strongest evidence came from his own account of uneasiness when everything was going smoothly. He wanted to be constantly in a turmoil of events, struggling to extricate himself from an immediately threatening crisis, or else he wanted to be trying a dangerous piece of surgery or working toward a crucial scientific experiment that entailed the risk of wrecking his career. We inferred that he still experienced anxiety with respect to his own competence and that he needed threatening situations in order to keep proving that he could conquer them. Even when he went on a summer vacation he busied himself with riding because it scared him to ride on horseback. It is possible that Hale would become very uneasy if he were forced to take a long vacation. But it seems unlikely that he will ever lack the opportunity to be more or less in his preferred state of turmoil. He is in a profession that knows no unemployment and that rarely can keep up with the full demands upon it. The element of neurotic trend in his working life might render him vulnerable under certain conditions, but these conditions do not seem likely to occur.

Neurotic Breakdown.—This example leads us directly to a consideration of *neurotic breakdown*. A person may be said to arrive at neurotic breakdown when anxieties, inhibitions, symptoms and general distress so overwhelm him that he feels unable to go on without help. That he reaches such a crisis must be attributed to a progressive shifting of the various forces at work within him. His established equilibrium fails and he cannot immediately reach a new one that permits a continuation of his usual pattern of life. What happens can be roughly schematized as follows. (1) Possibly there is an intensification of pressures that serve to reanimate the danger situations of childhood. In his home life or at his work the person is increasingly exposed to circumstances that awaken sexual fantasies, aggressive urges, or feelings of inferiority that caused him great anxiety during his childhood years. (2) Possibly his defensive operations are weakened, either by a general depletion of energy or by the blocking of a favored neurotic trend. (3) Possibly, on the other hand, there is an intensification of defensive operations in order to control increasing threats. These defensive operations themselves become so burdensome that the person cannot simultaneously sustain them and maintain his normal life. [21]

In studying the case of Joseph Kidd we had occasion to observe this kind of shifting in the internal balance of forces as a consequence of changing external conditions. Between the ages of ten and eighteen Kidd progressively lost his contact with friends of his own age. He had been using his companions as a source of security and esteem, as a life-giving force in his development. As his social income shrank he became increasingly exposed to the infantile dangers of being alone and unrecognized. His few remaining opportunities for affectionate esteem, especially his relationship with Mildred, were pursued with the violent intensity of neurotic trends. He could not subdue his anxiety through Mildred, who showed displeasure at his dependence and hunger for esteem. He could not subdue it through college friends because he obtained too slow and small a recognition in the various roles he attempted to play. He could not subdue it at home because his parents had become discouraged at the failure of his early promise. The threat of isolation and esteem famine thus steadily mounted, and the avenues for controlling it by seeking supportive relationships were progressively blocked off. Kidd did not quite reach neurotic breakdown, but he came fairly close to it, and his history is instructive as an example of the relevant dynamic processes.

Constructive Build-up.—Our account of neurotic breakdown at once suggests a converse process which might be described as *constructive build-up*. If circumstances can bring about the failure of an established equilibrium they can also produce an improvement in the existing level of adaptation. Conditions may change in such a way as (1) to decrease the reanimation of childhood anxieties, (2) to strengthen the effectiveness of essential defensive processes, and (3) to lighten the total burden of defense so that energies are more free for other purposes. This mode of analysis is particularly helpful in understanding those episodes in a person's life when things suddenly seem to go unusually well so that he feels a real surge of productivity and happiness. The earlier part of Kidd's military ex-

---

[21] For a fuller exposition of neurotic breakdown see White, R. W., *The Abnormal Personality, op. cit.*, pp. 270-275.

perience and his successful building of the flower studio can be cited as illustrating the general principles. These were also shown in Hale's conversion from advertising to medicine and in his recovery from the problems that beset him during his initial year at medical school. Perhaps the best example of constructive build-up, however, is to be found in the period of Joyce Kingsley's history that followed her falling in love with Rennie and her election to the presidency of student government. This episode was discussed in some detail in the previous chapter. [22]

For the most part we can regard neurotic breakdown and constructive build-up as converse processes, but there is an important difference in their relation to other facts of personality. When a person is moving in the direction of neurotic breakdown he becomes less free to pursue other interests, more paralyzed with regard to ego functions, more constricted to a preoccupation with his own symptoms and distresses. The neurotic aspects of his personality assume increasing predominance. When a person is moving in the opposite direction the range and freedom of his activities is in constant increase. Anxieties and defenses play a decreasing part in the organization of his personality. In order to describe the course of constructive build-up, therefore, we need to have an array of concepts that will cover the many activities of life that do not belong in the categories of neurotic anxiety and defense.

SUBLIMATION

To close our survey of the psychodynamic view of man we shall take brief notice of the concept of *sublimation*. This concept originated with Freud and has been developed primarily by workers interested in disordered personalities. It is therefore hardly more than a catchword intended to cover great areas of personality that are not of much concern to the psychiatrist. The concept of sublimation attempts to account for the origin and development of constructive human interests. It undertakes to trace the connection between basic human drives and those complex adult activities that flower in the arts, in science, in social action, in home life, and in all the other forms of special interest that make up the richly variegated canvas of human experience. We may well suspect at the outset that a single concept will not prove equal to the task.

The Freudian theory of psychosexual development is somewhat

[22] See pages 259-261.

uncompromising with regard to basic drives. It does not, of course, reject obvious drives such as hunger and thirst, but it does take the position that sexual striving—the obtaining of pleasure from stimulation of the sensitive oral, anal, and genital zones—constitutes the child's deepest preoccupation and supplies the needed energy for all those later elaborations of interest that are not directly connected with nourishment and the preservation of life. Most adult interests have no obvious relation to childhood sexual preoccupations. They seem to be determined by a wider array of developed motives and by a large number of objective considerations. By utilizing the concept of sublimation, however, it becomes possible to deduce a chain of events that connects mature interests with psychosexual roots. It is the fate of infantile erotic interests, such as sucking and biting, retaining or smearing feces, exhibiting the genitals, investigating the genital structure of other children, or asking questions about reproduction and childbirth, to fall under the constraint of adult displeasure. The energies thus trapped may cause considerable difficulty in development, but they may be liberated again by sublimation. The concept implies that the energies are deflected to new objects and new purposes which are free from social disapproval and therefore do not create anxiety. The child who is spanked for smearing feces at home may be praised for smearing finger-paints in beautiful patterns at school. His anal fascination has been sublimated, and the process may go on through many stages until he becomes a noted artist.[23]

The concept of sublimation was first proposed in connection with Freud's psychosexual theory, but its value is not altogether cancelled when one takes a less restricted view of childhood motivation. Suppose we feel that curiosity deserves status as an independent motive quite apart from zonal pleasures. Curiosity sometimes brings about danger and parental displeasure, and the concept of sublimation might well be appropriate in explaining the deflection of this urge into approved scientific interests. Sublimation is too simple a way of explaining the full growth of interests, but it serves to keep our attention on an extremely important problem in the development of personality.

In studying the case of Hartley Hale we were impressed by the

---

[23] A summary of the psychoanalytic view is given by O. Fenichel, *The Psychoanalytic Theory of Neurosis*, New York, W. W. Norton and Co., 1945, pp. 141-143.

early origin and enduring force of the interests that ultimately became focalized on biological research. It is possible now to point out a connection between the later interest and certain psychosexual preoccupations in early childhood. The connection is of course hypothetical; our methods of study did not permit us to recover enough early memories for a convincing demonstration. We might infer, nevertheless, that Hale's curiosity became greatly excited over the question of sexual intercourse between his parents. He told us of listening apprehensively from the next room when they went to bed, fearing that he would soon hear a quarrel. It is not uncommon for children to believe that what they overhear of parental intercourse signifies violence of some kind. We recall that somewhat later Hale eagerly read books about sex, acquiring a precocious knowledge of the subject, and that for the sake of his high-school gossip sheet he tried to spy upon amorous couples in parked cars. There is indeed evidence that Hale was specifically curious about sexual relationships, and by using the concept of sublimation we can propose that this specific curiosity was the root of his later urge to learn more and more about the human body. There is no way to be sure, however, that this was the sole or even the main root.

The greatest shortcoming in the theory of sublimation lies in the later rather than the earlier stages of what it tries to explain. The deflection of childhood interests to new and safer objects of a similar kind is certainly a legitimate conception. Trouble begins when we try to carry the process indefinitely onward to the developed interests of adult life. That a child who smeared his feces gets a similar kind of satisfaction out of smearing finger paints does not put a great strain on credulity, but his later career as an artist would certainly seem to contain many more kinds of gratification than it would be possible to trace to the anal period. The extent to which our artist, standing at his easel and "smearing" colors on to his canvas, is still securing gratification for something he was not allowed to do at the age of three must be open to considerable question. Psychoanalytic theory recognizes the difficulty by suggesting that the character of the original energy becomes changed, but this is too small a concession to give the concept much elasticity in describing the complexities of adult life. According to a proposal by Allport the energies become so greatly changed that it is misleading to identify them at all with childhood motives. Allport's principle of the *functional autonomy of motives* "regards adult motives as infinitely varied, and as self-sustaining *contemporary* systems, growing out of antecedent systems but functionally independent of them. . . . Earlier purposes lead into later purposes, but are abandoned in their favor." [24] We can sometimes enhance understanding by looking for the thread of historical continuity, but we must always explore motives as they actually work in the present, even if this makes the task of analysis many times more difficult.

It is understandable that the psychodynamic outlook should be incomplete with respect to the upper reaches of natural growth. The psychodynamic study of man has made a noteworthy contribution to knowledge, but it has not altogether transcended its origins in the psychiatric consulting room. It has partly filled, but partly left open, the central gap in our knowledge of human nature, the gap which must ultimately be closed if we are to achieve something better than a partial understanding.

SUGGESTIONS FOR FURTHER READING

Freud in his *New Introductory Lectures on Psychoanalysis* (New York, W. W. Norton & Co., 1933) gave his more or less final views on the ego, the superego, anxiety, and the stages of psychosexual development; see especially chs. 3 and 4. The psychosexual stages and their effects on development are presented with great clarity in J. F. Brown's *The Psychodynamics of Abnormal Behavior* (New York & London, McGraw-Hill Book Co., 1940), chs. 10 and 11. A scholarly and encyclopedic guide to the literature on psychoanalysis will be found in O. Fenichel's *The Psychoanalytic Theory of Neuroses* (New York, W. W. Norton & Co., 1945); in relation to normal development see especially chs. 4 and 5 (developmental stages), ch. 6 (the superego), ch. 9 (defense mechanisms and sublimation), and ch. 20 (character disorders).

In a brilliant new book Erik H. Erikson (*Childhood and Society*, New York, W. W. Norton & Co., 1950) gives a thoughtful reconsideration of the theory of infantile sexuality and sets forth, under the heading "The Growth of the Ego," his views on ego-identity. See especially chs. 2, 6 and 7.

The topic of parent-child relationships is conveniently sum-

[24] Allport, G. W., *Personality: A Psychological Interpretation*, New York, Henry Holt and Co., 1937, p. 194.

marized in a recent book by P. M. Symonds, *The Dynamics of Parent-Child Relationships* (New York, Bureau of Publications, Teachers College, Columbia University, 1949). Karen Horney's concept of neurotic trends is most explicitly set forth in her book, *Self-Analysis* (New York, W. W. Norton & Co., 1942), ch. 2. Neurotic trends and neurotic breakdown are discussed by R. W. White in *The Abnormal Personality* (New York, The Ronald Press Co., 1948), ch. 7.

9. The Process of Natural Growth

> Organic growth and repair have their counterpart in
> the personality in the process of renewal: a continued
> making over of ideas and attitudes, of sentiments and
> plans, so that the person will overcome the animal
> tendency to repetition, fixation, automatism.
>
> LEWIS MUMFORD

Up to this point we have been conducting two parallel investigations. On the one hand we have made a painstaking attempt to
understand in detail the lives of Hartley Hale, Joseph Kidd, and
Joyce Kingsley. On the other hand we have tried to evaluate some
of the leading ideas about personality that have issued from the social sciences, biological research, and the psychodynamic study of
man. Our findings fully confirm the value of a threefold approach
to the understanding of lives. Our three subjects would have been
strangely misinterpreted if we had failed to consider the shaping influence of the culture, social class, group experiences, and occupational and other roles. They would have been strangely disembodied
if we had omitted all reference to drive, the learning process, temperament, and the nature of their abilities. They would have been
peculiarly depersonalized if we had left out the special impact of
their parents and the details of their struggle to master anxiety
and find outlets for their interests. All three sources provided us
with indispensible information. One can take a narrower view only
at the risk of talking plain nonsense about human nature.

Although our insight has been greatly benefited by a combined
social, biological, and psychodynamic approach, we have also experienced certain enduring frustrations. It has bothered us that
general concepts such as social class and occupation, drive and motive, psychosexual stage and parental attitude, have required so
many qualifications in order to fit the individual case. We have repeatedly found that general concepts did not help us to understand
process or change, which always had to be described with reference
to many particulars. It has also been confusing to realize that so

many forces operate at once in a given personality, producing an elaborate lattice of interconnected events rather than a simple model of cause and effect. But perhaps our most recurrent difficulty has been that of accounting for natural growth. We kept finding ourselves in a trap: carefully explaining the more rigid, crippled, and irrational features of our subjects' personalities while simply taking for granted the constructive side of their development. It seems imperative to devote more thought to what happens *when lives are in progress*.

In attempting to correct the limitations of present understanding it is important not to throw overboard what we have already learned. Nothing can be gained by asserting that natural growth calls for a new point of view or a wholly new set of concepts. Arrested and unarrested development are not two classes of events; they represent different outcomes of lawful process under different conditions. Our task in this chapter is to think more specifically about the conditions under which natural growth takes place.

TOWARD A POSITIVE CONCEPTION OF NATURAL GROWTH

In attempting to give substance to the idea of natural growth we must shape our thinking in such a way as to accommodate certain broad facts. We must take serious account of the following points: (1) that the person undergoes more or less *continuous change*; (2) that the person is acted upon by a multiplicity of influences to which he necessarily makes a *selective response;* and (3) that the person not only receives influences but takes *action on the environment*. Man is not static, nor is he passive and helpless. It will also be necessary, because our examples of growth include the years of young adulthood, to consider seriously (4) the *nature of the reality* in which adult development occurs. For various reasons these broad facts have usually been pushed to one side in theorizing about personality.

1. In the field of psychopathology it is now generally recognized that emotional disorders can be traced to blocks in the learning process. As we saw in the last chapter, these blocks are produced by defenses against anxiety, and the specific task of psychotherapy is to liquidate this anxiety so that development can be resumed. It is implicit in this account that normal growth signifies unblocked learning, a process of *continuous change*. The personality is a system that normally undergoes continuous reorganization with the

passage of time. Yet although change is implicit in our thinking it is rarely made an important feature of actual case studies. Even workers with a strong historical orientation tend to build final cross-sectional pictures of their subjects at some point in time—usually the time when the patient arrived at the physician's office in search of help. Furthermore, when one's purpose is to treat emotionally disordered people, it is natural to become preoccupied with what has not changed and what is difficult to change in the patient's personality. Finally, it is always easier to understand fixed things than things that do not remain the same. For these reasons change has been seriously neglected in the study of individual lives. Clearly the concepts we need in order to deal with natural growth must be concepts about change.

2. Each individual is acted upon by a great multiplicity of influences. Social forces, biological forces, psychodynamic forces all compete in the shaping of a given personality. Quite naturally the scientific investigator has tried to use cause-effect models, studying single forces and trying to work out their specific effects on development. Inadvertently this way of simplifying things is sometimes carried over into an unjustified generalization: that personality can be understood as a direct reflection of its shaping forces. The case studies in this book are sufficient in themselves to dispel this notion. No person can equally reflect all the forces that impinge upon him. They are too numerous, too inconsistent, too productive of conflict to be received with passive acquiescence. A person is a nexus of competing and conflicting influences to which he must *respond selectively*, creating for himself a workable synthesis. He is inevitably the scene of frustration and conflict, and he can avoid hopeless confusion only by becoming an active transformer of his experience. Clearly the concepts we need in order to understand natural growth must be such as to encompass the highly selective nature of the response to shaping influences.

3. No one doubts the general principle that there is a constant interaction between the person and his environment. This implies both that the environment acts on the person and that the person *acts on the environment*. Scientific workers, however, have been loathe to examine the second part of the transaction, preferring to regard the person as the thing to be explained and the environment as the thing that explained him. Thus a social role tends to be perceived only as something that moulds the person; little thought has

been bestowed on the way social roles become transformed through the innovations of those who play them. Similarly, parental attitudes have been described chiefly as producing certain effects on the child's personality; little attention has been paid to the effects of the child's response on parental attitudes. The fact is that people very definitely affect their environments, even in childhood, and that what happens next in their development is often determined by these effects. Clearly the concepts we need in order to understand natural growth must include the action of the person on his surroundings.

4. The *nature of the reality* in which adult development takes place can be specified only in the most general terms. Each person's real situation differs from every other person's, and even within a single culture there may seem to be few points in common. The question of reality must be raised, however, because there is a tendency to make unwitting assumptions which seriously misrepresent the conditions of adult life. Mental health is often identified with being flexible and adaptable, ready for anything, an all-around person with versatile skills and interests. This prescription is merely the opposite of the blockings, constrictions, and impaired self-confidence that are so common in disordered personalities; it was never intended to carry implications about the nature of reality. It clearly implies, nevertheless, that reality chiefly demands sudden changes, abrupt dislocations, and a boundless capacity to react to novel and unexpected situations. One might say that it depicts the life of a traveling salesman who constantly meets new people in new territories and who shifts from company to company so that he has to keep learning the merits of new goods. Under some social and occupational circumstances there is much truth in this picture, but it certainly does not cover all the conditions of adult life. After adolescence a person starts to become a full partner in the social system. He begins to take on responsibilities that will last all his life. He cannot avoid concentrating his energies on a small number of ongoing interests, giving up many bright paths that all seemed possible while he was in school. He becomes committed, and he must make a go of his life with one wife, one home, one family of children, one line of work, and perhaps one chief circle of acquaintances. Sometimes there is very little demand for quick change in an adult's life. What is needed is a capacity for steady growth within a relatively constant framework of activities and re-

lationships. Our images of adult reality must include not only that of the foot-loose traveling salesman but also that of the man who works in the same institution for forty-five years. They must include not only that of the versatile girl who can command the admiration of every partner at a dance but also that of the wife who can command the admiration of one husband all the way from wedding to golden wedding. Some features of life call for the broadening of experience; others require its deepening. Clearly the concepts we need in order to understand natural growth must be equal to both aspects of development.

Having taken these preliminary steps toward a positive conception of natural growth, we shall proceed to set forth certain ideas concerning growth trends. As in previous chapters, we shall concentrate on leading ideas rather than attempting an exhaustive description. Episodes of growth drawn from our case studies will serve to illustrate the general trends. In utilizing our cases to provide examples we are not necessarily claiming that our subjects are unusual specimens of normality, health, or maturity. It is not relevant to our purpose to pass an overall judgment of this kind, nor is it in any event a particularly useful way to look at personality. Neurotics are not neurotic with respect to every feature of their lives; conversely, healthy people cannot be expected to be equally healthy in every department. In certain respects and on certain occasions our subjects have exhibited natural growth. This is sufficient to justify their use for purposes of illustration.

In keeping with the idea that our concepts should have to do with *change*, we choose to describe them under the heading of *growth trends*. A growth trend implies a direction of development; it can be described either by indicating the general direction of change or by setting up an ideal picture of the ultimate end point. Thus we might speak of a trend toward increasing rationality, or we might create the ideal type of a completely rational man. As between these alternative modes of description our preference is strongly for the direction of change. Ideal end points are utterly unreal in anything so complex as human personality, and it is very difficult to keep them from being mistaken for ethical goals. Our growth trends are named according to a direction of change: we speak, for instance, of the stabilizing of ego identity, or the freeing of personal relationships, or the humanizing of values. These directions may be judged "good" in the sense that we judge any natural development of capacities to be "good"—even the eruption of teeth or the mastery of locomotion. Let us not hastily conclude, however, that the logical end points of these developments define a perfect state of virtue. Ethics cannot be settled so simply.

In describing growth trends we shall consider not only the direction of change but also the *process* of change. Growth in a given direction takes place under certain conditions and through certain types of experience. It is not just something that happens because we grow older. If in addition to designating trends we can identify the crucial conditions under which development occurs, we shall be taking a definite step forward in the understanding of natural growth.

GROWTH TRENDS: 1. THE STABILIZING OF EGO IDENTITY

The concept of *ego system* is indispensable for understanding the more organized and enduring features of growth. As we saw in the last chapter, the ego was introduced into dynamic psychology by Freud and assigned a position somewhat like that of umpire among contending forces. It was amplified in one direction by Murray, who described the planning, goal-setting and executive operations that were implicit in the concept, and in a slightly different direction by Erikson, who emphasized ego identity as the central point of organization. As used here, the ego system includes both of these amplifications and also absorbs what is intended by the concepts of self and self-picture. The ego system is obviously complex; its growth can be described in a good many different ways. We shall concentrate here on one important aspect of this growth: a trend toward the *stabilizing of ego identity*.

Ego identity refers to the self or the person one feels oneself to be. In infancy the sense of identity is little developed, but progressive experience brings sharper outline and clearer definition. As we have seen, ego identity is never entirely a social product. It is par'
constructed from within, having perhaps its first basis in what experienced as "I" and "me" in contrast to what is "not me." Gradually the sense of identity becomes a fuller and richer establishment, compounded of bodily sensations, feelings, images of one's body, the sound of one's name, the continuity of one's memories, and an increasing number of social judgments delivered through the words and behavior of others. During adolescence there is a time when ego identity becomes heavily dependent on the judgments of

one's peers. "The danger of this stage," says Erikson, "is role diffusion. It is primarily the inability to settle on an occupational identity which disturbs young people. To keep themselves together they temporarily overidentify, to the point of apparent complete loss of identity, with the heroes of cliques and crowds." [1] Once this difficult period has been traversed, however, ego identity can continue its development along less diffuse channels.

Direction of Growth.—There are many vicissitudes in the development of ego identity, but the overall trend is toward an increase of stability. When one takes a long enough span of time, continuing well into adulthood as we have done with the cases presented here, ego identity can be seen to become not only more sharp and clear but also more consistent and free from transient influences. It becomes increasingly determined by accumulated personal experience. In this way it progressively gains autonomy from the daily impact of social judgments and experiences of success and failure. To be called a coward by a kindergarten playmate may be an extremely upsetting experience; one is not sure to what extent the epithet may be deserved. To be called a coward at the age of thirty is quite another matter. It may be upsetting if the person feels that others have discovered a weakness he was trying to hide, but it will not be upsetting at all if the person knows that it is not true. The point is that at thirty a person pretty much knows whether or not he is a coward; he can make a self-judgment on the basis of his accumulated experience, and he knows that this judgment is sounder than the one arriving from outside. Even praise is not accepted, as we saw in Hale's case, when inner judgment cannot agree that it was deserved. A similar trend can be observed with respect to the evaluation of successes and failures. The single incident progressively loses its power to send self-esteem into the sky or into the depths. Accumulated experience, organized as an increasingly stable set of self-feelings and self-estimates, more and more outweighs the impact of new events.

It is not an objection to this way of looking at the matter to say that with some people ego identity does not seem to grow more stable over the years. Any theory about growth makes the allowance that fixation and regression can occur. It makes the further allowance that conditions may not always be favorable for extensive

---

[1] Erikson, E. H. *Childhood and Society,* New York, W. W. Norton & Co., 1950, p. 228.

growth. In giving the *stabilizing of ego identity* its status as a growth trend, we are suggesting that change in this direction represents an increasingly full realization of capacities for development. It results, moreover, in a greater capacity to exert an influence on the surrounding world. As ego identity grows more stably autonomous, the person becomes capable of having a more consistent and lasting effect upon his environment. The more sure he becomes about his own nature and peculiarities, the more solid is the nucleus from which his activity proceeds.

Of our three subjects, Joseph Kidd ranks as the greatest authority on the earlier growth of ego identity. Because this aspect of growth was peculiarly difficult for him, and because of a serious setback during his later school and college years, Kidd became sharply conscious of the whole process and was able to give us an unusually vivid first-hand account. His description of himself at eighteen as "acting out personalities," "observing people and copying them," then falling back to a "childish attitude to make myself noticeable," deserves to be considered a classic account of a frustrated search for ego identity. Kidd staked out the ensuing trend of his development in two neat summaries given a decade apart. At nineteen he said, "I can't make a decision on my own and back it up; it's always guided by some factor outside my own intellect." At twenty-nine he expressed himself as follows: "It dawned on me after a while that I was knowing what I wanted. I was able to make up my mind." It is worth while to sketch again his progress between these two points.

Kidd's growth was aided by the temporary suspension of parental demands which resulted from his entrance into military service. He was able to drop a whole series of goals and pretensions that had never been invested with a substantial amount of self-feeling. Freed from pressure to study at college and prepare for medical school, permitted to leave all major decisions in other hands, he regressed for a while to the happy atmosphere of adventurous and irresponsible companionship which he had once enjoyed with neighborhood boys. In this way he recovered contact with true interests of his own and began testing his initiative with a great deal more persistence than had characterized his early trying out of "personalities." When he could carry through a hard day's work on a common task, he became aware of an increase of poise and confidence in his relationships with the other men, a thing he deeply wanted to achieve. Presently he ventured on experiments in "corning" and found that it was not impossible for him to be effective in getting what he wanted from other people. When he was commissioned an officer, however, his growing self-confidence went out from under him; he found it impossible to muster the decisiveness needed to direct and discipline the men under his command. He had again been placed in a position that did not "feel right" in the sense of freely enlisting his own desires, which were, after all, "to be *with* other fellows, not *over* them." When reassigned he was able to pick up his own development once more, so that by the time he undertook to manage the building of his father's new business establishment he was able, albeit a little nervously, to seek out information, choose and reject propositions, and require that things be done to suit him.

It was while building the flower studio that Kidd became clearly aware of knowing what he wanted and making up his own mind. The building stood in his mind as the payment of a debt owed by a son to parents whom he had in some respects disappointed. By paying the debt he freed himself from their lingering expectations, thus removing the chief remaining obstacle to the stabilizing of his own ego identity. He had managed to lay a sufficient basis of assertiveness so that he did not feel wholly unable to go after the things he really wanted. He had managed also to clarify an image of himself as a small independent business man and a friendly, likeable fellow. The flower studio stood as an enduring monument to his ideas and his labors. It represented the longest and biggest attempt he had ever made to exert an influence on his environment, and its success was of great value in further stabilizing his identity.

Process of Growth.—When we turn from the *direction* of change to the *process* of change, our focus of attention shifts to the single steps that cumulatively make up a growth trend. We become interested in the conditions under which the stability of ego identity receives an increment of natural growth. We shall not engage ourselves with such vaguely defined conditions as an atmosphere of parental acceptance, which could probably be reduced, after all, through sufficient study to a set of specific incidents. Rather, our concern will be to consider the steps in learning that appear to be most crucial with respect to the growth trend in question. Although we speak of continuous change and cumulative development, it would certainly be arbitrary to interpret these expressions literally as meaning an unbroken growth through time. Growth trends occur through specific incidents which are sometimes well-separated in time. Some incidents, moreover, are much more important than others, even to the extent of producing an astonishing transformation. Hartley Hale gave us an example in the famous "backbone incident," and Joyce Kingsley assigned rather special importance to her singlehanded rebellion at the western army post.

One type of event that often contributes to the stabilizing of ego identity is placement in an occupational status or in some other socially recognized position. Social roles provide us with a means of establishing identity. They also provide us with opportunities for action whereby we further define and stabilize ourselves. Hale's sense of identity began to assume a more definite form as soon as he decided to go to medical school, and his identification with his occupational role proceeded at a rapid pace when he had a chance to enjoy the privileges and utilize the opportunities provided by his profession. Similarly, Joyce Kingsley used her position as president of student government as a means of defining part of her identity and as a platform for effective action. In general it can be said that the stabilizing process owes much to those enduring roles which are characteristic of adult life. As a person shapes his behavior into his occupational role, his marital role, and his parental role, for example, his experience begins to accumulate more and more selectively. The stored-up sources of his stability come increasingly out of behavior within roles. Under stable social conditions much strength can thus be borrowed from the environment through consistent playing of consistently defined roles.

It is not possible, however, to understand the stabilizing process without taking into account the interest and initiative that a person brings to any proffered role. We can take as an example the episode during which Hartley Hale reached his decision to become a doctor. He was greatly helped in reaching this decision by his perceptive and outspoken friend, but he did not accept any of his friend's judgments at face value, arguing far into the night that the whole proposal was poppycock. He utilized his friend's observations, nevertheless, and the long-drawn-out nocturnal session amounted in fact to a profound attempt on Hale's part to imagine himself alternately in the roles of advertising man and physician in order to see which role could absorb the greater portion of his preferences and interests. Medicine won the battle because it took in his interest in biology and because it appealed to his desire to be taken seriously as the giver of profoundly needed services. Hale found that he could identify "harder," so to speak, with the role of doctor, and he made his choice on this basis even though it meant a longer and more difficult education and an income not as great as he hoped to make in advertising. His ego identity was more stable from that day forward.

That interest and initiative are indispensable is well revealed in Kidd's history as an army officer. Here we witness the failure of a well-defined and generally much coveted position to stabilize the behavior of its occupant. Kidd was not interested in being an officer. He made little attempt to overcome his distaste for issuing commands and administering discipline. It was impossible for him to adopt the proffered identity or to behave in such a way as to strengthen it. His interests were slowly moving him toward an entirely different ego identity, and the role of officer, which would have deflected this development, had no more than a transient negative effect on his stabilization.

It must be remembered, furthermore, that social roles do not define individual identities in a precise or sufficient sense. If a person's sense of identity consisted of nothing except that he was a doctor it could hardly be called well-stabilized. Within any one social role there is room for a great deal of individuality. Three vice-presidents in a bank, for example, might bring very different skills and very different personal interests into the company, each making his own special contribution to the enterprise. This point is well illustrated in the case of Hartley Hale, whose ego identity went far beyond what was implied by his role. Within the general framework of being a doctor he had preferred orthopedic surgery, come to favor a radical attitude toward surgical intervention, taken a stand for rapid and efficient ward rounds, devoted a good share of his time to research, selected one particular field of research, and so forth. All of these represent options within the physician's role, but they are all vital parts of Hale's ego identity. They determine, moreover, the particular channels along which his ego identity is translated into action.

Consideration of the part played by social roles thus leads us to perceive the types of experience that are most conducive to stabilizing one's ego identity. Stated schematically, any episode has this effect which serves to heighten the efficacy of accumulated personal experience as against new outside judgments, fresh experiences of success and failure, or new objects of possible identification. This heightened efficacy results most readily from a situation of choice in which there are immediate pressures on either side. Decision necessarily turns on becoming more aware of personal preference and of the things for which one really wants one's life to stand. Perhaps our best illustration is to be found in Joyce's collision with the authorities at the military post on the West Coast. When the youthful magazine editors asked her to present their grievances, she was faced with a considerable challenge. If she kept still, she would preserve her job, save a great deal of unpleasantness, and spare herself the criticism of her friends for being too zealously righteous. But she had strong convictions about leaders who let a mixed group of adolescents run wild and who carelessly interfered with the only activity that embodied one's serious responsibility toward young people. Joyce was forced back to her basic values. She found out what was more important to her and she proceeded to take a stand for it. The result was a permanent sharpening and stabilizing of her ego identity.

Suppose that Joyce had failed, receiving only ridicule and effecting no real change at the post: would we then say that the experience did *not* contribute toward stabilizing her ego identity? We do not know just how she would have been affected, and we believe in general that learning takes place most readily in connection with reward. But it is an essential part of our concept that a stable identity is not overthrown by single experiences of failure. Had this been the first moral stand Joyce had ever taken, she might have been badly upset by failure, possibly questioning whether she really believed in the defeated values. She might have called herself a fool for taking such a stand; she might have accepted from others the judgment that she had been unduly self-righteous. As stabilization increases, however, there is less chance of such a wholesale reaction. It is quite possible that Joyce would not have abandoned her values in the face of defeat; rather, she might have felt them confirmed, and judged only that her timing or her method had been poor. Failure and frustration can contribute a great deal to the stabilizing of ego identity when they are not so overwhelming as to destroy the basis of confidence. The person one feels oneself to be becomes stably established only through discarding a number of persons one gradually feels oneself not to be. These discards make it possible to throw much more energy along the main line, so that identity comes to be increasingly founded on one's better potentialities.

Obviously no single growth trend can do justice to everything that happens in the ego system. The trend we have described in this section resembles in certain respects, though not entirely, McClelland's concept of a trend toward *self-consistency*, a trend that has been given central importance in Lecky's theory of personality. [2] Two somewhat different aspects of growth have been described by Allport under the headings *extension of the self* and *self-objectification*. Extension of the self signifies that a person has "a variety of autonomous interests," that he devotes himself to friends, family, children, cultural interests, work, and so forth, all of which have objective value beyond his immediate pleasure or satisfaction. Self-objectification refers to "that peculiar detachment of the mature person when he surveys his own pretensions in relation to his abilities, his present objectives in relation to possible objectives for himself, his own equipment in comparison with the equipment of others, and his opinion of himself in relation to the opinions others hold of him." [3] These trends are discernible in our subjects and are important in understanding them. The stabilizing of ego identity is but one of several ways in which the ego system proceeds toward full development.

GROWTH TRENDS: 2. THE FREEING OF
PERSONAL RELATIONSHIPS

The second growth trend to be selected for discussion lies in the sphere of personal relationships. Like many other aspects of human behavior, personal relationships are deeply colored by their childhood history. They start very early under circumstances that are not altogether auspicious. The infant's first relationships are with people upon whom he is dependent for all the comforts and necessities of life. Never again will the situation be so one-sided, yet it is here, with basic security always at stake, that the infant lays down his first patterns of human interaction. For some time the child's social learning takes place within the family circle,

[2] McClelland, D. W., *Personality*, New York, William Sloane Associates, 1951, pp. 542-559; Lecky, P., *Self-Consistency: A Theory of Personality*, New York, Island Press, 1945.

[3] Allport, G. W., *Personality: A Psychological Interpretation*, New York, Henry Holt & Co., 1937, ch. 8.

which may be full of affection and esteem but which always contains possibilities for frustration, rivalry, jealousy, and hate. When a child first moves out into the world, he starts to use an already practiced repertory of social behavior. He treats the nursery-school teacher as if she were his mother, the other children as if they were brothers and sisters. He does not, as we sometimes put it, respond to them fully in their own right as new individuals; as a result, his responses are often poorly fitted to the new circumstances.

Responding to people in their own right as new individuals is not easy even for the most socially seasoned adult. It is a difficult human achievement. Our social learning is forever lagging behind the demands put upon it, and our most alert and sensitive responses are apt to reveal bits of inappropriate historical coloring. To some extent this lag results from the inherent difficulties that attend learning in a social situation. When we learn something like the multiplication table, or the way an internal combustion motor is put together, we can at least concentrate on what we are trying to learn. In a social situation, on the other hand, several things are likely to be going on at once. Social interactions have a content as well as an emotional undertone. We are apt to be doing something with the other person, or talking about something, so that our learning is by no means confined to the process of interaction. When someone talks about a trip he has taken, for instance, we respond simultaneously to the contents of his description and to the attitude he displays toward us. Perhaps a very "subjective" listener will respond wholly to the attitude, searching the narrator's manner and tone of voice for proof of affection, condescension, or distaste, and recalling nothing about the geography of the trip. Perhaps a very "objective" listener will come away with a full knowledge of the itinerary but no impression whatever of the person who took the trip. These extremes serve to point up the dilemma of social learning. Most of our social interacting is learned under conditions of high distraction. We do not fully perceive either the other person or ourselves, and this circumstance tends to favor the persistence of old attitudes rather than the learning of new ones.

In view of this weakness in the typical learning situation, and in view of the high emotional stakes that are often involved, it is no wonder that personal relationships are easily injured by anxiety and defenses. Anxiety adds to the distraction; defenses freeze the repertory of safe social behavior and block the attempting of new responses. Suppose that a person has learned to cover social discomfort by fast, superficial chattering, thus avoiding both the silences that would make him anxious and the serious discussions that would challenge his competence. His discomfort forbids him to stop chattering; thus he never learns how people would respond to him, or how he would respond to them, in any other kind of interaction. Social learning is peculiarly vulnerable to the workings of anxiety and defense.

Many students of psychopathology define a neurosis as essentially a disturbance in interpersonal relationships. It follows from this that the cure of neurosis involves *new learning* in interpersonal relationships. Information that is relevant to our second growth trend can be gained by briefly examining the well-studied process of psychotherapy.

Social Growth in Psychotherapy.—When we conceive of neurosis as being based on a defensive block in the learning process, psychotherapy falls into focus as a matter of removing defensive blocks so that learning can be resumed. The growth that goes on during and after a period of psychotherapy is therefore no different in principle from the normal course of development when important blocks have not been present. The essence of psychotherapy is to provide a situation in which the patient will feel progressively less anxious, less defensive, more able to put out new feelers in social behavior and thus to enlarge his capacity for personal relationships. The process has been studied intensively, especially since Freud developed the technique of psychoanalysis, and it is now fairly well understood. It can be translated, as Dollard and Miller have recently shown, into the concepts of a theory of learning originally derived from much simpler facts.[4]

The central feature of the therapeutic situation is the attitude taken by the therapist. This attitude is best described as *permissive*. The therapist accepts with composure and interest whatever the patient has to say. He shows that he considers it important, and he receives it without disapproval, criticism, or censure. He encourages the patient to talk freely even about embarrassing and frightening things, which he does not treat as if they betokened inferiority or wickedness. This is new and surprising; probably the patient has never before encountered such tolerance for his personal problems.

[4] Dollard, J., & Miller, N. E., *Personality and Psychotherapy*, New York, McGraw-Hill Book Co., 1950, Chs. 14-20.

As a result he becomes able to talk of more and more things, including experiences long forgotten and feelings long banished from his awareness. To be able to talk this way creates a new kind of human relationship. Because he receives such consistently permissive responses, the patient dares to increase the range of his feelings toward both the therapist and the other people in his life.

As time advances, however, the situation undergoes something of a change. The patient learns to relax a great many of his defenses, but this leads him to experience with renewed vividness the feelings that prevailed before his development became blocked. Let us suppose that his difficulties have lain chiefly in relationships with competitive people and that his development with respect to such people became blocked in childhood because of anxieties that sprang from trying to compete with a brother. After a while the patient finds himself feeling highly competitive toward the therapist, perhaps also extremely anxious about it. This is the *transference,* a reanimation of the crucial feelings that surrounded the earlier conflict. These feelings, whether of love, dependence, jealousy, hate or fear, are often experienced with great vividness and intensity. This time, however, they find a new reception. The therapist may point them out and interpret them, thus exposing their inappropriateness in the current situation, but he does not receive them in such a way as to create new cause for anxiety. Instead of being choked down again by fear, the feelings are named and brought under rational control so that they can contribute to a whole chain of new learnings. The process of therapy is a slow one, but its individal steps can all be conceived as acts of social learning. The permissiveness of the therapist's behavior makes it possible for the patient to try out an increasing range of formerly "dangerous" acts and feelings, until eventually he has reappraised even the original dangers that long ago blocked his development.

The process of cure does not take place, however, entirely during the therapeutic hours. The patient's improvement would indeed be fragile if it depended upon a permissiveness of response that is almost never found elsewhere in life. As he begins to feel greater freedom in his personal relationship with the therapist, the patient tries out his new behavior on other people and becomes able to increase his range even when the reception is not permissive. Except for the fact that the therapist stands ready to offer encouragement when these experiments receive a setback, the outside learning that accompanies psychotherapy is simply a natural course of growth. The patient belatedly makes the kind of growth that would have gone on through childhood and young adulthood if anxiety and defense had not effected a block. The therapist has provided the rare permissive atmosphere necessary to break the block, but the really vital learning must eventually be accomplished in the patient's own social orbit.

Direction of Growth.—The second of our growth trends moves in a direction which we shall now describe as the freeing of personal relationships. Under reasonably favorable circumstances the natural growth of personality moves in the direction of human relationships that are less anxious, less defensive, less burdened by inappropriate past reactions, more friendly, more spontaneous, more warm, and more respectful. Social interaction becomes more free not only from neurotic trends but also from the impulsive inconsiderateness and egocentricity of youth. The person learns not to be so immersed in his own behavior, so intent on the impression he is making or the point he is trying to put across, that he fails to perceive the people around him. He becomes increasingly able to interact, responding in a way that is related to their responses. As he moves in this direction he develops a greater range and flexibility of responses. He notices more things in the people with whom he interacts and becomes more ready to make a place for their characteristics in his own behavior. In this way he comes to interact more fully with other people, making more points of contact with them. Common interests emerge more quickly in new relationships, develop more lastingly in old ones. The person moves in the direction of increased capacity to live in real relationship with the people immediately around him.

In studying the trend toward the freeing of personal relationships we should concentrate primarily on the people who are important in a given life, those with whom there is frequent and significant interaction. Meeting new people and taking part in gatherings of acquaintances contribute to this growth trend but do not constitute its central events. We should notice also that the trend does not typically consist of a flat generalized increase of capacity to interact with every kind of person. The development proceeds partly by selection and concentration. Friendships are pursued when there are congenial similarities of interest and outlook, but people with whom interaction proves difficult are dropped out of the orbit.

With subjects in the age range of those described in this book it is instructive to begin with the growth of their relationship to parents. Then come their spouses or potential spouses, their children, their intimate friends, their colleagues at work, and the people they frequently meet in their neighborhood and community. With some people there is a lasting desire for novelty in human relationships, and it is important to study their growth in their own chosen direction. We must here confine ourselves, however, to a very few examples, and our clearest ones come from relationships with family members and friends.

Joyce Kingsley proved to be our most lucid informant concerning the freeing of personal relationships. In the first study she described in great detail, though not with much insight, her strong identification with her parents and their values. Indirectly, she gave evidence of marked dependence on her mother and of covert resentment against certain features of the parental regime. She also reported her difficulties in achieving real friendships with people of her own age, and she gave us reason, in her free associations, to suspect that these difficulties were occasioned by feelings of superiority and hostility. Five years later Joyce had become much more aware of what went on in her personal relationships. Through returning to the family home after a period of absence she had come to realize the force of her dependence on her mother, though she was not able to do very much to change it. She saw her parents in a new objective light and could be critical both of their behavior and of their values. With fine shrewdness she had sensed the poisoning of her social relationships by anxiety-based feelings of moral superiority. Here she had found it possible to venture a wider range of social behavior which had distinctly increased her capacity for interaction. Joyce's history clearly exhibits the trend toward the freeing of personal relationships, even though, as she herself put it, she still has "a long way to go."

Process of Growth.—In general, the situation that is most conducive to change is one in which the other person responds unexpectedly, thus disrupting one's own habituated way of behaving. Children learn that other children are not mere assistants in their games when the assistants rebel and prove to have desires of their own. Children learn that other children are not enemies when the supposed enemies show friendly interest and kindness. Similarly, in the course of psychotherapy the patient learns to be unafraid because his behavior is greeted with boundless permissiveness and understanding. When faced with such surprises one learns to observe the other person, to understand and respect him, and one becomes more aware of one's own action. The next attempt at interaction will be a little different, and differences may accumulate in such a way as to constitute a decided trend toward the freeing of personal relationships.

An example of the first step is provided by Joyce Kingsley's difficulties over her husband's departure from religion. Joyce attempted to meet this astounding development by utilizing her well-practiced argumentative and dominating modes of behavior. These efforts came to naught, and she was forced to observe Renn more closely. She discovered his strong trait of independence, his determination to work out the problem for himself, and his unwillingness to be hurried. Because she cared deeply about Renn, she was obliged to respect these wishes and hold in check her own desire to argue him back into the fold. This particular experience upset her for quite a while, but her patient waiting was a completely new response which represented a broadening of her capacity for personal relationship. She had learned to respect another person's convictions in the way that she wanted her own convictions to be respected.

If a person's social behavior is not too heavily bound by defenses against anxiety, it tends to become more varied as experience accumulates. Each occasion on which the other person's behavior has to be observed adds an increment of knowledge about human diversity. It also adds an increment of variation to the repertory of social behavior. This sort of growth by increments is well shown in Joyce's account of her increasing tolerance and friendliness toward others. She described her growth as proceeding steadily though slowly, a little at a time, without sharp or striking incidents.

There are times, however, when a growth trend moves ahead by sudden jumps. Such occasions correspond to the "learning by insight" first emphasized by the Gestalt school of psychologists.[5] The other person is perceived first in one way, then in an entirely different way, the change representing a sudden reorganization of the perceptual field. Hartley Hale's attitude toward his eldest daughter seems to have undergone one of these abrupt reorganizations. He felt nothing but irritation at the child's disobedience until

[5] Kohler, W. *The Mentality of Apes*, New York, Harcourt, Brace & Co., 1927.

he suddenly realized how much it resembled his own stubborn independence at a like age. He thenceforth grasped the inner meaning of the little girl's behavior and became much better able to treat her with an appropriate amount of patience. Hale's learning exhibited *empathy*, which in this connection means experiencing the same feelings as another person through having been in the same situation oneself. He realized why his daughter rebelled because he had "been there" himself. In a study of nursery school children Lois Murphy showed that empathy was very much influenced by personal past experience. A child who had once had a broken arm, for instance, would display special solicitude when another child arrived with an arm in a sling.[6] The capacity to produce new behavior in social situations is thus favorably affected by having a large *empathic range*, a rich store of experiences which can be used as a basis for understanding the meaning of another person's behavior. Sometimes a person can use the tragedies in his own life as a means of understanding other people's tragedies.

The two growth trends thus far described prove to be not unrelated. One of the things that contributes to the freeing of personal relationships is the stabilizing of ego identity. This is nowhere better exemplified than in our subjects' attitudes toward their parents. Joseph Kidd was always a child in his father's presence until he went away to military service and began to construct a more definite identity of his own. Upon his return he was able gradually to treat his father in the new way that was more appropriate to their respective ages. He began to collect bad debts, manage accounts, figure taxes, and generally take over initiative in the business, until at last he assumed full responsibility for the new shop which his father needed but lacked the energy to procure. Instead of asking for pocket money Kidd found himself giving his father pocket money out of the funds now subjected to orderly bookkeeping. To some extent Kidd freed this relationship from past distortions by actually working with his father and finding that in the end his father responded favorably when things were done for him. But it is doubtful whether Kidd would have advanced so rapidly if he had not been away for four years building a personality of his own. Interactions between parents and children rarely change as fast as would be warranted by the children's growth. A period

[6] Murphy, L. B. *Social Behavior and Child Personality*, New York, Columbia University Press, 1937, ch. 9.

of absence is therefore often of great benefit in putting things on a new footing. As the children become adults and stabilize their own identities they are apt to view their parents more objectively, with a more dispassionate criticism, and at the same time with a warmer and more empathic appreciation.

GROWTH TRENDS: 3. THE DEEPENING OF INTERESTS

Interests play a curiously small part in current thinking about personality. They have often been crudely "measured" for purposes of vocational guidance, but little attempt has been made to formulate their place in the growth of personality. Interests do not present themselves as clinical problems, and they are hard to describe in a systematic way. Perhaps they have also suffered from our frequent habit of describing personality at a fixed point in time. Interests are not static; it is of their very essence that they constantly move forward and almost never reach final goals. Thus it happens that the scientist, typically a person of the strongest interests, has found few ways to study this elusive topic. Yet interests are often of tremendous importance in the personal economy of happiness. The loss of opportunities to pursue them can sometimes be an irreparable catastrophe.

In the last chapter we mentioned Freud's theory of *sublimation*, which was an attempt to derive all interests from the libidinal preoccupations of the first few years of life. We also listened to the criticism of this view contained in Allport's theory of the *functional autonomy of motives*, which regards earlier satisfactions as being abandoned in favor of later ones. What is needed to decide upon the merits of such theories is a great deal more empirical evidence than is presently available. It is easy to study interests without utilizing the proper methods for uncovering possible infantile roots. It is also easy to talk about them as if the infantile roots alone determined the later evolution. The true picture can emerge only through extensive case studies. Our methods in this book are not equal to answering the crucial questions about early origins, but we can at least indicate a growth trend which appears highly important in understanding the natural development of interests.

The nature of interests was well set forth in one of John Dewey's notable contributions to education. An interest, he said, was always connected with an activity which engaged a person in a whole-hearted fashion.

Interest is not some one thing; it is a name for the fact that a course of action, an occupation, or pursuit absorbs the powers of an individual in a thorough-going way. But an activity cannot go on in a void. It requires material, subject-matter, conditions upon which to operate. On the other hand, it requires certain tendencies, habits, powers on the part of the self. Wherever there is genuine interest, there is an identification of these two things. The person acting finds his own well-being bound up with the development of an object to its own issue. If the activity goes a certain way, then a subject-matter is carried to a certain result, and a person achieves a certain satisfaction.[7]

Direction of Growth.—The growth trend with which we are now concerned may be said to take a direction toward the state of affairs described by Dewey. It is a trend toward increasing absorption in the object of interest, increasing identification of one's tendencies with "development of an object to its own issue." The absorption of a scientist in his experiments, an artist in his painting, a musician in his composition, a craftsman in his work, all serve to illustrate advanced points in this development. It is a common experience with creative people that they lose themselves in their work. Even the creatures of their fancy, such as the characters in a novel or the themes in a musical composition, acquire an almost autonomous existence, refusing at times to come out right, so that their creator must pace the floor or walk across the fields while waiting for them to assume a satisfactory shape. Similarly, the solution of a mathematical problem is often experienced as having to work itself out. Such instances are extreme, but they highlight the nature of an important trend in growth. Under reasonably favorable circumstances a person becomes increasingly capable of having his energies absorbed in the needs and properties of the objects with which he is working.

In speaking of a trend toward the *deepening* of interests we have in mind this increased capacity for absorption. Interests often enough grow broader as well as deeper, but our concern here is with one particular quality rather than with quantity or extensiveness. We are also not referring to the amount of time a person devotes to his interests; a trend toward deepening does not imply that he spends more and more of his hours in a state of absorption until at last everything else is excluded. The trend we have in mind

---

[7] Dewey, J., *Interest and Effort in Education*, Boston, Houghton Mifflin Co., 1913, p. 65.

is away from a state in which interests are casual, quickly dropped, pursued only from motives that do not become identified with advancement of the object. It is toward a state in which the sense of reward comes from doing something for its own sake. Our examples need not be so extreme as the artist or scientist. We can think instead of a man who allows himself to be nominated for the water board in a small town. At first he is motivated by a desire to participate in a necessary public service, to see his name in the town report, and to feel that he has the esteem of the citizens. Ten years later he may have become greatly interested in precipitation and watersheds, location of reservoirs, piping and pumping systems, filters and purifiers, and the economic side of a water supply. He has built up a store of knowledge and expertness. He is interested in making the town water system a better water system, and he might not care too much if through a printer's error his name was left out of the town report.

Of the three subjects studied in this book Hartley Hale had the most to teach us about interests. Two things were impressive in his early childhood: an eagerness to master physical objects and a strong curiosity about sex. We found reason to relate his curiosity to the problem of his parents' sexual relationships, and thus to the frustrations of the Oedipus situation. No satisfactory clues could be found to the precise origin of his interest in mastery; we noticed, however, that the interest was present in his earliest memories and that it received considerable encouragement from his parents. From these childhood beginnings it proved possible to trace a more or less continuous course of development that finally culminated in biology and medical research. Mechanical interests and sexual curiosity took separate courses through his high school years, but it seems not unlikely that the profound interest awakened by his first biology course came from a combining of the hitherto separate strands. Hale learned quite early to subordinate his immediate desires to the requirements of his objects. He abandoned the vision of a perpetual motion machine and settled for a boat that would go twice around the bath tub. He kept at the building of radios until he made a set that would work. Although in most respects he tended to be quick and impatient, his research career was marked by willingness to wait for years, if necessary, in order to develop the apparatus and strategy required to answer a single question. It was a crowning stroke of good fortune for Hale that his developing interests lent themselves so readily to the demands of the profession of medicine.[8]

Process of Growth.—There are no doubt many circumstances that favor the deepening of interests. Hale called attention to one of these when telling about the teachers who had encouraged his scientific pursuits. When a teacher disregarded his outward cockiness and expressed faith in his serious abilities, he became aware of a sudden increase in his capacity to become absorbed in scientific studies. Others have reported similar experiences, especially during adolescence: the encouraging interest of an older person seemed to give them needed assurance to pursue activities requiring detachment from the daily round of life. Adolescence is a period of intense loyalty to groups, intense conformity to the prevailing youth culture. Anyone who chooses to pursue an individual interest might therefore be expected to feel a need for special outside support. It seems likely, however, that something more is involved. Hale emphasized the fact that his favorite teachers disregarded his competitive aggressiveness.

Another of our subjects, not reported in this book, made the matter even clearer both through his behavior and through his responses on the Thematic Apperception Test. He indicated that creative interest always suffered when he felt competitive, hostile, or under the necessity to prove that he was not inferior. When the self was threatened and required defense, there was no energy left over to be expended on creative tasks. This man also responded very well to the interest of one of his teachers. Apparently the teacher's acceptance of him as a promising equal released him from the necessity of defense and allowed him to let his energies flow forth in new directions. We are entitled to suggest that the deepening of interests is favored by circumstances that abrogate anxiety and cancel expensive defenses. The peace of mind that goes with security and the rewards that come from encouragement are important aids to constructive growth.

The process of deepening occurs through satisfying transactions with objects of interest. It is characteristic of interesting objects that they offer an endless series of problems and challenges. One can never exhaust the things to be learned in a field of science or the obstacles to be overcome in research. One can never run

[8] For an account of the growth of artistic interests see Anne Roe, Artists and Their Work, *Journal of Personality*, 1946, Vol. 15, pp. 1-40.

through the possibilities of enjoyment and expression in art, literature, or music. People whose hobbies have grown to well-nigh professional proportions give ample testimony to the inexhaustibility of interesting things. Thus it is possible for satisfying transactions to go on and on, and this tends to build up funds of knowledge and expertness that make the person equal to still more difficult transactions. Just as growth in personal relationships makes one increasingly responsive to the characteristics of individual people, so growth in interests makes one increasingly alert to the properties of individual objects. Interests grow deeper through the cumulative effects of learning.

Occasionally the deepening of an interest occurs quite suddenly. In a way that almost resembles a religious conversion, a person "discovers his field" and goes forward with exuberant enthusiasm. Hartley Hale had an experience of this kind when he shifted his vocational plan from advertising to medicine. We can offer the guess that these sudden bursts of interest occur when several separate lines of previous interest become merged in a new unified activity, or when frustrated lines find their first real opportunity for free development. Our material provides these guesses, however, with only a small underpinning of facts.

The deepening of interests has a great deal to do with effectiveness and happiness in one's occupation. A person may want to become a doctor for many reasons: prestige, social status, money, identification with the white-coated heroes of the moving picture screen, a zeal to banish suffering, perhaps even a private mission to conquer the disease that has prematurely taken away a beloved relative. These can be powerful motives, but in themselves they do not make a good doctor. Granted a sufficient level of ability, the crucial thing is the possibility of becoming more and more deeply interested in the detailed subject-matter and daily activities of medicine. Whatever the initial motives, they will not produce a good doctor unless they can be channeled to support a deepening interest in the details of a doctor's arduous life. There were people who shook their heads dubiously over the idea that Hartley Hale, hellion of his high school, was going to be a physician. Yet he became a very good physician because there was no limit to his capacity for interest in medicine.

Anne Roe has made studies of artists, physicists, biologists, and several other groups of professional workers. If one examines the findings of psychological tests there proves to be a good deal of variation within each professional group and only a small number of marked differences between groups. The distinctive thing about these people seems to be that quite early in life they got interested in the subject matter they later pursued as a vocation. The cumulative deepening of interest was the thing that guided them to their careers and that largely determined their success.[9]

GROWTH TRENDS: 4. THE HUMANIZING OF VALUES

In earlier times it was not infrequently assumed that moral conscience was an innate human faculty. It is more in line with a scientific approach to assume that this "faculty" has a traceable history and that its development depends upon lawful processes of learning. Freud's doctrine of the superego reflected a searching attempt to uncover the childhood roots of what in later life would be called conscience and a system of values. Freud exposed the irrational origins of what we would like to consider one of the most rational features of our adult lives. Piaget's studies of moral judgments in children added greatly to the picture of early irrationality. The young child's understanding cannot fully grasp the meaning of moral values, which are therefore interpreted in a literal fashion that often departs widely from adult intentions. All in all, values get a bad start in early life. They are accepted under a certain duress, they are misunderstood, they are taken over wholesale by identification, they are rejected wholesale in a phase of negativism, and they may well become a bone of contention in contests between parents and children. Out of such beginnings must we fashion the moral conscience which Kant considered to be one of the strongest proofs of the greatness of God.

Direction of Growth.—In choosing to call our fourth growth trend the humanizing of values we are somewhat guided by Piaget's notable studies.[10] Piaget traced the evolution of the child's moral judgment between the seventh and fifteenth years. He demonstrated a trend from a literal belief in rules, almost as if they had an independent physical existence, to an attitude of relativity, in which precepts

[9] Roe, A., *op. cit.*, and also Psychological Examinations of Eminent Biologists, *Journal of Consulting Psychology*, 1949, Vol. 13, pp. 225-246; Personality and Vocation, *Transactions of the New York Academy of Science*, 1947, Vol. 9, pp. 257-267.

[10] Piaget, J. *The Moral Judgment of the Child*, New York, Harcourt, Brace & Co., 1932.

were perceived in relation to the social purposes they were designed to serve. Younger children did not grasp the fact that the rules for a game of marbles depended on mutual agreement and were adopted to make the game interesting and fair. They considered the rules to have an absolute existence which precluded any kind of alteration. Older children conceived the rules of a game much as adults would conceive them, but they were not always lucid about the meaning of more complex values. Piaget pointed out that the growth trend could not be conceived simply as a maturing of intellectual capacity. It depended upon experience in social interaction whereby the child came to perceive for himself the consequences of precepts and their violation.

The growth trend observed in the study of somewhat older subjects is in a sense a continuation of Piaget's trend toward relativism. We prefer to call it a *humanizing* of values in order to emphasize the following facts: (1) the person increasingly discovers the human meaning of values and their relation to the achievement of social purposes, and (2) he increasingly brings to bear his own experiences and his own motives in affirming and promoting a value system. The overall trend, starting from childhood, might be described as a trend from absolute received values to a personally wrought value system. This does not mean that the person creates his value system without benefit of historical tradition. It does not necessarily mean that he substantially changes the content of his received values. The growth trend implies that his values, whatever their content, become increasingly his own, increasingly a reflection of his own experiences and purposes.

Hartley Hale as an undergraduate did not believe in socialized medicine because the midwestern Republicans amongst whom he had grown up were generally opposed to socialization. At thirty-three he did not believe in socialized medicine because he had experienced great benefit under a system of individual freedom and believed on highly specific grounds that medical progress would eventually be crippled by state control. Whether or not one agrees with Hale, it is clear that his values became more humanized. They were more closely in touch both with his own ongoing interests and with the needs of sick people as he perceived them.

As we have already indicated, Joyce Kingsley proved to be an unusually illuminating authority on the humanizing of values. As a college senior she was a staunch advocate of the whole parental value system, even down to the details of national and local politics. She discussed values in the first person plural, as if she felt no need to discriminate her own views from those that emanated from the two ends of the family dining room table. Her value system was the "good foundation," built for her by her parents, on which she expected to construct her life. Five years later she made it clear that she had been inspecting the "good foundation." Her personal relationships had been marred by difficulties that seemed traceable to defects in the received value system. She had begun to think of improvements which she hoped to practice in the bringing up of her own children, and she had begun to find new meaning, through her personal experience in social work training, for the doctrine of freedom of choice that formed part of her religious tradition.

Process of Growth.—The general situation that leads to the humanizing of values is one in which existing values become an occasion for conflict. Perhaps a value that has been automatically accepted is challenged by a competing value. The person then faces the choice of espousing the new value or affirming the old one, and even if he chooses the latter course, as Hale did when challenged by socialized medicine, his affirming represents a new perception of what is involved and a new enlisting of motives that are really his own. Sometimes in such a conflict the person finds that the new value captures his personal loyalty. He then shifts to it, realizing more clearly than before what is implied both by the new value and by the old one. Joyce seems to have taken some such step when she changed from wanting to be a school teacher to wanting to be a counselor of misunderstood adolescents. Sometimes growth comes about when a person in the course of acting upon his usual values produces an unexpected and unwelcome result. Intending to be upright he finds that he has been cruel, or supposing that he is friendly and obliging he learns that he has been taken for a financial ride. This kind of thing happened to Joyce when she realized that her righteous administration of student government prevented her from having intimate friends.

In the humanizing of values, as in the freeing of personal relationships, an important place is occupied by the concept of *empathic range*. Often a marked growth occurs through sudden empathic identification with some new aspect of a value conflict. The process can best be illustrated by drawing an unusually clear example from our case files. A young woman in college was the younger of two

children in a business family of highly conservative outlook. She felt
that her brother was very much the favorite child and that she had
been treated quite unfairly at home. During the wartime shortage of
hospital personnel she spent a summer as a volunteer aide in a community hospital near her home. She was astonished and outraged
when she realized that patients in private rooms were given far
more care and attention than the patients in the wards. Nurses
sprang to answer the private-room bell calls while ward patients
might be kept waiting for half an hour. She suddenly began to question an economic system which produced so much unfairness in
ministering to the common needs of the sick. It was clear that this
challenging of received values became possible for her because of
a powerful empathic response toward the ward patients. As a victim of domestic unfairness she burned with wrath at the plight
of the less favored sick people. Empathy is often of crucial significance in breaking the hold of an unexamined value system. It
enlarges one's personal outlook and makes it possible to see the
conflicting human claims that offer the real challenge to any value
system.

The trend toward the humanizing of values does not take account of everything that happens in the growth of value systems.
It needs to be supplemented by another trend, one that has been
described by Allport as moving toward a *unifying philosophy of
life*. Allport comments as follows on the nature of this philosophy:

> Such a philosophy is not necessarily articulate, at least not
> always articulate in words. The preacher, by virtue of his
> training, is usually more articulate than the busy country doc-
> tor, the poet more so than the engineer, but any of these per-
> sonalities, if actually mature, participates and reflects, lives and
> laughs, according to some embracing philosophy of life devel-
> oped to his own satisfaction and representing to himself his
> place in the scheme of things.[11]

The trend we have been describing here does not carry any implication about a unified result. It often happens, in fact, that when a
person begins to use his own experience to humanize a well-knit
system of received values his philosophy for a time becomes much
less unified. This was the case with our hospital aide; she violently
rejected the economic philosophy of her parents when she perceived

[11] Allport, G. W., *Personality, op. cit.*, ch. 8.

one of its unfair consequences, but the job of thinking out her own economic philosophy proved slow and disturbing, so that for a time her views were neither stable nor consistent. Allport's remarks on a unified philosophy call attention to another aspect of development, one in which the person tries to make his humanized values work together in a common cause. The three subjects in this book exhibit to a certain extent the unifying trend, but perhaps our best example is to be found in Joyce Kingsley's father, who rejected a materialistic outlook and built up for himself a religious philosophy which drew cooperation, freedom, and spiritual needs into a unified whole.

The importance of analyzing a person's implicit philosophy is shown in a recent study by Smith, Bruner, and White on the relationship of opinions to other features of personality.[12] To some extent, opinions reflect external influences, but close scrutiny shows that individual experience comes in at certain points to give them a definite personal coloring. It is important to distinguish between opinions that are passively borrowed and those that represent humanized values. Any attempt to predict the future course of a person's opinions must take full account of this distinction.

MENTAL HEALTH RECONSIDERED: THE PERILS OF ADJUSTMENT

At this point we return to a more general theme. Our study has taught us something about the natural growth of personality, and we must now inquire how these findings bear on current ideas about human nature. In particular we must consider the impact of existing knowledge about personality upon the general values and ideals of our time, and we need to ask seriously whether these ideals should be reconsidered in the light of what we have learned about natural growth.

Ideals derived largely from the study of behavior disorders have crystallized into three concepts: *mental health, adjustment,* and *emotional maturity.* These ideals have come to occupy a prominent and influential place in our thinking. In part their prominence comes from the prestige that is currently accorded to science and medicine. In part it comes from the decline of religion and ethics as guides to personal conduct. In part it comes from the confusion

[12] Smith, M. B., Bruner, J. S., & White, R. W. *Opinions and Personality,* New York, to be published, 1953.

ın secular values other than those derived from science. Mental health, adjustment, and emotional maturity are thus tending to fill an ideological vacuum, expanding beyond their appropriate realm and becoming major goals and ethical values. "The maturity concept," writes Overstreet, "is central to our whole enterprise of living. This is what our past wisdoms have been leading up to." [13] If these ideals are going to be considered as the culmination of past wisdoms, it is certainly essential to give them the closest scrutiny. For they are anything but inert ideas. They have a direct point of application in child training, guidance, and teaching, and they are being used every day to influence the development of personality.

In content these three ideals are less different than might be expected. Mental health is strictly an extension of the medical concept of health, and it can be defined only in the negative sense of not having anything wrong with you. Actually most writers on the subject go a little further and speak of optimal mental health, but in so doing they tend to step over into the concept of emotional maturity.[14] Adjustment is generally used in the sense of biological adaptation, referring to the efforts made by a person to maintain himself in his physical and social environment. Emotional maturity lends itself to more positive statement, pointing to qualities which an adult can acquire by outgrowing the ways of his childhood. In Saul's book on the subject we find several criteria of emotional maturity which could be related to our growth trends: for example, "from parasitic dependence to independence of the parents," "freedom from the constellation of inferiority, egotism, and competitiveness," "construction of own conscience," "attaining a firm sense of reality." [15] Yet these statements contain little elaboration of the mature end of the scale, and it is hard to make them sound like a description of real life. Emotional maturity still means little more than a clean bill of mental health.

The truth is that none of these three ideals has been derived from the contemplation of successful life-patterns. They all spring

---

[13] Overstreet, H. A. *The Mature Mind,* New York, W. W. Norton & Co., 1949, p. 14.

[14] Ten criteria of optimum mental health, one of them being "adequate emotional maturity," are given in a representative statement by Thorpe, L. P., *The Psychology of Mental Health,* New York, The Ronald Press Co., 1950, pp. 116-117.

[15] Saul, L. J., *Emotional Maturity,* Philadelphia, J. B. Lippincott Co., 1947, pp. 7-17.

from the mental hospital and psychiatric consulting room, from studies of the sick aspects of sick people. For the most part they are simply the logical opposites of the things that are troubling sick people, things like dependence, inferiority, competitiveness, a harsh superego, a failure to test the reality behind delusional and hallucinatory experiences. When one adds up mental health, adjustment, and emotional maturity to form the image of an ideal life one is impressed that the authors of these concepts have themselves been weak in reality testing. They have not tried to make a direct study of mentally healthy, well-adjusted, emotionally mature behavior, and their image of perfection fits very poorly the lives of people who have made important contributions to civilization.

We need to pursue a little further, and quite seriously, our remarks about reality testing. There is a more grave charge that must be made against these ideals. They are never stated in such a way as to include the actual conditions under which growth in adulthood takes place. They are presented as a list of general traits which suggest that the person is equal to anything. "The individual has faith in his ability to succeed," says one account of mental health; "he believes he will do reasonably well whatever he undertakes." It is hard to detect in this and similar statements any recognition of the real conditions under which adult life is lived. There is little hint of the problems involved in being happy and creative in one particular life-pattern with its enduring commitments and inescapable restrictions as well as its rewards and its changes. Indeed, there is no such thing as a general pattern of mental health and emotional maturity—everything depends on the conditions under which the life is being lived. What is one man's meat is another man's poison, and there is certainly no one pattern of traits that would be equally "healthy" in a surgeon, a composer of music, a personnel manager, and a shifter of scenery on a moving-picture lot.

But this is not all. Our charge against the ideals of mental health, adjustment, and emotional maturity must become still more grave. These ideals imply, no doubt unintentionally but nevertheless with great repetitive insistence, that it is a person's job to adjust himself to the forces around him. "He establishes socially approved goals and makes reasonable progress toward attaining them"; no hint that he should ever criticize socially approved goals or try to formulate better ones. "He achieves a fundamental harmony with his environment"; no suggestion that he should ever take a stand against his environment or try to change it for the better. In all this thinking there is an implicit assumption that the physical and social environment is fixed and unchangeable, that the strong and the healthy can adjust themselves to it, that only the weak, the immature, the dependent, the egotistical, and the otherwise neurotically burdened people fail to take its demands in their stride. The doctrine that started as preventive medicine has become a slogan for iron-bound social conformity. In attempting to prevent mental breakdown, moreover, it has actually encouraged another kind of developmental tragedy. It has enshrined as its ideal the person who all-too-successfully adjusts to narrowing channels, monotonous routines, imposed restrictions, and the pressure to fulfil roles, a course of action that can succeed only at the cost of his power to object, to grow, to improve the roles, to enjoy, to invent, to act as a constructive force—in short, to have any creative front in his development. Breakdown is a tragedy, but adjustment can also be a tragedy.

We owe to Erich Fromm a very illuminating description of what happens to a life that is dominated by the marketing orientation.[16] Fromm related this orientation to present economic conditions, especially the increased size, impersonality, and incalculability of markets. The individual person, a mere item on the market for jobs, feels himself to be a commodity and tries to develop traits of personality that will keep him constantly saleable. He must even keep his personality in fashion, according to the patterns transmitted on the screen and in the advertising pages. His self-esteem is dependent upon conditions beyond his control; he fears set-backs, relentlessly strives for success, suffers a constant need for confirmation of his worth by other people. His ego identity is but little founded on his own powers and accomplishments, being almost wholly defined by the opinions of others. When he thinks of other people, it is in their saleable aspects, not for their range of individual qualities, and this renders all social interactions superficial. Even his thinking is affected, becoming a scramble to grasp such knowledge as might increase his commodity value. "The marketing personality," Fromm concludes, "must be free of all individuality."

The marketing orientation is encouraged by present economic

[16] Fromm, E. *Man For Himself*, New York, Rinehart & Co., 1947, pp. 67-82.

conditions. It sets an increasingly dangerous trap for the growth of personality. But the ideals of mental health, adjustment, and emotional maturity have done nothing to warn us against this trap. They have failed dismally as guides in this problem because they do not suggest in any proper way man's resources for continuing to develop even when hard pressed by economic and social circumstances. They lack concepts that have to do with the cumulative deepening and enrichment of experience. They do not suggest that a person can increase his power of changing things constructively while still fulfilling the obligations of partnership in society. They lack concepts about interests and about the special patterns of life that develop in connection with special interests. They do not encourage us to consider the many different ways in which lives can become happily and productively organized. They urge us to play a safe game for mental health and to take no chances with deviation. One might even say that they show little sympathy for adventure, and this is indeed a serious charge if one agrees with Whitehead that "without adventure civilization is in full decay."

GUIDANCE RECONSIDERED: THE NURTURING OF GROWTH

The ideals of mental health, adjustment, and emotional maturity have a strong and direct impact on the culture. They are being used not only as guides to personal conduct but also as doctrine for all those who are responsible for bringing up children: parents, teachers, and professional workers trained to give counsel and treatment. Our study of natural growth has caused us to believe that these ideals are open to considerable question. Perhaps we are justified in going a step further and considering the implications of our point of view for child rearing and child guidance.

It is well to remember that case studies such as the ones reported in this book cannot yield decisive information as regards child rearing methods or the atmosphere of the home. It would be highly valuable to compare methods of punishment, for example, or parental attitudes such as acceptance and rejection, in a series of case histories that included both healthy and disordered individuals. But for this purpose our material is unsuitable. We depend too much on our subjects' reconstructions of their childhood histories; and while it is important to know how they remember the atmosphere of their homes, we can never be sure that their reports quite correspond to the actual facts as an independent observer might have perceived them. Our findings therefore cannot be used to suggest how parents should behave or how programs of child guidance should proceed. We must use them only for a much more general purpose.

It is possible, nevertheless, to reconsider certain goals of child training in the light of those larger ideas that have emerged from our study. We have suggested that current ideals—mental health, adjustment, emotional maturity—have been conceived negatively rather than positively, as logical opposites of neurotic and psychotic conditions rather than as patterns designed to maximize constructive development. We have further suggested that these ideals seriously neglect the questions of continuous change, selective response to shaping forces, and the child's capacity to influence both the environment and his own destiny. Let us now examine the consequences of this one-sidedness and see whether we can take a fresh view of child rearing, even if only in a quite general sense.

One of the things which parents have been given to understand is that they have a tremendous influence on their children's emotional lives. They are responsible for implanting cultural values and producing socialized behavior, yet they are also the first objects of their child's loves, hates, and anxieties. Everything hangs on the way they handle the crucial episodes in training; everything depends on the emotional atmosphere they manage to create in the home. There is a substantial amount of truth in this outlook, but when it is not counterbalanced by any sense of the child's own activity, his desire to grow and his power to act selectively, its effect on parents can be extremely terrifying. There is evidence today of widespread intimidation of parents. They are afraid of doing the wrong thing, creating the wrong atmosphere, not being themselves mature, and thus permanently blighting their child's development. The task of producing healthy, happy, confident children often rests in the hands of people rendered tense and anxious by their huge responsibility and their feeling of awesome power. Take, for example, the question of parental rejection. Many a parent has come to have a terrible dread of showing annoyance at a child, even of feeling annoyance, because he has been taught that the child will read the signs, feel rejected, and go to emotional ruin. Only recently have workers like Baruch perceived the spreading scope of this dread and begun to reassure parents that their children will not be wrecked by displays of anger.[17] Children can be quite resourceful in resisting ruin by their parents.

Another thing that has served to intimidate parents is the implication that any failure in wise guidance pushes the child straight toward neurosis or psychosis. It is not just that one method of training is better than another; the penalty for using the poorer method is that the child will become mentally or emotionally sick. Supposing themselves to be confronted by this grim alternative, parents become apprehensively eager to stamp out "unhealthy" traits in their children and to produce the opposite traits. When the relation between repression and neurosis first became a part of common knowledge, many parents concluded that all discipline and restraint were evil. If a child refrained from tearing the nursery to pieces it was a danger signal of neurosis. Only later did it appear that a lack of clear discipline could itself provoke anxiety in children too young to restrain their own unruly impulses. A current example of intimidation is the attitude often taken by parents toward social adjustment. If a child shows an inclination to stay by himself he is deemed to be well on the way toward schizophrenia, and his parents rush to the rescue by pushing him into an unceasing round of social contacts. Current teaching has robbed many parents of the courage to wait for social growth and of the insight that solitude can be used constructively.

Thus it comes about that the intimidated parent of our time strives desperately to produce in his children a pattern of traits conceived to offer protection against neurosis and psychosis. His anxiety eventually produces a parental neurotic trend. His desire for "healthy" traits becomes indiscriminate and insatiable, and he feels anxious at even a hint of the opposite traits. As a result, the pattern of "healthy" traits becomes a complete end in itself, an imperative, a "must" for safe development. Individual variation from the preferred pattern is viewed with distinct alarm. Children must stick to the straight and narrow way toward healthy adjustment.

Certainly we cannot blame parents if they have drawn frightening conclusions from what is today available in the way of scientific knowledge. We cannot blame them for not knowing that the frontier of science moves forward jaggedly, giving no more than a partial view of its subject matter. But if we have been right in emphasizing the importance of interest, activity, initiative and new learning, the

[17] Baruch, D. W. *New Ways in Discipline*, New York, Whittlesey House, 1949.

parental attitudes we have just described are likely to have an altogether disastrous effect. Designed merely to avert emotional disorder, they are in danger of blocking the very trends that lead to constructive and original development. Some interests represent individual peculiarities which cause a child to be different from other children. These are all too apt to fall under the parental ban on deviations from mental health. Other interests, such as social interest, are highly approved but are pushed so enthusiastically by the parents that the child scarcely has a chance to mobilize his own interest or to exert his own initiative. The intimidated parent is under pressure to crush the child's individual interests and to run away with his social interests. Neither policy is conducive to natural growth.

According to the ideas developed in this book, the task of rearing and guiding children can best be represented by the metaphor of raising plants. This should be encouraging, because raising plants is one of mankind's most successful activities. Perhaps the success comes from the fact that the husbandman does not try to thrust impossible patterns on his plants. He respects their peculiarities, tries to provide suitable conditions, protects them from the more serious kinds of injury—but he lets the plants do the growing. He does not poke at the seed in order to make it sprout more quickly, nor does he seize the shoot when it breaks ground and try to pull open the first leaves by hand. Neither does he trim the leaves of different kinds of plants in order to have them all look alike. The attitude of the husbandman is appropriate in dealing with children. It is the children who must do the growing, and they can do it only through the push of their own budding interests.

Parents who are not intimidated can respect unusual interests in their children. They will not be afraid of deviations from neighbor patterns, and they will therefore not crush nascent interests, like Hartley Hale's in mechanical objects and radios, which may later evolve into professional activities of the utmost value for mankind. They will also be able to await the sprouting of interests which do not come quickly to the surface, even if this means that the child drops behind other children or falls below group norms. They will wait for social interest to manifest itself, for instance, so that the seeking of social contact shall come from the child's own motives and contribute to his initiative and ego identity. It will be recalled that Hartley Hale was anything but appreciative when his mother tried to find him suitable friends. It was not that he did not want friends; he merely wanted them to be of his own choosing, the products of his own social initiative, even if it cost him effort and frustration to find them.

The nurturing of growth requires the long patience of the husbandman rather than the hasty intervention of the mechanic. It requires waiting for impulse to declare itself, for interest to appear, for initiative to come forth. It calls for a tolerant attitude toward individuality, respect for the unique pattern that unfolds in every case. It demands confidence that in the long run individuality will be an asset, not a handicap, and that it will lead both to a happier life and to a better world than if the goal had been set at conformity, pleasantness, marketability, or a pattern that is merely the empty logical opposite of mental and emotional disorder.

IN CONCLUSION

It is a tragic fact of our time that we have become afraid both of our society and of human nature. The march of events has created this fear. The optimism of the nineteenth century, with its vision of unending progress through invention and business enterprise, has given place to a confused apprehension that the world order is falling to pieces and that civilization may soon be shaken to its foundations. Living in a crowded and impersonal society, barraged with information about facts far and near over which we have no control, each of us today is made relentlessly aware of his smallness and helplessness. We have become painfully conscious of the frequency of emotional strains and breakdowns under pressure of today's stressful conditions. We have had terrifying wars and seen many other ways in which man exhibits an inability to deal with his nature and manage his technical inventions.

Thus far the scientific study of man has unwittingly contributed to the trend toward apprehension and uncertainty. All three views of man—the social, the biological, and the psychodynamic—display that one-sided determinism which selectively views the person as the hapless product of forces and which shuns the corresponding study of the person taking action to change these forces. And we have insisted in this book that these approaches are sound; they reveal truth, and they therefore properly warn us not to face the future with blind optimism and a buoyant disregard for the difficult nature of the human undertaking. But equally we have insisted that some attempt should be made to examine the gap in the scientific account so that natural growth and the activity of the person can be put back into the story. This gap should be filled in the interest of full knowledge, but there is all the more reason to urge filling it when we reflect that precisely here lie the very facts about human nature that offer man the hope of influencing his own destiny. Lewis Mumford calls man "the unfinished animal" and says, "Unlike other organisms, the final stage of his growth is not determined by his biological past: it rests with himself and is partly determined by his own plans for the future." [18] Even though he be a nexus of biological, psychodynamic, social and cultural forces, a person serves to some extent as a transforming and redistributing center, responding selectively to create a new synthesis. Under reasonably favorable circumstances personality tends to continue its growth, strengthen its individuality, and assert its power to change the surrounding world. Man is capable of natural growth, and no fact about him is more important for his ultimate welfare.

The hopeful thing about the scientific study of shaping forces is that man will use his knowledge to prevent himself from being excessively shaped. The more he learns about the silent imperatives of culture and social class, the tyrannies of group expectation and social roles, the demandingness of drives, the subtle slanting of behavior by natural temperament and ability, the heavy impress of childhood training and parental attitudes, the crippling action of anxiety and primitive defense—the more he can perceive and weigh these forces that mould him, the less does he need to be their slave. And he is certainly justified in going a step further and studying the positive side of his capacity for constructive change.

SUGGESTIONS FOR FURTHER READING

The concept of growth trends is widely used in developmental psychology, but research interest has been largely confined to the earlier and simpler manifestations of growth rather than its continuation in adult life. Andras Angyal (*Foundations for a Science of Personality*, New York, The Commonwealth Fund, 1941) suggested two very general growth trends which extend throughout most of life, the trend toward increasing autonomy and the trend

[18] Mumford, L., *The Conduct of Life*, New York, Harcourt, Brace & Co., 1951, p. 36.

toward homonomy; see especially chs. 2 and 6. The continuing of growth is the subject of two chapters in G. W. Allport's *Personality: A Psychological Interpretation* (New York, Henry Holt & Co., 1937); the transformation of motives is discussed in ch. 7, the mature personality in ch. 8. Allport includes a brief description of C. Bühler's studies of life histories, studies which emphasize prolonged purposive striving toward distant goals. R. B. Cattell in *Personality: A Systematic Theoretical and Factual Study* (New York & London, McGraw-Hill Book Co., 1950) devotes a section (pp. 610–616) to the topic of personality trends in maturity and makes reference to several pertinent research studies.

Prominence is given to growth stages in Jean Piaget's monumental studies of child development. Of particular relevance to this chapter is his book, *The Moral Judgment of the Child* (New York, Harcourt, Brace & Co., 1932), which describes trends that are by no means confined to childhood. On the special topic of social growth in psychotherapy the outstanding reference is J. Dollard & N. E. Miller, *Personality and Psychotherapy* (New York & London, McGraw-Hill Book Co., 1950), chs. 14–20.

LIST OF REFERENCES

ABRAHAM, K. *Selected Papers*. London: Hogarth Press, 1927.

ALLPORT, G. W. *Personality: A Psychological Interpretation*. New York: Henry Holt & Co., 1937.

ANDERSON, H. H., AND ANDERSON, G. L. *An Introduction to Projective Techniques*. New York: Prentice-Hall, 1951.

ANGYAL, ANDRAS. *Foundations for a Science of Personality*. New York: The Commonwealth Fund, 1941.

BALDWIN, A. L., KALHORN, J., AND BREESE, F. H. Patterns of Parent Behavior, *Psychological Monographs*, 1945, Vol. 58, No. 3.

BARKER, R. G., KOUNIN, J., AND WRIGHT, H. W. *Child Behavior and Development*. New York: McGraw-Hill Book Co., 1934.

BARUCH, D. W. *New Ways in Discipline*. New York: Whittlesey House, 1949.

BERNREUTER, R. G. The Theory and Construction of the Personality Inventory, *Journal of Social Psychology*, 1933, Vol. 4, pp. 387-405.

BLOS, PETER. *The Adolescent Personality*. New York & London: D. Appleton-Century Co., 1941.

BROWN, J. F. *The Psychodynamics of Abnormal Behavior*. New York: McGraw-Hill Book Co., 1940.

BÜHLER, C. *The Child and His Family*. New York: Longmans Green & Co., 1940.

CATTELL, R. B. *Personality: A Systematic Theoretical and Factual Study*. New York & London: McGraw-Hill Book Co., 1950.

CENTERS, RICHARD. *The Psychology of Social Classes*. Princeton, N. J.: Princeton University Press, 1949.

COMMAGER, H. S. *The American Mind: An Interpretation of American Thought and Character Since the 1880's*. New Haven: Yale University Press, 1950.

COOLEY, C. H. *Human Nature and the Social Order*. New York: Chas. Scribner's Sons, 1902.

——— *Social Organization*. New York: Chas. Scribner's Sons, 1909.

DARLING, R. B. Autonomic Action in Relation to Personality Traits of Children, *Journal of Abnormal and Social Psychology*, 1940, Vol. 35, pp. 246-260.

DAVIS, A., AND DOLLARD, J. *Children of Bondage*. New York: American Council on Education, 1940.

DEWEY, J. *Interest and Effort in Education*. Boston: Houghton Mifflin Co., 1913.

DOLLARD, J., AND MILLER, N. E. *Personality and Psychotherapy: An Analysis in Terms of Learning, Thinking, and Culture*. New York: McGraw-Hill Book Co., 1950.

ERIKSON, E. H. *Childhood and Society*. New York: W. W. Norton & Co., 1950.

FENICHEL, O. *The Psychoanalytic Theory of Neurosis*. New York: W. W. Norton & Co., 1945.

FREUD, ANNA. *The Ego and the Mechanisms of Defense*. London: Hogarth Press, 1937.

FREUD, S. *Collected Papers*. London: Hogarth Press, 1924.

——— *New Introductory Lectures on Psychoanalysis*. New York: W. W. Norton & Co., 1933.

FROMM, E. *Man For Himself*. New York: Rinehart & Co., 1947.

GESELL, A., et al. *Biographies of Child Development*. New York: Paul B. Hoeber, 1939.

GRINKER, R. R., AND SPIEGEL, J. P. *Men Under Stress*. Philadelphia: P. Blakiston Co., 1945.

HANFMANN, E., AND KASANIN, J. Conceptual Thinking in Schizophrenia, *Nervous and Mental Disease Monographs*, 1942, No. 67.

HAVIGHURST, R. J., AND TABA, H. *Adolescent Character and Personality*. New York: Wiley & Sons, 1949.

HENRY, W. E. The Business Executive: The Psychodynamics of a Social Role. *American Journal of Sociology*, 1949, Vol. 54, pp. 286-291.

HILGARD, E. R. *Theories of Learning*. New York: Appleton-Century-Crofts, 1948.

HOLLINGSHEAD, A. B. *Elmtown's Youth: The Impact of Social Classes on Adolescents*. New York: John Wiley & Sons, 1949.

HORNEY, K. *The Neurotic Personality of Our Time*. New York: W. W. Norton & Co., 1937.

——— *Self Analysis*. New York: W. W. Norton & Co., 1942.

HUGHES, E. C. Personality Types and the Division of Labor, *American Journal of Sociology*, 1928, Vol. 33, pp. 754-768.

HUNT, J. McV. (ed.) *Personality and the Behavior Disorders*. New York: The Ronald Press Co., 1944. 2 Vols.

JONES, H. E. *Development in Adolescence: Approaches to the Study of the Individual*. New York: Appleton-Century Co., 1933.

JOST, H., AND SONTAG, L. W. The Genetic Factor in Autonomic Nervous System Function, *Psychosomatic Medicine*, 1944, Vol. 6, pp. 308-310.

KLINEBERG, O., ASCH, S. E., AND BLOCK, H. An Experimental Study of Constitutional Types, *Genetic Psychology Monographs*, 1934, Vol. 16, pp. 145-221.

KLUCKHOHN, C. *Mirror for Man: The Relation of Anthropology to Modern Life*. New York: Whittlesey House, 1949.

————, AND MURRAY, H. A. (eds.) *Personality in Nature, Culture and Society*. New York: Alfred A. Knopf, 1948.

KÖHLER, W. *The Mentality of Apes*. New York: Harcourt, Brace & Co., 1927.

KRETSCHMER, E. *Physique and Character*. London: Kegan Paul, 1925.

LECKY, P. *Self-Consistency: A Theory of Personality*. New York: Island Press, 1945.

LERNER, E. The Problem of Perspective in Moral Reasoning, *American Journal of Sociology*, 1937, Vol. 43, pp. 249-269.

LEVY, D. M. *Maternal Overprotection*. New York: Columbia University Press, 1943.

LEWIN, K., LIPPITT, R., AND WHITE, R. K. Patterns of Aggressive Behavior in Experimentally Created "Social Climates," *Journal of Social Psychology*, 1939, Vol. 10, pp. 279-300.

LINTON, RALPH. *The Cultural Background of Personality*. New York & London: D. Appleton-Century Co., 1945.

LYND, R. S. *Knowledge for What? The Place of Social Science in American Culture*. Princeton, N. J.: Princeton University Press, 1948.

MASSERMAN, J. H. *Principles of Dynamic Psychiatry*. Philadelphia: W. B. Saunders Co., 1946.

McCLELLAND, D. C. *Personality*. New York: Wm. Sloane Associates, 1951.

MEAD, G. H. *Mind, Self, and Society*. Chicago: University of Chicago Press, 1934.

MEAD, M. *And Keep Your Powder Dry: An Anthropologist Looks at America*. New York: William Morrow & Co., 1942.

MICHAELS, J. J., AND PORTER, R. T. Psychiatric and Social Implications of Contrasts Between Psychopathic Personality and Obsessive-Compulsive Neurosis, *Journal of Nervous and Mental Diseases*, 1949, Vol. 109, pp. 122-132.

MORGAN, C. T., AND STELLAR, E. *Physiological Psychology*. 2nd Edition, New York & London: McGraw-Hill Book Co., 1950.

MUMFORD, L. *The Conduct of Life*. New York: Harcourt, Brace & Co., 1951.

MURPHY, G. *Personality: A Biosocial Approach to Origins and Structure*. New York: Harper & Bros., 1947.

MURPHY, L. B. *Social Behavior and Child Personality*. New York: Columbia University Press, 1937.

MURRAY, H. A. *Explorations in Personality*. New York & London: Oxford University Press, 1938.

NEWCOMB, T. M. *Social Psychology*. New York: Dryden Press, 1950.

OVERSTREET, H. A. *The Mature Mind*. New York: W. W. Norton & Co., 1949.

O.S.S. ASSESSMENT STAFF. *Assessment of Men*. New York: Rinehart & Co., 1948.

PARSONS, T. *The Social System*. Glencoe, Ill.: The Free Press, 1951.

PENNINGTON, L. A., AND BERG, I. A. *An Introduction to Clinical Psychology*. New York: The Ronald Press Co., 1948.

PIAGET, J. *The Moral Judgment of the Child*. New York: Harcourt, Brace & Co., 1932.

—— *The Psychology of Intelligence*. New York: Harcourt, Brace & Co., 1950.

RAVVEN, R. M. *The Phrase Association Interview*. 1951, unpublished thesis, Harvard College Library, Cambridge, Mass.

RIESMAN, D. *The Lonely Crowd: A Study of the Changing American Character*. New Haven: Yale University Press, 1950.

ROE, A. Artists and Their Work, *Journal of Personality*, 1946, Vol. 15, pp. 1-40.

—— Personality and Vocation, *Transactions of the New York Academy of Science*, 1947, Vol. 9, pp. 257-267.

—— Psychological Examinations of Eminent Biologists, *Journal of Consulting Psychology*, 1949, Vol. 13, pp. 225-246.

ROSENZWEIG, S., AND KOGAN, K. L. *Psychodiagnosis*. New York: Grune & Stratton, 1949.

SAUL, L. J. *Emotional Maturity*. Philadelphia: J. B. Lippincott Co., 1947.

SELTZER, C. C. The Relationship Between the Masculine Component and Personality, *American Journal of Physical Anthropology*, 1945, Vol. 3, pp. 33-47.

————, WELLS, F. L., AND McTERMAN, E. B. A Relationship Between Sheldonian Somatotype and Psychotype, *Journal of Personality*, 1948, Vol. 16, pp. 431-436.

SHELDON, W. H., STEVENS, S. S., AND TUCKER, W. B. *The Varieties of Human Physique*. New York: Harper & Bros., 1940.

SHELDON, W. H., AND STEVENS, S. S. *The Varieties of Temperament*. New York: Harper & Bros., 1942.

SHERIF, M., AND CANTRIL, H. *The Psychology of Ego-Involvements*. New York: John Wiley & Sons, 1947.

SHIRLEY, M. *The First Two Years: A Study of Twenty-five Babies*. Minneapolis: University of Minnesota Press, 1933. 3 Vols.

SMITH, M. B., BRUNER, J. S., AND WHITE, R. W. *Opinions and Personality*. (To be published in 1953.)

STODDARD, G. D. *The Meaning of Intelligence*. New York: The Macmillan Co., 1943.

SYMONDS, P. M. *The Dynamics of Human Adjustment*. New York: D. Appleton-Century Co., 1946.

———— *The Psychology of Parent-Child Relationships*. New York: D. Appleton-Century Co., 1939.

THOMAS, W. I. *The Unadjusted Girl*. Boston: Little, Brown & Co., 1923.

THORPE, L. P., AND KATZ, B. *The Psychology of Abnormal Behavior*. New York: The Ronald Press Co., 1948.

———— *The Psychology of Mental Health*. New York: The Ronald Press Co., 1950.

TRYON, R. C. Genetic Differences in Maze Learning Ability in Rats, *Yearbook of the National Society for Studies in Education*, 1940, Vol. 39, pp. 111-119.

WARNER, W. L., AND ASSOCIATES. *Democracy in Jonesville: A Study in Quality and Inequality*. New York: Harper & Bros., 1949.

WHITE, R. W. The Personality of Joseph Kidd, *Character & Personality*, 1943, Vol. II, pp. 183-208, 318-360.

———— *The Abnormal Personality*. New York: The Ronald Press Co., 1948.

WHYTE, W. F. *Street Corner Society*. Chicago: University of Chicago Press, 1943.

Index